NETWORKING

A Guide to European Volu

Brian Harvey is a researcher and writer living in Dublin. He worked for the Simon Community in Ireland, and subsequently became research consultant to the European Provisional Working Group against Poverty. His work on homelessness and poverty issues has been widely published.

The Voice of the Voluntary Sector

NCVO aims to promote the common interests of voluntary organisations and to provide a range of resources that will increase their effectiveness.

Established in 1991 as the representative body for the voluntary sector in England, NCVO has some 600 members involved in all areas of voluntary and social action. It is also in daily contact with thousands of other voluntary bodies and groups, as well as government departments, local authorities and the business sector. NCVO has helped to set up several new organisations, including the Charities Aid Foundation (1974), the National Association of Citizens Advice Bureaux (1978) and the National Association of Councils for Voluntary Service (1991).

Community Development Foundation

CDF was set up in 1968 to pioneer new forms of community development.

CDF aims to strengthen communities by ensuring the effective participation of people in determining the conditions which affect their lives through:

- influencing policy making

- promoting best practice

- providing support for community initiatives

It does this through a broad programme which includes consultancies, training, local action projects, publications, conferences and research.

Networking in Europe

A Guide to European Voluntary Organisations

Brian Harvey

NCVO Publications and Community Development Foundation

Published by
NCVO Publications (incorporating Bedford Square Press)
imprint of the
National Council for Voluntary Organisations
26 Bedford Square, London WC1B 3HU and by
Community Development Foundation
60 Highbury Grove, London N5 2AG

First published 1992

© NCVO, CDF and European Briefing Unit of the University of Bradford, 1992

Typeset in house
Printed in Great Britain by J.W. Arrowsmith Ltd, Bristol
Cover printed by The Heyford Press, Wellingborough
Printed on recycled paper

A catalogue record for this book is available from the British Library.

ISBN 0 7199 1338 1

CONTENTS

4   European Networks: Origins and Roles

5   Different European Networks

6   The Voluntary Sector in Other European Countries

7   Information on Europe and How to Get It

8   Conclusions

Appendix

LIST OF TABLES

FOREWORD

The role of the voluntary sector in British society is so established that reassessing it and learning about voluntary organisations in other countries may seem superfluous. Yet that is what this guide is about.

When we began the project, we had expected the staff of voluntary organisations to be the most likely readers. During the process of collecting and analysing information, however, we saw that the book would be welcomed by a wider audience. Other sectors, particularly local authorities, have a growing interest in its subject matter. We also became aware of a strong interest in the guide among organisations on the Continent.

These signals reaffirmed the decision of our three organisations to initiate the undertaking. The implications of the single European market and the expanding links among organisations across Europe apply as much to the voluntary sector as any other. This is the immediate context which will, we think, make the guide an invaluable reference point for development staff, managers, researchers and others.

We have been extremely fortunate to have had Brian Harvey to collect the information and write the guide. His experience and skills have been impressive. We are also very grateful to the advisory group established for the project and chaired by CDF's northern director, Paul Henderson: Peter Kuenstler (CEI Ltd), Margareta Holmstedt (European Briefing Unit, University of Bradford), Bill Seary (European Social Action Network), Marilyn Taylor (School for Advanced Urban Studies, University of Bristol), and Nigel Tarling (NCVO).

We should like to thank the Joseph Rowntree Charitable Trust and the Calouste Gulbenkian Foundation for the financial support which made this project possible.

David Thomas
Chief Executive, Community Development Foundation

Judy Weleminsky
Director, National Council for Voluntary Organisations

Professor Kenneth Dyson
Head of European Studies Department, University of Bradford

INTRODUCTION

This guide aims to provide information about the work of voluntary sector associations, federations and networks in Europe. Voluntary organisations in Britain may be interested in joining some of them - or at least in finding out more about them. These organisations might also be interested in European programmes providing information and opportunities to influence policy and social change - whether that be that through the European Communities or the other institutions of Europe.

The guide will complement the existing literature, notably Ann Davison and Bill Seary's *Grants from Europe: how to get money and influence policy* (Bedford Square Press). Readers more interested in the financial, project and grant-aid aspects of the European Communities should consult *Grants from Europe*, using the references provided. Another guide of special interest to readers will be *Changing Europe - challenges facing the voluntary and community sectors in the 1990s*, by Sean Baine, John Benington and Jill Russell, also published by Bedford Square Press. Baine, Benington and Russell analyse the likely effect of the single European market -and what it means for everyone involved in the voluntary sector and social services.

While this guide includes practical information, it is not, nor is it intended to be, an exhaustive or comprehensive directory of all the organisations, institutions and bodies encountered by the researcher. It is a guide, not a directory. There is a strong 'information orientation' in the presentation of the book. Readers are introduced to subjects, groups, organisations and networks, and then encouraged and invited to carry out their own further research and investigations. With this in mind, a sign ■ is used to refer the reader to further information, reading or other publication. Chapter 1 discusses the present political context for the voluntary sector in Europe. Chapter 2 describes the main European institutions - not just those of the European Communities, but those of the Council of Europe, the United Nations and the Nordic Council. The specialised programmes of the European Communities are described in chapter 3, where European foundations of interest to the voluntary sector are presented. The reader is introduced to the world of the new European networks of voluntary organisations in Europe in chapter 4; the networks are listed in detail in chapter 5. The voluntary sector in each of the other EC countries is the subject of chapter 6: not only is there an account of the origins of the voluntary sector in those countries, but key voluntary organisations in each field are highlighted. Chapter 7 confronts the problem faced by many voluntary organisations in Britain: what is the best way of keeping up to date with information on current developments in Europe? Finally, there is a listing in the appendix of over one hundred networks - and the main voluntary organisations in other European countries.

Because of the rapid pace of change in Europe, there is the danger that what one writes may be overtaken by events. Developments in Europe are described as they stood in January 1992. Likewise, while every effort has been made to ensure accuracy, addresses and phone numbers can change swiftly and become out of date. Fax, minitel and electronic mail numbers have been provided wherever possible. The mention of a particular organisation in the guide implies neither approval nor disapproval.

Finally, I would like to thank all those many persons, organisations and institutions who gave so very generously of their time and information, and whom I met in the course of preparing this guide. Their help is enormously appreciated.

Brian Harvey

GLOSSARY AND ACRONYMS

A foremost objective of this guide is that it be written in plain English. The use of Eurospeak, acronyms and other obfuscating terminology has been kept to a minimum. A few terms which recur throughout the text are defined here.

Benelux   Belgium, the Netherlands and Luxembourg.

ECOSOC   The Economic and Social Council of the United Nations.

ECU   European Currency Unit, the notional currency in which the European Communities transact their business. It may well become the future European currency. An écu is the old French word for a crown or a shield.

HMSO   Her Majesty's Stationery Office, where many of the publications referred to can be obtained.

MECU   million ECU.

network   an international association, union, federation, grouping of organisations, experts, or individuals to share information and a common course of action on a problem or issue.

NGO   non-governmental organisation: the term in use in continental Europe comparable to 'voluntary organisation' or possibly 'charity' in Britain. In addition to general associations and organisations, it also includes lobbying groups and professional bodies – in this case, those concerned with social issues.

observatory   a French-derived concept which is of broader scope than 'a monitoring body' would suggest in English. An observatory looks out and observes what is going on in a particular field – such as poverty or family policy – and reports back what it sees (some observatories have subsections called antennae!).

sector   an area of work for voluntary organisations, for example, the youth sector, elderly people, refugees and migrants.

SMEs   small and medium-size enterprises.

structural funds   those funds of the European Communities designed to improve the infrastructure of the EC – the regional fund, the social fund, and the agricultural guidance fund (European Agricultural Guidance Fund), also called FEOGA.

subsidiarity   the principle whereby decisions should be taken and services should be delivered at the lowest possible level in society: national government should not do what local government could do as well, if not better. This is a disingenuous explanation for a nineteenth-century word which suddenly came back into favour in the late 1980s after many people thought it had been buried in arcane history books. In practice, it can mean exactly what politicians want it to mean. It is cited by the proponents of administrative decentralisation; equally it is cited as a hands-off argument by some national governments to argue that Europe should not deal with social issues, since national governments are better equipped to deal with social issues. Subsidiarity was invented by the nineteenth-century papacy to ward off creeping socialism and government intervention in the affairs of the family and the church. It was a popular concept among corporatists in the 1930s. In its most current application in the field of European social policy it is now invoked by the Commission to mean that the EC is entitled to lay down minimum social standards – but leave it to the member states to work out how they should be reached.

the Six the original six members of the European Communities.
the Twelve the present twelve members of the European Communities.
zero-rating the manner in which some goods have a zero (0) per cent value added tax rate.

Other Notes

- The phrase 'European Communities' is used in the plural, it being legally correct, rather than European Community, which is more popular (but inaccurate).

- The term *central* Europe (rather than eastern Europe) is used to refer to the countries Poland, Czechoslovakia, Hungary, Rumania, Bulgaria, and the former German Democratic Republic (GDR). The new title for the USSR, the Commonwealth of Independent States (CIS), is used.

- Telephone numbers outside Britain given in the guide are the numbers to be dialled after 010, which is the number required for a caller in Britain to get an international line.

- For some European addresses (e.g. in France and Italy), the practice of putting the street number after the address is followed, hence avenue Général de Gaulle 12, rather than 12, avenue Général de Gaulle.

- Where groups of networks or foundations are examined together, they are generally reviewed in alphabetical order.

1

Europe: Setting the Scene

Europe is now undergoing a period of far-reaching change. The shape of Europe as we will know it in the first half of the next century may well be governed by decisions taken now and in this decade. The communist governments of central Europe crumbled before the popular revolutions of 1989: these countries are now in the midst of profound and painful social transformation as they attempt to build democratic institutions and adjust to mixed economies. The European Communities, which began as a limited attempt in six countries to construct a common market in the trade of goods in the 1950s, have now emerged as an embryonic United States of Europe, one which the central European countries and even the neutral nations of Europe are clamouring to join.

The path towards European political union has raised profound distrust about the quality of life in the new Europe. With 50m poor, over 14m unemployed, and countless others who have derived precious little benefit from the grand design now unfolding before them, serious doubts about our European future deserve an answer. Only in the past five years have the European institutions begun to consider seriously the social dimension of the society of the twenty-first century now in the making. The role which voluntary and community organisations could play in this process is perhaps the greatest challenge they could ever face –and is one of the key themes of this guide.

This chapter briefly reviews some of the special concerns which voluntary organisations may address in considering their role in Europe. These include:

- How did we reach the present situation in Europe?

- The meaning of the completion of the single market;

- The Fundamental Charter of Social Rights: will there be an effective social dimension to the European Communities?

- The dangers of 'Fortress Europe';

- New members of the European Communities; and

HISTORY - HOW DID WE GET HERE?

Twice this century Europe has been at war, and after each cataclysm the leaders of the European national states swore that such a tragedy would never recur. The attempts to rebuild Europe after 1945 met with lasting success, not least as a result of the efforts of the French leaders Robert Schuman and Jean Monnet to establish a community of nations which combined economic self-interest with mechanisms that were specifically designed to ensure co-operation between nations, most especially the great rivals, France and Germany (a less stated, but nonetheless present reason, was the desire to control Germany in the uncertain postwar political environment). They wished to create positive international institutions which would promote economic co-operation and generate economic growth. From the very start, the EC was also driven by federalist notions that these institutions could lead ultimately to a United States of Europe. Accordingly, three European Communities were created: the first, the European Coal and Steel Community was set up in 1951.

The European Coal and Steel Community pooled German and French steel production under a single authority, within an organisation open to others to join. In the event, Italy, Belgium, Luxembourg, and the Netherlands joined the Community as well. The Treaties of Rome in 1957 set up two more Communities: the European Atomic Energy Community (also known as Euratom), and the European Economic Community (also known as the EEC). The EEC's aims were ambitious: they were to strengthen peace, achieve economic integration, harmonious and balanced economic development, and to work towards 'an ever-closer union of the peoples of Europe'. Each of the Communities was run by a Council of government ministers, and an executive Commission.

The organisational structure of the three Communities was merged in 1967, so that there was only one Commission and one Council for all three, though constitutionally three Communities continued to exist. British membership of the Communities was blocked for years by French President Charles de Gaulle, and Britain did not join until 1973, the same time as Ireland and Denmark. Greece joined the Communities in 1981, followed by Spain and Portugal in 1986.

The period 1973 –86 was a difficult one, dominated by disagreements over finance, priorities and procedures. The new members took some time to settle in, and Britain long remained unenthusiastic about its membership. Europe's economic performance was sluggish, weakened by the two recessions of 1974 and 1980. Two measures were put forward to clear the logjam in the mid-1980s. First, the Treaty of Rome was amended and revised in 1987 by the Single European Act (SEA) which speeded up decision-making procedures in the EC, and gave the Communities new authority in the areas of research, the environment and social policy. These proposals owed much to Commission President Jacques Delors and European Parliamentarian Altiero Spinelli. Delors came from French President François Mitterrand's socialist government, and was appointed to head up the Commission in 1985. Jacques Delors is now considered the mastermind of the new Europe, and his many admirers consider him the most influential individual in western Europe.

COMPLETION OF THE SINGLE MARKET – WHAT DOES IT ACTUALLY MEAN?

Second, it was decided to turn the twelve states into a single economic unit, a single market. A core assumption in this process was the notion of European inefficiency. Central to the analysis of Europe's place in the world in the early 1980s was the supposition that Europe was an inefficient competitor with the United States and the Pacific rim economies, principally Japan. Europe was inefficient, it was held, not only because of its old industries, but because of barriers of language, trade, bureaucracy, customs and borders, all of which slowed economic performance. Trade was impeded by red tape, local regulations, and rules against foreign competition. French companies did not learn from Spanish companies; local employment creation experiences in Greece were not relayed to Portugal, which might emulate them – all because they did not know about them or because barriers of language and distance stood in the way. The European Commission-inspired report by Paulo Cecchini (*Research on the cost of non-Europe*) held out the promise that if Europe could wipe out the non-trade barriers to its economic development, then its economic performance would improve markedly. Abolish these barriers, and Europe would be wealthy once more. This not only explained the commitment to the single market, but also the sharing of information, ideas, policies and practice, often through information networks.

The single market is based on four freedoms of movement: those of goods, capital, people and services. Free movement of goods has been a reality in Europe for many years, and the process of 1992 has been more about the elimination of the non-trading barriers and red tape, and about eliminating national policies which distort competition among the member states.

3

Agreement has been reached on the ending of border customs formalities on 1 January 1993. The same date should see the introduction of a standard VAT rate of 15 per cent, though rates may not be aligned in respect of all goods until 1996. In addition to the standard rate, there will be a low rate of 5 per cent for a common list of items, several of which are currently zero-rated, such as food, children's clothes and books. Although the decision has been formally taken to end zero-rating in 1996, it is unlikely that discussion on this issue is over.

One of the many fears engendered by the single market is that work, capital and industry will be increasingly centred on the golden triangle of Paris, Brussels and Frankfurt, and that the peripheral areas of the European Communities will suffer accordingly. Biotechnology and continued improvements in production methods mean that less and less land will be needed to meet the food needs of the European Communities: it is predicted that millions of hectares of agricultural land may go out of production by 2020, about 10 per cent of the total farmed at present.

The EC budget for 1991 was 58.5 billion ECU and is expected to rise to 65 billion ECU in 1992. The funding of agriculture is likely to decline as a proportion of the EC budget over the next few years. It fell from 81 per cent in 1973 to 67 per cent in 1989, and reform of the Common Agricultural Policy will mean its further decline, thus giving more scope for regional policy (currently 10 per cent of the total budget), and social policy (7 per cent of the total).

Despite the steady removal of these non-trading barriers, despite all the information-sharing programmes and networks, Europe's economic performance is still considered weak. Unemployment in the EC in late 1991 stood at 9.1 per cent of the workforce, no less than 14.2m people; much worse than Europe's chief rival, the United States, where unemployment was in the order of 5 per cent.

■ *Grants from Europe*, 13-18.

■ Paulo Cecchini: *The European challenge 1992 –the benefits of a single market*. Wildwood House, 1988 (summary of *Research on the cost of the non-Europe*).

THE CHARTER OF FUNDAMENTAL SOCIAL RIGHTS

The Charter of Fundamental Social Rights was adopted by the European heads of government meeting (Britain excepted) at their summit held in

Strasbourg in December 1989. The Charter of Fundamental Social Rights (not to be confused with the Social Charter of the Council of Europe) articulated aspirations for social progress to accompany the completion of the internal market in 1992. These were:

- the free circulation of workers;

- fair remuneration and a decent wage;

- minimum income and appropriate social assistance;

- freedom of association and collective negotiation;

- opportunities for professional training;

- equality of men and women;

- rights to information, consultation and participation for workers;

- minimum income for elderly people;

- the protection of health and safety at work; and

- protection of children, adolescents, elderly people, and people with learning difficulties.

Having declared these goals, the Commission was then invited to submit proposals ('an action programme with a set of related instruments') as to how these aspirations could be translated into reality. Forty eight such proposals were presented by the Commission in 1990. The Commission was instructed to report, at regular intervals, on the progress being achieved towards the implementation of these objectives.

Two early targets for Commission action were a minimum wage and a minimum income: several countries in Europe do not have a basic minimum wage – Britain being a notable example. Others, such as Greece, do not have rights to a basic minimum income, and several countries introduced such rights only recently (for example, France, Spain and Luxembourg). The Commission's intention is to harmonise these two elements between the member states, so that there is greater convergence (a favourite Commission phrase) in the way in which the different social security systems of the EC evolve.

The first draft recommendation was on a basic minimum income: it was published by the Commission in May 1991. Being a recommendation, it cannot have legal force, but will be a base line on which the performance of different states can be measured and adjudged. The recommendation was designed to lay down an 'individual basic right to a guarantee of sufficient benefits and resources', Eurospeak for a basic minimum income. The recommendation proposed that a basic minimum income be without time limit, that it be 'sufficient to cover essential needs beyond subsistence levels', that those concerned also receive counselling and legal aid, that claimants are informed of their rights, and that there be an efficient, fast and free independent appeals machinery.

Although this recommendation is geared towards the four states which lack a basic minimum income without time limit (Italy, Greece, Portugal and Spain), it is the intention of the Commission that the recommendation improve the national social security provisions in the other eight states as well, achieving greater convergence in the various social security systems in the Communities. This is intended to take effect in 1996, but being a recommendation it is not legally binding. However, the Commission is understood to favour a legally-binding directive should it not be acted on.

The Commission also published three proposals to improve training, social security, pensions, health and holiday entitlements for atypical workers (the term applied to part-time workers), designed to give them rights comparable to full-time workers; and a fourth to improve the position of pregnant women at work, ensuring 16 weeks' maternity leave. These proposals ran into strong resistance from the social affairs ministers of the EC in the course of 1991. Despite delays, pressure for the European Charter of Fundamental Social Rights to be an effective instrument of social policy is likely to be maintained by the Commission and the Parliament in the course of the next few years: indeed, presenting the Commission's programme to the Parliament in 1991, Commission President Jacques Delors went out of his way to rebuke those who had held up progress to date.

A draft directive on mobility and transport was adopted by the Commission in February 1991: it requires public transport to be modified so as to enable disabled people to use it, or personal aid to be provided by specially trained staff. If adopted, member states must introduce the necessary legislation, regulations or administrative measures to comply with this directive before 1993.

'FORTRESS EUROPE'?

Two words play a pivotal role in the debate on Fortress Europe: Schengen and TREVI. These two words are of vital importance to the 15m migrants now in the EC, and the 1.5m migrants whose position is considered to be irregular or illegal. A total of 500,000 people applied for asylum in Europe in 1990, and a European Commission-sponsored study has predicted that as many as two million people from the southern and eastern Mediterranean will settle in the Communities before the year 2000.

Schengen is a small, otherwise obscure, border town in Luxembourg, and the chosen place since 1985 for meetings between the governments of the

Benelux countries and later, France, Italy and Germany for their discussions on the consequences of the abolition of internal borders in advance of 1993. At first sight, the holding of such meetings is innocuous: governments wish to review controls over customs, transit and travel arrangements in their six states (now eight, after Spain and Portugal joined) when, as is expected, frontier checks are eliminated. Nor is there necessarily anything wrong in these meetings being secret: most intergovernmental meetings are. But several concerns have arisen. Not only are meetings behind closed doors, but their decisions have always been kept closely under wraps. What little is made public identifies the problems of migration with those of 'security', which suggests a guilt by association. Similarly, illegal immigration and the illegal importation of narcotics are twinned. Ethnic minorities fear they will be harassed in the name of security and illegal movement. The currently understood line of thinking at Schengen is that border customs checks should be replaced by random 'security' checks anywhere in the member states – but the fear among migrants is that such checks will be targeted at 'foreign-looking' people.

Schengen has also examined the harmonisation of asylum policies – again, not an unreasonable exercise. The problem is that the procedures for harmonisation have been agreed, but not the criteria. Harmonisation is the procedure whereby a person refused asylum in one of the six is automatically refused in the other states. But the criteria in the states are different – relatively liberal in Germany, not so liberal in the Netherlands. Again, migrant groups fear that Germany and the other liberal states will become stricter, so as to conform to the levels of the strictest states, for fear of otherwise attracting 'their' asylum seekers.

The TREVI anti-terrorism group (established in 1975) is similar in nature, except that it takes place at the level of the Twelve. Meetings are attended by high-ranking officials of the Departments of Justice or the Interior. TREVI, like Schengen, is technically not an EC group, since the issues it deals with are claimed to be officially outside EC competence. It has nourished the ambition of setting up a European police agency, analogous to the American Federal Bureau of Investigation. What concerns migrant groups is its approach of considering combined methods of dealing with drug-traffickers, terrorists and international crime (which is illegal) in the same way as irregular immigrants, refugees and asylum seekers (which is not necessarily illegal).

The outcome of the TREVI and Schengen discussion remains unclear, and groups concerned with ethnic minorities have argued for movement procedures that will not disadvantage minorities or residents who are not EC citizens. This may be a more serious problem in countries other than Britain. British *citizens*, black or white, have been free to work in other parts of Europe without impediment since 1968, and this is not under threat or consideration. Problems arise when we examine the position of British non-citizen *residents*, who must obtain a visa to visit other EC member states; and the greater numbers of immigrant workers in France and Germany. Most such workers, likewise, are residents without citizenship or the vote.

Some experts believe that the Schengen and TREVI debate is far from over, that a 'fortress Europe' is far from inevitable, and that effective lobbying by migrants groups and related bodies could still ensure that the 1992 process makes things easier, rather than more difficult for minorities. The European Parliament has taken a sympathetic view on the issue, publishing a landmark report on racism and xenophobia in 1989. Parliament, like migrants' organisations, dislikes the manner in which the Schengen and TREVI process have taken place outside its control, especially when Schengen and TREVI have dealt with matters that are otherwise EC concerns. Some groups concerned with migrants believe that the key to the issues is to make Schengen and TREVI amenable to EC influence, accountability and control, in other words an EC policy matter, rather than a secretive intergovernmental affair.The Charter of Fundamental Social Rights spoke of the responsibility of member states to guarantee that third country residents should enjoy treatment comparable to citizens. Organisations working with migrants, ethnic minorities and asylum seekers are generally pessimistic about the outcome of the Schengen and TREVI discussions. In the pipeline is a new EC convention on asylum and free movement: it will ensure that a visa issued in one country is respected in another, but will not adopt the European Parliament's proposal for a European residents' card.

■ *Grants from Europe*, 60-3, 68-71.

NEW MEMBERS OF THE EUROPEAN COMMUNITIES

Negotiations concluded during 1991 on the creation of a common economic area (European Economic Space), between the EC and the six non-EC European Free Trade Area (EFTA) countries. This European Economic Space is based on the principle of free movement of people, goods, capital and services – but without the costly Common Agricultural Policy. A text on the creation of a 'cohesion fund', which would bridge the gap between EFTA and the poorer areas of the Communities, was agreed.

Since 1990, discussions have been under way between the EC and Hungary, the Czech and Slovak Federal Republic, and Poland for treaties of association with the EC. Similar discussions may shortly be opened with the newly independent Baltic states. Association treaties would regularise the relationships between the Communities and these countries, state the limits of the movement of trade, labour and capital, and, possibly, pave the way for EC membership by the end of the 1990s. Six countries have now joined the queue at the door for admission to the Communities: Turkey, Morocco, Austria, Cyprus, Malta and Sweden. Sweden's application is expected to lead to membership in 1995. The accession of just some of these members could change the shape and evolution of the EC as we now know it.

Further evidence of the moves towards European integration came with the historic Treaty of Paris in November 1990, which marked the culmination of the work of the Conference for Security and Co-operation in Europe (CSCE). Thirty-four nations attended to mark the end of the cold war and agreed in principal to the creation of the 'common European home from the Atlantic to the Urals'. A parliamentary assembly is to be instituted to progress the concept.

EUROPEAN COMMUNITIES AND CHARITY LAW

Under article 58 of the Treaty of Rome, non-profit organisations are specifically excluded from the rigours of European company law. Tax concessions available to charities in England and Wales have not been interfered with.

But charities are ultimately threatened by the European Commission's plans to bring virtually everything that moves into the VAT net, and to have as few items zero-rated for VAT as possible. At present, a number of items which charities purchase are zero-rated (e.g. fund-raising materials and medical research equipment). Ending these concessions could cost UK charities up to £40m a year; ending zero-rating generally could cost as much as £750m a year. The heads of government meeting of June 1991 agreed that zero-rating of VAT should end in 1996, and that zero-rated goods could go on either the new standard rate of 15 per cent or the special lower rate of 5 per cent. These tax issues are clearly of concern to voluntary organisations in the medium term, as are proposals to modify article 58. Charities are thought to be safe from the VAT threat until at least 1996.

■ See Charities Tax Reform Group, chapter 3.

2

Europe: Institutions

This chapter describes the institutional context for the voluntary sector in Europe. Learning about institutions and how they work is not the most gripping of subjects; nevertheless institutions are important for voluntary and community organisations anxious to find out more about Europe and the bodies with which they will ultimately be doing business. Some of the main institutions, especially those of greatest interest to the voluntary sector, are outlined. Fuller descriptions of how these institutions work in all their permutations and ramifications are available in other guides, and devotees of institutional analysis should refer to them. The descriptions given here are merely starting points.

Those international institutions that voluntary organisations are most likely to meet in some shape or form – the Council of Europe, the United Nations, the Nordic Council, the Organisation for Economic Co-operation and Development (OECD), the European Free Trade Association, the European Communities, and the new institutions of the Charter of Paris – are included. Although the institutions of the European Communities have now overwhelmingly become the most important of these bodies, they are by no means the only ones which should be considered. Others have a rich history of their own, and could be of much interest to voluntary organisations. However, the European Communities are likely to be the first point of interest to the voluntary sector.

THE EUROPEAN COMMUNITIES

The European Communities built on the experience of international bodies like the League of Nations in the interwar years, and on that of the United Nations and the Council of Europe in the postwar period. They were the outcome of a long period of deliberation in the years following the surrender of Germany in 1945. They did not, as it were, emerge from the blue, but were rooted in the experience of many politicians, statesmen and leaders in trying to get countries to work together to achieve common ends.

The European Communities broke fresh ground in a number of areas, principally in the complexity of the organisational arrangements which they adopted. Hitherto, international bodies had been seen by governments as a place where their ministers could discuss common problems, make progress if there was agreement, but let the matter go if there was not. The treaty establishing the Communities laid down that there should be:

- A Council of Ministers;

- A Commission, or civil service;

- A parliamentary assembly, later called the European Parliament;

- An economic and social committee, to act as its advisory upper house; and

- A court of justice, to adjudicate disputes and enforce EC law.

Unlike previous international organisations, governments could not adopt a take-it-or-leave-it position to common problems: there was an underlying assumption that problems and differences between the member states would be worked at, and even voted on, until they were resolved. And so it was. The formative years of the EC were devoted to providing a benign environment for trade through the elimination of customs barriers between the six member states; and to making Europe self-sufficient in food production. This was achieved through the Common Agricultural Policy (CAP) which guaranteed a minimum price to farmers for basic agricultural products. That having been done, the EC enlarged its role to reduce disparities between its regions (by introducing a regional development fund), and to provide support for the better training of the workforce (through the social fund).

■ See *Grants from Europe*, 1–6.

The Council of Ministers

The Council of Ministers is the most powerful decision-making body in the Communities after the twice-a-year summit meetings of heads of governments (Prime Ministers or Presidents), sometimes also called the 'European Council'. The phrase 'Council of Ministers' actually covers a number of possible meetings: the meetings of foreign affairs ministers (the original Council of Ministers); the meeting of agricultural ministers to decide on farm prices (generally called the council of agriculture ministers) and so on. Not all categories of ministers meet, and those that do vary in the scope and importance of their meetings. For example, labour ministers meet as the

Council of Social Affairs Ministers to co-ordinate the drive against unemployment in the EC. The housing ministers of the EC met for the first time in 1989, and assemble only once a year.

Decisions of the Council of Ministers can be made on some issues by weighted majority vote (the UK has ten votes, Luxembourg only two), but in practice any nation can veto something which it considers to affect a 'vital national interest'. This veto arrangement was introduced in the 1960s at a meeting in Luxembourg, and is called the Luxembourg compromise.

The meetings of the Council of Ministers are presided over by each country in turn for a period of six months. For example, the UK holds the presidency of the Council of Ministers in the second half of 1992. The question of which country holds the presidency at any time is of more than academic or administrative interest, for the presiding country is primarily responsible for deciding on the agenda of the meetings during its presidency.

The Council has a general secretariat.

■ General Secretariat, Council of Ministers, rue de la Loi 170, B.1048 Brussels, Tel. 322 234 6111.

The business of Council meetings is prepared not just by the country holding the presidency of the European Communities at any given moment, but by the committee of permanent representatives in Brussels, called COREPER. Staffed by public servants, COREPER consists of each member state's ambassador to the European Communities and his or her supporting team. The UK representative, called UK-REP, can be contacted at UK-REP, Chancery, Rond-Point Schuman 6, B.1040 Brussels, Tel. 322 230 6205.

The Commission

Despite being referred to as the 'civil service' of the Communities, the Commission is much more powerful than a Whitehall Civil Service Department. It is more accurately referred to as the engine of the Communities, for the Commission is expected to take the lead in proposing legislation, action plans, programmes and policy. Thus not only does it execute policy, but it has an important role in the formulation and development of policy – in effect, a role of political leadership. It is often expected to take the lead in presenting new policies. Generally, it is reckoned that about 80 per cent of proposals emanating from the Commission become law or take effect in some manner or other.

The Commission consists of 17 members, or commissioners: two from each of the large member states (France, Germany, Italy, Spain and the UK), and one from each of the others. The Commission is appointed for four years at a time, Commissioners being nominated by member governments, and the

President being agreed by all. The current president, Jacques Delors, is French, and will probably come to be considered as the most dynamic ever appointed. The British Commissioners are appointed by the government, and there is a tradition of one being appointed from each of the two main political parties. The present UK Commissioners are Leon Brittan (Commissioner for Competition) and Bruce Millan (Commissioner for Regional Affairs). Each Commissioner is advised by a small group of about six to eight confidants whom he or she appoints: they are referred to as the *cabinet* (a French word for a close circle of advisers).

The structure of the Commission is modelled on the French administrative system. What would be the equivalent of departments are called Directorates-General. The Commission has 23 Directorates-General (referred to in shorthand as DGs), subdivided into directorates (A, B, C, D, etc.), divisions and sections. The Directorates-General carry out the decisions of the Commission. This system is reckoned to be efficient, but its weak point is the lack of cross-linkages. Popular misconceptions to the contrary notwithstanding, the number of officials employed by the Commission is small, most are overworked, and individuals carry substantial responsibilities.

The Commission has one address (rue de la loi 200, B.1049 Brussels, Tel. 322 235 1111), even though some of its offices are located in nearby streets. The Commission has a general secretariat, legal service, spokesman's service for the press (Tel. 322 235 2233), and interpreting service in addition to the 23 directorates. The Directorates-General, the DGs, always have a Roman numeral after their name. These directorates do not correspond neatly to national government departments, but from the point of view of the voluntary sector the most important are:

- DG V: Employment, industrial relations and social affairs;

- DG VI: Agriculture and rural development;

- DG VIII: Development;

- DG X: Information, communication and culture;

- DG XI: Environment, consumer protection and nuclear safety;

- DG XVI: Regional policy;

- DG XXII: Co-ordination of structural policies; and

- DG XXIII: Enterprise policy, commerce, tourism and the social economy.

The Directorate-General with which many voluntary and community organisations will find themselves doing business is DG V, the Directorate-General of social affairs. Two of its departments are called units, one of which is responsible for women's equality, and the other for the position of people with learning difficulties (HELIOS).

■ The Equal Opportunities Unit, Directorate-General V, Commission of the European Communities, rue de la loi 200, B.1040 Brussels, Tel. 322 235 5717, Fax 322 235 0129.

There is also the Task Force for Human Resources, Education, Training and Youth. The task force has responsibility for a number of specialised training programmes and exchange schemes. It is in effect a proto-directorate, and it is expected that when it is larger it will eventually float free to become DG XXIV. It uses the main Commission address and phone number.

The European Parliament

One of the difficulties in coming to grips with the Parliament is that it has no fixed abode. The precise location of the Parliament has, for many years, been the victim of a three-cornered dispute between Luxembourg (backed by the Luxembourgeois), Strasbourg (backed by the French), and Brussels (backed by the Belgians). In practice, most of the out-of-session work is done in Brussels, near to the core institutions of the Communities; and most parliamentary sessions (which take place generally during the second week of each month) are now held in Strasbourg. The Belgian government is pressing hard for Brussels to become the parliament's permanent location. Most of the staff of the political groupings in the Parliament are located in Brussels, but the permanent secretariat and library are located in Luxembourg. Some new MEPs have not even been to the official headquarters in Luxembourg, though the importance of the library in Luxembourg should not be underestimated, for researchers and parliament staff investigating current social issues will make use of material sent there by voluntary organisations.

■ The European Parliament, L.2929 Luxembourg, Tel. 352 43001, Fax 352 437009.

■ The European Parliament, rue Belliard 89-91, B.1047 Brussels, Tel. 322 234 1111, Fax 322 230 6933.

■ The European Parliament, Palais de l'Europe, Strasbourg, Tel. 33 881 74001, Fax 33 8825 6501.

■ *Grants from Europe*, 6-8.

The Political Groupings

The European Parliament of 518 MEPs has party divisions, just as Westminster has. However, there are more groupings than in Westminster and, on policy positions at least, there can be quite an overlap between them. The three main groupings are:

• The socialist group (to which the Labour party belongs);

• The christian democrat group, called the European People's Party (EPP); and

• The liberals, democrats and reformists.

The socialist group is the largest, with 180 members. This number includes the 46 Labour MEPs elected to the European Parliament in June 1989. The 32 Tory MEPs belong to the 34-strong European Democrats group (the other two are from Denmark), though discussions are under way which could lead to the Tories joining the European People's Party.

The European People's Party (121 members) brings together the main conservative or Christian Democrat parties of the EC. Three new groups emerged following the elections of June 1989. The Greens, with 29 members, comprise the Green MEPs whose core comes from Germany, France and Italy. Another new group is the Group of the United European Left, based on the old Italian Communist Party, now called the PDS. A third, smaller grouping is Left Unity, whose largest element is the French Communist Party.

The groups are provided with secretarial, administrative and research support. The socialist group, for example, has 135 officials. Many are temporary, and are recruited directly by the national parties concerned. These staff are important, performing a combination of press work, briefings, research and correspondence roles. Some staff are attached to the work of particular committees. Each parliamentary group normally meets twice a month – once in Brussels, and once during the parliamentary session in Strasbourg – to plan its work and to receive delegations.

At the same time, the structure provided by the groups should not be overstated. Divisions and votes in the European Parliament are much less rigid than at Westminster, for several reasons. The Parliament does not elect the government, so there is no pressure on a particular grouping to 'get its legislation through'. Parliament is much less homogeneous than many of the national parliaments. Party divisions are, in many instances, superseded by regional or sectoral interests: for example, the MEPs representing agricultural areas may act together, crossing the range of party divisions. The parties themselves cross a spectrum of positions: the Christian Democrats extend from conservatives to left-of-centre Christian Socialists. No party has an absolute overall majority in the Parliament, so concerted efforts must involve several parties working together (generally the Socialist Group with an untidy mixture of the other groups to its left, or together with the Christian Democrats). And one thing that brings all parliamentarians together is their desire for more power over the Council of Ministers and the Commission (the absence of such control they term the 'democratic deficit').

Parliamentary Committees

Much of the Parliament's detailed work takes place through 18 committees, of which the most important ones for the voluntary sector are:

- Agriculture and rural development (chair: Franco Borgo, Italy, Christian Democrat);

- Budgets (chair: Thomas von der Vring, Germany, Socialist Group);

- Development co-operation (chair: Henri Saby, France, Socialist Group);

- Environment, health, consumer protection (chair: Ken Collins, UK, Socialist Group);

- Legal affairs and citizen's rights (chair: Graf Franz von Stauffenberg, Germany, Christian Democrat);

- Regional policy and regional planning (chair: Antoni Diaz, Spain, Left);

- Social affairs (chair: Wim van Velsen, Netherlands, Socialist Group);

- Women's affairs (chair: Christine Crawley, UK, Socialist Group);

- Youth, culture, education, media and sport (chair: Antonio la Pergola, Italy, Socialist Group).

The women's committee of the Parliament is one of the most active. It has adopted strategic, long-term objectives, attempting to improve the women's agenda within the Charter of Fundamental Social Rights, and to promote childcare provisions and the development of women's studies. The women's committee can be contacted through its secretariat in Luxembourg or its chair, Christine Crawley MEP.

■ Committee on Women's Rights, European Parliament, L.2929 Luxembourg, Tel. 352 43001;

■ Ms Christine Crawley MEP, Birmingham District Labour Party, 16 Bristol Street, Birmingham B5 7AA, Tel. 021 622 2270, Fax 021 666 7332.

The Social Affairs Committee can be contacted through its chair, Wim Van Velsen.

■ Wim van Velsen, European Parliament, Bureau Van Maerfant 207, B.1040 Brussels.

The Socialist Group is the largest in the European Parliament. Its key political objectives are 'creating a social Europe, without which the single market is unacceptable; halting the destruction of the environment; establishing economic and monetary union; and creating a true European identity for the peoples of East and West'.

■ The Socialist Group in the European Parliament, rue Belliard 79-113, B.1047 Brussels, Tel. 322 234 2111, Fax 322 230 6664, or, during Parliamentary sessions, Tel. 33 88 17 4134.

The group publishes *European Labour Forum* (established 1990), a quarterly 40-page journal.

■ *European Labour Forum*, c/o Spokesman, Bertrand Russell House, Gamble Street, Nottingham NG7 4ET.

The next largest grouping is the Christian Democrat (CD), based on one of the longest political traditions in Europe. The two most powerful blocs within the CD group come from the governing Christian Democrat parties of Germany and Italy. The CD group is called the European People's Party (EPP, or PPE in French). The Liberal, Democratic and Reformist Group of the Parliament is the third largest in the Parliament, with 49 members from 10 countries. The largest single member is the French Republican party of former President Valéry Giscard d'Estaing. The group has contributed actively to the debate on the Charter of Fundamental Social Rights.

■ The Liberal, Democratic and Reformist Group in the European Parliament, rue Belliard 97-113, B.1047 Brussels, Tel. 322 234 2111, Fax 322 230 2485.

Intergroups

In addition to committees, there are intergroups of MEPs. These are cross-party groupings of MEPs pursuing particular interests or issues. They have no constitutional or legal standing within the Parliament, but they can be important. There are now about 50 intergroups, but their number is unlikely to increase substantially.

A number of intergroups deal with social issues. An example is the intergroup on ageing, which was promoted by Eurolink Age, the European network of organisations concerned with elderly people. It is a cross-party group of 100 MEPs, though only about one-third attend meetings. The meetings of the intergroup are convened by Eurolink Age, which helps to secure the passage of resolutions and reports through parliament. Several Commissioners have spoken to the intergroup. The group has contributed to the approval of a European Year of the Elderly (1993), an action plan for elderly people, and an increase in funding of projects for elderly people. Secretary is Belgian MEP Marijke Van Hemeldonck.

Intergroups of interest to voluntary organisations include:

- Animal welfare (chair: Mary Banotti, Ireland, European People's Party);

- Consumers (Chair: Pauline Green, UK, Socialist);

- Disabled people (chair: Derek Prag, UK, Conservative);

- Family policies;

- Rural areas;

- Islands, peripheral and maritime regions; and

- Social economy and co-operatives.

- See 'Intergroups' in *European Citizen* No 4, Oct/Nov 1990, available from ECAS, rue du Trône 98, B.1050, Brussels, Tel. 322 512 9360, Fax 322 512 6673.

Petitioning the Parliament

It is possible to petition the European parliament. Any citizen who believes he or she has suffered under EC law or been the victim of unfair treatment is entitled to send a written petition to the petitions committee of the Parliament. There were 785 petitions in 1990-1, of which 103 came from the UK (the second highest number, after Germany). Belgian physiotherapists have used petitions to ensure France recognised their professional qualification; another successful action led to Greece dropping its practice of charging foreigners higher prices for entry to museums! Besides the threat of legal action which petitions may bring, they can also be of publicity value.

The Economic and Social Committee

The Economic and Social Committee has the dubious distinction of being the least influential of the EC institutions! The Economic and Social Committee, is, like many of the other EC institutions, a French device modelled on the Republic's own Economic and Social Committee, in effect a third house to its parliament. The role of the Economic and Social Committee is to give opinions (they are formally called opinions) on EC measures, policies and proposals. The committee must be consulted by the Council and the Commission in certain specified areas, which include social policy; it may be consulted on others; and it can proffer its own views on anything it wishes (this is called an 'own initiative opinion'). The committee presents over 100 opinions a year, and a smaller number of special reports each year. The large countries, like Britain, have 24 members, while a small country such as Luxembourg has only 6.

Generally, however, the Economic and Social Committee reflects the interests of three groupings: employers, trade unions and sectoral interests (agriculture, trade and the professions). The committee is appointed by the member governments of the EC every four years, and the present term lasts until 1994. It is unusual for representatives of UK voluntary organisations to be appointed to the Economic and Social Committee, though a recent member is Sue Slipman of the National Council of One-parent Families.

There are two means whereby voluntary organisations may influence the Economic and Social Committee: the first is to approach the rapporteur of an upcoming opinion so that the opinion may reflect its position; and the second is to persuade the committee to appoint one of its members or nominees as an 'expert' to assist the rapporteur (the rapporteur can be assisted by up to four experts).

Recent reports from the Committee include *The economic and social situation in the EC, Consumer information, Declining industrial areas*, and *The future of rural society*. The committee works in nine sections: (i) economic affairs; (ii) external relations; (iii) social, family, educational and cultural affairs; (iv) environment, public health and consumer affairs; (v) agriculture, regional development; (vi) industry; (vii)transport; (viii) energy; and (ix) research.

■ The Economic and Social Committee, rue Ravenstein 2, B.1000 Brussels, Tel. 322 519 9011, Fax 322 513 4893.

The European Court of Justice (ECJ)

Thirteen judges are appointed to the Court of Justice. Their decisions are binding. Matters can be referred to the Court by the Commission if it believes a member state is in breach of the treaties establishing the Communities; by one state with a grievance against another for breaching the treaties; or brought there by individuals or organisations in the member states if they believe that their rights under the treaties have been abridged. National courts can refer questions of EC law to the Court for a ruling – and they often do so if they believe that European law will sooner or later become relevant to the outcome of the case.

The procedures of the European Court can be slow and the intricacies of European law convoluted. Nevertheless, some voluntary and community organisations have helped their clients to bring their cases there for adjudication.

■ The European Court of Justice, Palais de la Cour de Justice, L.2929 Luxembourg, Tel. 352 43031, Fax 352 4303 2600.

The work of the Court of Justice is based on both the Treaty of Rome (and its subsequent amendments), and on the legislation prepared by the Commission and subsequently approved by the other organs of the European Communities. As a general statement, EC law takes precedence over national law, unless the national government can subsequently persuade the Court that EC law has no particular competence in the particular field (generally, the Commission will not prepare legislation likely to exceed its competence). This has produced a situation in which in any EC country, two bodies of law now exist side by side, EC law and national law, the former taking precedence – a situation which has, not unexpectedly, furnished much of the heat in the discussion as to the manner in which EC membership abridges a nation's sovereignty.

Most EC legislation has concerned economic, rather than social, matters. It has concentrated on what is called competition policy – breaking down national legislation preventing the free movement of companies and trade. National governments have been reluctant to let the Commission prepare legislation in the social area, preferring to keep social affairs a national concern. In the social arena, the Commission has been invited to prepare non-binding recommendations, rather than binding legislation. The shining exception to all of this has been in the area of women's rights: the uncomplicated declaration in the Treaty affirming the right of women to obtain equal pay has led to a series of court judgments in a number of countries striking down discrimination in the areas of social security and employment-related entitlements.

■ Detail on current ECJ cases is given in the *Bulletin of the European Communities* and *Welfare Rights Bulletin*, published by the Child Poverty Action Group (CPAG).

■ See especially chapter 7: Information on Europe and how to get it.

Lobbying the EC: the Points of Influence

As is the case with most political institutions elsewhere in the world, there is no one single point in the European Communities where political pressure is always decisive for the lobbyist – whether the lobbyist be a voluntary organisation, a network, or a commercial body. Political activity and lobbying in the EC is often a confusing mosaic of defensive actions (preventing EC action in a particular area), monitoring (acting as the eyes and ears for one's members, tipping them off about developments which may prove positive, or neutral or negative), and pro-active action. Granted that most voluntary organisations wish to expand EC competence, activity, funding and interest in social affairs, this means that most voluntary organisations find themselves (or at least *should* find themselves!) in a pro-active role. Because the Commission is the EC institution which initiates legislation and determines the broad brush strokes of funding priorities, it is the focus of the energies of most voluntary organisations, which make a point of building up relationships in the directorate-general of greatest relevance to their cause.

It is the aspiration of every voluntary organisation, network or lobby to persuade the Commission to draft legislation, present action plans, and concoct specialised programmes – and then see their smooth passage through the other European institutions into reality. Indeed, as a rough rule of thumb, 80 per cent of Commission legislation, recommendations and proposals do see the light of day – but that guideline has to be qualified: the Commission has a shrewd sense of what it thinks is likely to get through, and frames its proposals accordingly. Consequently, the more sophisticated voluntary organisations and networks will devote efforts to building up a consensus for their viewpoint among the other bodies that are an integral part of the European political decision-making machinery. They will ensure there is a vocal group of MEPs to argue their case; they will bring the Economic and Social Committee round to their side by persuading it to adopt an opinion that endorses their position; and the network's parent organisations in the member states will lose no time persuading their minister or their government that forthcoming EC proposals in the area concerned should be favoured. There is evidence that some adversarial voluntary organisations are giving attention not only to the bringing of test cases to the European Court of Justice, but also that they are finding ways whereby they can report their government to the Commission for being in breach of provisions of the Treaties (thereby leading to the Commission taking infringement procedures in the Court of Justice).

In lobbying the EC, the more professional voluntary organisations and networks will use a broad-front strategy in canvassing support for their proposals. The EC has generally proved itself not to be amendable to one point of pressure alone – the successful campaigns have won through because they have worked diligently to find backing from as many sources of pressure as possible.

■ *Grants from Europe*, 25–8.

Structural Funds

For the period 1989-93, a total of 60 billion ECU are being devoted to what are termed the structural funds. Almost all of this goes into three funds:

- Agricultural Guidance Fund (EAGGF, more commonly called FEOGA);
- European Regional Development Fund (ERDF); and
- European Social Fund (ESF).

These are allocated on the basis of agreements between the Commission and the member states, called Community Support Frameworks (CSFs). Regional spending was a priority within the European Communities 1991 budget. The ten least developed regions of the EC entered the 1990s with incomes less than one third of the average of the 10 richest regions. The contrasts between the regions were evident when the Commission published its fourth periodic report on the regions in February 1991. There are 171 'regions' in the EC, and, taking 100 as the average, the gross domestic product varies between Groningen (Netherlands) at 183.1, and Voreio Aigaio (Greece) at 39.9. The lowest UK regions are Northern Ireland (80.6) and Merseyside (86.1), and the highest is Greater London at 164.0. A total of 75 per cent of all research and development in the EC takes place in just three countries: Germany, France and the UK.

The EC structural funds work toward five objectives. These distinctions are technical, and enormously important, because some programmes are available only in particular regions. Objectives 1, 2 and 5b refer to specific geographical areas; objectives 3 and 4 refer to groups in need. Objectives 3 and 4 can, theoretically, apply to any region or part of the EC; in practice, some areas have benefited more than others. The objectives are as follows:

- objective 1 - Areas where GNP is lower than 75 per cent of the EC average. These are Ireland, south and west Spain, Corsica, southern Italy, all of Greece, the former east Germany, overseas French territories, and all of Portugal;
- objective 2 - Regions affected by serious industrial decline;
- objective 3 - Long-term unemployment;
- objective 4 - Vocational training of young people; and
- objective 5 - (5a) agricultural reconstruction; (5b) areas where rural development (agriculture, forestry and fishing) is a priority.

Strangely, maps of the different objective areas are not easy to come by, but one is published in the Commission's document *Guide to the reform of the structural funds*. This shows how Northern Ireland (together with the rest of Ireland) is an objective 1 area. Objective 2 areas in the UK are quite small, comprising parts of south Wales, parts of the north-east, and a swathe from Merseyside to Manchester. Objective 3 areas which have benefited from the structural funds take in most of the rest of Wales and a large central band of the country from the midlands up to and including central Scotland. Objective 5b areas are parts of Devon and Cornwall, parts of Dyfed, Powys and Gwynedd, parts of Dumfries and Galloway, and the Highlands and Islands.

■ Commission of the European Communities: *Guide to the reform of the structural funds*. Brussels, 1989. ISBN 92-826-0029-7.

An understanding of the objective areas is vital, for these categories determine how EC money flows into the different areas of the EC. Some specialised EC programmes simply do not apply to areas outside the objective 1 area. Obviously, the UK as a whole does badly out of the objective 1 money, only Northern Ireland being able to benefit, but does far better out of other allocations. For example, the UK received 38.3 per cent of all the objective 2 allocations over 1989–93, by far the most generous allocation in the EC.

■ The specialised programmes of the European Communities, chapter 3.

■ *Grants from Europe*, 40–8.

The Special Institutions

Besides the principal political institutions of the European Communities (Parliament, Council of Ministers, Commission, Economic and Social Committee) there are three permanent institutions: the European Investment Bank (EIB) in Luxembourg; the European Centre for Vocational Training (CEDEFOP) in Berlin; and the European Foundation for the Improvement of Living and Working Conditions (European Foundation, in short), in Dublin. Two more are in the process of formation: the European Environment Agency (EEA) and the Health and Safety Agency (HSA). These bodies are to be distinguished from the specialised programmes of the Communities, which may run from year to year or over three, four, or five year periods, but which may or may not be renewed.

The European Investment Bank (EIB)
The European Investment Bank was created by the Treaty of Rome to foster greater economic and social cohesion in the EC, and forms an integral part of the Treaty. All member states subscribe to its capital, which stands at 57.6

billion ECU. Its aims include the economic advancement of less favoured areas, the improvement of transport and telecommunications, protection of the environment, urban development, the promotion of SMEs, and enhancing the competitiveness of industry.

While not a commercial profit-making bank, the EIB is required to adhere to the rules of strict banking management. The EIB finances projects outside the EC, such as in the African, Pacific and Caribbean states, 12 mediterranean countries and, more recently, Poland and Hungary. Loans (generally at fixed rates) may not normally exceed 50 per cent of investment costs. Duration of loans is generally 7-12 years (industrial projects) and up to 20 years (infrastructural projects). Loans totalled 12.7 billion ECU in 1990.

The UK is the second highest user of the European Investment Bank, with loans totalling 1,652 MECU in 1989 (Italy is the principal user, at 3,734 MECU). The UK loans, which were for private companies, went to industry (450.2 MECU), SMEs (58.1 MECU), transport (305.7 MECU, including the channel tunnel), energy (211.6 MECU) and the modernisation of water supply companies (431.8 MECU). Spending in the environmental area rose from 1.7 billion ECU in 1989 to 2.2 billion ECU in 1990, most going on water treatment plants, cleaning up dirty industry, and improving the quality of drinking water. 7,400 SMEs received loans of over two billion ECU. The bank's annual report (with summary) is available on request: it also publishes a leaflet outlining its work and the monthly *EIB Information*.

The relevance of the EIB to the voluntary sector is limited, although it is an important body in the picture of EC funding and financing. Although EIB loans to the UK were for private companies, the pattern of allocation varies according to member state: in other countries loans went to public enterprises and local and regional authorities. Voluntary organisations can, at least in principle, point their statutory partners in the direction of the EIB for project funding. There are also moves to encourage the scope of EIB funding towards projects with a more social dimension.

■ European Investment Bank, Blvd Konrad Adenauer 100, L-2950 Luxembourg, Tel. 352 43791, Fax 437704.

■ European Investment Bank, 68 Pall Mall, London SW1W 5ES, Tel. 071 839 3351, Fax 071 930 9929.

The European Bank for Reconstruction and Development (EBRD)

The European Investment Bank is not to be confused with the European Bank for Reconstruction and Development (EBRD), agreed in May 1990, launched in April 1991 and located in the London docklands. Conceived by President Mitterrand of France in the aftermath of the revolutions in central Europe in 1989, it is mainly designed to fund private sector projects in central Europe. Capitalised at 10 billion ECU, it is much smaller than the European Investment

Bank. Thirty-nine states are shareholders, plus the European Investment Bank on behalf of the European Communities. Its chief executive is a Mitterrand adviser, Jacques Attali.

The European Foundation for the Improvement of Living and Working Conditions
The European Foundation for the Improvement of Living and Working Conditions must have the most protracted title of all the European institutions, though in shorthand it is often referred to as 'The European Foundation', or even 'The Foundation'. The title tells a story, which is that outside the economic sphere, the social policy competence of the European Communities is limited, in the words of the Treaty, to the improvement of living and working conditions.

The European Foundation was set up in 1976 in Dublin, Ireland, in an old Georgian house on the outskirts of the city. Its board consists of the representatives of employers (one per country), trade unions (one per country) and government (one per country, generally a representative of the national Department of Labour). Its agenda is determined by the board, and it is organised according to four-year long rolling programmes, the present one expiring in 1992. The issues of importance selected by the board are progressed through research, documentation and information activities. Social issues have, since the mid-1980s, assumed a greater importance in the Foundation's work. Its budget is 9 MECU.

The Foundation's research reports are weighty. They have been rewritten in a series of information booklets which are available in all the principal EC languages. The following issues are addressed by some of the present rolling programme:

• industrial relations;

• new forms of work, and the social impact of shiftworking;

• safety at work;

• hazardous wastes, and how factories protect the local environment;

• young people leaving home, including housing projects for young people;

• technologies in the future (biotechnology, the electronic home); and

• the contribution of local action to the development of disadvantaged urban areas.

A new project of the Foundation is Eurocounsel – an action research network involving six countries (Denmark, UK, Ireland, Germany, Spain and Italy). The project began its first 18-month phase of operations in 1991, and may last 36 months altogether. Its purpose is to monitor and analyse the effectiveness of counselling services in helping the long-term unemployed, and look at means whereby these services can be made more effective. Contact either the Foundation or:

■ CEI Consultants, Brussels, rue Belliard 205, B.1047 Brussels, Tel. 322 230 6068, Fax 322 230 7176.

The Foundation will be of interest to the voluntary sector for two reasons. First, its conferences on specialised themes provide opportunities for experts, practitioners, projects, researchers and policy-makers to come together to discuss common themes, share information and perhaps find partners. One of the strengths of the Foundation's social research is that it is rooted in and connected to, local studies, projects and action. Second, the Foundation's publications provide a valuable European context for social issues. The Foundation's publications have an analytical (rather than a statistical) bent, stating problems, noting projects, comparing the approaches of different countries, and looking at ways forward. Publications include *Social change and local action – coping with disadvantage in urban areas, The paths of young people toward autonomy, Living conditions in urban areas, Locally-based responses to long-term unemployment,* and *Activities for the long-term unemployed* (by country). Titles published in 1991 included *Part-time work in the European Communities* and *Public services – working for the consumer.* The onus is very much on the voluntary sector to make itself known to the Foundation.

The Foundation has a library, publications, and a new-look bimonthly newsletter, *News from the Foundation.*

■ European Foundation for the Improvement of Living and Working Conditions, Loughlinstown House, Shankill, co Dublin, Ireland, Tel. 353 1 282 6888, Fax 353 1 282 6456.

The European Centre for the Development of Vocational Training (CEDEFOP)

CEDEFOP was in some senses a twin institution to the European Foundation, being set up at a similar time (1975), comparable in size, and with parallel rolling programmes. CEDEFOP is located in Berlin. The legal basis of the centre is article 118 of the Treaty, which gives the Commission responsibility for promoting close co-operation in the member states in the social field, particularly in matters related to vocational training. CEDEFOP works closely with the national vocational training agencies in each of the member states. Its board consists of representatives of trade unions (one per country), representatives of employers' organisations (one per country), and representatives of the national governments (one per country), and it has a staff of 60.

CEDEFOP has three main tasks:

26

- information on developments in vocational training in the Twelve;

- research into new vocational training initiatives, with a focus on innovation; and

- consultation: bringing together the different bodies concerned with training.

CEDEFOP's programme is organised according to action guidelines, those at present in force until 1992. CEDEFOP's role has expanded because of the commitment of the European Communities to a free labour market – an essential element of which is that qualifications gained in one country should be recognised automatically in another. Unless qualifications are so recognised, free movement of labour is a theoretical possibility only. As a result, one of its main undertakings is preparing a set of comparative tables whereby professional qualifications for one country and another can be compared. In Eurospeak, this is called 'comparability'. Thus far, comparability studies have covered the catering industry, vehicle repair, construction, agriculture, electric and electronic engineering, and textiles/clothing. Ultimately, the purpose of this work is to create an EC system for the mutual recognition of diplomas, certificates and qualifications, and the establishment of a European Training Pass.

CEDEFOP has examined the position of groups vulnerable to the free labour market, and where improved vocational training opportunities are vital. It is carrying out research into the training needs of women, migrants, people with learning difficulties, and those isolated in backward regions. It organises study visits and assists transnational projects.

CEDEFOP has a portfolio of publications: *Vocational Training* (12 ECU/year), *CEDEFOP News*, *CEDEFOP Press* and *CEDEFOP Flash*, as well as a substantial book list.

■ CEDEFOP, Jean Monnet House, Bundesallee 22, D.1000 Berlin 15, Germany, Tel. 49 30 88 4120, Fax 49 30 884 12 222.

The European Environment Agency (EEA) and the Health and Safety Agency (HSA)
The European Environment Agency is expected to be set up in 1992, when agreement is reached on its location. One of its functions will be to monitor the growing battery of EC standards in the environmental area, ranging from the management of hazardous waste to limits on car exhaust emissions, and the elimination of CFCs. A European-wide, standardised environmental system, code-named CORINNE, is already in place. Also projected is a Health and Safety Agency, possibly to be located in Greece. Its function will be to supply the EC and the member states with technical and scientific information

in the field of health and safety at work, information that will be used as a basis for Commission directives and other legal instruments.

How are Decisions Actually Taken in the EC?

Not only have the European Communities grown in size since their inception, but their scope, objectives and orientation were redefined in 1987 by the Single European Act. This Act:

* committed the Communities to the completion of the single market;

* enlarged the competence of the Communities; and

* laid down new procedures for decision-making.

The new procedures for decision-making revised the means whereby decisions were reached in the Communities. They are called the 'SEA Co-operation procedure'. Under the co-operation procedure, proposals (for legislation, recommendation or whatever) go from the Commission to the Parliament for an opinion, called a first reading. The Council then makes known its view (called a 'common position'), and sends the proposal back to the Parliament for a second reading. The Parliament has three months in which to endorse, amend or reject the proposal in its new form. Then things get really complicated.

If the Parliament approves the proposal, the Council then confirms it, and the matter is settled. If the Parliament rejects the proposal, the Council may override the objection by unanimous vote. Should the Parliament amend the proposal, the Commission then recommends a course of action to the Council. If the Council fails to act within three months of receiving suggested amendments, then the proposal lapses.

This is a gross oversimplification of the co-operation procedure: such a description fails to do justice to its tortuous Byzantine complexities. The procedure has been designed to produce results, and, by building in incentives for the three elements to co-operate, end the pre-1987 stalemates. In the first eighteen months of the co-operation procedure, the Commission accepted in whole or in part 60 per cent of the Parliament's amendments, and 60 per cent on the second reading. The Council accepted 44 per cent of first reading amendments and 23 per cent of second reading amendments. From the point of view of the voluntary organisations, it means that the opportunities for influencing decision-making are multiple, and they can have many more openings than would be the case in national parliaments. At the same time, voluntary organisations and the European networks to which some belong need to be quick off the mark if they are to take advantage of the 'co-operation procedure'.

The processes of European decision-making were revised for the third time in 1991 and led to agreement in principle by the Twelve to form a European Political, Economic and Monetary Union. The accord was signed by the heads of government meeting in Maastricht, Netherlands in December 1991.

The main terms of the Union treaty were:

- a common currency by the year 1999 at the latest;

- a European central bank (the EUROFED);

- procedures to establish a common security and foreign policy; and

- the concept of common Union citizenship.

Increased powers for the Parliament were agreed although these fell short of what the Parliament had hoped. Parliament was granted new powers of enquiry, petition and the right to reject proposals from the Council of Ministers in a number of areas. Parliament was also made responsible for the appointment of an ombudsman to whom any citizen could complain about maladministration by the institutions of the Communities.

The powers, competences and funding arrangements of the Communities were redefined and extended in the following areas:

- education and training;

- research and development;

- environment;

- transeuropean transport;

- health;

- culture;

- rural development;

- consumer protection; and

- development co-operation.

The UK obtained special provision to opt out of the single currency arrangements. The UK refused to sign the social section of the Union treaty. As a result, the other eleven states made a legal arrangement to sign the social section as separate treaty, and proceed without the UK.

OTHER EUROPEAN INSTITUTIONS

Council of Europe

The voluntary sector tends to focus most of its attention on the institutions of the European Communities, because of their proximity, influence and the scale of their information output. An older institution, the Council of Europe, is often overlooked. Not only is the Council relevant to the work of the voluntary sector, but it may provide easier access for the voluntary sector and its networks than the EC institutions.

Ten countries formed the original Council of Europe in 1949, and it now has 25 members, although these include some very small states, such as San Marino and Liechtenstein. The Council of Europe had ambitious aims – Winston Churchill envisioned it as an embryonic United States of Europe. The Council includes the Scandinavian countries, Austria and Turkey. The Council has four main institutions (some of which in the fullness of time became a model for the European Communities):

- Committee of Ministers (normally the Minister for Foreign Affairs or a permanent representative appointed to represent the Minister);
- Parliamentary Assembly of 184 members, including 18 from the UK;
- Secretariat, which presents a programme of work; and
- the European Court of Human Rights, with seven judges.

The Council of Europe, which is located in Strasbourg, has little power but is nonetheless influential. The Council of Ministers can make binding decisions, but rarely does so. The parliamentary assembly may recommend action, but cannot require it. The Council of Europe became the first political, institutional bridge to central Europe when Hungary became a member in 1990. The Czech and Slovak Federal Republic has joined, and Poland is becoming a full member. Members of the assembly are appointed by national parliaments, generally according to party strengths there: they are not directly elected.

■ The Council of Europe, Palais de l'Europe, F 67006 Strasbourg Cedex, France, Tel. 33 88 41 2000, Fax 33 8841 2781/33 8836 7057/33 8837 3259.

■ London Press & Information Office, Tel. 071 720 8781.

European Court of Human Rights and the Human Rights Commission

The Council of Europe's influence has been most durable in the area of human rights. The Council of Europe's *European Convention on Human Rights* (1950) not only enables one state to sue another for breaches of human rights, but, under certain circumstances, empowers citizens to sue their governments for such breaches. Between 1955 and 1980, ten governments and 9,016 individuals took advantage of these procedures. Complaints go first to the Human Rights Commission, and then to the European Court of Human Rights for final decision. The human rights orientation of the convention has led both individuals and voluntary organisations to consider it an attractive instrument for the advancement of grievances, with, in some respects, more scope than the EC's European Court of Justice.

The Court of Human Rights has the power to bind member states to carry out its decisions. Cases taken to the Court have led to the establishment of a right of persons detained in a psychiatric hospital to have access to a court; to the abolition of birching; to the decriminalisation of homosexuality; and to the extension of press freedoms. In a famous 1979 judgment, the Court ruled that all citizens had a right to legal aid – and required member states to establish schemes of legal aid and advice. Human rights abuses in Turkey in the early 1980s were highlighted by the Court. At the same time, it is worth noting that this process (like most international law) is slow, and depends on national governments for their implementation (although recalcitrant governments can be brought back to court for non-compliance).

The European Court of Human Rights should not be confused with the European Court of Justice, which is an institution of the European Communities.

■ The Human Rights Commission; the European Court of Human Rights, Palais de l'Europe, 67006 Strasbourg, France, Tel. 33 88 614 961.

Council of Europe and NGOs

The Council of Europe welcomed the involvement of international non-governmental organisations in its work at an early stage. These NGOs had to be *international*, rather than just important national NGOs from individual countries – and this very requirement may have encouraged NGOs to come together on an international basis. The General Secretary of the Council in her preface to the directory of NGOs published by the Council of Europe in 1989 praised 'their dynamism, imaginativeness and competence....NGOs act both as a stimulus and a sounding board for international co-operation, denouncing shortcomings, encouraging further progress, and disseminating results.'

In 1952 the Council of Europe devised what it termed consultative status and encouraged international NGOs, with members functioning in a minimum number of countries, to apply. The Council drew up nine fields of activity, and NGOs could apply to be consulted under any one or a number of these headings. These are:

Council of Europe: defined fields of activity for voluntary organisations

- Human rights and fundamental freedoms;

- Media;

- Social and socio-economic problems;

- Education, culture and sport;

- Youth;

- Health;

- Heritage and environment;

- Local and regional government; and

- Legal co-operation.

To fulfil the requirements of consultative status, international NGOs must:

- have aims compatible with those of the Council of Europe;

- be 'representative of its field of activity';

- be 'interested in European problems'; and

- be a 'structured international organisation'.

NGOs co-operate with the Council through the provision of opinions, views, information and advice; by acting as consultants to studies organised by the Council; and by making presentations (either written or oral) to the Council's Parliamentary or intergovernmental committees.

A formal structure has evolved which places the contribution of NGOs to the Council on an official footing:

- the plenary conference of NGOs. This is an annual conference of all NGOs having consultative status. It elects a 25-strong Liaison Committee of NGOs;

- the Liaison Committee of NGOs, established in 1976. It meets three times a year and is responsible for contact with and representations to the Council of Europe secretariat;

- the parliamentarians/NGOs joint committee, established in 1979; and

- sectoral meetings. Three sectoral meetings are held during the parliamentary sessions. One concerns human rights.

The precise effect of NGOs in influencing the Council of Europe is difficult to gauge. NGOs have made a specific contribution to Council of Europe initiatives such as the *European convention on the legal status of migrant workers* and the *European campaign for the countryside 1987-8*. The question of detention in prison became a lively issue following a 1985 Society of Friends study by Mirjam Berg. With the assistance of the Council's Directorate of Legal Affairs, she carried out an examination of the record of member governments in observing pre-trial standards for remand prisoners. Her critical report was later quoted extensively by organisations concerned with penal reform.

In 1985, the Committee of Ministers of the Council of Europe adopted a recommendation on voluntary work in social welfare activities. It proposed greater consultation between the voluntary sector and the public authorities, tax exemptions and income tax relief to recognised volunteers' organisations, and the removal of obstacles which might prevent the unemployed doing voluntary work. A lengthy, 46-point 1990 recommendation by the Council of Europe Committee of Ministers concerned violence within the family: it outlined principles of good practice for member states and their national, regional and local authorities in responding to the problems of violence within the home, especially as it affected elderly people, women and children. Like many such exhortations, its value is likely to lie in the use made of it by voluntary organisations in pressing for improvements in their respective member states.

European youth organisations have a direct channel to the Council of Europe through the European Youth Centre and the European Youth Foundation.

■ See: networks of youth organisations, chapter 5.

In 1986, the Council of Europe opened for signature the *European convention on the recognition of the legal personality of international non-governmental organisations*. This applies to international associations, foundations and other private institutions functioning in at least two member states, and which have a basic constitutional structure.

■ NGO section, Council of Europe, B.P. 431/R6, F.67006 Strasbourg Cedex, France, Tel. 33 8861 4961, Fax 33 8836 7057.

Council of Europe and Social Issues

Twelve years after it came into existence, the Council of Europe signed the *European Social Charter* (1961), not to be confused with the *Charter of Fundamental Social Rights* (1989) agreed by the members of the European Communities (except Britain). The charter itemises rights in the areas of employment, social security, freedom of association and protection for migrant workers. The charter is supervised in two-year cycles by what is termed the Committee of Independent Experts. The charter is not enforceable in the manner of the *European Convention on Human Rights*, but it is not unimportant. The charter, for example, lays down the right to 'decent remuneration'. As a result, the Council defined a 'decency threshold', set at 68 per cent of the average wage of all men and women in the workforce. The Committee of Independent Experts has been damning of those countries (not least Britain) where low pay rates bring many workers below the 68 per cent level. Some voluntary organisations (the Low Pay Unit is an example) have been effective in quoting the committee's reports in an effort to persuade their governments to improve their policies and practices, but the full potential of working with the committee of independent experts has probably not been reached.

Council of Europe and Regional Policy

The Council of Europe was early to recognise the importance of regional policy in the construction of Europe. In 1957 it set up a representative body for the local authorities in Europe which in time matured as the Standing Conference of Local and Regional Authorities in Europe (CLRAE). Two recent initiatives are worth noting. First, CLRAE is currently promoting a European Charter of Regional and Minority Languages. Second, CLRAE adopted in 1989 a significant resolution which asserted the positive values of community development, asked its member organisations to recognise its potential, and declared its support for steps to set up a European association for community development.

Nordic Council

The Nordic Council (established 1952) is barely known outside Scandinavia, which is a pity, since it demonstrates mechanisms of intergovernmental and interparliamentary co-operation which have, by all accounts, enjoyed a much smoother passage than the institutions of the European Communities in the course of their evolution. The Council comprises Denmark, Sweden, Finland, Greenland, Iceland, Norway, the Faroes and Åland. The Council consists of:

- Nordic Council of Ministers;

- Nordic Council (consisting of 87 parliamentarians); and

- Six standing committees (economic, legal, communications, cultural, social and environmental, budget and control).

The Council meets for a week each year, generally the first week in March, taking it in turn to convene in each of the different Nordic capitals. In between, the work of the Council is carried on by a Presidium. Recommendations from the council go to the Ministers and the member governments for action. The council has been involved in the setting up of research institutes into such matters as atomic physics and volcanoes. The Council of Ministers oversees the work of the Nordic Investment Bank.

The Nordic Council works in a more consensual manner than the European Communities, which may be easier because of the political similarities of the nordic states. There is also a closer mesh between the national governments, the Council of Ministers, the Nordic Council of parliamentarians and the parliamentarians of the national assemblies. The Nordic Council has worked towards the convergence of policies in the Scandinavian countries, such as freedom of movement; regulations have been agreed covering family law, the sale of goods and business competition. There are about 100 'joint instruments', as they are termed, to implement the decisions of the Nordic Council, all funded from the joint Nordic budget. Some of the most recent initiatives of the Council have been similar in form to those of the EC, environmental programmes to save the Baltic sea being a prime example.

Mirroring the European Communities in reverse, the Nordic Council reached agreement on social policy before almost anything else. Under the Nordic Social Security Convention, 1955, a citizen from one Nordic country living in another has full social security rights there. The Council issues a three-year working programme, the present one being *Norden in Europe until 1992*. A newsletter, *Norden*, reports on developments in the Nordic Council of Ministers.

■ The Nordic Council, Tyrgatan 7, S-104 32 Stockholm, Sweden, Tel. 46 814 3820.

■ (for *Norden*) Nordic Council of Ministers, Store Standstraede 18, DK 1255 Copenhagen, Denmark, Tel/Fax 45 3311 4711, night Fax 45 3311 5232.

The European Free Trade Association (EFTA)

The European Free Trade Association was founded in Stockholm in 1960, and comprised many of the then non-EC countries of western Europe. It was subsequently depleted when several of its members, including the UK, left to join the EC. Present members of EFTA are Austria, Finland, Iceland, Norway, Sweden and Switzerland. Its objective has been similar to that of the EC: the liberalisation of trade. EFTA has never adopted institutions comparable to those of the European Communities.

■ See New members of the European Communities (p. 9).

■ European Free Trade Association (EFTA), 9 rue de Varembé, 2111 Geneva 20, Switzerland, Tel. 41 22 34 9000.

OECD (Organisation for Economic Co-operation and Development)

The Organisation for Economic Co-operation and Development, OECD, established in 1961, comprises 24 industrialised countries. As well as the EC countries, the OECD includes Scandinavia, Turkey, the United States, Canada, Japan, Australia, New Zealand, Austria and Switzerland.
The OECD has three declared aims:

• the promotion of economic growth and development;

• the promotion of economic and social welfare; and

• the stimulation of help to the developing nations.

The OECD is funded by its member countries. Its headquarters are in Paris, and its official languages are English and French. Its supreme body is its Council which consists of one representative for each country. The Council meets weekly. Each country maintains a permanent delegation to the OECD which operates like a normal diplomatic mission and is headed by an ambassador. The Council produces legally binding decisions (although these are rare) and recommendations. Most of the work of the OECD is carried out in 150 specialised committees, expert groups and working parties. The OECD has nine directorates, one of which is responsible for social affairs, manpower and education.
The OECD is important to the voluntary sector because of its information work and because, like the Council of Europe, it has consultative status for NGOs. NGO consultative status, introduced in 1962, is poorly developed, and

has been little advertised. So far, only five organisations have consultative status. These are:

- The Business and Industry Advisory Committee (BIAC);
- The Trade Union Advisory Committee (TUAC);
- The International Association of Crafts and Small and Medium Size Enterprises;
- The International Federation of Agricultural Producers; and
- The European Confederation of Agriculture.

The OECD often asks for advice from the International Labour Organisation, the EC, and the International Social Security Association (ISSA) but this is generally on a case-by-case basis. The OECD tries to avoid formal procedures and voluntary organisations are welcome to contact the secretariat. Contact it directly for further information and/or a publications catalogue:

■ OECD, rue André Pascal 2, 75775 Paris Cedex 16, France, Tel. 33 1 4524 8200, Fax 33 1 4524 9098/8500.

United Nations (UN)

The United Nations Organisation was conceived in the final days of the Second World War, and its creators had ambitions that exceeded those of the League of Nations in the 1930s. Not only was it to have a global peace-keeping role, but it was seen as an international body which would carry out international programmes of benefit to all the world's citizens. Furthermore, on the urging of Eleanor Roosevelt, wife of the President of the United States, voluntary organisations were visualised as playing an important part in this process. Several bodies of the United Nations make provision for consultative status with international NGOs.

The United Nations set up a number of agencies to address some of the key problems of the world. Several of these are located in Europe or have regional offices in Europe:

- The Food and Agriculture Organisation (FAO), located in Rome;
- The United Nations Scientific and Cultural Organisation (UNESCO), located in Paris;
- The World Health Organisation (WHO), with a regional office in Copenhagen; and

- The United Nations High Commissioner for Refugees (UNHCR), located in Geneva with a regional office in Brussels.

The European regional offices of the United Nations are located in Geneva and Vienna (the latter being termed the United Nations Office at Vienna (UNOV), located in the Vienna International Centre). The glass palaces of UNO Vienna (24,000 windows, it boasts!) tower over the east bank of the Danube, a stylish European riposte to the UN's illustrious headquarters building in New York. UN city Vienna, as the tourist bureau touts UNOV, is the centre of social policy development work (that includes women's rights), and has responsibility for drug control. The office incorporates the Centre for Social Development and Humanitarian Affairs (CSDHA). UNOV administers a number of UN trust funds, principally those concerned with ageing, disability and youth. CSDHA monitors trends in social welfare and advises national governments on social developments. The five priority areas in the Centre's work are elderly people, the advancement of women, disabled people, young people and criminal justice.

■ Publications: *International Social Development Review.*

UNOV is the focal point for European voluntary, community, and non-governmental organisations having consultative status with UN bodies. UNOV processes applications for accreditation and makes arrangements for meetings between them and the UN secretariat. No fewer than 900 NGOs are accredited to the UN, and a listing is available from UNOV (*Vienna-based NGO interest groups and NGO representatives accredited at the United Nations (Vienna)).*

■ United Nations Office at Vienna, Vienna International Centre, PO Box 500, Vienna, Austria, Tel. 43 1 211 310, Fax 43 1 232 156, 431 963 4879.

■ United Nations Food and Agriculture Organisation, via delle Terme di Caracalla, I-00100 Rome, Italy.

■ United Nations Information Centre for Britain and Ireland, Ship House, 20 Buckingham Gate, London SW1E 6LB.

■ The United Nations Association, 3 Whitehall Court, London SW1A 2EL.

■ The United Nations, United Nations Plaza, New York, New York 10017.

United Nations Economic and Social Council (ECOSOC)

The role of the United Nations Economic and Social Council (ECOSOC) is to carry out studies, make recommendations, and submit reports to the UN on economic and social matters, particularly in the area of human rights and fundamental freedoms.

Consultative status at ECOSOC is provided at a number of different levels, these different tiers representing different entitlements, such as the right to send observers, or the right to submit papers for circulation as UN documents. A subcommittee of ECOSOC decides whether to approve consultative status for an NGO and at what level. There is category I, II, III, etc. (at UNESCO it goes A, B, etc.). Category I applies to organisations whose competence covers most of the fields of interest of ECOSOC; category II is for bodies whose competence and interest covers only some of the fields of interest of ECOSOC. Examples of category I international non-governmental organisations are the International Council of Voluntary Agencies (ICVA), the International Union of Local Authorities (IULA) and the League of Red Cross Societies. Examples of category II are Amnesty, Rehabilitation International and the Salvation Army.

The Council of ECOSOC consists of 54 members, elected on rotation from UN member governments. ECOSOC holds two month-long sessions each year, one in New York and the other in Geneva. Between sessions, the work of ECOSOC is carried out by six functional commissions (which include commissions on social development, the status of women and human rights); regional commissions (there is one for Europe); and standing committees (there is one on the role of NGOs).

United Nations High Commissioner for Refugees (UNHCR)

The work of several UN agencies is likely to be of especial interest to voluntary organisations concerned with social issues. The United Nations High Commissioner for Refugees (UNHCR) (established 1949) deals with refugee problems throughout the world, with the exception of Palestinian refugees, who are the responsibility of its Relief and Works Agency (UNRWA). The function of the High Commissioner, within the framework of international conventions protecting persons fleeing a country where they face a 'well-founded fear of persecution', is to assist refugees and promote their assimilation into new national communities. The founding statute stresses that its work must be humanitarian, social and non-political. The budget of UNHCR is in the order of $450m, most of which is spent on emergency relief, voluntary repatriation, re-integration programmes, education, counselling, legal assistance and rehabilitation.

The Brussels office has a staff of 15 and is in contact with the Refugee Council and the European Consultation on Refugees and Exiles (ECRE) in Britain. It discusses refugee and asylum policy with the institutions of the EC, particularly the Schengen agreement. The public information office in Geneva publishes an informative monthly newsletter, called simply *Refugees* and other printed and audio-visual material. There is a Documentation Centre on Refugees (DCR), library and reading room at 5-7 avenue de la Paix, 1201 Geneva. The UNHCR has direct contact with over 200 non-governmental organisations working with refugees. Despite its location in Europe, the European region absorbs the smallest portion of the overall budget: Africa is the largest single area of spending.

■ United Nations High Commissioner for Refugees (UNHCR), PO Box 2500, CH 1211 Geneva 2, Switzerland, Tel. 41 22 739 8111, Fax 41 22 731 9546.

■ rue Van Eyck 11a, B.1050 Brussels, Tel. 322 649 0151, Fax 322 641 9005.

United Nations Educational, Scientific and Cultural Organisation (UNESCO)

Britain left UNESCO in 1985 because it was considered to be adopting too political a role. One-third of UNESCO's budget is spent on educational work, and the rest on natural sciences, culture and communications. Educational work is concentrated on the struggle against illiteracy, and improving access to primary education in developing countries. The work of UNESCO is documented in its monthly newsletter, *UNESCO Courier*.

Over 500 voluntary organisations have a working relationship with UNESCO, which is classified in three categories: 43 organisations have consultative status, 263 have 'informative and consultative relationships' and 263 information only.

■ UNESCO, place de Fontenoy, F.75700 Paris, France, Tel. 331 4568 1000, Fax 331 4273 0401.

World Health Organisation (WHO)

The regional office of the World Health Organisation (established 1948) is located in Denmark. A total of 32 countries belong to the European region. The function of WHO is to work with national governments to raise health standards consistently throughout Europe, in order to achieve lower mortality and disability rates, by setting targets and reporting on progress towards their achievement (the *Health for all by the year 2000* programme).

WHO Europe runs what is called the Healthy Cities Programme in conjunction with 30 urban local authorities in Europe (London, Liverpool, Glasgow and Belfast are the UK participants), these being linked in turn to a further 300 cities under national healthy cities programmes. These are all now grouped under what is called EURONET.

WHO publications, principally in the *Strategy for health for all by the year 2000* series should be of interest to voluntary organisations: situation reports on health in Europe cover such issues as disability, AIDS, smoking and environmental health, combining statistical information with analysis of government policies. Its country reports describe the health and social services of all European countries, and attempt to measure their achievements. WHO has a comprehensive publications catalogue (available from Copenhagen), though books must be ordered through its UK agent, which is HMSO. A list of published documents is available in a separate catalogue.

■ World Health Organisation – Regional Office for Europe, 8 Scherfigsvej, DK 2100 Copenhagen, Denmark, Tel. 45 3129 0111, Fax 45 3118 1120, e-mail DKA110.

■ HMSO, PO Box 276, London SW8 5DT, Tel. 071 873 8372, Fax 071 873 8463.

International Labour Organisation (ILO)

The ILO was the first specialised agency of the United Nations, dating from 1919, having been proposed by Germany as part of the armistice arrangements ending the First World War. Its structure is quite different from other UN bodies, being a tripartite consultative body involving governments, employers and trade unions (its working methods are described as *tripartism*). There is a built-in role for employers and trade union representatives in the ILO. Each member state sends four voting delegates to its conference: two represent government, one the employers, and one the workers.

The stated objectives of the ILO are the promotion of human and trade union rights, and the improvement of living and working conditions. This is done through the preparation of binding conventions on labour and employment standards, which member states are invited to ratify; and recommendations, which they are urged to honour. The operation of these conventions is monitored by a Committee of Experts to which governments must report and to which comments by non-governmental organisations are invited. The UK has ratified 80 of the ILO's 171 Conventions. They cover such matters as minimum wages, maximum hours of work, discrimination, freedom of association and dangerous occupations. The ILO has also taken an important role in promoting improved national social security cover for workers and the unemployed.

The ILO has a liaison office in Brussels to maintain contact with the European institutions, and the trade unions and employers' organisations represented there. The ILO has a an excellent library, database and documentation centre. The ILO Institute for Labour Studies is located in Geneva and it runs an advanced vocational training centre in Turin. Recent ILO programmes have promoted the participation of women in using the industrial relations machinery.

The ILO has a $1.5m publishing programme of books and periodicals: the latter include such titles as *International Labour Review*, *Official Bulletin*, *Women at Work* and the *Bulletin of Labour Statistics*. The ILO has close links with the International Social Security Association. Procedures have been laid down for consultation with international NGOs (or networks): the ILO has what is called a *Special List* of NGOs with which it has, in effect, consultative status. Other NGOs can apply to attend particular ILO conferences or meetings. Details of both procedures are available on request.

■ ILO, route des Morillons 4, CH-1211 Geneva 22, Switzerland, Tel. 41 22 799 6111.

■ ILO Bureau de Liaison, 40 rue Aimé Smekens, B.1040 Brussels, Tel. 322 736 5942, Fax 322 735 4825.

■ ILO London, Vincent House, Vincent Square, London SW1P 2NB, Tel. 071 828 6401.

UN Conventions

The practice of adopting conventions is not unique to the ILO: it is followed by the UN itself. A stream of conventions, declarations and protocols have been adopted by the UN since 1948. Two conventions adopted by the General Assembly of the United Nations in recent years will be of especial interest to voluntary organisations: these are the *Convention on the rights of the child* (1989), and the *International convention on the protection of the rights of all migrant workers and members of their families* (1990). Both are now open for signature by the UN member states. Both conventions require member states to report to the UN on how they honour the conventions, and make provision for people to complain if their rights are being violated in their state. Legally speaking, this does not seem to provide the complainant with a strong basis for changing the practice of his or her member government; in practice, change or improvement takes place because of the ability of individuals or organisations to highlight their grievances in the media. Reporting one's country to the UN is a campaigning strategy hitherto little used by voluntary organisations.

■ *Proclaiming migrants rights: the new international convention on the protection of the rights of all migrant workers and members of their families.* Churches Committee for Migrants in Europe, rue Joseph II 174, B.1040 Brussels, Tel. 322 230 2011, Fax 322 231 1413.

North Atlantic Treaty Organisation (NATO)

NATO is a collective defence alliance of 14 European countries (including the UK) with the United States and Canada. Its role is currently under re-evaluation, following the demise of its rival, the Warsaw Pact, in 1991. NATO has a parliamentary assembly of 188 members, drawn from the parliaments of its member countries, which meets twice a year. Several pacifist groups have attempted to begin a dialogue with the Assembly in the hope of persuading it to look at non-violent alternatives to problems of defence.

■ North Atlantic Assembly, International Section, place du Petit Sablon 3, B.1000 Brussels, Tel. 322 728 4111.

■ Public relations section: 322 728 4997. It arranges tours and study visits.

Western European Union (WEU)

The Western European Union (established 1955) is mentioned from time to time in discussions and debates about the future of Europe. The WEU consists of the NATO members of the EC, with the exception of Denmark and Greece (Ireland is not a NATO member). Its aims are to promote the co-ordination of security and defence among its nine members. The WEU has a parliamentary assembly of 108 members.

■ Parliamentary Assembly of the Western European Union, 9 Grosvenor Place, London SW1X 7HL, Tel. 071 235 5351.

International Organisation for Migration (IOM)

Since 1951 there has been a government-based international agency concerned with migration. The International Organisation for Migration (IOM) works with governments and voluntary agencies to ensure the 'orderly migration of persons in need of international migration services'. IOM has a staff of 140 in its Geneva headquarters in Switzerland, and between 1951 and 1989 helped over four million persons. Its on-the-ground work includes the provision of resettlement programmes, language and orientation courses and medical services. IOM provides advisory services on migration policy and legislation: its academic review, *International Migration*, plays a role in current research on migration issues.

Membership of IOM is open to member states, observer states (Britain is an observer, rather than a member), international governmental organisations and international non-governmental organisations (the Red Cross being such an example). IOM's European work revolves around resettling immigrants from CIS: this could well grow in importance.

■ IOM Brussels, rue Belliard 65, B. 1047 Brussels, Tel. 322 230 6055, Fax 322 230 0763.

■ IOM office, Cranmer House, 3rd floor, 39 Brixton Road, London SW9 6DD, Tel. 071 735 6197/8.

Charter of Paris (1990)

The most recent institutions in the architecture of Europe are those in the process of construction following the Charter of Paris in 1990. Likely to be considered in the course of time as one of the landmark European peace treaties after Vienna (1815) and Versailles (1919), 34 nations came together in Paris in November 1990 to sign the end of the cold war. They did so under the auspices of the Conference of Security and Co-operation in Europe (CSCE), first held in Helsinki in 1975, and designed to regulate the postwar world. The treaty involves:

• a Parliamentary Assembly, likely to be modelled on the Council of Europe;

• a human rights mechanism;

• an affirmation that the distinct identities of national minorities will be protected;

• a commitment to economic, environmental, social and scientific co-operation;

• a CSCE secretariat in Prague; and

• a Conflict Prevention Centre in Vienna.

None of these elements was elaborated at the signing of the Treaty. The human rights mechanism would entitle individuals to raise grievances at an international level, and entitle one state to raise human rights matters with another; it would be policed by a roster of eminent persons involved in human rights issues. At this stage, it is not intended to adopt legally binding conventions, and the governments of the 34 are exploring means whereby mechanisms can, if possible, make a reality of its aspirations through non-legalistic means.

3

European Programmes and Foundations

UK government departments run programmes, schemes and initiatives directly from their central and regional offices: the 23 directorates of the European Communities have not built up bureaucratic empires on this model. Instead, they run specialised programmes which are subcontracted to management groups, consultancies, networks, correspondents and institutions. These are then given programme titles and acronyms. Some are funding programmes, others are information networks, some have a policy and advisory role; many are an uneasy combination of the three. Most provide opportunities for contact and influence for the voluntary sector. Some have liaison groups with voluntary organisations; in all cases, recommendations from the specialised programmes are fed back into the institutions of the Communities, and to the Commission in particular.

This chapter describes these specialised programmes, and then goes on to review the main European foundations, institutes and bodies promoting co-operation in Europe. Chapter 3 then looks at smaller societies and groups promoting greater contact with Europe, before concluding with a glance at some of the British organisations now locating in Brussels. All provide routes into Europe in some shape or form – routes that will lead to information, political influence or working partnerships for voluntary organisations.

SPECIALISED PROGRAMMES OF THE EUROPEAN COMMUNITIES

Voluntary organisations generally do not warm to the devolving of specialised programmes to consultancies, management groups, 'technical support teams' and institutions for two reasons: a distrust of management 'experts' and the ideologies with which they may be associated and because it may be difficult to hold them accountable. However, the circumstances in which these programmes arise are worth examining. Specialised programmes have a time limit – normally in the order of three years. This gives them an experimental character, which means that they can be renewed if they prove successful, or abandoned if not. They do not become a permanent part of the bureaucratic structure, a matter to which European governments are sensitive. As a general rule, the specialised programmes are run by agencies which have both organisational and promotional skills. They have a commitment to publications, output of information and accessibility by voluntary organisations (and any others who may be interested). How effective they are in influencing EC policy is difficult to judge.

The EC institutions have been reluctant to establish permanent agencies and institutions. In the field of social policy, there have been only two: the European Foundation for the Improvement of Living and Working Conditions, in Dublin, and the European Centre for Vocational Training (CEDEFOP), in Berlin. Some specialised programmes have proved popular and have been renewed. There is now an extensive range of specialised programmes in operation, to the extent that the Commission has been accused of setting up a programme where in other countries governments set up committees. It is even said that there is a Commission official whose full-time job is to dream up acronyms for the specialised programmes! Some of the programmes discussed may not be readily usable by the voluntary sector, but voluntary organisations will come across them and hear about them from time to time.

The specialised programmes vary in their scale: some are quite small and are designed with a limited catchment group in mind. Others are broad. For that reason, the amount of money being spent is indicated, and where possible, the number of projects operational or the number of people involved. Some recent programmes (like the Horizon, NOW and Euroform programmes) are transnational funding schemes. Some specialised programmes combine many different elements – funding, information and policy. As a result of these diverse purposes, they can be difficult to disentangle. A further organisational complication is that some are run exclusively from Brussels; others, by contrast, from national government departments, and some from a combination of the two.

A number of specialised programmes have advisory committees. As well as advising the programmes in question, they serve as a liaison point between the programmes, the Commission, the 12 national governments and other interested persons. The purpose of such advisory committees is, in the Commission's view, to ensure convergence between what it is trying to do and what national governments are trying to do. For voluntary organisations, these advisory committees are important, not because of their power (they have little) but their influence: they serve as an information route into the Commission. Voluntary organisations wishing to make known their activities and policies may well wish to consider putting members of the advisory committees on their mailing lists – and ask to be sent material in return.

■ Details of advisory committees from the National Council for Voluntary Organisations, 26 Bedford Square, London WC1B 3HU, Tel. 071 636 4066, Fax 071 436 3188.

The listing of programmes includes most of the programmes that could, in some shape or form, be of interest to voluntary and community organisations, or individuals within them. Programmes in the fields of advanced technology, agriculture, industry and SMEs have not been included. The listings here give only an outline of the programmes concerned: some programmes are enormously detailed, with elaborate criteria, and for that reason should be followed up with further enquiries. It is very much up to voluntary and community organisations themselves to pursue whichever programmes seem of the greatest interest to them.

Some notes of caution. First, although programmes may have a particular start date, sometimes they do not actually get under way until the following year. The process of devising a programme, the reaching of agreement between the Parliament and the Council of Ministers as to its level of funding, and the appointment of technical support teams to run the programme in question can take a number of years. Thus programmes are listed which are not yet up and running, although they have passed well beyond the aspirational stage. Second, a number of programmes are co-funded; they require co-funding from national, regional or local authorities. Although voluntary organisations are welcome as initiators of projects, because EC funding may be limited to 50 per cent of the cost of the project, voluntary organisations must either meet the balance themselves, or find a partner in the statutory sector. In the case of other specialised programmes, approval is required from national 'agents' appointed to supervise the programme in question (either a technical support agency or a government department). Third, programmes differ between the closed and the on-going. The first category is those programmes that have a single, start-of-programme deadline for the submission of project applications (generally six months after the programme is approved). Even if a project misses the deadline, voluntary organisations may still find the programme to be a useful source of information, and may be in a better position to apply for the next phase, even if it is possibly three years down the line. Open programmes are on-going, either taking applications for projects or participation all the time or on an annual basis.

Some voluntary organisations have obtained European Commission funding for research studies and conferences without the requirement for matching funding. The Commission is in a position to spend small amounts of money on information studies and conferences bringing together the main European 'actors' in areas where the Communities have competence, or are developing an interest. It is up to voluntary organisations to put forward such proposals to the appropriate Directorate-General, outlining the area concerned, how it relates to the competence and activities of the Commission, how such a project would advance these issues, the expected outcomes, and a proposed budget. Such applications are treated on a case-by-case basis.

A new Euro-word appeared in the early 1990s: the concept of the 'observatory'. The European Commission has now established a number of observatories. This does not indicate a sudden interest by the Commission in star-gazing: the term suggests the idea of institutes which observe social, or regional, events taking place and report back on what they see. There are now observatories on cross-border co-operation, homelessness, the family, employment, and 'social exclusion' (Eurospeak for poverty). A branch unit of an observatory is called an antenna.

A problem which voluntary organisations face in coming to terms with European programmes is the quality of language used in the explanatory documents. Some of the documents have not benefited in the course of translation and retranslation, and reaching a precise understanding of exactly which programme is intended for whom, in what way and exactly what it means can be a testing undertaking. Some programmes overlap each other, and distinctions between each are not readily evident. There are even suggestions that the EC has come to perceive this problem itself: to give one example, the MIRIAM programme (information on rural development) is partly an information programme to explain how all the other rural development programmes actually work! Perhaps there is a script here for a Brussels version of *Yes, Minister* ('Yes, Commissioner')? Voluntary organisations that find difficulty with explanatory memoranda about programmes can sometimes do worse than go back to the original Council decision approving a particular programme: although legalistic in their wording, original documents sometimes have a clarity of language and conceptualisation lacking in their more garrulous successors.

Another word of caution about terminology: some of the specialised programmes are also termed networks – and they should not be confused with the networks of non-governmental voluntary organisations in the EC described in chapter 5. ERGO and ELISE, for example, are sometimes called networks, but for the sake of clarity they are termed programmes here. Despite that, some of these programmes have spawned a number of networks (the LEDA programme calls them 'mini-networks'), which in practice comprise voluntary organisations. The European Regional Fund began in

1991 to fund the first of up to 60 networks which involve combinations of voluntary organisations, business and the local authorities. These involve mini-networks and sub-networks.

Finally, dispelling many popular conceptions about the lack of British interest or involvement in Europe, most specialised programmes indicate that take-up by British organisations is high.

Before looking at the smaller, specialised programmes, it is worth setting them in the context of the structural funds.

General European Programmes Operating in the UK

The main funding programmes are unappealingly termed 'the structural funds' which comprise the Agricultural Guarantee Funds (EAGGF or FEOGA), the European Social Fund (ESF); and the European Regional Development Fund (ERDF).

Three Whitehall Departments have a large-scale involvement in the implementation of European programmes in the UK: the Department of Trade and Industry (DTI), which has general responsibility for the completion of the single market; the Department of Education and Science (DES), which has responsibility for some of the specialised education programmes, such as LINGUA; and the Department of Employment (DE), which is responsible for the European Social Fund.

European Social Fund

The Department of Employment has responsibility for administering the European Social Fund, one of the EC's programmes of greatest interest to the voluntary sector. Despite its title ('social'), it is in reality a fund for training.

The social fund, valued at four billion ECU for 1991, was devised to promote job opportunities for workers within the meaning of article 123 of the Treaty which describes its purpose as 'to improve employment opportunities for workers in the common market and to contribute thereby to raising the standard of living...it shall have the task of rendering the employment of workers easier and of increasing their geographical and occupational mobility within the Communities'. The value of the social fund to the UK is 1.025 billion ECU for 1990–2.

The ESF includes a voluntary sector programme. In 1987, about 150 local voluntary sector projects received ESF funding totalling about £15m. The voluntary sector programme was worth about £23m in 1991, or about 8.5 per cent of the UK allocation. The programme is administered by the National Council for Voluntary Organisations (NCVO), which is advised by a National Advisory Committee (NAC) which represents Scotland, Wales, and six English regions (London, central, southern, Yorkshire and Humberside, northern and northwestern). NCVO receives what the EC terms a technical assistance budget for its work in administering this budget. NCVO's role is limited to the allocation of funds under EC objective areas 3 and 4 (objectives 1, 2 and 5b being dealt with regionally). The principal problem in operating the ESF has been inordinate delay in waiting for payments from Brussels to come through, which has made the running of projects problematic.

■ Department of Employment –European Social Fund Unit, 6th floor, Civil Service College, 11 Belgrave Road, London SW1V 1RB, Tel. 071 834 6644.

■ Ms Christine Evans, National Council for Voluntary Organisations, 26 Bedford Square, London WC1B 3HU, Tel. 071 636 4066, Fax 071 436 3188.

There is a an advisory committee to the Commission on the operation of the European Social Fund.

■ UK representative: Ms. Rachel Green, Department of Employment, Social Fund Unit, 6th floor, Civil Service College, 11 Belgrave Road, London SW1V 1RB, Tel. 071 834 6644.

■ *Grants from Europe*, 43-5.

Strathclyde Community Business Ltd has been a user of the ESF since 1987: the company aims to create self-sustaining jobs for local unemployed people in areas of high unemployment (20-50 per cent), and to be a focus for community economic development. There is a strong emphasis on control of the scheme by local people. Details of this experience (which have been very mixed) are available from:

■ Strathclyde Community Business, 6 Harmony Row, Govan, Glasgow G51 3BA, Tel. 041 445 6363, Fax 041 445 4272.

Principal Regional Programmes
Specialised EC regional programmes channel finance from the European Regional Development Fund (ERDF) into the different objective 1, 2, 3, 4 and 5 regions.

Table 1 Principal EC regional programmes

Name	Field of activity	Budget	Remarks
VALOREN	Endogenous energy	400 MECU (1987-91)	N. Ireland eligible
RESIDER	Steel areas	300 MECU	50 per cent funding
RENAVAL	Shipbuilding areas	1990-3	
RECHAR	Coal-mining areas of UK and Germany	600 MECU (1990-4)	Fourteen UK areas eligible
ENVIREG	Environmental protection	500 MECU (1990-3)	N. Ireland and mediterranean
STRIDE	Research in manufacturing	400 MECU	N.Ireland eligible
INTERREG	Cross-border co-operation	800 MECU	Border regions in Ireland
REGIS	Peripheral areas	200 MECU	
TELMATIQUE	Telecommunications improvements	200 MECU	N. Ireland eligible
STAR	Advanced telecommunications for SMEs	1991-	
PRISMA	Product standards	100 MECU	Management advice
REGEN	Energy for regions	300 MECU	

Many parts of the UK are ineligible for some of the programmes in Table 1: some apply only to Northern Ireland, since it is designated an objective 1 area. But several areas have benefited from RENAVAL, such as Fife, Plymouth, parts of the north-east, and Middlesbrough. The process here is that possible areas for assistance are identified by the Commission, and funding may then be allocated following receipt of applications from the member government. Similarly, RECHAR was designed to bring economic activity back to coal-mining areas which have suffered high job losses, such as parts of the UK and Germany. Fourteen UK counties are eligible, and projects have included environmental restoration, the training of young people, and the creation of SMEs. A new programme, RETEX, was announced during 1991. It will provide help to the textile-producing regions of the EC. It is possible for voluntary organisations to put up projects for funding through these programmes and to pursue them with the directorate-general for regional affairs, and their local authorities and national governments.

■ DG XVI/A/2, Commission of the European Communities, rue de la loi 200, B. 1049 Brussels, Tel. 322 235 4628, Fax 322 235 0149.

■ *Grants from Europe*, 45–8.

Consulting with the Regions
Mechanisms have recently come into play which enable the local authorities to have an input into decision-making in the Communities. Since 1988 there has been a Consultative Council of Local and Regional Authorities with the European Communities. It has 42 elected members, of whom six come from the UK.

■ Local Government International Bureau, 35 Great Smith Street, London SW1P 3BJ, Tel. 071 222 1636, Fax 071 233 2179.

Specialised Regional Networks

During 1991, 18 MECU from the European Regional Development Fund (ERDF) were allocated for the construction of the first 12 of as many as 60 networks designed to improve information flow in the Communities (Table 2). These networks are co-funded between the Commission and groups of local authorities.

Quartiers en crise (best translated as 'old cities in crisis') is the name of a new 1.167 MECU network launched by the Commission in 1991 for urban areas in decline. It involves 25 cities from 10 member states, and is designed to respond to what it describes as a two-tier Europe which 'is a reality in many European cities where the poorest become increasingly marginalised'. UK cities that have participated in the pilot programme for *Quartiers en crise* are Paisley and Belfast.

The purpose of the network is to understand better the reasons for urban decline, and to stimulate co-operation between European towns and cities on this issue. The network will function through seminars, research, study meetings and a magazine.

■ *Quartiers en crise*, LSA, Prinsegracht 51, 2512 EX Den Haag, Netherlands, Tel. 31 70 380 4431, Fax 31 70 380 9973.

Table 2 New regional networks and their funding in MECU

Chambers of Commerce and development agencies	4.34
Tourism and maritime transport in the regions	3.5
Co-operation between the regions of the Atlantic coast	3.575
Communications technologies	2.961
Ouverture: liaison with central Europe	8.667
Co-operation between universities and regional and local authorities	8.667
Commission des villes: economic and technological co-operation for medium-sized towns, with five mini-networks	1.108
Best practice in public transport	0.55
Eurocities, with three mini-networks	1.0
Quartiers en crise: decaying urban neighbourhoods, involving 25 cities	1.167
Co-operation between cities of automobile producers	0.801
POLIS: road traffic informatics	2.2

Some of these networks also reflect the growing interest of the Commission in the future of cities in Europe. The tireless environment Commissioner Carlo Ripa di Meana pushed through a green paper on the urban environment during 1990-1, which is likely to lead by the mid-1990s to a more vigorous EC role in such issues as urban zoning, planning, traffic management and the conservation of the urban architecture and natural environment. This in turn may lead to Brussels having more direct links with the local authorities in Europe, bypassing national governments.

Community Education and Vocational Training

There are 14 specialised programmes currently running which are designed to promote cross-European training and educational experiences (Table 3). They vary in scale: ERASMUS has over 73,000 applications a year, while the ARION programme provides only 700 grants a year. LINGUA sets up language training opportunities for teachers, while the exchange of young workers scheme provides placements for study and training. Some programmes are based on individuals making applications; others depend on organisations making the necessary arrangements. Voluntary organisations may wish to consider which are most appropriate for them as organisations, or for individuals within their organisations.

■ *Grants from Europe*, 72–85.

Table 3 Specialised programmes in community education and vocational training

ERASMUS II	1990–4	Students in higher education
COMETT II	1990–4	Universities and SMEs
TEMPUS	1990–5	Training, with central Europe
Youth for Europe II	1992–	Exchanges for 15–25-year-olds
PETRA II	1992–5	Vocational training
Exchange of young workers IV	1984–	Exchanges for young workers aged 18–28
EUROTEC NET II	1990–4	Improving training through technology
ARION	1978–	Education policy-makers
LINGUA	1990–4	Teachers and students
DELTA II	1991–2	Technology to improve learning
EURYCLEE		New information technologies
Education of the children of migrant workers	1977–	15 pilot schemes for primary and secondary schools with migrant children
FORCE	1991–4	Adult training
EURYDICE	1980–	Information about education

ERASMUS is for students in higher education. Its objective is to increase the mobility of students in higher education. It provides grants to enable university students (postgraduate and undergraduate) to spend time training in other member states. The students who avail most of ERASMUS are engineering students, followed by students of languages and the social sciences. Nearly two-thirds of the total take-up has been from Britain, France and Germany. Its budget is 74 MECU a year.

■ ERASMUS, rue d'Arlon 15, B.1040 Brussels, Tel. 322 233 0111, Fax 322 233 0150.

COMETT II is for students in higher education. It focuses on university co-operation to improve training in the area of new technologies; transnational placements for students in enterprises; and the creation of transnational and sectoral networks in advanced technology training projects. Projects must involve both university and enterprises (preferably SMEs). COMETT II is open to the EFTA countries. There were 1,320 projects in phase I (50 per cent were from France and the UK). The budget is 230 MECU.

■ COMETT Technical Assistance Unit, ave. de Cortenberg 71, B.1040 Brussels, Tel. 322 733 9755.

Trans European Mobility Scheme for University Students (TEMPUS) is a 300 MECU programme for training co-operation with the central European countries. Priority countries are Poland and Hungary; followed by the Czech and Slovak Federal Republic, Rumania and Bulgaria. This is to be achieved through placements and exchanges called Joint European Projects (JEPs). Eligible projects include those concerning environmental protection, social sciences and agriculture. JEPs must involve two EC countries and one central European country. Awards go as high as 200,000 ECU but most will be much smaller. There are mobility grants for teachers, administrators and trainers from enterprises, for training assignments, visits and practical placements. Youth exchanges are funded up to 10,000 ECU per project. TEMPUS is aimed at university students, teachers and enterprises (including SMEs, professional bodies, public and local authorities).

■ EC Tempus office, rue de Trèves 45, B.1040 Brussels, Tel. 322 238 7833.

Youth for Europe is a programme of youth exchanges geared towards improving an understanding of the economic, social and cultural life of another member state, and the position of young people in it. There are study visits for youth leaders. Disabled people are now encouraged to use the scheme. The scale of the programme is 180,000 young people, and it is budgeted at 10 MECU in 1992, rising to 15 MECU in 1994. The programme enables young people to live and work in another member state for a period of up to six months, with grants of up to 500 ECU a month. The programme is run by the European Communities' Youth Exchange Bureau, a technical assistance body which runs Youth for Europe and the programme for the exchange of young workers.

■ European Communities Youth Exchange Bureau, place du Luxembourg 2-3, B.1040 Brussels, Tel. 322 511 1510, Fax 322 511 1960.

Partnership in Training and Research (PETRA) (established 1987) is subtitled the 'action programme for the vocational training of young people in their preparation for adult and working life'. Its objective is to ensure that all young people who so wish can receive two or more years' vocational training after leaving their full-time compulsory education. It concentrates on organisations working with young people undergoing vocational training and makes provision for extending the provision of vocational training, improving its quality and adapting training to new needs. There are four distinct elements:

- The European Network of Transnational Partnerships (ENTP): this provides grants of up to 10,000 ECU to enable a small number of projects to identify partners in other member states so they can address common problems (contact grants); and up to 30,000 ECU to enable such partnerships to continue their joint work (partnership grants). More than 350 projects are now estimated to be part of the network. Initiatives must be innovative in character, of value to other member states, and be capable of dissemination.

- Youth Initiative Projects (YIPs). These provide grants of up to 10,000 ECU to encourage youth projects concerned with training, the development of employment opportunities, and youth information. They are managed and controlled by young people themselves. About 150 YIPs are funded each year.

- Research partnerships. Grants of up to 25,000 ECU are available to organisations nominated by member states to study the improvement of vocational training. About 40 such research partnerships have been funded.

- Study visit programme. This is available for vocational training specialists, and about 300 such study visits have now been funded.

PETRA II is budgeted at 177 MECU, much of which will provide subsistence allowances, 75 per cent travel costs and preparatory costs such as language training.

■ PETRA UK: National Policy Co-ordinator of the PETRA programme, Department of Employment, Room 355, Caxton House, Tothill Street, London SW1H 9NF, Tel. 071 273 3000, Fax 071 273 5124.

PETRA is funded through the Commission's Task Force on Human Resources. It is administered by IFAPLAN, an independent German institute for applied social research and planning. IFAPLAN publishes information on PETRA, including a PETRA YEARBOOK.

■ PETRA, IFAPLAN, square Ambiorix 32, B.1040 Brussels, Tel. 322 230 7106, Fax 322 230 7167.

The exchange of young workers programme aims to help young workers (aged 18-28), through exchanges, to develop their work knowledge and experience through study training periods (three weeks to three months) or schemes for four to sixteen months. Funding arrangements make provision for 75 per cent of travel costs and a flat rate subsidy. Between 1984 and 1989 7,759 young people benefited from the programme, 3,044 of whom were in 1989. The 1990 budget was 5.5 MECU.

▪ Exchange of young workers programme, European Communities Youth Exchange Bureau, place du Luxembourg 2-3, B.1040 Brussels, Tel. 322 511 1510, Fax 322 511 1960.

The purpose of EUROTECNET II is to adapt vocational training to technological change; to assist in the design of future training in such a way that the new technologies are incorporated into training; and to improve access to training in new technologies for disadvantaged and marginalised groups, such as young people, women and the unemployed. This is done through the dissemination of information on vocational training which involves the new technologies; research and analysis; and networks of projects. There are 135 demonstration projects. The current budget is 28.5 MECU.

▪ EUROTECNET II, rue des deux Églises 37, B.1040 Brussels, Tel. 322 230 5378, Fax 322 230 0254.

▪ Eurotechnet II UK Advisory Committee, Department of Employment, Caxton House, Tothill Street, London SWIH 9NF, Tel. 071 273 5397, Fax 071 273 5475.

ARION is a small-scale programme for education policy-makers and experts, aimed at improving understanding of different education systems through study visits of up to one week at a time. Since 1978 3,200 study visits have been funded. About 700 grants were made in 1991.

▪ ARION Programme Assistance Unit, Paedagogischer Austauschdienst, Nassestraße 8, D.5300 Bonn 1, Germany.

The purpose of the 200 MECU LINGUA programme is to promote a substantial improvement in the teaching and learning of foreign languages in the EC for teachers and students in secondary education by language training through exchanges.

▪ LINGUA Technical Support Team, place du Luxembourg 2-3, B.1040 Brussels, Tel. 322 511 4218.

▪ In the UK, Tel. 071 224 1477 (for England and Wales); 031 447 8024 (for Scotland); and 0232 664 418 (Northern Ireland).

DELTA (Development of Learning Through Technological Advance) hopes to develop technologies that facilitate learning.

■ Commission of the European Communities, DG XIII, rue de la loi 200, B.1049 Brussels, Tel. 322 235 1111, Fax 322 235 0147.

EURYCLEE is a new programme specialising in the field of new information technologies in education.

■ National Council for Educational Technology, 3 Devonshire Street, London W1N 2BA.

The Education of the Children of Migrant Workers is one of the EC's older programmes, geared towards primary and secondary schools with migrant children. Its objectives are to improve the integration of migrant children into the education system. There are 15 pilot projects, including one in Nottingham. Studies and exchanges have been carried out concerning the education of children whose parents have no fixed abode (children of travelling people and gypsies); and on measures to combat illiteracy and skills problems for early school leavers. Its budget was 1.2 MECU in 1990.

■ Education of the Children of Migrant Workers, EWH, Im Fort 7, D-6740 Landau, Germany.

FORCE is for workers, and representatives of employers and workers in companies, or the self-employed, not the unemployed or those returning to the workforce. Its declared objectives are the improvement of adult training; innovation in management training; and training initiatives that support transnational partnerships. It surveys and forecasts future demands for skills, occupations and qualifications through partnership arrangements and international exchange schemes for durations of between 12 and 24 months. FORCE provides project grants: the maximum grant for large projects is 200,000 ECU; 7,500 ECU for exchange grants.

■ the Department of Employment (the 'national co-ordination unit') or:

■ FORCE, rue du Nord 34, B.1000 Brussels, Tel. 322 209 1311, Fax 322 209 1320.

Pickup Europe is linked to the FORCE: its brief is to work with Training and Enterprise Councils (TECs) to improve the training services that will prepare British industry for 1992. Pickup Europe has 23 regional centres in the UK. It publishes *Pickup bulletin*, and *Europe's money: a guide to the budget of the European Communities, 1991*.

■ The Pickup Europe Unit, South Bank Polytechnic, Borough Road, London SE1 0AA, Tel. 071 633 9249, Fax 071 261 9426.

EURYDICE, the Education Information Network in the European Community, facilitates the exchange of information about the different national education systems. There is a national correspondent in each state, generally located in the national department of education. The 1990 budget was 1.8 MECU (1990).

■ EURYDICE European Unit, rue Archimède 17, B.1040 Brussels, Tel. 322 230 0382, Fax 322 230 6562.

The Department of Education and Science (DES) has a briefing pack on all the specialised EC educational programmes.

■ The Department of Education and Science (DES), International Relations Division, Grove House, 2- 8 Orange Street, London WC2H 7WE, Tel. 071 321 0433.

Women

Specialised programmes for women operate within the context of the 150 MECU-worth third action plan to promote equality of opportunity for women and men (1991-5). The third action plan is a development of the first two action plans (1982-5 and 1986-90 respectively) and includes a number of new ideas. The present plan involves legislation and other measures in the areas of sexual discrimination, parental leave and social security; and the promotion of vocational training opportunities. A number of advisory and funding networks come under the auspices of this programme: these concern equal opportunities, diversification of occupational choices, women in the labour force (the NOW programme), women and television, women and local employment initiatives, childcare and training (IRIS).

■ *Equal opportunities for women and men: the third medium-term community action programme, 1991-5. Women of Europe* supplement no.34. Available from the Women's Information Service, Commission of the European Communities, rue de la loi 200, B.1049 Brussels.

■ *Grants from Europe, 56-9.*

IRIS
IRIS is subtitled the European Network of Training Schemes for Women. The present programme (phase I) runs from 1988 to 1992. It aims to ensure that women have access to quality vocational training through inter-programme exchange visits, national and transnational seminars and transnational partnerships.

There are now over 330 members, of whom 80 per cent train women-only, the balance predominantly concerned with meeting the training needs of women. Most of the programmes are aimed at unemployed women, women returning to the labour market and socially disadvantaged women. Just over half are geared for those aged over 25. Some 36 per cent of programmes concern the new technologies, followed by commerce, hotels, catering and tourism (20 per cent) and enterprise creation (20 per cent). Other projects are for manufacturing (18 per cent), office work (17 per cent), manual trades (15 per cent) and crafts (13 per cent). Details of the projects are listed in the IRIS directory.

Any vocational training programme for women satisfying the selection criteria can become a member of IRIS: as a result, it has full access to IRIS information (bulletin, directory, database, seminars, etc.), inter-programme exchanges, partnership and publicity grants. In return, it must keep IRIS up to date with its own activities. In 1989, there were 48 inter-programme exchanges. IRIS funds publicity grants to promote model programmes. The budget is 500,000 ECU per year. IRIS publishes an annual report, a quarterly bulletin and special dossiers.

The European Commission has overall responsibility for IRIS. The Centre for Research into European Women (CREW) manages and runs IRIS for the Commission. The Commission's working group on vocational training for women includes two representatives from each member state. One comes from the national training organisation and the other from the national equality body or its equivalent:

■ Mr John Sharman, Equal Opportunities Commission, Overseas House, Quay Street, Manchester M3 3HN, Tel. 061 833 9244, Fax 061 835 1657.

■ Ms Ann Greengrass, Training Agency, c/o Moorfoot, Porterbreask House, Block A/1, Sheffield S1 4PQ, Tel. 0742 704 166, Fax 0742 758 316.

■ The IRIS unit, Centre for Research into European Women (CREW), rue de la Tourelle 21, B.1040 Brussels, Tel. 322 230 5158, Fax 322 230 6230, e-mail MCR1:CREW.

NOW

NOW is a new 120 MECU flagship programme, billed with HORIZON and EUROFORM, for long-term unemployed women, women seeking to re-enter the workforce, women threatened by unemployment and the entire female working population in the poorer countries. Its objectives are the promotion of women's qualifications, changes in the enterprise culture to enable women to create their own businesses and co-operatives, the re-integration of women into the regular labour market (rather than temporary and unstable jobs), the promotion of structures that will provide childcare facilities, transnational partnerships and exchanges of experiences. This is done through the co-funding of projects by the EC and the national authorities.

The Commission's research has shown that although women may wish to opt for setting up self-employed activities and SMEs, the survival rate of these businesses is low, mainly because of the lack of training and know-how. NOW hopes to address this situation by providing help for the setting up of self-employed activities and SMEs run by women. NOW also provides support for the provision of childcare facilities, including their running and equipment costs and training for childcare workers.

■ NOW, Commission of the European Communities, rue de la loi 200, B.1049 Brussels, Tel. 322 235 1111.

Childcare Network of the European Commission

The EC childcare network deals with questions of access to childcare services, and the quality of these services. The network has one member from each state, and meets three times a year. The network was initially invited to put forward proposals on the development of childcare policies and provision, which it did in 1988. The network proposed a framework directive requiring member states to publicly fund childcare services for children up to the age of 10. Although this proposal received support from the women's committee of the European Parliament, no such directive was forthcoming; instead the Commission opted for a non-binding recommendation to member states to provide more childcare facilities for working parents.

The UK part of the network, in the course of organising its views and comments for the Commission, held a number of consultation meetings with the main childcare organisations. Several UK childcare action projects were undertaken over 1989-90. These included the following themes: men as carers, partnership nurseries and support services for own home care. The network now has publications available on childcare policies and provision, both in the UK and in the rest of Europe. UK member:

■ Dr Bronwen Cohen, Director, Scottish Child and Family Alliance/Clann agus Teaghlaichean an Albainn, 55 Albany Street, Edinburgh, Tel. 031 557 2780, Fax 031 556 5925.

■ The network co-ordinator: Peter Moss, Thomas Coram Research Unit, 41 Brunswick Square, London WC1, Tel. 071 278 2424.

There is an advisory committee on equal opportunities, with representatives from each of the member states. In addition to these national representatives, there are representatives from European trade unions, employers, public enterprises and agriculture. The UK national representatives are:

■ Mrs Joanna Foster, Chair, Equal Opportunities Commission, Overseas House, Quay Street, Manchester M3 3HN, Tel. 061 833 9244.

■ Ms June O'Dell, Deputy Chair, Equal Opportunities Commission, Overseas House, Quay Street, Manchester M3 3HN, Tel. 061 833 9244.

Employment

Unemployment in the EC stood at 9.1 per cent in 1991, and was forecast to rise to 9.25 per cent in 1992. Table 4 lists the six main EC programmes in the area of employment promotion.

Table 4 EC specialised employment programmes

ELISE	LEI	SPEC	ERGO	LEDA	Euroform

Note: both the present ELISE and ERGO programmes closed in autumn 1991, and their successor programmes have not yet been established, although it is anticipated they will be merged and resume in some form.

■ *Grants from Europe*, 39-50.

European Information Exchange Network on Local Development and Local Employment Initiatives (ELISE)

Many years ago, the European Communities identified local employment projects as a valuable means of combating unemployment, and they are clearly attractive to voluntary organisations as part of the process of community development. ELISE sets out to collect, process and distribute information on local employment initiatives throughout the Twelve. ELISE does this by means of:

- Three databanks (devoted to publications, projects and organisations);

- An information service;

- Research;

- Press service;

- An on-line journal updated every Monday;

- Project profiles; and

- A directory of local development agencies.

ELISE's project profiles may be of special interest to voluntary and community organisations. They are folders describing innovative and unusual projects in the member states, full of ideas, information and possible contacts. Two recent ones were devoted to housing and social integration and

63

employment. Full membership of ELISE costs 1,000 ECU. Although a programme concerned with local employment initiatives might not be the most obvious place to expect this, ELISE has a range of information relevant to voluntary and community organisations. *ELISE News* is the 10-times-a-year information bulletin. It is well presented, up-to-date, clearly written, and provides names and addresses for further enquiries. It normally runs a page on the development of European networks. Subscriptions for non-members cost 80 ECU. In addition to reporting on local employment initiatives, it carries several pages on EC initiatives and developments. Its coverage of networks of voluntary organisations, their activities and news of European voluntary organisations is unique. ELISE is managed by AEIDL.

■ ELISE, rue Breydel 34, B.1040 Brussels, Tel. 322 230 5234, Fax 322 230 3482.

The European Communities' Support Programme for Women's Local Employment Initiatives (LEI)

This programme should be of considerable interest to community groups promoting the participation of women in local enterprise projects. Because of its success under the second programme for equality (1986-90), this programme is being continued as part of the EC's third action programme on equal opportunities between men and women (1991-5).

LEI offers start-up grants (1991 budget, 1.5 MECU) and technical support, by means of a transnational network of experts, to women starting businesses and other initiatives to create jobs for women. Over the period 1987-90, some 600 women's initiatives received start-up grants under this programme, covering sectors such as organic horticulture, processing, data-banking, desktop publishing, design and marketing.

Grants range from 1500 to 7500 ECU, but they can often make the difference for women facing difficulties in raising sufficient capital and credibility in their applications for bank loans. Initiatives by women in marginalised categories (migrants, lone-parents, disabled) receive priority.

■ Caroline Turner, co-ordinator, Breakthrough, 14 Victor Hugo Street, 54625 Thessaloniki, Greece, Tel & Fax 30 31 535 658.

■ Eva Eberhardt, Equal Opportunities Unit, Commission of the European Communities, rue de la loi 200, B.1049 Brussels, Tel. 322 236 3221, Fax 322 235 0129.

There is a network of experts supporting women's local employment initiatives. In the UK the contact is:

■ Ms Alicia Bruce, CEI Consultants, 42 Frederick Street, Edinburgh EH2 1EX, Tel. 031 225 3144.

European Group for Local Employment Initiatives (EGLEI)
EGLEI is a related, independent network of independent local employment initiatives with over 50 members, involving study visits and cross-national comparisons of local enterprises. Membership costs 500 ECU. Lancashire Enterprises and Fife region are two of the UK members.

■ European Group for Local Employment Initiatives (EGLEI), rue des Échevins 72, B.1050 Brussels, Tel/Fax 322 646 7831.

Support Programme for Employment Creation (SPEC)
SPEC is a new joint programme between the Commission and the International Union of Local Authorities (IULA) to co-finance pilot innovative local and regional employment creation projects. Information and advice projects can receive grant-aid of up to 10,000 ECU; the ceiling for projects involving training, job creation, industrial restructuring or relocation measures can be 20,000 ECU. SPEC, which runs from 1990 to 1992, gives priority to objective 1 areas, objective 2 areas (declining industrial areas), objective 5b areas (underdeveloped rural areas) and cross-border areas. The 1992 budget is 5 MECU.

■ Commission of the European Communities, Directorate-General V, rue de la loi 200, B.1049 Brussels, Tel. 322 235 1111 (Mr Potamianos);

■ International Union of Local Authorities, PO Box 90646, 2509 LP The Hague, Netherlands, Tel. 31 32 7032 44032, Fax 31 31 7032 46916;

■ Local Regional Development Planning, impasse du Pré, B.1040 Brussels.

ERGO
ERGO is the European Communities' Action Programme in favour of the long-term unemployed. It aims to establish a selective inventory of programmes and projects that benefit long-term unemployed people, pointing out examples of good practice, and encourage projects to learn from each other. Issues arising are then communicated to those responsible for planning and implementing national programmes for assisting the long-term unemployed. There are national correspondents in each country who report back on developments in their countries. The programme is implemented by CEI Consultants. The first phase ran from 1989 to October 1991.

ERGO is a small-scale programme: its budget is 1.5 MECU a year. ERGO has a database of 1,600 local initiatives to help the unemployed and has 103 evaluations of local projects. It also has a publications portfolio which includes video and newsletter. The video studies a number of different initiatives against unemployment, comparing two projects: one in Derry (Northern Ireland), the other in Italy. *Work again* is a series of publications 'showing that in a number of fields interesting and practical things are being done with or for long-term unemployed people'. They describe 15 projects in the areas of health and welfare, arts, culture, energy conservation, the environment, housing and construction and rural development and are available for £3. ERGO NEWS is available on request: it has an unusual broadsheet format with information on local projects and news on EC developments and new programmes. Prior to the end of the present phase of the programme, a database of 1,700 locally-based projects fighting long-term unemployment was opened, accompanied by a directory of these 1,700 local projects.

■ ERGO, rue Belliard 205, B.1047 Brussels, Tel. 322 230 6068, Fax 322 230 7176.

The UK national correspondent:

■ Ms Alicia Bruce, CEI Consultants, 42 Frederick Street, Edinburgh EH2 1EX, Tel. 031 225 3144, Fax 031 226 2259.

Local Employment Development Action (LEDA)
LEDA is one of the few specialised programmes located in the UK. It is an experimental action and research programme based on pilot projects: it provides technical assistance and advice, and funds exchanges between projects. LEDA was launched in 1986 and expanded in 1988, although its budget remains small, at 1 MECU per year. Its purpose is to define strategies for local job creation schemes, and research into the operation of local employment markets. LEDA comprises 24 pilot areas which are subdivided into rural, mixed urban and rural, declining industrial communities and urban centres. It hopes to identify good practices in local strategies, and find ways of making local programmes more effective. It is not a funding programme, but one which spreads know-how, gives expert advice and provides some management training. LEDA-supported projects have been directed at stemming decline in rural areas, underdevelopment in peripheral areas. UK pilot areas are Dundee and Nottingham.

The LEDA projects are organised in five mini-networks: enterprise partnership, analysis of local markets, culture and human resources in development, local development organisations and tourism initiatives.

LEDA has an appealing publications portfolio including conference reports, policy reports, *LEDA Newsletter* and *Magazine*.

■ LEDA, Local and Regional Development Planning, South Bank Technopark, London Road, London SE1 6LN, Tel. 071 922 8835, Fax 071 261 1166.

■ LEDA, rue Franklin 106, B.1040 Brussels, Tel. 322 732 4250, Fax 322 732 4973.

Euroform

Euroform is the second of a three-part set of funding programmes which run with HORIZON and NOW. Begun in 1991, it is aimed at the long-term unemployed, apprentices, young people and persons threatened by unemployment. Euroform, budgeted at 300 MECU, is based on joint funding between the EC and national authorities of transnational training schemes, exchanges and partnerships of trainers and apprentices, the development of new qualifications, skills and employment opportunities. Priority is given to poorer regions of the EC.

In addition to specialised programmes promoting employment creation, the Communities have set up numerous programmes to help the development of industry, focusing on small and medium-sized enterprises (SMEs). These include the 90 MECU SPRINT programme (new technologies for SMEs), IMPACT 2 (information services for the single market), VALUE (information concerning SMEs), and TEDIS (electronic data exchange in industry).

Two networks in the field of business, training and employment creation
EUROCO is a new network of training organisations for the long-term young unemployed based in Germany, Belgium and the Netherlands, originally focused on yacht construction projects. Similar projects in the UK, Denmark, Spain, Portugal, Ireland and Poland have joined or are joining. It is designed to give young people the opportunity to broaden their training experiences by exchanges with other countries.

■ EUROCO, PO Box 5247, NL-2000 CE Haarlem, Netherlands, Tel. 31 23 310 503.

EUROCREATION is a French-based organisation concentrating on helping young people in the 18 –35 age group. Since 1985, it has supported over 200 projects in the fields of business, new technologies, the arts and environment. It is a project incubator, providing financial aid and identifying other funding sources and maintaining contact between projects.

■ EUROCREATION, rue Debelleyme 3, F.75003 Paris, France, Tel. 33 1 4029 9246.

Environment

The work of the European Communities in the environmental field expanded enormously in the late 1980s and early 1990s and is expected to continue to be a growth area.

Table 5 Specialised environmental programmes

REWARD	STEP	ACE	MEDSPA	NORSPA	ACNAT	LIFE

In addition, there are Pilot Projects to Conserve the Communities' Architectural Heritage, and an environmental clearing house, ELEICH.

■ *Grants from Europe*, 101-10.

REWARD is a programme of research into recycling of waste, including recycling technologies, and fuel and energy production from waste.

■ REWARD programme, DG XIII/E-1, rue Montoyer 75, B.1040 Brussels, Tel. 322 236 3024, Fax 322 235 0147.

The Science and Technology for the Environment Programme (STEP) is a programme for the protection and conservation of Europe's environmental heritage, technology for environment protection and dealing with technological hazards.

■ STEP programme, DG XIII/E-1, rue Montoyer 75, B.1040 Brussels, Tel. 322 236 3024, Fax 322 235 0147.

The 24 MECU Action by the Communities relating to the Environment (ACE) runs from 1990 to 1994. Its purpose is to develop clean technologies, and to encourage conservation and the creation of nature protection areas through demonstration projects.

■ ACE, Commission of the European Communities, Directorate-General for Environment, consumer protection & nuclear safety, rue de la loi 200, B.1049 Brussels, Tel. 322 236 1388.

MEDSPA is a programme (25 MECU in 1991-2) for the Mediterranean coastline. It will run from 1991 to 1996, and provide funding for waste removal projects, recycling and pollution control. Similarly, NORSPA (10 MECU) funds pilot projects (1991-3) in the North Sea, the Irish Sea and the Baltic. The programmes will encourage the use of new clean technologies, the protection of habitats, and administrative structures to ensure standards are met.

■ Commission of the European Communities, Directorate-General for Environment, consumer protection & nuclear safety, rue de la loi 200, B.1049 Brussels, Tel. 322 236 1388.

Further details are awaited on ACNAT and LIFE. ACNAT (Community action to conserve nature) is a new 50 MECU programme to preserve habitats.

LIFE has been described as a new 'funding instrument' and has been heralded as 'the beginning of an operational fund to allow the Communities to implement a real environmental policy'. An initial 31 MECU has been allocated to the LIFE programme. It will finance priority environmental projects through co-funding, subsidies and loans, and may subsume the MEDSPA, NORSPA and ACNAT programmes.

Pilot Projects to Conserve the Communities' Architectural Heritage
There are Pilot Projects to Conserve the Communities' Architectural Heritage, running from 1989 to 1993. The pilot projects have a budget of 2.4 MECU/year, operating on the basis of funding of between 1 and 40 per cent of the projects concerned. The Commission is most interested in projects that illustrate an area or region's architectural heritage by reason of its artistic or historical interest. Projects in 1992 give priority to public spaces and historical buildings. A project must receive public funding at least equivalent to that of the EC's funding.

■ Pilot Projects to Conserve the Communities' Architectural Heritage, Cultural Action Division, Office JECL 2/116, Commission of the European Communities, rue de la loi 200, B.1049 Brussels, Tel. 322 235 9095.

European Local Environmental Information Clearing House (ELEICH)
ELEICH will be of interest to groups concerned with local and community development, housing renewal and environmental action. Dating from 1987, ELEICH is funded jointly by the Commission of the European Communities and the Department of the Environment. It provides computerised information on local environmental action programmes, 'a single source of information for all those working in the environmental field in Europe'. Membership costs between £25 and £85 (plus VAT), depending on category. ELEICH provides data-sheets on such diverse projects as pedestrianisation, recycling, landscaping, urban renewal, disabled access, traffic management and nature in cities. ELEICH also provides a twinning service, linking British voluntary and statutory organisations with counterparts in Europe who face similar environmental problems. Some assistance towards expenses is provided.

■ ELEICH, 393 Corn Exchange Building, Manchester M4 3HN, Tel. 061 839 1589, Fax 061 236 5836.

General Fund
The Commission has a general fund for information, training and education in environmental awareness; for environmental projects; and for 25 per cent subsidies to European environmental organisations. NGOs, local and

regional authorities are invited to apply: applications are taken in March, June and October.

■ Commission of the European Communities, DG XI C 4, rue de la loi 200, B.1049 Brussels, Tel. 322 235 111, Fax 322 235 0144 (Mr Jankowski).

Rural Development

Two programmes, MIRIAM and LEADER, have been developed by the Commission to respond to the problems affecting rural areas of the Communities. These problems have been identified as population loss (the flight from the land), economic and industrial underdevelopment and poor environmental planning.

■ *Grants from Europe*, 17–18.

Model Scheme for Information on Rural Development Initiatives and Agricultural Markets (MIRIAM)

MIRIAM's objective is to set up an information network to encourage rural development. One hundred centres are planned throughout rural Europe. This network is based on eight existing experimental information centres, called *carrefours* (from the French word for crossroads). The first and thus far only UK *carrefour* is located in the Scottish Agricultural College, Perth, Scotland.

MIRIAM centres provide local development teams and community development groups with information on EC programmes, 'helping to guide them through the EC maze', foster the starting up of projects, and 'collect the expectations of rural areas'. MIRIAM also has a function of explaining the Common Agricultural Policy, and other agricultural policies, to farmers. MIRIAM's budget was 50 MECU in the first year, thereafter 20 MECU a year.

■ Carrefour Scotland, Scottish Agricultural College, Cleve Gardens, Oakbank Road, Perth PH1 1HF, Tel. 0738 36611, Fax 0738 27860.

■ DG X (Information), Commission of the European Communities, rue de la loi 200, B.1049 Brussels, Tel. 322 235 2902, Fax 322 236 0752.

MIRIAM is accompanied by ORA (Opportunities for Rural Areas), a 14 MECU programme (1991-4) to study the possibilities of information technology in improving the quality of rural life – though the Commission's approach has been criticised as one of trying to persuade farmers to 'replace feed troughs with satellite dishes'.

Liaison between Actions for the Development of the Rural Economy (LEADER)

LEADER's purpose is the acquisition of expertise in rural development. It is a three-year programme over the period 1990 –3 for objective 1 and 5b areas. The 400 Mecu LEADER programme is designed to improve the development potential of rural areas through local initiatives. LEADER operates through local rural development action groups drawn from 'leading figures in the local economy and society' which take responsibility for the handling of funds and investment. According to the Commission, 'many areas are handicapped by incapacity to exploit local resources, plan and support promoters of projects or make use of national and EC aid schemes. These failures stem primarily from the lack of local organisation and local encouragement of development.'

LEADER will provide support for the organisation of rural development, vocational training, rural tourism, small firms, craft enterprises, local services and the exploitation and marketing of local agricultural projects. Support and funding will go to local groups which may be either based on voluntary organisations or local authorities or a combination of the two. Areas suitable for the LEADER programme are defined as between 5,000 and 100,000 people. About 100 groups will be financed. These local groups will be encouraged and funded to use new technologies in their work.

■ Commission of the European Communities, DG VI (Agriculture), rue de la loi 200, B.1049, Brussels, Tel. 322 235 1111, Fax 322 235 0132.

European Support Centre for Rural Economic Activities (CESAR)

CESAR was opened by the Commission in 1991. It is described as a prototype resource forum for rural areas where economic development has been slow, concentrating on helping SMEs and the local authorities.

■ CESAR, rue de l'Ermitage 1, B.5561 Celles (Houyet), Belgium, Tel. 32 8266 6143, Fax 32 8266 6015.

Disabled People

It is estimated that as many as 30m European citizens, about a tenth of the population of the Communities, suffer from some kind of physical or mental disability or handicap. The first European action programme in favour of the disabled was launched in 1983: 19 local projects which promoted the social integration of the disabled were supported. HELIOS has since become the flagship specialised programme to help disabled people. TIDE is a much smaller, new programme. HORIZON is a new catch-all programme for disabled people, migrants and the long-term unemployed.

■ *Grants from Europe, 64-7.*

71

Handicapped People in the European Communities Living Independently in an Open Society (HELIOS)

HELIOS (established 1988) is named after the Greek word for sunshine. The present programme is to be succeeded by HELIOS III (1992-6). It aims to 'bring a common European approach to a range of disability issues such as employment, vocational training, independent living, mobility, access and housing'. There are four areas of practical co-operation with local services: the network of rehabilitation centres, the network of local model activities (LMAs), the information and documentation service and HANDYNET. An international jury decides the annual HELIOS European Independent Living Awards for organisations that best promote access to buildings, transport and housing. HELIOS's budget is 19 MECU.

HELIOS services a network of 50 rehabilitation centres of which six are in Britain (list available from HELIOS) with a variety of seminars and an annual conference. Eighty local pilot schemes are involved in local model activities (LMAs) covering three sectors of provision: school integration, economic integration and social integration. Each sub-network has a study visit programme, seminars and a theme-based conference. The information service edits the magazine (circulation 45,000) and holds a comprehensive stock of EC documents and texts. HANDYNET is a computerised database in nine languages, with information on technical aids for disabled people, products and legislation. It has a national data collection and co-ordination centre which in the UK is:

■ The Disabled Living Foundation, 380–384 Harrow Road, London W9 2HU, Tel. 071 289 6111.

HELIOS has two means of communication between the voluntary and national governments: an advisory committee and a liaison group. They act as a bridge between the representative organisations of disabled people and the relevant government ministries. Several international networks are represented on the liaison group: Action Européenne des Handicapés, Disabled People International, European Blind Union, the European Regional Secretariat of the World Union of the Deaf, Eurolink Age, the International League of Societies for Persons with Mental Handicap, Rehabilitation International, the European Association for Special Education, Mobility International and FIMITEC (Fédération Internationale des Mutilés, Invalides du Travail et Invalides Civiles). The UK government representatives on both the liaison group and the advisory committee are:

■ Department of Health, Alexander Fleming House, Room B 1509, Elephant and Castle, London SE1 6BY, Tel. 071 912 4125, Fax 071 407 7154.

■ Tom Gawn, Department of Employment, The Training Agency, Employment Rehabilitation Service (Room 908), Moorfoot, Sheffield S1 4PQ, Tel. 0742 594 492, Fax 0742 758 316.

■ See chapter 6: networks of European organisations working with disabled people.

In addition to the advisory committee and the liaison group, there is an annual meeting between the Commission and 27 national and international organisations concerned with disability. This is called the dialogue group. Each organisation appoints two representatives, and there is a growing tendency for these representatives to be disabled people. Sign language and braille are available at the annual meeting of the dialogue group, which the Commission funds.

HELIOS aims to be 'a driving force for EC legislation for people with disabilities' and it has urged legislation in the areas of employment, technical aids, integration in education, mobility and transport. HELIOS publishes a free-of-charge 16-page A4 colour magazine (circulation 45,000), covering all aspects of HELIOS, reporting on events and developments at European level in the field of disability, including the activities of NGOs. The magazine has included directories of HELIOS projects, including the participating UK projects, and could be a useful source of information for groups in Britain wishing to learn about disabled people in other European countries.

■ HELIOS, ave de Cortenberg 79, B.1040 Brussels, Tel. 322 735 4105, Fax 322 735 1671.

The EC Secretariat for Sports for the Disabled funds games for disabled people. It holds a databank on sports for disabled people and has a promotional film.

■ EC Secretariat for Sports for the Disabled, Heijenoordseweg 5, 6813 GG Arnhem, Netherlands, Tel. 31 85 526 726.

Technology for Socio-economic Integration of the Disabled and Elderly (TIDE)
TIDE is designed to improve communications and rehabilitation technology for disabled people. Its first budget in 1991 was 8 MECU.

■ TIDE, Commission of the European Communities, rue de la loi 200, B.1049 Brussels, Tel. 322 235 1111.

HORIZON
HORIZON is a new (adopted in December 1990) programme for disabled people, migrants and the long-term unemployed. It co-finances projects for these groups, together with national and regional authorities. It is budgeted

at 180 MECU for 1990–3. Its aim is to promote access to vocational training and to employment for persons with serious handicaps resulting from physical or mental impairments and other 'disadvantaged' categories ('persons suffering from specific difficulties which hinder or act as a brake on their economic and social integration'). There has been controversy over the way in which HORIZON attempts to mesh programmes for disabled people and the socially disadvantaged. HORIZON's aims are to improve access to the labour market for these groups through vocational training in the new technologies, distance learning, resettlement in the labour force and exchanges of experience and know-how.

For people with learning difficulties, HORIZON transnational exchanges must involve partners from objective 1 regions: aid is provided for the creation of SMEs, start up services, pilot projects to improve access to buildings and transport, technical aids and information networks. For the disadvantaged, HORIZON makes provision for transnational pilot projects involving guidance and counselling, vocational training, staff exchanges, language training and start-up services for SMEs.

■ HORIZON, European Communities Branch, Department of Employment, Caxton House, Tothill Street, London SW1H 9NF, Tel. 071 834 6644, Fax 071 828 7041.

■ Commission of the European Communities, Directorate-General V, rue de la loi 200, B.1049 Brussels, Tel. 322 235 1111.

Social Security and Anti-Poverty

One of the ways in which the European Communities have had the closest contact with the voluntary and community sector is through the anti-poverty programmes. These date from the mid-1970s. The anti-poverty programmes have frequently been criticised by the voluntary sector as being an inadequate response to the scale of the problem of European poverty; their working methods have come under close scrutiny; and individual projects have not been without funding and financial difficulties. Yet the ability of the Communities to run three consecutive such programmes (Table 6), sometimes in the teeth of opposition by national governments, has to be reckoned as an achievement in itself.

The persistence of high levels of poverty has been cited by critics as the weakest point in the process of European integration. The number of Europeans below the poverty line in 1989 was 50m people. Many attributed this to the low levels of economic development in some of the southern countries; to the shakeout of traditional European industries; and to the general rise in European unemployment. Radical critics attributed these distressing levels of poverty to governments pursuing policies which promoted inequality, and to EC agricultural policies which drove people from the land.

In response, the European Communities chose to finance model projects, rather than to promote across-the-board measures to alleviate poverty. The Commission hoped that a European picture of poverty would emerge, and that effective transnational measures against poverty would be taken as a natural result. Voluntary organisations were given co-funding for anti-poverty projects, generally on a basis of 55 per cent Commission funding and 45 per cent funding from national governments or local or regional authorities.

In addition to funding individual projects, the Commission invested resources in ensuring that lessons from one project were shared with other projects. For example, in the second programme, which saw the funding of 91 projects, there was a 'central information clearing house' (its Eurospeak title was 'the centre for the animation, diffusion and dissemination of information'!) in Cologne. The projects were grouped into themes (the elderly, the long-term unemployed, urban poverty, rural poverty, single parents, etc.): theme groups were required to meet to share their findings. Again, it was hoped that this would create a multiplier effect: the lessons learned from one project would be applied to another.

Research studies complemented the work of the local projects. Indeed, the anti-poverty programmes generated a considerable amount of literature. The first and second programmes produced end-of-programme reports (the second not until spring 1991); the work of projects was documented; and under the second anti-poverty programme, individual studies were done of poverty in each state. In the course of the second programme, studies were launched into what was termed 'new poverty' –identifying the 'new' poor of the 1980s, such as the long-term unemployed, one-parent families and the victims of cutbacks in public spending by national governments.

The first programme was termed The First European programme of pilot schemes to combat poverty; then there was the Second programme of the European Communities against poverty; and then there was the 'medium-term community action plan to foster the economic and social integration of the least privileged groups in society', sensibly called *Poverty 3* in shorthand. There has also been a shift in the nature of the projects funded. Reports from the second programme stressed the importance of voluntary-statutory co-ordination in the struggle against poverty. *Poverty 3* projects were expected to combine partners from the voluntary and the statutory sector.

Poverty 3 projects were selected in the course of 1990: it is closed to new applicants. Despite that, its importance should not be underestimated.

Table 6 The title, scale and dates of the three anti-poverty programmes

Title of programme	Dates	MECU
First European programme of pilot schemes to combat poverty	1975–80	20
Second EC programme against poverty	1985–9	29
Poverty 3	1990–3	55

Under *Poverty 3*, 39 projects are funded which are divided into two main groups: large-scale model actions – subdivided into rural and urban (27 projects) and innovative initiatives (12 projects). There are three model actions in the UK: the Liverpool Toxteth Pilot Project, the Brownlow Community Trust in Craigavon, Northern Ireland, and the Pilton Pilot Project in Edinburgh. There is one innovatory initiative, the Single Parent Action Network in Bristol.

An elaborate infrastructure is in place supporting the *Poverty 3* programme consisting of a central unit and research and development units. The central unit, which is located in Lille, is responsible for the co-ordination of all the 39 projects; animation of the projects; evaluation of the projects; information about them; and the research issues arising. It has published a directory describing all the projects, and a book outlining the programme, *Europe against poverty*. The unit has a workshop programme to promote communication between the projects over the period 1991-4, and although the main participants will be the projects, other persons, projects, and groups (including voluntary organisations) may be invited to participate.

■ *Poverty 3* central unit, EEIG A&R, rue Jacquemars Giélée 60, F-59800 Lille Cedex, France, Tel. 33 2054 3527, Fax 33 2030 7252.

In each country (except Benelux which are grouped together, and Germany and Denmark which are grouped together) there is a research and development unit (RDU) which co-ordinates the projects in each country, and extracts the policy and research issues arising from their work. The *Poverty 3* programme is a valuable source of information; its RDUs and its central unit are interested in what is going on in the poverty field outside the projects; and its final report will be instrumental in determining the shape, nature and orientation of Poverty 4 (if there is to be such a thing!). For the British RDU, contact:

■ John Benington, Local Government Centre, Warwick Business School, The University of Warwick, Coventry CV4 7AL, Tel. 0203 524 109, Fax 0203 523 719.

There is a liaison committee between the European Commission and the national governments which not only oversees the operation of *Poverty 3* but also examines the much broader issues concerning European anti-poverty policy. Technically, it is called the Advisory committee on the economic and social integration of the least favoured groups: it consists of one representative from each national government, generally an official from the Department of Social Security or its equivalent.

■ Ms Louise Maderson, Department of Social Security, Room 10146, The Adelphi, 1-11 John Adam Street, London WC2N 6HT, Tel. 071 962 8411, Fax 071 962 3437.

■ See also: European Anti-Poverty Network, EAPN.

■ *Grants from Europe*, 51–5.

SOME OTHER SPECIALISED PROGRAMMES...

AIDS

It is expected that there may be up to 150,000 AIDS cases in the EC by 1992. A 9 MECU action plan against AIDS in the EC was approved by the European Parliament in May 1991. It proposes information campaigns, training and exchanges of experts and data collection. The EC already funds campaigns against AIDS in the developing countries.

Information and Media Programmes

SYMBIOSIS is an information programme drawn up by Directorate-General X of the Commission in 1990 to inform the ordinary citizen about the 1992 programme. Still at a design stage, it hopes to distribute information about the single market and the implications of its completion through non-governmental organisations and networks, and through the local authorities.

■ SYMBIOSIS, Commission of the European Communities, Directorate-General for Information, communication and culture, rue de la loi 200, B.1049 Brussels, Tel. 322 235 4995.

The Media and the Audio-Visual Industry: MEDIA and MAP-TV

Measures to encourage the development of the audio-visual industry represent a new area of interest in the European Communities: a European action programme to develop the audio-visual industry was adopted in 1990. Its French-inspired origins lie in the need to protect an indigenous European audio-visual industry from powerful American influence and competition. The MEDIA programme was launched in 1991 with a 20 MECU budget line to take it to 1995. Its aim is to stimulate audio-visual activity, from creation to marketing, and to strengthen networks of makers and distributors.

Within MEDIA, there is a 700,000 ECU sub-programme to preserve and redistribute archival material called MAP-TV (Memory-Archives-Programme). The sub-programme will pay for colouring, new sound tracks and electronic preservation of the archives of Europe –and could be of some value to local groups aware of old documentaries of their communities.

■ Commission of the European Communities, DG X (Information, communication and culture), rue de la loi 200, B.1049 Brussels, Tel. 322 235 1111, Fax 322 236 0752.

The European Communities, Central Europe, and the CIS: PHARE

The first agreements between the European Communities and the former Council for Mutual Economic Assistance (CMEA) were signed in 1988. A 10-year agreement with Hungary was agreed in 1988 with a view to the rapid dismantling of trade barriers between the EC and Hungary. In July 1990, Hungary expressed the aspiration that it would become a full member of the Communities by 1995.

PHARE is the name of a specialised programme to help development in the central European economies, to which the European Communities are contributing 785 MECU in 1992. In 1991, 220 MECU were allocated to Poland for the modernisation of its financial sector, training and professional guidance, environmental protection projects, agriculture, health care and education. The PHARE programme also provided financial assistance to

Hungary of 140 MECU for training and education, environmental protection and energy projects. A further 500 MECU were allocated to the other countries covered by PHARE, namely Bulgaria, the Czech and Slovak Federal Republic, Rumania and Yugoslavia. Under PHARE, there will be BIC Networks (Business and Innovation Centres Networks) in Poland, Hungary, and the Czech and Slovak Federal Republic.

PHARE is a funding programme supervised by Directorate-General I, and responds to requests for funding from the governments of central Europe on a case-by-case basis.

OBSERVATORIES

When the French government decentralised its administration in the 1980s, a number of 'observatories' were set up to comment on the process of decentralisation and report back on what they saw unfolding. The Commission adopted this model in 1990.

Table 7 European Observatories

	Location	Management Body
Social exclusion	Bath	University of Bath
National family policies	Leuven	Catholic University
Homelessness	Brussels	FEANTSA
Social security	Leuven	MISSOC
Cross-border co-operation	Gronau	Association of European Border Regions
Employment	Brussels	SYSDEM and MISEP

The European Observatory on Social Exclusion

Following a Council of Ministers resolution on social exclusion (a French-derived term that translates best into English as poverty), the European Commission established a European observatory on national policies to combat social exclusion. The observatory involves 12 national correspondents and is co-ordinated at a technical level by Graham Room, Centre for Research in European Social and Employment Policy, at the University of Bath. The first annual report (a summary of which is also available), was published in 1991, in English, French and German, with 40 pages of data, analysis and comment. The observatory works in close collaboration with the *Poverty 3* programme and with other observatories in the social field which have been set up by the Commission.

■ European observatory on social exclusion, University of Bath, Claverton Down, Bath BA2 7AY, Tel. 0225 826826, Fax 0225 826381.

European Observatory on National Family Policies

The European observatory on national family policies was set up by the Communities to 'draft an annual report presenting significant measures and data showing the trends and guidelines of policies in the member states'. Its first annual report, detailing trends over 1988 -9, was published in June 1990, with information on the economic situation of families, the housing situation for families, and changes in family law in the member states. The observatory is helped by a number of national correspondents: in the UK they are Malcolm Wicks and Kathleen Kiernan of the Family Policy Studies Centre, London.

■ The European observatory on national family policies, Department of Sociology, Catholic University, E. van Evenstraat 2C, B.3000 Leuven, Belgium, Tel. 32 16 283111.

■ Malcolm Wicks, Family Policy Studies Centre, 231 Baker Street, London NW1 6XE, Tel. 071 486 8211.

European Observatory on Homelessness

The function of the European observatory on homelessness is to collect basic information on homelessness in each of the member states, and on the type of organisations working with the homeless. Policies to help homeless people have, in part, been frustrated by lack of clear definitions of homelessness, and by lack of standardised information on the number of homeless people in the different countries. The European observatory has begun this process of information-collection with a view to a 1992 first report. The work of the observatory has been delegated to the European Federation of National Organisations Working with the Homeless, FEANTSA. There are national correspondents in each country, and three expert advisers (from Italy, Belgium and Ireland).

■ European observatory on homelessness, FEANTSA, 1 rue Defacqz/17, B.1050 Brussels, Tel. 322 538 6669, Fax 322 539 4174.

The Observatory on Social Security: MISSOC (Mutual Information System on Social Protection)

MISSOC reflects an early attempt to grapple with the implications of European political union for the harmonisation of social security policies levels. Article 118 of the Treaty promotes *co-operation* in the field of social policy. As a first step, the Commission began to compile comparative tables of systems of social security in the EC. These tables were largely statistical in nature. MISSOC is designed to take this process a stage further by providing overviews of the systems of social security and public assistance, noting changes in policy and practice, making proposals for reform, with policy analysis.

It is intended that MISSOC hold a databank on social security systems in the member states, and that it publish an annual policy assessment of the development of national policies, with reports on each country. Information is supplied through national correspondents in each country, generally from the national department of social security.

■ MISSOC, Observatory on social security, Tiensestraat 41, B.3000 Leuven, Belgium, Tel. 320 1623 9338.

The European Observatory for Cross-border Co-operation (LACE)

In 1990, the European Communities established an observatory for cross-border co-operation, also titled the LACE project (Linkage, Assistance, Co-operation for the European regions). LACE examines the problems for border regions associated with the completion of the internal market, such as currency alignment, the removal of customs barriers, road and rail traffic, and shared environmental problems.

LACE hopes to promote relationships between border populations and the economic and infrastructural development of border areas. LACE hopes to do this by exchanging information and experience, by technical assistance and advice, and by helping border areas design cross-border projects. It can help border regions make proposals to the INTERREG programme (above). LACE is setting up a database on cross-border projects, issues and problems, which will be available in 1993. LACE can cover up to 75 per cent of the costs of individual activities in objective 1 areas (which would include border areas in Ireland). The LACE programme is managed by the Association of European Border Regions (AEBR), with 66 per cent EC funding.

■ European Observatory for cross-border co-operation (LACE), Enschederstraße 362, D.4432 Gronau, Germany, Tel. 49 2562 25062, Fax 49 2562 1639.

European Observatory on Employment

The European observatory on employment consists of two distinct elements: SYSDEM and MISEP. SYSDEM reports on the European pattern of employment change, MISEP on changes in policies and practice at national level.

Système Européenne de Documentation sur l'Emploi (SYSDEM)
SYSDEM is a new programme to collect information on employment trends, skills shortages and labour mobility with a view to encouraging early and appropriate policy responses at European and national level. SYSDEM is based on national correspondents, generally located in universities or institutes, and has an information unit/documentation centre and an analysis unit. It publishes a 20-page A4 quarterly *SYSDEM Bulletin*.

■ SYSDEM, square de Meeûs, B.1040 Brussels, Tel. 322 511 2058, Fax 322 511 2522.

■ SYSDEM c/0 ECOTEC Research & Consulting, 28-34 Albert Street, Birmingham B4 7UD, Tel. 021 616 1010, Fax 021 616 1099.

Mutual Information System on Employment Policies (MISEP)
MISEP (established 1982) is the system whereby information on employment policies within the member states is exchanged. It disseminates those measures, policies and actions adopted by the member states that promote and improve employment. MISEP provides what it calls Basic Information Reports (BIRs) summarising labour policies in each of the member states, costing 6 ECU for each country, or 50 ECU for all. This includes details of relevant institutions, legal framework and procedures, measures and initiatives, information and research.

The magazine of MISEP is called *InforMISEP*, and is compiled on the basis of information prepared by national correspondents of whom there is one in each member state. InforMISEP is a quarterly, A4, 24-page magazine outlining employment policies, with reports from each country. Of interest to voluntary organisations concerned with unemployment are articles and information that focus on its nature and the measures taken to counteract it. InforMISEP no. 34, for example, carried tables on the level and nature of unemployment assistance schemes in other countries. There are reports on services for the unemployed and, for example, signing-on arrangements. Voluntary organisations may be interested in employment initiatives and measures to help the unemployed that may be worth emulating in Britain. The UK national correspondent is Ms Jeanie Cruickshank, Department of Employment.

■ MISEP Secretariat, Institute for Policy Research, PO Box 985, 2300 AZ Leiden, Netherlands, Tel. 31 71 253 737, Fax 31 71 253 702.

Observatory on Ageing

Steps are being taken towards a European policy observatory on ageing. National reports on social and economic policies affecting older people are now being compiled.

■ Prof. Alan Walker, Department of Sociological Studies, University of Sheffield, Sheffield S10 2TN.

EUROPEAN FOUNDATIONS, RESEARCH BODIES, INSTITUTES AND SIMILAR INSTITUTIONS

In addition to official, government-sponsored, or EC-based institutions, there are research bodies, foundations and other organisations in Europe which are of relevance and interest to the voluntary sector. In Europe, the term 'foundation' is used widely to describe bodies that combine research activities, information work, grant-giving, networking and publishing. In central Europe, bodies that would in Britain be described as national voluntary organisations term themselves 'foundations'.

AEIDL

AEIDL is the European Association for Information on Local Development, specialising in the production and communication of information on regional and local economic development, SMEs, and social affairs.

■ AEIDL, rue Breydel 34, B.1040 Brussels, Tel. 322 230 5234, Fax 322 230 3482.

Centre d'Information et d'Études sur les Migrations Internationales (CIEMI)

The Centre d'Information et d'Études sur les Migrations Internationales (CIEMI), or Centre for the Study of International Migrations is a prestigious Catholic research centre in Paris. It has written briefing papers on migration, including one on Schengen.

■ Centre d'Information et d'Études sur les Migrations Internationales (CIEMI), rue de Montreuil 46, F.75011 Paris, France, Tel. 331 4372 4934.

Centre for European Policy Studies (CEPS)

The Centre for European Policy Studies (CEPS) (established 1983) describes itself as a 'think tank, research centre and meeting place'. Its publication list includes books, papers, research reports and two yearbooks, one of which is an annual review of EC affairs. Its publications have an economic and political focus, dealing with such matters as monetary union and the consequences for the EC of German unification. It is currently widening its research to new areas, such as the EFTA countries, central Europe and Russia. CEPS runs conferences, lunchtime seminars and briefings. Membership costs from 75 ECU (individual) to 10,000 ECU (corporate). Fees include library access.

■ Centre for European Policy Studies, rue Ducale 33, B.1000 Brussels, Tel. 322 513 4088, Fax 322 511 5960.

Centre for Local Economic Strategies (CLES)

The Centre for Local Economic Strategies (CLES) has published *Local authorities and 1992*, describing the process of the single market and how it relates to the work of UK local authorities.

■ Centre for Local Economic Strategies (CLES), Alberton House, St Mary's Parsonage, Manchester M3 2WJ, Tel. 061 834 7036, Fax 061 835 1589.

Centre for Research into European Women (CREW)

The Centre for Research into European Women (CREW) was founded in 1980, and specialises in consultancy and research into equal opportunities in the fields of employment, enterprise creation and training. CREW publications include *CREW Reports*, a monthly magazine published in English and French, giving in-depth analysis of European and national employment and social policy, especially as it affects women. Subscription rates range from £11 to £37.50 a year, according to category. Since 1988, CREW has co-ordinated IRIS, the European network of training schemes for women for the European Commission.

■ The Centre for Research into European Women (CREW), rue de la Tourelle 21, B.1040 Brussels, Tel. 322 230 5158, Fax 322 230 6230, e-mail MCR1:CREW.

European Association for the Development of Women's Information and Training (EUDIFF)

The European Association for the Development of Women's Information and Training (EUDIFF) (established 1990) is a new professional network designed to improve the flow of information about the situation, rights, and means of advancement of women in Europe.

■ European Association for the Development of Women's Information and Training (EUDIFF), rue du Jura 7, F.75013 Paris, France, Tel. 331 4331 7700.

European Bureau for Lesser Used Languages

The European Bureau for Lesser Used Languages (established 1984), located in Dublin, is the concrete recognition by the European Communities that, among its 340 million citizens, close on 50m speak a language other than the nine working languages (since 1991 Catalan has been an official language, but not a working language requiring translation into all documents). In the case of the UK, this includes Welsh, Cornish (*kernewek*), Scots gallic and Irish. There are minority languages in every member state with the exception of Portugal. Although the best known are languages like Basque and Breton, the Bureau recognises no fewer than 31 minority languages, from *friesian* (northern Germany) to *turke bileyorum* (in the eastern borders of Greece).

The European Bureau for Lesser Known Languages is not a formal EC institution, but an independent association working closely with the Commission. Its budget is small and it has only three staff. Funding comes from the Commission and the Irish and Luxembourg governments. The Bureau has concentrated on study visits, helping MEPs with a commitment to lesser-known languages, and on compiling a linguistic map of Europe. It has held an international youth conference of speakers of lesser known languages, another on how radio and television can promote lesser known languages; is promoting publishing of children's books in lesser known languages; and is setting up an information network. One of the UK members is Comunn na Gàidhlig in Inverness. The bureau has a magazine called *Bulletin*.

■ European Bureau for Lesser Known Languages, 10 Sráid Haiste íocht, Baile Atha Cliath 2 (Dublin), Ireland, Tel. 353 1 612205, 353 1 618743, Fax 353 1 766840.

■ Dafydd Orwig, Cilcafan, Braichmelyn, Bethesda, Gwynedd LL57 3RD.

■ Comunn na Gàidhlig, 109 sraid na h-Eaglaise, Inbhirnis IV1 1EY, Tel. 0463 234138.

European Centre for Regional Development (Centre Européen de Développement Régional) (CEDRE)

The European Centre for Regional Development is the European organisation for interregional development and co-operation in scientific, technical and economic areas. Its present programme involves promoting co-operation in the areas of transport, the islands of Europe, environmentally friendly agriculture, and SMEs. Its work is linked to that of the Assembly of the European Regions (AER) through a co-operation agreement.

■ CEDRE, Immeuble Europe, place des Halles 33, F.67000 Strasbourg, France, Tel. 33 88 22 3883.

European Centre for Social Welfare Policy and Research

The European Centre for Social Welfare Policy and Research aims to promote co-operation among governments, organisations and agencies concerned with social welfare issues. It collaborates closely with the United Nations Centre for Social Development and Humanitarian Affairs. It fosters the exchange of information and carries out research. Publications include *Eurosocial newsletter* (three times a year, no charge), reports, research and occasional papers. It has three interesting databases: INFUSE (Information Uses in Social Welfare Policy); AIDSINST; and MANAGAIDS. INFUSE is a challenging joint programme with the Israeli Ministry of Labour and Social Affairs, designed to bring together all published and unpublished documentation on social welfare planning and research. AIDSINST and

MANAGAIDS will provide a complete list of AIDS services and institutions in ten European countries, including the UK.

■ The European Centre for Social Welfare Policy and Research, Berggasse 17, A.1090 Vienna, Austria, Tel. 431 45050, Fax 431 45 0519, e-mail BITNET X θ 261 DAA @ WIUNI11.

European Citizen Action Service (ECAS)

The European Citizen Action Service is a non-profit-making lobbying, information and action service in Brussels specifically designed to help the voluntary and community sector. Formally launched in May 1990 after a market survey conducted the previous year found that over 400 voluntary organisations in Europe indicated their support for some kind of citizens' lobby in the European Communities, it describes its aims as 'to advise, inform, and strengthen the position of the voluntary, non-governmental organisations (NGOs) in relation to the European institutions'. ECAS hopes to be 'a focal point for many NGOs in their dealings with the EC, and, by doing so, correct the imbalance between lobbying on behalf of business and lobbying on behalf of the public interest'. Two individuals were guiding forces in the evolution of ECAS – Tony Venables, former director of the European Consumer Bureau (BEUC), and Marie Spaak, who came from the United Nations High Commissioner for Refugees.

Growth areas in the work of ECAS involve helping delegations to meet MEPs, putting people in contact across borders, and helping people to lobby internationally. ECAS is giving consideration to setting up a satellite office in Strasbourg which can follow the Parliament more closely. On the information front, it profiles directorates of the Commission and alerts people to forthcoming meetings. It is very aware of the danger of overloading people who already receive a high volume of European information.

ECAS has 200 members, of which 60 per cent come from the UK. Most of the others are from the northern countries, and southern members are coming in slowly. It has a mailing list of up to 7,000 names and voluntary organisations across Europe. Interest in ECAS comes in four main categories: citizens' rights, health issues, social affairs and culture.

Its magazine, *European Citizen*, is a no-frills, neatly-presented, serious 20-page magazine outlining issues in Europe that are of interest to voluntary and community organisations. The section 'EC round-up' reviews current developments, and the work of the Parliament in Strasbourg; there are features and profiles, for example on 'EC and disability', 'EC and health', and so on.

ECAS has begun coalition-building in the areas of child welfare, health and the revision of the Common Agricultural Policy, bringing together voluntary organisations involved in these issues.

Membership costs of ECAS are on three scales: corresponding member – 150 ECU; associate member – 1200 ECU; and full member – 4300 ECU. Corresponding members receive the publications of ECAS and general information on the development of EC programmes and legislation. Associate members are entitled to advice about how to approach EC institutions, to reports of particular interest to their sector, and to the use of office space in Brussels. Full members receive a personalised service, a watching brief on specific issues and decisions and legal advice. Although the membership rates have struck many in the voluntary and community sector as expensive, ECAS stated from the start that it did not want to cut corners by providing an under-rate service. ECAS has also been generous in giving advice gratis to new voluntary organisations discovering Europe and its institutions for the first time.

■ ECAS, rue du Trône 98, B.1050 Brussels, Tel. 322 512 9360, Fax 322 512 6673.

European Cultural Foundation (ECF)

Robert Schuman, the political father of the European Communities, was the first President of the European Cultural Foundation in 1954. It is based in the Netherlands, and describes its aims as 'to promote cultural activities throughout the continent, with the aim of encouraging transnational co-operation and stimulating awareness among European citizens of the culture they have in common'. The European Cultural Foundation concentrates its efforts in education, the arts, environment, the media, social issues, and east-west relations. Its board has 42 members drawn from 18 countries, and includes two representatives of the Council of Europe. There is a 13-strong staff. Funding comes from the Dutch lottery and football pools, and from research contracts. There is a national committee of the foundation in the UK. Several years ago, the foundation mapped a scenario of the Europe of the future which was published as Peter Hall's *Europe 2000*.

The foundation operates a grants scheme for projects designed to enhance the awareness of the European dimension of society today. Grants must involve projects covering at least three European countries, last for a year, and must comprise only half the cost involved. The grants budget in 1988 was 2.4m guilders. The secretariat distributes general information brochures, a newsletter, list of grants awarded, list of publications, and guidelines for grants.

■ European Cultural Foundation, Jan van Goyenkade 5, 1075 HN Amsterdam, Netherlands, Tel. 31 20 76 0222, Fax 31 20 752231.

The foundation has sponsored the setting up of no less then ten institutes which include:

Institutes of the European Cultural Foundation

• European Institute of Education and Social Policy (Paris)

• European Institute for Environmental Policy (Bonn, Paris, London, Brussels)

• European Institute for the Media (Manchester)

• European Centre for Work and Society (Maastricht, Netherlands)

• European Co-operation Fund (Brussels)

• Central and East European Publishing Project (Oxford).

The European Institute of Education and Social Policy (established 1975) is a Paris-based body set up by the Foundation together with the Commission of the European Communities and the International Council for Educational Development, New York. It focuses on higher education and vocational and scientific training in Europe. It publishes the *European Journal of Education*. It administers, in Brussels, the EC programmes Erasmus and Eurydice.

■ European Institute of Education and Social Policy, Université de Paris IX-Dauphine, place du Maréchal de Lattre de Tassigny 1, 75116 Paris, France, Tel. 331 4505 1410, Fax 331 4553 8134.

The European Institute for Environmental Policy (established 1976) undertakes comparative studies on environmental policies and promotes co-operation on environmental issues. Specific research tasks are carried out for the European Commission, the European Parliament, national governments and industry. For example, it assesses the implementation of EC environmental directives on the discharges of mercury and cadmium, and publishes a directory of EC legislation in the environmental area. The Institute has four separate legs – in Bonn (Institut für Europäische Umweltpolitik), London, Paris (Institut pour une Politique européenne de l'Environnement) and Arnhem (Netherlands) (Institut voor Europees Milieubelied). The Institute is noted for its familiarity with EC environment directives and being up to date in developments in EC policy.

■ Institute for European Environmental Policy, 3 Endsleigh Street, London WC1H 0DD, Tel. 071 388 0326, Fax 071 388 2826.

The European Institute for the Media (established 1983) is a forum for decision-makers in the media in Europe. Its aims are to foster programme quality and encourage co-operation between the media of the different states.

■ European Institute for the Media, Manchester University, Manchester M13 9PL, Tel. 061 273 6055, Fax 061 273 8788.

The European Centre for Work and Society (ECWS) was founded in 1979 by the Queen Juliana Foundation in the Netherlands and the European Cultural Foundation. It undertakes comparative research and organises conferences on a wide range of social issues of general concern: unemployment, changing patterns of work, the integration of minority groups and migrants, and the assimilation of elderly people. It administers two EC programmes: MISEP and EUROTECNET. It is promoting an initiative for migrants' associations called MAINE (Migrants' Associations Information Network in Europe). It has a range of reports and publishes *ECWS News*.

■ European Centre for Work and Society, Hoogbrugstraat 43, 6221 CP Maastricht, Netherlands, Tel. 31 43 21 6724, Fax 31 43 25 5712.

The European Co-operation Fund (established 1977) is dedicated to the improvement of relationships between the peoples of western and central Europe. One project, Concorde east/west brings young musicians together. The fund is contactable by way of the European Foundation Centre (see below). The Central and East European Publishing Project supports the publication and dissemination of literary and academic works as well as periodicals from central Europe in their original languages and in translation.

■ Central and East European Publishing Project, St Anthony's College Annexe, Belsyre Court, 57 Woodstock Road, Oxford OX2 6HQ, Tel. 0865 310793, Fax 0865 311021.

International Fund for the Promotion of Culture

Founded in 1974, the International Fund for the Promotion of Culture is a UN-derived, UNESCO-sponsored international agency located in Paris. It claims to be 'the first international mechanism devoted wholly to the funding of cultural activities. It is the only body within UNESCO directly accessible to private and public institutions, groups and individuals. It can respond quickly to fresh ideas...' The International Fund for the Promotion of Culture has a brief which takes in music, dance, drama, literature, painting, architecture and crafts, areas which will be of interest to community organisations. Funding comes from UN member states and from trusts and similar institutions.

Innovative projects supported by the Fund have included an international drama workshop between companies in Denmark, Poland, the Czech and Slovak Federal Republic, and Wales; a community education and resource centre; a marketing scheme for traditional textiles in Alentjo, Portugal; and the Euro-Arab summer university. The Fund states that it gives priority to 'experiment, innovation and new talent'. It will look for well-managed projects that can eventually pay their own way. It prefers action-orientated research.

■ International Fund for the Promotion of Culture, UNESCO, 75700 Paris, France, Tel. 331 4568 1000.

European Foundation Centre (EFC)

The European Foundation Centre (EFC) (established 1989) is a networking service for grant-giving bodies. It does not itself provide grants, though it can help match applicants with suitable donors. It describes its aims as to 'encourage partnership between foundations, corporations and governments in meeting the needs of the citizen in pluralistic civil societies'.

Its interests at present are in a common European statute for voluntary organisations, the compiling of an overall picture of the voluntary sector and its size and its scale in Europe, and the development of contact with foundations in central Europe. A directory of European grant-giving foundations is being compiled.

UK members include the Charities Aid Foundation (a founder member) and the Prince's Trust. Some of the most prominent European foundations are members: Fondazione Giovanni Agnelli (Italy), American Express Foundation (US), the King Baudouin Foundation (Belgium), the Queen Juliana Foundation (Netherlands), Alexander von Humboldt Stiftung (Germany), Fundación Santa María (Spain), Alexander S Onassis Foundation (Greece), United Way, Fondaçao Iriente (Portugal) and the Fondation de France. It has special guest members and associate members from central Europe. Membership is open to European grant-makers and international grant-makers with a European programme: costs range from 500 ECU (publications only) to 10,000 ECU (full membership).

EFC publications include *EFC news*, *EFC monitor*, *EFC profile* and *EFC communiqués*. These provide summaries and news of EC programmes and developments affecting the voluntary sector. The centre also has a library. The director is John Richardson.

■ European Foundation Centre (EFC), rue de la Concorde 51, B.1050 Brussels, Tel. 322 512 8938, Fax 322 512 3265.

■ Funding opportunities for voluntary organisations in Europe, chapter 7.

European Institute for Social Security

The European Institute for Social Security (established 1968) is an institution for international co-operation between specialists in social security. It has 17 national sections and 300 researchers as members. It organises colloquia on social security, the proceedings of which are published in its yearbook. Research on comparative aspects of social security is carried out on contract for the Council of Europe and the EC. It operates the MISSOC programme for the European Commission. Membership costs BF 1200 (individuals) or BF 12,000 (institutions).

■ European Institute of Social Security, Tiensestraat 41, B.3000 Leuven, Belgium, Tel. 320 1623 9338.

International Association for Intercultural Education

The International Association for Intercultural Education (IAIE) is a Dutch-based body bringing together organisations interested in the multi-cultural, multi-ethnic aspects of education. It has a wide membership across Europe, and a system of national correspondents in different countries. UK members include university colleges, polytechnics and education centres, particularly those sectors concerned with racial equality and community and race relations.

■ International Association for Intercultural Education, Sumaltralaan 37, 1217 GP Hilversum, Netherlands, Tel. 313 54 7375, or the UK national correspondent: Jagdish Gundara, Centre for Multicultural Education, University of London Institute of Education, 20 Bedford Way, London WC1H 0AL, Tel. 071 636 1500.

International Institute of Humanitarian Law

Based in Italy, the International Institute of Humanitarian Law is primarily interested in legal matters affecting the victims of war, but has taken an especial interest in the law on migration, asylum and refugees. The Institute works through teaching, research, conferences and publications. It runs annual courses on humanitarian law and on international refugee law for government civil servants. It has a specialised library, and publishes a yearbook. It has provision both for full and associate membership. It has an academic Commission on Migration. It collaborates closely with the Red Cross, and has consultative status at the Council of Europe.

- International Institute of Humanitarian Law, Villa Ormond, Corso Cavallotti 115, 18038 San Remo, Italy, Tel. 39 184 541848, Fax 39 184 541600.

International Social Security Association

The International Social Security Association (ISSA) (established 1947) brings together government departments, centralised institutions and national federations which administer social security systems in 118 countries. Its aims are to promote the technical and administrative improvement of social security systems. UK affiliates are the Department of Social Security (Great Britain) and the Department of Health and Social Services (Northern Ireland). It works closely with the the UN's Economic and Social Council (ECOSOC), the International Labour Organisation (ILO) and the Council of Europe. It carries out research and training; distributes and publishes literature; and organises conferences.

- International Social Security Association (ISSA), Case postale 1, CH 1211 Geneva 22, Switzerland, Tel. 41 22 799 6617, Fax 41 22 798 6385.

International Social Service (ISS)

ISS is a Geneva-based service concerned with migration issues originally founded by the Young Women's Christian Association (YWCA) in 1921. It seeks to find solutions, on a case-by-case basis, of problems which arise as a consequence of migration or residence in a foreign country. It endeavours to procure legal documents, assists in the adaptation of migrants, and makes studies of the problems underlying migration. It has consultative status with the Economic and Social Council of the United Nations and with the Council of Europe. International Social Service has what it terms 'national units' in a number of countries.

- International Social Service, Cranmer House, 39 Brixton Road, London SW9 6DD, Tel. 071 735 8941/4, Fax 071 582 0696.

- International Social Service, quai du Seujet 32, CH 1201 Geneva, Switzerland, Tel. 41 22 731 7455, Fax 41 22 738 0949.

FOUNDATIONS, RESEARCH BODIES, INSTITUTES AND SIMILAR BODIES RELEVANT TO EUROPE LOCATED IN BRITAIN

There are a number of foundations, research bodies, publishing houses, and institutes concerned with Europe which either grew up in Britain, or have come to be based here. Some provide information on events taking place in Europe as part of their general programme of information-giving, or as part of community and adult education programmes. Others are more specifically geared to encouraging their clients to take advantage of funding and business opportunities in Europe. For voluntary organisations, they may provide a point of contact with Europe without having to go to the continent: because they are based here, they are much easier to reach. For others, they may be sources of valuable information. Either way, they offer routes into Europe. Voluntary organisations may also wish to consider linking with the European awareness programmes run by their local authorities. These programmes are reviewed first.

In some parts of the country, the initiative of providing information on Europe has been taken by chambers of commerce, in others by the local authorities, in some by education bodies, and in others by a combination. For example, Islington Chamber of Commerce ran an information programme partly funded through the Department of the Environment's urban programme, in co-operation with the local authority's European Liaison Officer, and with the Polytechnic of North London. One of the functions of the programme was to alert community and arts organisations to EC funding possibilities. Several local authorities have appointed European Liaison Officers. In 1989, the Council of the Western Isles established a *European desk* charged with providing information and advice to its elected members and council departments.

The Convention of Scottish Local Authorities (COSLA) carried out a 1989 study of the level of European information provision among its members. Although all the regions had discussed their future relationships with Europe, only one-third of the districts and islands had. The main findings were that:

- some towns had established twinning;

- several were involved in specialised EC programmes (for example SPRINT and PETRA);

- several had joined the Conference of Peripheral Maritime Regions (CPMR);

- many had appointed a European Liaison Officer; and

- several had run, or were considering running, European information weeks.

European information weeks have now been held in more than 25 localities. The organisers have now come together to form the organisation Relay Europe.

■ Convention of Scottish Local Authorities (COSLA), Rosebery House, 9 Haymarket Terrace, Edinburgh EH12 5XZ.

■ Relay Europe, Mithras House, Lewes Road, Brighton BN2 4AT, Tel. 0273 600 900.

Arkleton Trust

The Arkleton Trust has issued publications concerning rural development in other European countries. *Village Halls in Europe* (1990), for example, was a joint study with ACRE (Action with Communities in Rural England) of community facilities and their development in six European countries.

■ Arkleton Trust, Enstone, Oxford OX7 4HH, Tel. 0608 672255.

ARVAC

ARVAC stands for the Association of Researchers in Voluntary Action and Community Involvement: the association has overseas members in Denmark, Ireland, Portugal, Belgium and France.

■ ARVAC, Unit 29, Wivenhoe Business Centre, Brook Street, Wivenhoe, Essex CO7 9DP, Tel. 0206 824281.

CEI Consultants

CEI Consultants Ltd, until 1989 known as the Centre for Employment Initiatives, works in the area of local economic development. It has run the EC's ERGO programme and has built up considerable knowledge around local economic issues throughout Europe.

■ CEI Consultants Ltd, 42 Frederick Street, Edinburgh EH2 1EX, Tel. 031 225 3144, Fax 031 226 2259.

Centre for Economic Policy Research (CEPR)

The Centre for Economic Policy Research publishes discussion papers on economic development in Britain and Europe, some 330 being currently available. CEPR themes include the integration of the European Communities, and developments in central Europe.

■ Centre for Economic Policy Research, 6 Duke of York Street, London SW1Y 6LA, Tel. 071 930 2963, Fax 071 930 8454.

Centre for Research in Regional Economic Development (CRED)

The Centre for Research in Regional Economic Development (CRED) is an independent research group based on the University of Liverpool. It provides information and advice on local and regional economic development on a commercial basis.

■ CRED, Roxby Building, PO Box 147, Liverpool L69 3BX, Tel. 051 794 2855.

Centre for Voluntary Organisations at LSE

The Centre for Voluntary Organisations at the London School of Economics (LSE) provides postgraduate courses for the voluntary sector, training courses and workshops, and carries out research into the voluntary sector which includes cross-national comparisons.

■ Centre for Voluntary Organisations, London School of Economics, Houghton Street, London WC2A 2AE, Tel. 071 405 7686.

European Consortium for Political Research (ECPR)

There are now a countless number of European courses available in colleges. A research network concentrates on relationships between Britain and the European institutions: over 140 universities are involved in the work of the European Consortium for Political Research (ECPR) (established 1970): its aim is to foster collaboration between political science scholars. It holds workshops and summer schools and produces publications (*Political Science in Europe* and *ECPR News*). The workshops are intended to share the experiences and research of advanced students, younger members and well-established professors.

■ European Consortium for Political Research, University of Essex, Wivenhoe Park, Colchester, Essex C04 3SQ, Tel. 0206 872501.

European Human Rights Foundation

The European Human Rights Foundation is a small Netherlands-based foundation promoting human rights throughout the world. The foundation is open to receive grants and donations from individuals and organisations interested in promoting support for human rights: the main donor is the Commission of the European Communities, following the voting of such funds by the European Parliament. Forty-nine grants totalling 199,755 ECU were allocated in 1990, varying in size from 1000 ECU to 6400 ECU. Preference is given to action projects rather than research. The foundation is currently funding a study on access to legal services by people on low incomes in four EC countries.

■ Stichting European Human Rights Foundation, 95a Chancery Lane, London WC2A 1DT.

Gulbenkian Foundation

The Calouste Gulbenkian Foundation is a Portuguese-based Foundation which has a UK branch in London. Calouste Sarkis Gulbenkian was an Armenian who worked in Britain and settled in Lisbon. He died in 1955, and since then the Gulbenkian Foundation has been supporting charities in the areas of the arts, education and social welfare. The Anglo-Portuguese Cultural Relations Programme makes provision for the development of relationships with Portugal in the fields of language, culture and people.

■ Calouste Gulbenkian Foundation, 98 Portland Place, London W1N 4ET, Tel. 071 636 5313.

International Business Club

The International Business Club of Park Lane College is the hub of a network of small and medium sized enterprises (SMEs) in the EC, helping them to grow in the environment of the single market. The European Regional Fund has grant-aided the Club to run a network of SMEs from Britain, Denmark, Greece, France, Italy and Poland, which will involve the exchange of information, staff and managers.

■ International Business Club, Park Lane, Leeds LS3 1AA, Tel. 0532 42 2887.

School of Advanced Urban Studies in Bristol

The School of Advanced Urban Studies (SAUS) at the University of Bristol runs a programme of seminars concerned with European social affairs. The 1991 programme included such subjects as the European Social Fund, the Regional Development Fund and local government. SAUS has specialised in the urban environment and has taken part in a number of cross-national research projects. It is a leading centre for the training of local government officers.

■ School of Advanced Urban Studies (SAUS), Rodney Lodge, Grange Road, Bristol BS8 4EA, Tel. 0272 741117, Fax 0272 737308.

University Association for Contemporary European Studies (UACES)

Based in King's College, London, the UACES is a group of lecturers and researchers working on European issues. It has a conference and publications programme.

■ University Association for Contemporary European Studies (UACES), King's College London, Strand, London WC2R 2LS, Tel. 071 240 0206.

BRITAIN AND EUROPE: MAKING CONTACT

There are several ways in which British voluntary and community organisations and their members can get involved in Europe – linking to specialised programmes or foundations, joining networks and finding partners in the voluntary sector in other European countries. Informal opportunities exist, which give members of voluntary organisations the chance to explore Europe and get a taste of its different peoples and culture without necessarily binding those members to a long-term organisational commitment. These opportunities can be found in youth exchange schemes, town twinning, and workcamp programmes.

European Federation of Intercultural Learning (EFIL) and Intercultural Educational Programmes (IEP)

The European Federation of Intercultural Learning is a federation (established 1971) of 21 member organisations in 20 countries in Europe which promotes youth exchange programmes, concentrating on secondary school students. It operates a number of the EC exchange programmes such as Youth for Europe and the Programme for the exchange of young workers. IEP offers year-long placements for 16-18-year-olds in European and other countries as part of a cultural and education learning experience. It also operates the intercultural programmes of the AFS, the American Field Service.

■ EFIL, rue de la Montagne 36, B.1000 Brussels, Tel. 322 514 5250, Fax 322 514 2929 or

■ IEP, Ground floor, Arden House, Main Street, Bingley, West Yorkshire BN16 2NB, Tel. 0274 560677 Fax 0274 567675.

Prince's Trust

The Prince's Trust has operated a European programme since 1989. With 'Go and see' grants, it fills a gap in the market not met by the existing structured exchange programmes. 'Go and see' pays a small grant (possibly an airline ticket) to an individual with a good idea to visit a potential partner and see how they could work together in the future. A total of 153 grants were awarded in the first year of the scheme. France, Germany, the Netherlands and Italy are the most popular destinations; the principal themes of the new partnerships concern the arts, crafts, design, the environment and communications. Minority ethnic candidates and people with disabilities are welcome to apply. The Trust is developing new programmes with central Europe, especially Poland and Hungary.

■ The Prince's Trust, 8 Bedford Row, London WC1R 4BA, Tel. (European programme) 071 405 5799.

Study and Go-and-See Abroad

The British Council provides scholarships for study abroad. The Council publishes *Scholarships abroad* (£4.95) which lists scholarships administered by the Council. Most are designed with postgraduates in mind, but there are schemes for undergraduates. In most cases, there is no restriction on subject matter.

■ British Council, 10 Spring Gardens, London SW1A 2BN, Tel. 071 930 8466, Fax 071 839 6347.

Town Twinning

Town twinning is one of the most frequently used mechanisms whereby people from Britain can establish relationships with their counterparts in Europe. Town twinning in Britain is administered by the Local Government International Bureau. The total number of UK twinnings has now reached 1,540. Twinning is financially supported by the European Commission, to the tune of 3 MECU in 1991. Twinning often takes the form of exchanges between representatives of one town and its opposite number in the EC.

Under the Commission allocation of 3 MECU, priority is given to twinned towns which are disadvantaged because of their geographical location, because their languages are not widely used, and because their countries have recently joined the EC. Priority is given to new twinning, small twinned towns and twinning activities which take up new themes. Grants are made to the host town in respect of one particular event and to cover preparatory meetings. Of the fund 5 per cent is reserved for twinning arrangements with central European towns. Twinning grants range from 300 ECU to 5,000 ECU. The French-based World Federation of United Cities (FMCU) has recently taken the initiative in linking west European towns with Poland and the CIS.

Twinning can operate in different ways, its creativity depending on the individuals in each town concerned. In some cases, there are straightforward exchanges between councillors and officials; however some local authorities will arrange twinning around particular themes (for example, social services or community development), and will invite the voluntary sector to participate. Voluntary organisations may sometimes overlook the possibilities that can be opened up by contacting their local authority to encourage a new twinning arrangement (or to develop an existing one) and to make them part of an exchange arrangement. Some local authorities may well be receptive to new ideas for themes for a twinning arrangement.

■ Twinning Officer, Local Government International Bureau, 35 Great Smith Street, London SW1P 3BJ, Tel. 071 222 1636, Fax 071 233 2179.

■ Fédération Mondiale des Cités Unis (FMCU), rue d'Alsace 22, F 923000 Levallois Perret, France, Tel. 331 4739 3686.

Workcamps

A much-valued means of learning about other countries is to go on a workcamp there. From the point of view of voluntary organisations, workcamps seem of little value because they are undertaken by individuals rather than organisations. Workcamps provide opportunities for individuals to work in another country for periods of two to four weeks, generally during the summer holidays, on community and social schemes. Volunteers must find and pay their own way there, but will be provided with board and basic accommodation once there. Participants on international workcamps come from many countries, and some are devoted to studies of social themes, as well as practical work. Unlike some exchange schemes, twinning and placements, which can take months to set up, the procedure is relatively simple: a person applies, lists preferences of camps to go to, is allocated accordingly, and given instructions on how to get there. Camps are sponsored by voluntary organisations, community groups and local authorities. Participants generally recommend them as a positive and informal means of getting to know other countries, and for the individuals concerned they can be a first, useful exposure to working with people from other countries.

Perhaps the best known organisation for summer workcamps is International Voluntary Service (IVS). Its 1991 programme offered about 500 workcamps from Alaska to Samarkhand. Some camps are ecological, some help disabled people, and others work with children, refugees, minorities and orphans, though this list does no justice to the variety available.

■ International Voluntary Service (IVS), Old Hall, East Bergholt, Colchester CO7 6TQ, Tel. 0202 298215; IVS Scotland, St John's Church, Prince's Street, Edinburgh EH2 4BJ, Tel. 031 229 7318.

■ Community Service Volunteers, 237 Pentonville Road, London N1 9NJ, Tel. 071 278 6601.

Youth Exchange Centre

The funding system for youth exchanges is both more generous and more sophisticated than that of many other sectors. The principal organisation is the Youth Exchange Centre, which was integrated into the work of the British Council in March 1990. The Youth Exchange Centre is the UK agent for the

Youth for Europe programme (see p.99 above). The Youth Exchange Centre supports exchange work with the EC countries, the Commonwealth and central Europe. There has been a surge of interest in central European exchanges in the past two years, much facilitated by the easing there of travel restrictions. Exchanges are generally built on themes with a European dimension, the most common being environmental protection, social and political affairs, and the creative arts. Priority is given to young people who would not normally have the opportunity for an international experience.

The Youth Exchange Centre is financed by the Department of Education and Science, the Foreign and Commonwealth Office, and the European Commission. The work of the Youth Exchange Centre is promoted through the newsletter *Youth Exchange News* which publicises opportunities abroad and organisations seeking partners. Grants generally cover about 30 per cent of the gross costs of an exchange. A youth group is defined as comprising between 8 and 35 young people aged from 15 to 25 years. Visits must last for at least a week. Short study visits for youth leaders are also financed. The centre welcomes the participation in exchanges of minorities and disadvantaged groups.

■ Youth Exchange Centre, Seymour Mews House, Seymour Mews, London W1H 9PE, Tel. 071 487 5961, Fax 071 224 4506.

VOLUNTARY ORGANISATIONS PROMOTING EUROPEAN IDEALS

Several voluntary organisations, some of them long-established, exist to promote European ideals, or to further the political cause of European integration. Some are enthusiasts for a united Europe: but those who do not share their political objectives may still wish to consider them as valuable sources of information to learn about developments in Europe. Several run conferences and seminars where the future of Europe is discussed, and these may give new participants a flavour of how European political issues are developing. They can also provide a point of access to political decision-makers, since several such groups include MPs and important political figures as patrons, sponsors and activists.

Danish Cultural Institute

The Danish Cultural Institute was formed in 1940 to spread information about Denmark aboard, and to promote co-operation between Denmark and other countries. It is an independent body under the Ministry of Cultural Affairs. It arranges study tours and seminars, summer schools and specialised conferences, exhibitions and lectures. The institute has offices in Austria, Benelux, France, Britain, Italy, Germany and Latvia. All have libraries and information about Danish society, and welcome enquiries.

■ Danish Cultural Institute, 3 Doune Terrace, Edinburgh EH3 6DY, Tel. 031 225 7189, Fax 031 220 6162.

European Atlantic Group

The European Atlantic Group (established 1954) exists to promote better co-operation between European and Atlantic countries. It disseminates information on the European institutions, and runs a lecture programme on European themes. Many of these lectures attract leading European personalities and politicians.

■ European Atlantic Group, 6 Gertrude Street, London SW10 0JN, Tel. 071 352 1226.

European Atlantic Movement (TEAM)

TEAM (established 1985) encourages research and disseminates information about the European and Atlantic communities and their institutions. Its main activities are conferences and study tours. There is an annual Easter study tour of the European institutions (European Communities, Council of Europe and NATO).

■ European Atlantic Movement (TEAM), Well Court, 14-16 Farringdon Lane, London EC1R 3AU, Tel. 071 251 4254, Fax 071 253 0269.

European Educational Research Trust

The European Educational Research Trust (established 1962) promotes the study of other European countries, and establishes scholarships and grants for this purpose. So far, 14,000 individuals have benefited from grants from the European Educational Research Trust. It has also given financial support to organisations developing European work, study tours and exchanges.

■ European Educational Research Trust, Europe House, 1 Whitehall Place, London SW1A 2DA, Tel. 071 839 6622.

European Movement

The European Movement was formed to carry out the objectives of the first Congress of Europe, which, convened under the chairmanship of Winston Churchill in the Hague in 1948, called for a European political, economic and cultural union. It presents the annual *Women of Europe Award* for women who have contributed to the cultural, educational or political development of Europe. It welcomes members with or without political affiliations and sees itself as a broad church of people concerned with Europe. It organises conferences, arranges visits to the European institutions, publishes a newsletter (*Facts*), and runs a lecture programme. Membership costs from £5 to £20, according to category.

■ European Movement, Europe House, 1 Whitehall Place, London SW1A 2DA, Tel. 071 839 6622, Fax 071 925 2685.

Federal Trust

The Federal Trust for Education and Research (established 1945) is an educational charity concerned with European and world integration. Its study groups are concerned with the implications of economic and monetary union, the harmonisation of taxation, and alternative scenarios for the social and economic future of Europe. It has evening discussion groups, a publications list, and it encourages the study of federal systems of government at the Centre for Federal Studies at the University of Leicester. It has issued a video on the theme of Europe and the developing countries. Membership costs from £10 to £20, according to category.

■ Federal Trust, Europe House, 1 Whitehall Place, London SW1A 2DA, Tel. 071 839 6625.

Lothian Foundation

The Lothian Foundation aims to educate the public 'in ways of achieving better relations between the citizens of the European Communities and other peoples, particularly the United States, by educational activities which promote discussion and exchange of ideas and information'. Membership costs from £5 to £10, according to category. Its 1990 conference was on the theme 'A constitution for Europe – a comparative study of federal constitutions and plans for the united states of Europe'.

■ Lothian Foundation, Europe House, 1 Whitehall Place, London SW1A 2DA, Tel. 071 930 3413.

Young European Movement (YEM)

The Young European Movement 'aims to ensure that young people in the UK understand and support the arguments for the creation of a European Union, based on democratic decision-making and local autonomy'. It has a network of local groups, a programme of national events, and a series of publications. It belongs to the Jeunesse Européenne Fédéraliste, a body with members in 20 countries across Europe, east and west. The Young European Movement has organised visits to the institutions of the EC. Membership costs £5 a year, and it has a branch membership throughout the country. The YEM also provides a monthly newsletter, briefings, workshops and seminars.

■ Young European Movement, Europe House, 1 Whitehall Place, London SW1A 2DA, Tel. 071 839 6622, Fax 071 925 2685.

BRITISH ORGANISATIONS PROMOTING LINKS WITH EUROPEAN VOLUNTARY ORGANISATIONS

Several voluntary organisations in the UK already have an active involvement in European affairs, networks and organisations. Others are actively distributing information and news about Europe. This section discusses voluntary, community and other organisations in the UK which British organisations may wish to approach here first, before going on to contact networks in mainland Europe itself. For some groups, these may provide a useful, first, home-based point of contact and introduction to European affairs.

Charities Aid Foundation

The Charities Aid Foundation is an acknowledged expert on the voluntary sector in the countries of the European Communities and central Europe. It was co-founder of the European Foundation Centre in Brussels; and has opened offices in Prague.

■ Charities Aid Foundation, 48 Penbury Road, Tonbridge, Kent TN9 2JD, Tel. 0732 771 333, Fax 0732 350 570.

The Research and Statistics Unit of the Charities Aid Foundation prepares information and statistics on voluntary organisations there, and their tax and legislative environment.

■ Research and Statistics Unit, Charities Aid Foundation, 18 Doughty Street, London WC1N 2PL, Tel. 071 831 7798.

Charities Tax Reform Group

The Charities Tax Reform Group, similarly, has studied the tax implications for charities of the completion of the single market. It has contact with other voluntary organisations in Europe in its campaign to ensure that charities do not suffer from the harmonisation of VAT rates, or the end of zero-rating.

■ Charities Tax Reform Group, 9 Old Queen Street, London SW1H 9JA, Tel. 071 222 1265.

Civil Rights Forum

In the human rights area, two new networks have been set up in Britain to promote human rights in Europe. The *Civil Rights Forum* was launched by the National Council for Civil Liberties (now called more simply, Liberty) in 1990 'to ensure that civil liberties and human rights are defended and extended in a united Europe; to create awareness within the EC of the consequences for human and civil rights of EC policy; and to stimulate and influence policy-making within the EC'. It plans to do this by lobbying politicians and civil servants, by initiating research in the human rights area, and by working towards a European Civil Rights Forum. The Forum has working groups entitled Fortress Europe, Policing and Security, Data Protection, and the Social Charter. UK members include the National Council for Civil Liberties, the Joint Council for the Welfare of Immigrants, Charter 88, the Refugee Council, the Scottish Council for Civil Liberties, and the Committee for the Administration of Justice.

■ Civil Rights Forum, The National Council for Civil Liberties, 21 Tabard Street, London SE1 4LA, Tel. 071 403 3888, Fax 071 407 5354.

Community Development Foundation

The Community Development Foundation offers a European Service for community development agencies. It is at an initial stage, and hopes to advise both non-governmental organisations and local authorities concerned with community development and networks in Europe, lobbying, research, conferences, training and documentation.

■ European Service for Community Development Agencies, Community Development Foundation, 60 Highbury Grove, London N5 2AG, Tel. 071 226 5375, Fax 071 704 0313.

Consumer Health Information Consortium (CHIC)

CHIC is a body currently developing European links with health information centres in Europe.

■ Consumer Health Information Consortium, Highcroft Cottage, Romsey Road, Winchester SO22 5DH, Tel. 0962 849100, Fax 0962 849079.

Consumers in the European Community Group (CECG)

Consumers in the European Community Group (CECG) brings together 29 UK organisations with an interest in EC consumer affairs. It carries out research into consumer concerns and watches out for EC legislation and other proposals likely to affect consumers. Organisations involved include the Consumers' Association and the National Consumer Council. It works through the European Bureau of Consumer Unions (BEUC), and the EC's Consumer Consultative Council (CCC).

■ Consumers in the European Community Group (CECG), 24 Tufton Street, London SW1P 3RB, Tel. 071 222 2662, Fax 071 222 8586.

Cornish Bureau for European Relations (CoBER)

The Cornish Bureau for European Relations is an unusual initiative in one English county to develop relationships with the European Communities and other European countries. Its quarterly magazine *CoBER Covath* ('Covath' is a Cornish word for 'recorder') brings news of Europe to Cornwall.

■ CoBER, Old School House, Mylor Bridge, Falmouth, Cornwall TR11 5NA.

Euro Bureau

The Euro Bureau is a small organisation (established 1990) which helps community action groups find out about, lobby, and get grants from European institutions. It provides an information service and workshops, and has published a booklet called *Power in the European Parliament*. It concentrates on helping Asian people resident in EC countries.

■ Euro Bureau, 9 Bower Street, Stoke-on-Trent ST1 3BH, Tel. 0782 266712.

European Dialogue

European Dialogue is a new independent organisation 'whose purpose is to help bring into being a new Europe united not simply by a common market but by common rights for all its residents'. Its priorities are human rights, cultural diversity, social justice and environmental responsibility. Members so far include the National Council for Civil Liberties (Liberty), European Nuclear Disarmament, Charter 88, the Campaign for Nuclear Disarmament, the New Economics Foundation and the Socialist Society. Membership costs from £5 to £100, according to category.

■ European Dialogue, 11 Goodwin Street, London N4 3HQ, Tel. 071 272 9092.

Joint Council for the Welfare of Immigrants (JCWI)

The Joint Council for the Welfare of Immigrants has been developing an international programme of work in the area of immigration in Europe. The JCWI has published a directory of non-governmental organisations in other member states that work with ethnic minority communities on the issues of immigration and nationality law and policy. Edited by Ciaran O'Maolain, it is a unique and monumental work, listing community and solidarity organisations, and is available for £12 including P&P. Called *Ethnic minority and migrant organisations – European directory*, it is a must for British groups wishing to contact their opposite numbers in other parts of Europe.

■ Joint Council for the Welfare of Immigrants, 115 Old Street, London EC1V 9JR, Tel. 071 251 8706, Fax 071 253 3832.

Legislation Monitoring Service for Charities

The Legislation Monitoring Service for Charities has published a number of leaflets and guidance notes about the implications for charities of 1992.

■ Legislation Monitoring Service for Charities, 9 Old Queen Street, London SW1H 9JA, Tel. 071 222 1265, Fax 071 222 1250.

National Association for Development Education (NADEC)

The *National Association for Development Education* is represented on the European Development Education group of the Liaison Committee for NGOs concerned with development issues.

■ NADEC, 6 Endsleigh Street, London WC1H 0DX, Tel. 071 388 2670.

National Consumer Council

The National Consumer Council has published a directory of Consumer Advice Centres in the member states of the EC. It identifies and lists national and regional organisations, governmental and non-governmental, which provide consumer advice in the areas of debt, housing, employment, immigration and social security advice.

■ National Consumer Council, 20 Grosvenor Gardens, London SW1W 0DH, Tel. 071 730 3469.

National Women's Network for International Solidarity

Founded in 1985 following a conference on women, aid and development at Kent University, the National Women's Network for International Solidarity aims to inform and mobilise British women and women from other countries living in Britain around international issues, particularly those concerned with development. It is a small organisation, with neither office nor full-time staff. Its objectives are to facilitate lobbying on international issues as they affect women. Membership fees range from £3.50 to £65, according to category. At European level, the National Women's Network participates in Women in Development, Europe (WIDE), which has membership in 14 European countries. The National Women's Network publishes a monthly newsletter and has a members' register to promote contact between women sharing similar areas of interest.

■ National Women's Network for International Solidarity, Box 110, 190 Upper Street, London N1 1RQ.

Refugee Forum

The Refugee Forum (established 1984), a self-help umbrella organisation with 56 branches in Britain, has, together with the Migrant Rights Action Network, written a *European manifesto*. It is producing a guide to European bodies and agreements affecting migrant and refugee communities, and to the Schengen agreement. It has adopted a *Refugee Charter for Europe*, outlining the principles on which refugees should be treated.

The Refugee Forum in Britain has proposed, in conjunction with similar organisations in Europe, a European Refugee Charter whereby a refugee granted asylum by one member country would have the same rights of movement, social security and work as a national within any other country of the Communities. There should be, it says, an independent appeals system and legal rights for all those facing deportation, detention or repatriation. It is critical of state-funded refugee agencies.

■ The Refugee Forum, 54 Tavistock Place, London WC1, Tel. 071 482 3829.

Standing Conference on Racial Equality in Europe (SCORE)

The Standing Conference on Racial Equality in Europe (SCORE) was launched in Birmingham in November 1990 and attracted 132 member organisations in its first half year of work. Its objectives are to ensure that the completion of the single market 'does not have serious adverse and sinister implications for black people' and 'to ensure that the door to Europe does not close to black people, refugees, asylum seekers and third country nationals'. It strives for racial equality in Europe, legislation to outlaw racial harassment, and for links with like-minded groups in other parts of Europe. Membership costs £20 for national voluntary organisations and statutory bodies; £5 for small voluntary organisations.

■ Standing Conference on Racial Equality in Europe (SCORE), c/o Greater London Action for Racial Equality, St Margaret's House, 21 Old Ford Road, London E2 9PL, Tel. 081 983 1122.

Volunteer Centre

The Volunteer Centre has active contact with organisations concerned with volunteering in EC and other European countries. With the Community Development Foundation, it began work in 1990 in compiling a listing of voluntary sector contacts in Europe. It is intended that this be added to VOLNET, which is the on-line database for voluntary organisations in the UK. The Volunteer Centre has run conferences on the theme of volunteering in Europe.

■ Volunteer Centre, 29 Lower King's Road, Berkhamsted, Hertfordshire HP4 2AB, Tel. 0442 873311, Fax 0442 870852, e-mail Greennet/Voluk.

BRITISH ORGANISATIONS IN BRUSSELS

Several British newspapers, media and trade magazines have correspondents in Brussels. These include the *BBC*, *Mail, Mirror, Telegraph*, The *Financial Times*, The *Guardian*, The *Independent, Metal Bulletin, New Scientist*, The *Scotsman, The Times* and The *Sunday Times*. Most of the media are contactable at the International Press Centre.

■ International Press Centre (IPC), boulevard Charlemagne 1, B.1040 Brussels, Tel. 322 238 0811.

Confederation of British Industry (CBI)

The Brussels office of the CBI acts as the eyes and ears of the CBI in Britain, and is in a position to make representations to the EC institutions about the needs of British industry.

■ CBI Brussels office, rue Joseph II 40 bte 14, Brussels B.1040, Tel. 322 231 0465.

The CBI works closely with the Union of Industrial and Employers' Confederations, UNICE, which is perhaps the largest Euro-lobby.

■ UNICE, rue Joseph II 40 bte 4, B.1040 Brussels, Tel. 322 237 6511.

Representation of Local and Regional Authorities in Brussels

Local and regional authorities are increasingly finding it desirable – if not necessary – to set up shop in Brussels: partly to provide 'eyes and ears' to pick up developments that may be of interest to them, partly to ensure that their region obtains its rightful share of European regional, training and structural funds. Remarkably, the list of local and regional authorities with a presence in Brussels does not just include European ones, but American ones concerned to protect their interests. Not only are several American states represented, but even the Port Authority for the Delaware river in New Jersey!

Local authorities are coy about the work of their Brussels outposts, but details of the work of the city of Birmingham's European office are available. The office was set up in Brussels in 1984, and its activities include:

* learning, at as early a stage as possible, of upcoming EC legislation;

* ensuring that Birmingham obtains the fullest possible benefit of the structural funds and other funding programmes (e.g. student exchanges, support for SMEs);

* timely lobbying to prevent the negative effects of proposed legislation; and

* policy-making in regard to urban development, through the Eurocities association.

The German, Spanish and French regions have been perhaps the quickest off the mark, but Danish and British regional authorities have now been moving in. These are as follows:

■ Cornwall County Council, rue du Commerce/20-22 bte 12, B.1040 Brussels, Tel. 322 513 0235, Fax 322 512 2165.

■ City of Birmingham (European office), Chaussée St Pierre, B.1040 Brussels, Tel. 322 646 3821, Fax 322 646 1355.

■ Strathclyde Regional Council, avenue Albert-Elisabeth 12, B.1200 Brussels, Tel. 322 736 2667, Fax 322 733 7822.

■ Scottish Highlands and Islands, and Mid Wales, rue Franklin 113, B.1040 Brussels, Tel. 322 735 5873, Fax 322 735 5766.

Scotland Enterprise (formerly the Scottish Development Agency) is located in Brussels, but its purpose is different: its remit is to encourage industrial investment *inwards into Scotland* as part of the *Locate in Scotland* campaign. Brussels is merely a convenient location for the campaign.

4

The European Networks: Their Origins and Role

Voluntary and community organisations concerned with social policy have a long shopping list of concerns which they wish to address to the European institutions. They need to make an impact out of proportion to their size if they are to influence social policy and put what has been termed a 'human face' on the single market of 1992. There are three channels by which voluntary and community organisations try to influence the European institutions: their national governments, by setting up direct means of representation in Brussels itself, and by joining a European network.

About 20 sectors of voluntary organisations are now represented in Europe, mainly through international networks, federations, movements, associations and unions (the terminology varies according to the style and purpose of the organisation concerned). These include sectors such as social services, youth, family bodies, migrants and refugees, disabled people, regional and rural concerns, community development, and unemployed people. There is even a set of groupings dedicated to improving the position of the voluntary sector itself. In the course of time, the late 1980s and early 1990s may come to be seen as a period of explosive growth in the international voluntary movement.

These groups are sometimes referred to as 'the networks'. It is important to distinguish between large, organisationally sophisticated, professionally financed and staffed bodies, with statutes and constitutions on the one hand; and, on the other, a group of two or three researchers who meet together once or twice or year and who also call themselves a 'network'. Clearly, the importance, potential and weight of these two extremes will be quite different. A network, after all, if one considers the definition of the word, is 'an artery or a series of channels or passages that promote communication over a large area'. The term 'network' will be the one which is most used here.

■ *Grants from Europe*, 32-8.

This chapter looks at the voluntary sector in Brussels and its reasons for being there; questions its effectiveness; and briefly compares it with the other European lobby groups. It gives an account of the origins of European networks, and how voluntary organisations in Britain can locate them. It describes their structures, openness, and methods of work. It considers the benefits and costs of joining European networks.

WHAT DO EUROPEAN NETWORKS DO?

European networks reflect on matters of concern to their members, collect information about their field of work in the different European countries, and lobby the European institutions for improved social policies. This work is serviced by staff members (often two or three), acting under the instructions of executive committees elected by general assemblies of the members of the network.

Some networks are explicitly formed in order to protect and advance the interests of their members, clients and professional interests. Others exist to share models of policy and best practice. These are sometimes termed reflective networks: members reflect on their work - sometimes through an annual European conference -and go home, and, if they feel so moved, then put into practice the concepts and practices that they have learned from their European colleagues. Other networks are formed with the specific purpose of influencing the policy of the European Communities (or the Council of Europe or the UN, as the case may be) - preventing that which is undesirable, and arguing for the needs of their clients. These lobbying networks can be identified by two specific characteristics: they are located in Brussels, the centre of power in the European Communities; and they have a structure (generally involving staff), which enables the work of the organisation to proceed in between annual conferences.

These purposes - reflection, representation, lobbying - are by no means exclusive. Some networks will share all these three objectives to a greater or lesser degree. The EC liaison committee of the International Federation of Social Workers, for example, not only promotes the professional standing of its members (which includes the mutual recognition of social work qualifications across Europe), but has commented sharply on the need for and the nature of anti-poverty policies in Europe, these being the concerns of greatest interest to the clients of social workers.

There is a lack of scientific information to explain why voluntary organisations join networks, and how precise their calculations are as to the possible gains likely to arise from membership. Some voluntary organisations may join networks as part of their strategy to pursue social change at a number of levels; others join in order to obtain information. Some join networks in anticipation of future policy outcomes, perhaps many years in the future; others, for negative (but nonetheless legitimate) reasons such as to prevent groups adopting positions inimical to their interests. Many still reserve to themselves the right to do their own European lobbying independently, and are reluctant to devolve substantial powers to a European office.

Some European observers will caution voluntary organisations against a headlong rush into the wonderful world of networks, associations and euro-talk. Members of the European Parliament point out that they respond twice as fast to representations from their constituents as to those from the grisled lobbyists who besiege the parliament: MEPs are, after all, accountable to the former, not the latter. It is possible to wage successful Euro-campaigns without ever setting foot across the channel, still less by joining a network.

VOLUNTARY ORGANISATIONS IN BRUSSELS

Some *national* voluntary organisations have already set up shop in Brussels. The representative body of the six main German welfare organisations, the Bundesarbeitsgemeinschaft der Freien Wohlfahrtspflege (BAGFW), already has a Brussels office which it shares with another large German charity, Caritas (Deutsches Caritasverband). The other leading German NGO groupings are not far behind: the Evangelical Church (*Diakonie*) arrived in June 1991. The umbrella group for the smaller German welfare organisations, Paritätischer Wohlfahrtsverband, is, in addition to its lobbying work in Brussels, launching a broad-based coalition to pursue issues of concern with like-minded voluntary organisations in other parts of Europe: it is being designated *Europarität*. National voluntary organisations in other countries do not have comparable resources, and for this reason have pooled their efforts. For example, the Fondation de France, has together with other, similar large national umbrella voluntary organisations, established the European Social Action Network (ESAN), to ensure that the social concerns of the national voluntary sector are argued in Brussels.

■ Bundesarbeitsgemeinschaft der Freien Wohlfahrtspflege (BAGFW), ave de la Renaissance 1 bte 8, B.1040 Brussels, Tel. 322 732 3810, Fax 322 732 3848.

■ European Social Action Network (ESAN), rue du Trône 98, B.1050 Brussels, Tel. 322 512 7411, Fax 322 512 6673.

■ Europarität, Endenicherstraße 125, D.5300 Bonn 1, Germany, Tel. 49 228 98599 10/11, Fax 49 228 9859980.

WHERE CAN WE FIND THE NETWORKS?

One approach is to go to directories of networks in Europe. There are two official such directories, one of which is published by the Council of Europe and is entitled *International non-governmental organisations enjoying consultative status with the Council of Europe*. In order to be in the directory, the network concerned must, first of all, have consultative status, and, to do that, have membership in at least four of the European countries that are members of the Council. A total of 287 networks had consultative status with the Council of Europe in 1989: the directory lists 232.

There are advantages and disadvantages to using the Council of Europe directory. It is the only published directory of its kind, it covers a wide range of non-governmental organisations, and there are profiles of 232 networks in English and French (the two texts are alongside each other). On the other hand, the rapid pace of change means that it is dated; it covers groups well outside the interests of voluntary and community organisations engaged in social action; and, of course, it includes only those organisations that have consultative status with the Council of Europe. Many of the newer networks either have not sought such status, or have not yet progressed to the point that they might wish to do so.

■ The Council of Europe, Palais de l'Europe, F 67006 Strasbourg Cedex, France, Tel. 33 88 41 2000, Fax 33 88 41 2781.

A list of Vienna-based NGO interest groups and NGO representatives accredited at the United Nations (Vienna) is published by the United Nations. About 900 are included: they cover everything from the international association of beekeepers to scientists concerned about the applications of hydrogen energy. Nevertheless, it is up to date and does include several of the international networks concerned with social affairs.

■ United Nations Office at Vienna, Vienna International Centre, PO Box 500, A.1400 Vienna, Austria, Tel. 431 211310, Fax 431 232156.

In April 1989, the Conseil National de la Vie Associative (National Council for Voluntary Associations) compiled a directory of European networks of associations (*Les regroupements associatifs en Europe*, by Suzana Szabo). This listed each according to sector, and included information on location, fields of work, programme, finance and criteria for membership. Its format is a series of files in a folder, rather than a book, but it provides considerably more detail than the Council of Europe directory, and is more focused on the social affairs area.

■ Conseil National de la Vie Associative (CNVA), rue de Varenne 55, 75007 Paris, France, Tel. 331 4548 6400.

WHERE DID THE NETWORKS COME FROM?

Historically, European networks of NGOs have developed in four phases:

• before the Second World War;

• in the immediate postwar period, principally around the United Nations;

• during the 1960s, chiefly around the Council of Europe; and

• during the 1980s and early 1990s, mainly around the EC institutions.

Naturally, there have been overlapping periods in this process, and there is the danger of simplifying the process. Nevertheless, these periods should provide a useful structure.

One of the earliest examples of the voluntary sector working at international level is furnished by the Red Cross, now based in Geneva, which has functioned as an international organisation since 1863, and now has 146 affiliated national organisations. Although best known for disaster relief and assisting the victims of war, national organisations of the Red Cross are equally well known for the provision of health and social services and training. An early British example of an international organisation is the Salvation Army, which was established in 1865, began work in France in 1880, and spread to other parts of mainland Europe the following year, meeting on an international basis to co-ordinate its work. It has become well known throughout the world for its work with the homeless, with prisoners, and in disaster and emergency relief. The International Council on Social Welfare was established in 1928 to promote the work of those providing social services and to improve the quality of the service provided. These networks saw themselves as sharing issues and problems of common concern, and by doing so, enriching the quality of service their members provided in each country. Many of the networks of the 1990s have similar objectives.

The expansion of networks in the period after the Second World War is associated with the United Nations (UN). The UN located a regional office and a number of its key departments in Europe, and encouraged national governments and non-governmental organisations alike to come forward with their views so that their various programmes, particularly in the areas of health and social affairs, could be made more effective. Most of the UN offices were located in neutral Switzerland and Austria. As a result, many non-governmental organisations came together on an international basis so that they could present an international overview of the situation facing their particular clients.

The Council of Europe provided a specific focus for the expansion of another wave of international networks. By being limited to a smaller number of countries than the United Nations, by having specific areas of competence (even if little real power), and by having a direct political link back to national governments, the Council of Europe offered new opportunities to international networks. The potential of the Council was enhanced by its decision to recognise the role of international non-governmental organisations explicitly by the creation of its system of 'consultative status'.

The present wave of non-governmental organisations owes much to the expansion of the role of the European Communities in the 1980s. This was due both to the increasing interest of the European institutions in social affairs, and to pressure from voluntary organisations to make the European Communities more sensitive to social issues.

Some voluntary organisations, fearful of the consequences of the completion of the internal market, acted to ensure that the social dimension of the single market achievement would not be neglected. Others saw the new-found competence of the Communities in the social affairs arena as an opportunity to influence policy both at European level and in the individual member states. Other networks were, financially speaking, the offspring of the Commission of the European Communities: it gave them seed money so they could get themselves off the ground. There were two possible reasons for this: first, the Commission's preference to hear the different European social sectors on an international basis, rather than 12 individually; second, so as to gain support for its own ambitious agenda for the European social dimension for the future, and to legitimise its own activities in this area.

Partly because of these historical circumstances, networks differ in their orientation. Some, chiefly those which grew up around the United Nations, aim to include all European countries, north and south, east and west. Some of these, especially in the health field, term themselves regions of world federations. Those networks associated with the Council of Europe have a smaller membership, as often as not covering only the Council of Europe countries. Some of the newest networks are limited to countries of the European Communities. These distinctions are by no means exclusive. Some of the UN-orientated networks, for example, subsequently opened what were termed *liaison offices* in Brussels.

Most of the international networks around the European Communities appear to be led (led in the sense of inspired by, or comprised of people in senior staff or officer positions) in three countries: Britain, France and Ireland. Few networks owe their existence or persistence to the southern countries. This may reflect the fact that Spain, Greece and Portugal joined the EC in the 1980s, and have become exposed to European methods of working only more recently. Curiously, neither Germany nor Denmark have been to the fore in the creation of networks.

AIMS AND OBJECTIVES OF THE VOLUNTARY SECTOR IN EUROPE

It is difficult to make an assessment of which, if any, networks or lobbies are successful in advancing their aims and objectives. Few networks commit themselves, at least publicly, to precise short and medium-term political objectives, such as specific legislation, action plans, parliamentary resolutions or specialised programmes, or comment on their own progress in achieving these objectives. As a result, it is difficult for outsiders to measure what progress they are making. Several networks declare their objectives in very general terms, like 'representing the interests of our clients or our members': this may well be true, but such generalised aims are not a useful yardstick by which to measure their effectiveness. If challenged about the reasons for their involvement in Europe, organisations respond by voicing a diffuse concern about decisions being taken there which may be of concern to them. Others express an interest in ensuring their member organisations in the national states are able to benefit from the structural funds or other financial opportunities. Few present an interest in large-scale political objectives. Only a few organisations have made a contribution to the EC's future social objectives by forwarding submissions to the intergovernmental conference of 1990-1. Those that did include ECAS, which prepared a memorandum *Citizens' Europe and the revision of the EC treaties*, the European Federation for the Homeless (FEANTSA), the European Anti-Poverty Network (EAPN), the European Women's Lobby and the Churches' Committee on Migrants in Europe (CCME). In its memorandum, ECAS argued for a 10-point plan for an expansion of the competence of the European Communities, and a common European statute for voluntary organisations.

The presence in Brussels of leading German welfare organisations seems to be entirely defensive in nature. The conferences that led to their being established there referred to the 'dangers' of 1992: dangers that other welfare organisations may be able to compete with them for the provision of social services in Germany, and that their secure (critics might say cosy and privileged) position as providers of services might be outlawed under new competition laws.

BRUSSELS OR STRASBOURG? THE COMMISSION OR THE PARLIAMENT?

One lobby which has specifically attempted to plan long-term objectives is the lobby for elderly people, Eurolink Age. Conceived initially as a European wing to the lobbying efforts of Age Concern in Britain, and still deriving substantial funding from Age Concern, Eurolink Age has specific objectives in the fields of anti-discrimination legislation, anti-poverty projects for the elderly, a seniors' pass in Europe, and a rolling action plan for elderly people incorporating a number of short-term, medium-term and long-term elements. In pursuit of these objectives, it set up a Brussels office; in Strasbourg it services an intergroup of MEPs which has 80 nominal members (15-25 regulars) and meets four times a year.

The European Commission seems to be the focus of the work of most of the networks of voluntary organisations. Despite that, the networks have used the European Parliament to fortify their position. Some of the anti-poverty networks have several times persuaded MEPs to add budget lines, not only for a continuation of their own funding, but for funding special projects and activities which they have promoted. In 1990, the European Secretariat of the World Deaf Federation managed to persuade the Parliament to add 1.26 MECU to the Commission's proposed 5.5 MECU budget for projects for disabled people. The ability of the networks to flex their muscles in the Parliament has, one suspects, been part of the process of persuading the Commission of their seriousness and professionalism.

Eurolink Age employs a European Parliament Liaison Officer half-time on retainer in Strasbourg, in addition to its Brussels staff. It is one of the few networks to have such explicit links with the Parliament. Several MEPs have spoken of the animal welfare lobby as a model for others. Its three staff are deployed as follows: one liaises with MEPs, a second travels throughout the European Communities building up support for its issues of concern, and a third runs the lobby's office. One MEP reported that 'they seem to have a staff member permanently parked outside the entrance to the Parliament building'. The animal welfare lobby is very conscious of the level at which it pitches its proposals, being careful to be reasonable, and distance itself from the extreme wing of some animal welfare organisations. Its intergroup, chaired by Ms Mary Banotti MEP, is always well attended (about 30-40 MEPs attending as a rule). A vet, who is attached to the lobby, gives MEPs briefings of a technical nature when required. The animal welfare lobby appears to have achieved some success in restricting the transport of live animals, reducing animal experimentation, banning the trade in skins of endangered species, and controlling the fur trade, yet most of this appears to have been accomplished through the Parliament more than the other institutions. The lobby is strongly rooted in the constituencies of MEPs, whose voting behaviour on animal welfare issues is closely scrutinised and reported. MEPs voting favourably are courteously thanked by branches based in their constituencies; those who vote unfavourably are quickly confronted.

The Parliament and the Economic and Social Committee provide fora where issues can be raised, debated and promoted. But while Parliament can adopt resolutions and set the tone for the discussion of issues within the European institutions, it has little power to ensure their effective implementation. For this reason, the quality of the follow-up work by the networks has proved all-important. This includes ensuring that the relevant parliamentary debates are well publicised in the member state concerned, and making sure that the text adopted is used as the benchmark for effective lobbying at home.

A successful campaign of this sort followed the adoption by the European Parliament of a hard-hitting report on homelessness in 1987. Part of the report condemned the manner in which two states used vagrancy laws to lock up people for being homeless. Voluntary organisations in the two countries concerned (Belgium and Ireland) used the report to embarrass their national governments into suspending or repealing these laws. Another section of the report, prohibiting hospitals from discharging homeless people onto the streets without aftercare services, was quoted against Irish health boards which continued these practices. In other words, lobbying through networks at European level has proved as effective as the campaigning capacity of the members of the network in their home countries.

HOW DOES THE VOLUNTARY SECTOR COMPARE?

Voluntary organisations publicly draw attention to the small size and ineffectiveness of their 'lobby' compared to that of the business sector, which they believe to be much more professional and lavishly endowed with resources. There is little evidence to support this contention. It is true that the employers' confederation, UNICE, in Brussels has a staff of 30 people, but most business organisations, confederations and networks in Brussels are much smaller. Most have a staff of similar size to that of the voluntary sector networks. Most have difficulty in persuading their members that investment in a Brussels wing is worth their while: 'what are *we* getting out of this?' is a refrain raised just as frequently in the business community.

Although the voluntary sector finds this hard to credit, business lobbyists in Brussels do not see their work as a smooth passage, or that it gets its way on all, or even many issues. If it had its way, the single market would have been completed long ago, it argues, and it perceives itself as having in its view 'lost' a long series of battles over health issues (such as the restrictions on tobacco) and environmental standards (which it considers too high). The business lobby finds the Brussels atmosphere a much more difficult one in which to work than that of its national governments: the accessibility of the Commission means that it is much more open to lobbies that it does not have to contend with at home! The freer market in ideas in Brussels actually makes its work harder. Business lobbies point to the voluntary sector as being much more used to building coalitions and networks, something less familiar in its more hierarchical structures. Business lobbies can experience acute problems of cohesion traditionally considered the privilege of voluntary organisations: indeed the Common Market Automobile Constructors Association fell apart in 1990.

Nor is the voluntary sector necessarily 'poorer' than the business lobby. Some voluntary organisations (notably in the conservation and environment area) are believed to be able to raise considerable amounts of money; other networks have attracted substantial funding from the Commission for their information and research roles. In any case, size and resources have never been synonymous with effectiveness.

This is not to argue that the Commission is a neutral ground, a level playing field in which all the players are equal. Quite clearly, the single market and the thus far limited social achievements of the EC indicate that the Brussels environment has favoured some interest groups more than others. At the same time, the voluntary and community sector may not be the victim of the forces of European integration that it sometimes imagines itself to be. The growth in European networks of voluntary organisations and associations suggests that it may have strengths and capabilities which will stand to its advantage as key European decisions are taken over the next few years.

European Commission officials themselves argue that they respond best to lobbies which are clear about their objectives, which are both early and timely in their interventions, which pay attention to detail, and which supply accurate, reliable and factual information. They do not necessarily warm to lobbies simply because they are powerful in their home states or because they have glossy public relations.

HOW OPEN ARE THE NETWORKS?

Not everyone can join a network, federation or association. Some insist that only one organisation represent each country. This is difficult to enforce in practice, since many countries have strong regional divisions, not least Belgium, which is divided between the Dutch and the French tradition, each insisting on its right to representation. Other networks, particularly the more reflective ones which emphasise the diversity of experience of their membership, welcome all comers. Some networks or associations adopt the practice of having full members (who pay full rate and have full voting rights) and associate members (who pay a lower rate, receive the full range of publications, but have no voting rights). Membership fees not only vary widely, but are often quoted in different currencies - US dollars, Belgian francs, Austrian schillings being common; some of the newer networks set their fees in ECU.

This guide lists networks and associations which are open to new members and those that, for one reason or another, have more restricted membership. There are two reasons for including the second group. First, networks with restricted membership are often a valuable source of information and publications, and their information policy may be quite open as well as being prolific in quantity. Second, even if it is not possible to join, such networks and associations are generally open to being asked to raise issues, or even to have guest speakers address their meetings or participate in their debates.

Some European networks have been criticised for being elitist, that they are hard to get into, and that decisions in them are taken by a small number of people. At least two networks (The European Women's Lobby and the European Anti-Poverty Network) have taken steps to try avoid this danger by building up broad-based consultative mechanisms, and even creating electoral colleges in each of the member states.

WHAT KIND OF ORGANISATIONAL STRUCTURES DO THE NETWORKS HAVE?

Most international networks have a legal basis or structure to their work. This takes two forms. First, they have what in Britain is called a constitution but which in mainland Europe is referred to as *statutes*, or 'the statutes' of an organisation or network. Second, most networks register in the country where they are located as an international non-governmental organisation (INGO). The process of registration reflects the continental tradition whereby voluntary organisations legitimate themselves with the state in order to become official and legal. It dates to historical circumstances (different from Britain) whereby unless something was officially approved, it was automatically illegal. Such regulation is not usually considered oppressive and most networks feel uncomfortable without putting themselves, sooner rather than later, on a formal legal basis. British people still remain puzzled at the continental obsession with being registered.

Luxembourg and Belgium make special arrangements to facilitate the registration of international NGOs. To take the case of Belgium, the procedure is relatively straightforward. The NGO writes to the Belgian Minister for Justice applying to register as an NGO, enclosing a copy of its statutes and list of officers. When approval comes through, its registration is then published in the official Royal Gazette, called *Moniteur Belge*, along with a copy of the statutes. The Minister must be informed of the names, addresses and professions of the officers of the organisation, and of any changes that take place.

Networks differ from British voluntary organisations in their structure. Annual General Meetings (AGMs) are rare: European organisations generally have an AGM every second year, and it is called either a Congress or a General Assembly. The Assembly generally elects what is called an *administrative council* which consists of 12 to 15 *administrators* which meets two or three times a year. In practice, although the statutes may not require it, most organisations will aim to have each country represented on its administrative council. The administrative council in turn elects a small executive committee, sometimes called a *bureau*. This generally consists of five officers:

Officers of a European network

• president;

- two, sometimes three, vice-presidents;

- treasurer; and

- secretary.

The term president is used rather than that of chair. The executive committee is then responsible for the running of the organisation's office or staff. The staff will generally number around one, two or three, as often as not operating out of a small, cramped, bustling den as close to the Commission as possible. Staff members may be recruited locally in Belgium, but at least one will normally have come from one of the countries most influential in that particular network. Staff must be entrusted with a high level of responsibility, for distance and finance mean that the executive committees to which they work can only meet a few times a year. They must have the scope and ability to get on with the job.

European networks are funded from a number of sources. A small number of networks are almost 100 per cent funded by the European Commission: these are principally networks in the anti-poverty field, recognising that by their nature these groups have great difficulty financing themselves. Several networks receive Commission funding for specific projects – like a conference on a particular theme, or a research report, the quid pro quo being that the Commission is able to use the information and research and policy results arising. As a result, several networks contrive to attract Commission funding to cover about 40 per cent or so of their funding each year. Many networks rely on membership subscriptions, which in the case of some networks can be quite hefty. Some rely to a greater or lesser extent on grants from foundations or research bodies. Some networks have become quite adept at sharing office space with other networks or research institutes, and using other money-saving approaches familiar to voluntary organisations everywhere.

Corporate giving to voluntary organisations and networks in Europe thus far has been limited. More than one-third of corporate money going to voluntary organisations finds its way to voluntary organisations concerned with the arts and culture. Smaller amounts go to organisations and projects with employment, educational or environmental themes, but very few to groups otherwise attentive to social deprivation.

WHAT ARE THE BENEFITS AND DISADVANTAGES OF JOINING A NETWORK?

No studies are available which have analysed the benefits to British voluntary organisations of joining European networks, or how they have felt about the experience, so any comments here are speculative in nature. Joining a European network should lead to an enhanced understanding of how the European institutions work, and a much improved (possibly excessively large!) information flow about developments in the European Communities. It should also enable voluntary and community organisations in the UK to learn about how their counterparts in other European countries tackle similar problems, be it with more or less success than themselves. Networks may confirm individual members in the wisdom of the manner in which they approach their own work at home, reduce their sense of isolation, and give them greater confidence to undertake new approaches.

Participation in European networks also presents costs for voluntary organisations: these need to be carefully weighed. European work is time-consuming, and can mean that already over-committed staff or voluntary members of organisations will spend several days away from home base at a time. Working relationships in networks take years to establish, and making a network an effective lobbying force may take up to five years' hard work. It is a process that produces results in the medium term or the long term, but not in the short term. The membership of the voluntary organisation may grow impatient with a process that seems remote and unproductive, and has all the negative associations of junketing.

There are also financial costs. The cost of affiliating to a network, as we have seen, varies from the nominal to a level that absorbs a significant part of the organisation's budget. The second expense that needs to be taken into account is the cost of attending meetings. Some networks attract funding for specialised conferences or seminars, and the small number of directly funded Commission-sponsored networks are able to pay the full travel costs of their members. However, even those networks that are able to provide travel or participation costs generally do so on the basis of a subsequent refund. Participants invariably find themselves meeting some expenses themselves: these can add up and be a real problem for people on low incomes or for social security claimants.

The other matter which an organisation wishing to participate in a network may need to think through is the question of the internal implications.

Participation in a network means that the organisation will need to re-orientate itself towards a European focus. The organisation will need to adapt internally, make space within its staffing and agenda for European affairs, and ensure that its members acquire some basic knowledge of what Europe is about and why the organisation is taking part. Not all organisations give European affairs prominence in their internal discussions, even though some of their senior members may be actively involved in some of the new networks. By contrast, some organisations have a 'European affairs page' in their newsletter outlining European developments, and the nature of their participation in its various networks.

■ *Grants from Europe*, 120-4.

5

Different European Networks

One can categorise the networks in many different ways - according to function (lobbying or reflection); size; funding sources (Commission or membership); and scope (broad-based, or specific field of action), but here they are categorised according to sector.

VOLUNTARY SECTOR

There are a number of networks which are concerned with the voluntary sector in general. Over the past 20 years, networks concerned with voluntary organisations, volunteering, and what has even been termed 'voluntarism' have been coming together to share their experiences on a European basis.

Association pour le Volontariat

The *Association pour le Volontariat* was formed in Lucca, Italy, in 1989. It brings together national organisations concerned with voluntary work in France, Italy, Spain, Belgium and Denmark, the UK member being the Volunteer Centre. It hopes to carry out information, training, research and documentation concerning the voluntary sector, and represent the needs of the voluntary sector to the national and international authorities.

■ Association pour le Volontariat, rue Royale 11, B.1000 Brussels, Tel. 322 219 5370.

Comité Européen des Associations d'intérêt Général (CEDAG)

CEDAG was established in 1989 as the European Council for Voluntary Organisations to 'represent the interests of voluntary organisations in general to the European Commission'. CEDAG hopes to assist the cross-border co-operation of voluntary organisations. Its aims are to ensure that there is a common legal constitution for voluntary organisations in Europe, that voluntary organisations are specifically mentioned and consulted when EC legislation is prepared, and that EC legal and financial arrangements respect their needs and structures. It has built up an intergroup for the voluntary sector in the European Parliament, and works with DG XXIII (the social economy directorate) to press the Commission for special funding for the work of voluntary organisations. CEDAG has sixty-four members from nine different countries (there are nine UK members). Its main partner in the UK is the National Council for Voluntary Organisations.

■ CEDAG, rue de Varenne 18, 75007 Paris, France, Tel. 331 4549 0658, Fax 331 428 40484.

Volonteurope

Volonteurope (established 1981) is the association of organisations from EC countries concerned about the role of volunteers in social provision. Volonteurope has adopted a 10-point charter both to protect the role of volunteers in voluntary organisations, and list their responsibilities as well as rights. Its declared purpose is to 'encourage co-operation in the unpaid voluntary sector, to facilitate the flow of information, and to help promote an increase in the amount and effectiveness of volunteer work (broadly defined) within the countries of the EC'. Volonteurope has over 100 affiliate agencies, and the board is composed of two representatives from each country. Its current activities include workshops, training, exchanges, publications, and raising the profile of volunteering in the EC. A documentation centre is being established in Amsterdam in conjunction with the Institute of Social History. After four years of lobbying by Volonteurope, the European Commission allocated a sum of £36,000 in 1991 to develop exchanges between full-time volunteers in Europe.

The British national members are the volunteer bureaux and Community Service Volunteers. Volonteurope has a journal which goes out to 1,700 addresses. Journal no.7, for example, was devoted to the voluntary sector in central Europe. Volonteurope has members in all EC countries and beyond: its working language is English. Volonteurope is in the process of administrative reorganisation and has relocated in Brussels with the European Foundation Centre. It has recently established a youth network, called Volonteurope Youth. All agencies involved in volunteering are welcome.

- Volonteurope, rue de la Concorde 51, B.1050, Brussels.

- Community Service Volunteers, 237 Pentonville Road, London N1 9NJ, Tel. 071 278 6601, Fax 071 837 9621.

- International Association for Volunteer Effort, European Office, Centre National du Volontariat, rue des Poissonniers 130, F. 75018 Paris, France, Tel. 331 4264 9734.

RELIGIOUS ORGANISATIONS

To speak of a 'religious lobby' in Brussels is to seem pejorative. What, after all, could church networks be doing in Brussels? Yet a striking feature of the various lobbies, networks and associations there is the presence of mainly ecumenical international Christian associations. They do not appear to be there for the same reasons as religious bodies are in their member states, namely to protect their institutions (like schools and other establishments). The Brussels religious lobby is at least in some respects politically to the left of their member churches in the national states.

The religious networks are composed of wings of the existing, long-established European churches. Including them in a listing of networks may in one sense seem questionable: yet their lobbying methods, approaches and organisation mark them as more sophisticated than many networks in the voluntary sector, and networks of voluntary organisations could stand to gain much if they enlisted the religious lobby in their various causes.

COMECE stands for *Commission des Épiscopats de la Communauté Européenne* (Commission of the Bishops of the EC) and represents the views of the Catholic Bishops in Europe on all matters affecting the political, social, cultural and economic aspects of the evolution of Europe. It does so through its contacts with officials in the EC institutions and MEPs.

- COMECE, ave Père Damien 13, B.1150 Brussels, Tel. 322 771 3678, Fax 322 770 7654.

The European Ecumenical Commission for Church and Society (EECCS) is the protestant social justice umbrella organisation attempting to influence the policies of the European Communities. It is the approximate equivalent of COMECE. EECCS describes itself as 'a focus for discussion and joint efforts by member churches as they respond to the questions posed by the emerging new Europe'. There are secretariats in Brussels and Strasbourg. British members are the Church of England, the Church of Scotland, and the Council of Churches for Britain and Ireland.

■ European Ecumenical Commission for Church and Society (EECCS), Ecumenical Centre, rue Joseph II 174, B.1040 Brussels, Tel. 322 230 1732, Fax 322 231 1413.

There are several networks built around EECCS, such as the Churches' Committee for Migrants in Europe, and the European Contact Group on Urban Industrial Mission, which is active on unemployment and economic issues. Together with the William Temple Foundation in Manchester, the European Contact Group has created the West European Work and Economy Network (WEN), which has 400 affiliated members, researchers and policy-makers. Its 1990 conference addressed such issues as the crisis in European rural areas and the economic exploitation of black and migrant workers. The network has published a series of papers on the social implications of the completion of the internal market.

■ Revd Tony Addy, European Contact Group, 48 Peveril Crescent, Manchester M21 1WS, Tel. 061 881 6031.

The European Ecumenical Organisation for Development (EECOD), was formed in 1974. Its aim is to persuade the EC to adopt aid policies that are more just. One of its strengths is the involvement of the Catholic missionary orders of Africa. EECOD has campaigned vigorously on the negative effects which the Common Agricultural Policy has on small agricultural producers in developing countries. In 1989, EECOD brought to Brussels an ecumenical delegation of African Church leaders to plead their case. EECOD has observer status with the Council of Europe and attends meetings of the Council's bodies dealing with migration. EECOD's newsletter is entitled *Antenna*. The UK members are Christian Aid and the Catholic Institute for International Relations.

■ EECOD, Ecumenical Centre, rue Joseph II 174, B.1040 Brussels, Tel. 322 230 1732, Fax 322 231 1413.

The Jesuit-inspired OCIPE is the Catholic European Study and Information Centre. It was founded in 1956 by the Bishop of Strasbourg at the urging of lay persons working in the Council of Europe. It describes its objective as 'a more just Europe': accordingly its focus is on social issues, on which it carries out research, provides information and takes action. Recent conferences have been on the rights of children and the position of asylum seekers, migrants and the poor. It also runs public lectures and study days. OCIPE publishes *European Studies*, a recent edition of which was devoted to the social implications of the Charter of Fundamental Social Rights. OCIPE has six staff members in Brussels and three in Strasbourg. It has wasted no time in responding to the changes in central Europe and is currently opening offices in Warsaw and Budapest.

■ OCIPE (Brussels Office), rue de la loi 221, B.1040 Brussels, Tel. 322 231 0697 Fax 322 230 0556.

The Quaker Council for European Affairs (QCEA) exerts pressure out of all proportion to the small number of Quakers in Europe. A Quaker (Society of Friends) house was inaugurated in Brussels in 1979 in response to Friends insisting that contemporary social issues be addressed to decision-makers in the European Communities. The main areas of interest developed by QCEA are the arms trade, defence, social issues, refugees, migrants and relationships with the developing countries.

Some of the most durable work of the QCEA has been human rights work with the Council of Europe, where the Friends have consultative status. The QCEA report, *Waiting for justice* (Mirjam Berg), describing the conditions facing remand prisoners, led to a resolution in the Council of Europe's Parliamentary Assembly critical of the record of many member states, and to proposals for uniform European minimum standards for remand prisoners. The Council of Europe published a QCEA study on non-violent conflict resolution in school. It has also made progress in persuading European governments to recognise the right of conscientious objection to compulsory military service. The QCEA wrote the introduction to the Council of Europe's *Convention for the Prevention of Torture and Inhuman and Degrading Treatment or Punishment*.

The QCEA is one of the few networks to develop a working relationship with the North Atlantic Treaty Organisation, NATO. Searching for new means to promote security through non-aggressive means, the Quakers have begun a process of dialogue with NATO officials and some of the 188 parliamentary members of NATO. Groups of Quakers visit the NATO headquarters regularly, and Quaker House has twice been the venue for day-long discussions among international groups of Quakers, Mennonites and NATO diplomats and staff. A newsletter, *Around Europe*, is published ten times a year, the subscription for which costs 600BF. Associate membership costs 1200BF (about £20) and includes twice-yearly mailings, with documents and publications.

■ QCEA, square Ambiorix 50, B.1040 Brussels, Tel. 322 230 4935, Fax 322 230 6370, e-mail: greennet qcea.

VOLUNTARY ORGANISATIONS CONCERNED WITH DEVELOPMENT ISSUES

Several networks of voluntary organisations are concerned with development issues. They have located in Europe so as to influence European attitudes, policies and funding patterns towards the developing countries. The International Council of Voluntary Agencies (ICVA) goes back to 1962 and is a primary point of contact between development organisations and the United Nations. Voluntary organisations involved in development issues are considered an important, well-organised lobby. Seventeen European development associations came together in 1990 to form a new European Forum for North-South Solidarity.

■ European Forum for North-South Solidarity, rue Jonquoy 25, F.75014 Paris, France, Tel. 331 4539 0862, Fax 322 4539 7164 (temporary address).

■ *Grants from Europe*, 86-100.

The Association of Protestant Development Organisations in Europe (APRODEV)

APRODEV was formed in 1990 to influence the decisions of the European Communities in development policy, taking up such issues as the debt crisis and the role of non-governmental organisations in the south. Christian Aid is the UK member.

■ APRODEV, rue Joseph II 174, B.1040 Brussels, Tel. 322 231 0102, Fax 322 231 1413.

Euro Coopération Internationale pour le Développement et la Solidarité (EUROCIDSE)

CIDSE (established 1967) is the international catholic development organisation: translated, it means International Co-operation for Development and Solidarity. Its aims are to support the peoples of the developing countries in their struggle for their economic, social and political rights, and to influence all those concerned with development so as to ensure policies based on self-reliance, partnership and solidarity. Development education is an important aspect of its work. Its members are involved in 6,000 development programmes valued at $300m. UK members are Catholic Fund for Overseas Development (CAFOD) and the Scottish Catholic International Aid Fund (SCIAF). It was relaunched as EUROCIDSE in 1991.

■ CIDSE Secretariat General, ave des Arts 1-2 bte 6, B.1040 Brussels, Tel. 322 219 0080, Fax 322 218 3788.

EUROSTEP

EUROSTEP stands for European Solidarity towards Equal Participation of People, and brings together secular development NGOs. Its priorities are the debt crisis, and more just relationships between the industrialised and the developing countries.

■ EUROSTEP, rue Stévin, B.1040 Brussels, Tel. 322 231 1709, Fax 322 23 0348.

Handicap International

Handicap International is the umbrella group for French and Belgian solidarity missions of technicians, physiotherapists and medical doctors to developing countries, principally those in Africa and Indo-China. They run more than 60 rehabilitation centres in these countries, in co-operation with other international partners which include Save the Children Fund and Oxfam. Many of those using their rehabilitation centres are amputees and victims of war.

■ Handicap International, avenue Clays 111, B.1030 Brussels, Tel. 322 735 2008, Fax 322 735 2761.

International Council of Voluntary Agencies (ICVA)

The International Council of Voluntary Agencies is an independent, international association of non-governmental, non-profit-making organisations active in the field of humanitarian assistance and development co-operation. It was established in 1962 to promote the development of voluntary agencies, and today provides a permanent international liaison structure for voluntary agency consultation and co-operation. It also acts as a liaison body between the voluntary sector and intergovernmental organisations such as the United Nations High Commissioner for Refugees, the United Nations Relief and Works Agency for Palestine Refugees, the United Nations Development Programme and the World Bank.

ICVA supports the work of voluntary agencies in general, and member agencies in particular, in influencing national and international policies, protecting refugees and displaced persons, providing for relief and rehabilitation, and in fostering sustainable development. It has working groups on institutional development; refugees, displaced persons and migrants; and on sustainable development, environment and population.

British or British-based member organisations include ACORD, Actionaid, the British Refugee Council, HelpAge International, International Planned Parenthood Federation, Oxfam, Ockenden Venture, the Refugees Study Programme, the World Ort Union and the Salvation Army. It has a bi-monthly publication, *ICVA News*, and library and documentation centre.

■ International Council of Voluntary Agencies, rue Gautier 13, CH 1201 Geneva, Switzerland, Tel. 41 22 732 6600/1/2, Fax 41 22 738 9904.

International Workers Aid/Entraide Ouvrière

A specialised socialist-based network bringing together voluntary aid agencies is International Workers' Aid (established 1928), though it is better known by its German and French titles (*Internationales Arbeiter-Hilfswerk* and *Entraide Ouvrière* respectively). IWA has consultative status with the Council of Europe and the International Labour Organisation, and opened a Brussels liaison office in 1987. Workers' Aid co-ordinates members' projects in developing countries and brings the issues arising from development work to the attention of the European political institutions, principally the debt crisis facing the developing countries. The UK member is War on Want.

■ Entraide Ouvrière (Bureau de Liaison), rue Montagne aux Herbes Potagères 37, B.1000 Brussels, Tel. 322 219 4882, Fax 322 218 8415.

Médecins sans Frontières

One of the most active third-world charities is the medical help organisation *Médecins sans frontières* which sends young doctors abroad to provide medical help.

■ Médecins sans frontières (International Office), boulevard Léopold II 209, B.1080 Brussels, Tel. 322 426 5552, Fax 322 426 7536.

NGO Liaison Committee

Foremost of the networks concerned with development is the Liaison Committee (established 1976). Sponsored by the Commission, it brings

135

together up to 600 voluntary organisations concerned with development issues from all over Europe. Each country elects a national delegation of up to eight members to a general assembly, which in turn elects a twelve-strong liaison committee, which includes one person from each country. This committee, chosen for a three-year period, is the core of the network, and is in permanent contact with the two directorates of the Commission most concerned with development policy – VIII (Development) and VI (Agriculture).

The seventeenth assembly of development NGOs was held in April 1991. The EC's contribution to NGO operations in developing countries in 1990 totalled 318.5 MECU, of which one-third was food aid and one-quarter co-financed small-scale development projects. The 1991 general assembly was attended by representatives of EC institutions and NGO networks, and addressed by Commission Vice-President Manuel Marin and European Parliament President Enrique Baron Crespo.

The work of the liaison committee is divided into several areas: the education of public opinion about development issues, development policy, the promotion of NGOs in the developing countries themselves and the co-ordination of projects co-financed by NGOs and the European Communities. About 300 such projects are co-financed each year.

■ Comité de Liaison ONG, ave de Cortenberg 62, B.1040 Brussels, Tel. 322 736 4087, Fax 322 732 1934.

The liaison committee has five subcommittees: development education, emergency aid, volunteering, project finance and food matters. UK representatives on these subcommittees are drawn from OXFAM, CAFOD (Catholic Fund for Overseas Development) and Christian Aid.

POLITICAL GROUPINGS

The main political groupings in Europe, like the Socialists and Christian Democrats, are organised into federations in their own right. Campaigning voluntary organisations have approached the political groupings in order to gain support for their various causes, in addition to their work with individual Members of the European Parliament.

■ The political groupings in the European Parliament, chapter 2 of this volume.

Just as the political groupings are organised in European Federations, so too are their youth wings, and in some cases their women's groups. Some will be prepared to support the positions of voluntary organisations and pursue issues for them both within their own organisation and with their parent bodies. The youth wings of the political parties are active contributors to the European international youth organisations and bodies.

European Union of Women

Similarly, the women's wing of the European People's Party is organised into the European Union of Women (EUW). Its membership is drawn from women members of parliament, local authorities and public life from the Christian Democrat parties of 16 countries including those of the EC, Scandinavia, Austria and Switzerland. The EUW aims to promote the exchange of ideas, with discussion on practical issues of political and social reform, to strengthen international understanding and to help women take a greater part in the public life of their country: it has commissions on social affairs, migrants and refugees, economics, health and environment.

The UK section of the European Union of Women is the Conservative party, although the party is not yet a member of the Christian Democrats (the matter is under discussion). There are 58 branches in the different Euro-constituencies, where they play an active role in supporting the work of Conservative MEPs. They have about 3,000 members.

■ European Union of Women, Kärntnerstraße 51, A.1010 Vienna, Austria, Tel. 431 515 210, Fax 431 512 2468; European Union of Women, 392 Shakespeare Tower, Barbican, London EC2Y 8DR, Tel. 071 588 5745.

European Young Christian Democrats (EYCD)

The European Young Christian Democrats (EYCD) (established 1985) co-ordinates the work of the young members of the Christian Democrat organisations in Europe, both in the EC countries and the Council of Europe. Several central European countries (Poland, the Czech and Slovak Federal Republic and Hungary) are now represented as observers. Its work concentrates on debate, training, education and information activities. The EYCD runs a summer school, publishes a newsletter 10 times a year, and issues a magazine *CD Future*. There is no British member organisation, though this will certainly change if the Conservatives are admitted into the European People's Party.

■ European Young Christian Democrats, rue de la Victoire 16, B.1060 Brussels, Tel. 322 537 4147, Fax 322 537 9348.

Socialist International Women

Socialist International Women is the international organisation of women's groups in the socialist, social democratic and labour parties of the Socialist International. It was formed in 1907 and now has 68 member organisations, but does not accept individual membership. It is a non-governmental organisation with consultative status at the UN, UNESCO and ECOSOC. It publishes detailed conference reports which debate contemporary social issues affecting women.

The British affiliated organisation is Labour Party Women. The international secretariat is in London.

■ Socialist International Women, Maritime House, Old Town, Clapham, London SW4 0JW, Tel. 071 627 4449, Fax 071 720 4448.

WOMEN'S NETWORKS

There are 165m women in the European Communities, or 52 per cent of its population. Article 119 of the Treaty of Rome referred specifically to the right of women and men to equal pay for equal work. This has subsequently been interpreted by the Commission as laying the basis for a broad mandate of programmes to promote greater equality between men and women, and for the advancement of women's rights. The European Parliament first addressed women's issues by establishing an ad hoc committee on women's rights in 1979. This became a permanent committee in 1984. The European Commission's Third Action Programme on Equal Opportunities for Men and Women was adopted in 1991.

Two main women's bodies deal with the EC institutions: the European Network of Women (ENOW) and the European Women's Lobby (EWL). The newcomer to women's rights at European level may find the picture of women's lobby groups quite confusing, as both of these organisations pursue similar objectives, and have an overlapping membership. Despite that, they have different histories and are distinct. Because of their prominence in the EC, these two networks are described first.

■ *Grants from Europe*, 56-9.

European Network of Women (ENOW)

The European Network of Women was a voluntary sector initiative in 1983, comprising women's groups interested in pursuing issues at European level: it sees itself as both radical and critical. In 1988, ENOW organised the Women's Poverty Tribunal in Brussels in order to influence the agenda of the Commission's action programme for women so that it would include poverty affecting women. Before the conference, every country carried out research into women's poverty; afterwards, a set of proposals to alleviate women's poverty was published. The conference was attended by 170 women from nine member states. Its report was entitled *Women demand action from the EC* and included proposals in the area of women and work, women and benefits, and legislation.

ENOW is based on what are called 'national co-ordinations' in each country, and receives some funding from the European Commission for its activities. It is campaigning for the adoption and improvement of the EC directives that concern part-time work, temporary work and homemaking. Present priorities for ENOW include women, 1992 and the labour market; training; health at work; atypical work; and the caring professions. Membership is open to individuals, women's groups and national organisations, and costs between £7 and £35, according to category.

■ Secretariat, ENOW, rue Blanche 29, B.1050 Brussels, Tel. 322 537 7988, Fax. 322 537 5596.

European Women's Lobby (EWL)

The European Women's Lobby was started on the initiative of the women's section of the Commission. Like ENOW, it is based on national co-ordinations in each country, and it is up to each country to select or elect its representatives to the women's lobby. The Women's Lobby is funded principally by the Women's Information Service of the Commission, but raises some finance itself. The UK has a liaison committee of eight members which meets four times a year.

The European Women's Lobby is comparatively new. It traces its origins to a meeting organised by the Fawcett Society in London in 1986 which passed a resolution advocating the representation of women at European level. This conference was called the IVth European Colloquium for Women's Organisations, and on the UK side included the Women's National Commission, the Women's Interest Group of the National Council for Voluntary Organisations (subsequently – 1989 – the National Alliance of Women's Organisations), and the National Federation of Women's Institutes.

A structure was proposed which should 'exert influence and put effective pressure on European and national institutions in order to ensure that women's interests are more adequately defended and represented...in the context of a more united Europe'. Proposals for basic rules, structures and objectives were circulated to women's organisations in Europe over the next two years: the outcome was the first General Assembly of the European Women's Lobby, held in Brussels in September 1990. This 70-strong General Assembly adopted the current aims and objectives of the Lobby.

The objectives of the Lobby, as defined in its statutes, are to promote the interests of women in the European Communities, particularly migrant women, black women and women from ethnic minorities; to make proposals for a European social policy; and to influence the policies of the European Communities wherever it feels it has a specific contribution to make. It tabled two motions for the European intergovernmental conference (1990-1) and has prepared commentaries on four proposed directives affecting the welfare of women.

Each member state of the EC elects four members to the General Assembly of the European Women's Lobby. These delegates are chosen by the national co-ordinations. In the case of the UK, delegates are chosen according to a regional basis (England, Wales, Scotland, Northern Ireland). In the Netherlands, by contrast, the selection was according to sectors (feminists, ethnic minorities, health and traditional women's groups). Work between general assemblies is carried out by a bureau of 20 members meeting four times a year, which includes one representative from each member state. Day-to-day work is carried out by a secretariat in Brussels.

British members of the European Women's Lobby include the National Alliance of Women's Organisations, Women's Forum Scotland, Wales Women's European Network and the Northern Ireland Women's European Platform. The lobby has contact with the large number of different women's groups, associations and networks throughout Europe.

■ Eva Eberhardt, Place Quitelet 1a, B.1030 Brussels, Tel. 322 217 9020, or rue du Méridien 22, Brussels, Tel. 322 217 9020, Fax 322 219 8451.

Associated Countrywomen of the World (ACWW)

This is a much older organisation, constituted in its present form in 1933. ACWW describes itself as 'the largest international organisation of rural women and homemakers' with a membership of 500 women's societies (200 in Europe) in 70 countries. As well as representing the views and concerns of rural women, it works with the United Nations and UNESCO in water, nutrition, housing and agricultural projects in developing countries. ACWW has consultative status at the United Nations. Its quarterly magazine is *The*

Countrywoman. Membership costs between £10 and £50, according to category.

■ Associated Countrywomen of the World, ACWW, Vincent House, Vincent Square, London SW1P 2NB, Tel. 071 834 8635.

The European Forum of Socialist Feminists

This is a new network which functions through an annual conference, the first of which was held in 1985. A draft constitution is currently being agreed, which declares the organisation's aims to be 'to promote socialist feminism...with a European focus. It is committed to the involvement of black, ethnic minority and migrant women in Europe and seeks to build on links with women in other parts of the world.' Conference proceedings have occasionally been published. Membership is open to women aged 17 or over.

■ Claire Crocker, Membership Secretary, European Forum of Socialist Feminists, Garden Flat, 7 Acol Road, London NW6 3AA, Tel. 071 328 5108.

Women in Development, Europe (WIDE)

WIDE is the network for women concerned with development issues in Europe, and who are working for the improvement of the conditions facing women in the southern, developing countries. It seeks to promote public awareness of women's needs in the development process, to strengthen the programmes of NGOs helping women in the southern countries, and to ensure that EC aid to developing countries takes account of the needs of women. Membership costs from 10 to 100 ECU, according to category. It has members from 14 countries in Europe, offers an annual assembly and publishes a three-times-a-year bulletin. The national group in Britain belonging to WIDE is the National Women's Network for International Solidarity.

■ Women in Development, Europe, Irish Commission for Justice and Peace, 169 Booterstown Avenue, Blackrock, co Dublin, Ireland, Tel. 353 1 2884853.

World Union of Catholic Women's Organisations

This group was founded in 1910 and now has 90 affiliated organisations from 62 countries. This includes a European region. Its aims are to promote the greater involvement of women in their church and in society as a whole. It is

141

registered under Swiss law, but is headquartered in Paris. The Union has contributed to the work of the United Nations, the International Labour Organisation (ILO), and the Council of Europe, where it has consultative status. British member organisations include the Catholic Women's League, the Union of Catholic Mothers, and the National Board of Catholic Women.

■ World Union of Catholic Women's Organisations, rue Notre-Dame des Champs 20, 75006 Paris, France, Tel. 331 4544 2765, Fax 331 4284 0480.

ELDERLY PEOPLE

The principal European network for the elderly, Eurolink Age, was one of the first of the EC social interest group lobbies to become installed in Brussels and Strasbourg. Eurolink Age concentrates on policy issues. EURAG is a much broader, representative network involving the Council of Europe countries. Issues affecting the elderly in the European Communities are likely to grow in importance with the greying of Europe's population: elderly people comprise 100m people out of a European population of 320m.

■ *Grants from Europe*, 51-5.

EURAG

EURAG (established 1962), or European Federation for the Welfare of the Elderly, is a broad-based network based in Graz, Austria. With membership from 22 countries, it runs large international congresses attracting over 200 participants. EURAG has consultative status with the Council of Europe and ECOSOC. Membership costs AS 410 (individuals) or AS 3270 (organisations); information bulletins and newsletters are available separately, costing from AS 120 to AS 410. Recent special publications have covered such issues as housing for elderly people, the problems of older migrants, the very old and elderly women. EURAG formed a committee to take responsibility for contact with the European Communities in 1986, and opened a Brussels office two years later. Help the Aged is a British member of EURAG.

■ EURAG, General Secretariat, Schmiedgasse 26 (Amtshaus), A-8010 Graz, Austria, Tel. 43 316 872 3008, Fax 43 316 872 3019.

Eurolink Age

Subtitled 'a European network concerned with older people and issues of ageing' Eurolink Age (established 1981) is an umbrella group bringing together organisations from around the EC concerned with elderly people. It has a Council formed of 17 national groups concerned with the position of elderly people. The British members are Age Concern England and the British Society of Gerontology. Eurolink Age co-ordinated the 12 projects of the second European programme against poverty in the 'elderly' category, and in April 1991 set up a *Network of Older People in Poverty* consisting not only of the second programme projects but other anti-poverty projects for the elderly.

Eurolink Age publishes a first-class triennial *Bulletin*. Available on subscription in English and French, it reviews all European social and political issues affecting the elderly. A leaflet, *Older people in the European Communities – some basic facts*, and policy reports are also available.

Eurolink Age actively campaigned for an EC Programme for Elderly People (launched in 1991), an over-60s seniors' pass for travel and other concessions, a European Year of the Elderly (1993) and legislation against age discrimination. The first EC programme for the elderly, costing 2.4 MECU, was finally given the go-ahead at the end of 1990, and will involve studies of the problems facing the elderly, conferences on the role of the elderly, and a database of projects helping the elderly. Another Eurolink Age achievement was the start of high-level meetings in 1991 of government officials and the Commission to discuss improvements for the elderly in Europe (the UK is represented by the Department of Health). Eurolink Age has organised a number of seminars and conferences on themes affecting the elderly, for example, age and disability.

■ Eurolink Age, rue du Trône 98, B.1050 Brussels, Tel. 322 512 9360, Fax 322 512 6673.

■ Eurolink Age, 1268 London Road, London SW16 4EJ, Tel. 081 679 8000, Fax 081 679 6727.

The Network on Older People in Poverty, which is based on the London office, is publishing a booklet on older people in poverty in the EC, and is compiling a database of projects. The network has a system of national correspondents in each member state; the UK member is Tony Flynn.

■ Tony Flynn, Beth Johnson Foundation, Parkfield House, 64 Princes Road, Hartshill, Stoke-on-Trent ST4 7JL.

International Federation of Widows and Widowers Organisations (FIAV)

FIAV (established 1978) has 68 member organisations of varying size and interests. Membership takes in Africa and America as well as Europe. FIAV aims to ensure that member organisations concerned with the widowed, with grief and bereavement, keep in contact with each other through four means: a six-monthly newsletter, a conference every two years, by launching special projects, and by encouraging the setting up of self-help groups. Issues arising from the work are presented to the Council of Europe. A resource centre on grief and bereavement, which will be open to the public, is planned.

■ FIAV, rue Cambacorès 10, 75008 Paris, France, Tel. 331 4007 0432.

Fédération Internationale des Associations des Personnes Agées (FIAPA) (International Federation of Associations of Elderly Persons)

FIAPA (established 1980) is a French-based world-wide federation of associations of elderly people. It has consultative status with ECOSOC and the Council of Europe. It has membership in 30 countries. FIAPA promotes exchanges and the twinning of associations, as well as large international gatherings to consider particular aspects of ageing and the position of elderly people.

■ Fédération Internationale des Associations des Personnes Agées (FIAPA), rue d'Anjou 24, 75413 Paris Cedex 08, France, Tel. 331 4017 7350, Fax 331 4924 9128.

HelpAge International

HelpAge International is a network of 31 independent national or international organisations working with and for elderly people throughout the world, dedicated to the improvement of their quality of life. The activities of HelpAge members include the setting up of sheltered housing schemes and community care for elderly people; transport, training and opthalmic projects; and advice to government on services for elderly people. Two of its primary European members are Help the Aged UK and the DaneAge Foundation of Denmark. In Europe, where its office was opened in December 1990, HelpAge hopes to encourage the interest of the Communities in the welfare of elderly people.

■ HelpAge International, rue Froissart 123, B.1040 Brussels, Tel. 322 230 0872, Fax 322 231 1529.

CONSUMERS

The consumer lobby is considered one of the most professional lobbies on the social front in Brussels. There is one principal lobby group called BEUC (*Bureau Européen des Unions de Consommateurs*). With a staff of 12, and a budget of 900,000 ECU, it is certainly one of the best equipped. It handles an impressive volume of work, and deals with up to 60 pieces of European legislation at any given moment!

■ *Grants from Europe*, 116-19.

BEUC (Bureau Européen des Unions de Consommateurs)

There are two full members from the UK: the Consumers' Association and the National Consumer Council. BEUC has contributed to the evolution of a formal consumer policy and programme, the setting up of a directorate-general for the environment and the consumer in the Commission; and since 1983, there have been regular meetings of EC consumer ministers. It has a substantial publications portfolio. Issues raised by BEUC that will be of the greatest interest to community and voluntary organisations in the UK include environmental protection (phasing out of CFCs, green labelling) and health (medicines, food labelling and quality).

■ BEUC, 1st floor, ave de Trevuren 36/4, B.1000 Brussels, Tel. 322 735 5110, Fax 322 735 7455.

FAMILY ISSUES AND ORGANISATIONS

The titles 'family issues' or 'family organisations' may have a politically conservative ring to them, but European family organisations and networks have a progressive record in pressing for policies for the improvement of the position of women and children.

■ *Grants from Europe*, 51-5.

Confederation of Family Organisations in the European Community (COFACE) and the International Union of Family Organisations (IUFO)

For convenience, these two networks are described together. Formed in 1948, the International Union of Family Organisations (IUFO) contains within its membership more than 300 NGOs from 60 countries. Now based in Bonn, it has consultative status with ECOSOC and with the Council of Europe. UK members include the National Marriage Guidance Council, and the Catholic Marriage Advisory Council.

The Twelve are grouped within the Confederation of Family Organisations in the European Community (COFACE), which has been fully autonomous since 1979. In pressing for a family policy in the EC, COFACE notes that 'the family today is no longer the traditional nuclear family. It takes many forms and is influenced by a number of different beliefs and developments....The union of Europe's people assumes a positive stand against inequality. The care of children can create a particular inequality.'

COFACE is represented on the Consumer Consultative Council (CCC) of the EC and the Consultative Committees on the Common Agricultural Policy. It has well developed links with the Commission, the Parliament, and the Economic and Social Committee. In recent times it has proposed measures to promote sexual equality and child day-care centres, to respond to youth unemployment, and for consumer protection. UK members include Help the Aged, the National Council for Voluntary Organisations, SCAFA (Scottish Child and Family Alliance), the Consumers in the European Communities Group, the Institute of Family Studies (Wolverhampton Polytechnic) and the National Federation of Women's Institutes. COFACE has six staff in Brussels. COFACE is considered an influential and professional lobby group and is likely to reach even greater prominence in 1994, which has been declared 'International Year of the Family'. There is an intergroup on the family in the European Parliament, and the first meetings of government family ministers have been held. The Council of Family Ministers has examined, for example, the position of carers of the elderly and people with learning difficulties. A publications list is available.

■ COFACE, rue de Londres 17, B.1050 Brussels, Tel. 322 511 4179, Fax 322 514 4773.

European Network for One-parent Families

The Network for One-Parent Families arose from the second EC anti-poverty programme. The network was formed in 1990 and is organised in all 12 member states. It links with other anti-poverty and specialist networks, particularly recognising the specific needs of different races and cultures. Membership is open to practitioners from self-help groups, researchers and academics working on issues around the changing family. The network is one of the anti-poverty networks funded by the Commission of the EC. The objectives of the network include the exchange of information on trends in one-parent family life; to inform policy-makers in Europe of the needs and priorities of one-parent families and the promotion of practical examples of innovative service for one-parent families. The network reports on issues of employment, social security and childcare for one-parent families in Europe.

■ European Network for One-parent Families, 325 Bunratty Road, Coolock, Dublin 17, Ireland, Tel. 353 1 481872, Fax 353 1 481116.

■ The European observatory on national family policies, chapter 3 of this volume.

SOCIAL SERVICE ORGANISATIONS

Europe has a number of broad-based social service organisations, some of which have provided social services in countries where state welfare services have been poorly developed. The Red Cross, although associated in Britain with emergency and disaster relief, has long provided health and welfare services throughout Europe (including central Europe). Two leading Catholic charities, which are generally not well known in Britain, have taken lead roles in developing welfare services in the southern countries: these are Caritas and the Society of St Vincent de Paul. They are large, well-regarded and influential organisations in European terms. In some countries, they provide cradle-to-grave services for the poor. Their work with the poor has led to Caritas and St Vincent de Paul taking up critical positions on social policy. Caritas in Europe is entitled 'Eurocaritas'. The European Association of Organisations for Home Care and Help at Home is a new specialised network in this general field.

Caritas and Eurocaritas

The declared objective of Caritas International (established 1950) is 'to spread charity and justice throughout the world'. The three key elements of its work are emergency services, helping the developing countries and challenging social exclusion. It has consultative status with the Council of Europe, the ILO and UNESCO.

■ Caritas International, Palazzo San Calisto, V-00120 Città del Vaticano, Italy, Tel. 39 306 698 7197.

Eurocaritas assembles the national Caritas organisations at European level, and brings their common concerns to the attention primarily of DG V of the Commission, MEPs, and the Economic and Social Committee. Caritas operates in Belgium, Denmark, France, Spain, Portugal, Germany, the Netherlands and Luxembourg. Eurocaritas has encouraged its member organisations to take advantage of the European Social Fund; it has organised seminars on poverty and social problems in Europe, two examples being the position of refugees and training for young unemployed people.

■ Eurocaritas, rue du Commerce 70-72, B.1040 Brussels, Tel. 322 511 4255, Fax 322 514 4867.

European Association of Organisations for Home Care and Help at Home

This is a new network, formed as recently as November 1990. The secretariat is provided by the Belgian Yellow and White Cross. It aims to promote home care and help at home, the stimulation of contact between member organisations, advocating their interests to the European institutions, and promoting research in the field. Membership is open to non-profit home-care and home-help services which have a roll of more than 50 helpers or employees, and which provide more than a local service. Membership costs 230 ECU. Most EC countries are now represented: the UK founder member is Crossroads Care. A newsletter, *Home Care News*, is available separately for 10 ECU.

■ European Association of Organisations for Home Care and Help at Home, ave. Lacomblé 69, B.1040 Brussels, Tel. 322 739 3511, Fax 322 739 3599.

European Federation of the Communities of S. Egidio

The European Federation of the Communities of S. Egidio is a new (launched October 1991), lay, radical, catholic, Italian-based association, with 13,000 members in Europe, of whom 11,000 are in Italy. It is a movement of students, workers and professionals providing services for the poor, and acting as a force of solidarity and social change. Its members work with the elderly, people with learning difficulties, the homeless, gypsies and abandoned and abused children. It has three European hubs – one in Rome for the southern countries; Würzburg for Germany, Austria and Switzerland; and a hub in Belgium for the other northern countries, including Britain.

■ European Federation of the Communities of S. Egidio, Vereiniging voor Solidariteit, Lombardenstraat 28, 2000 Antwerp, Belgium, Tel. 323 231 4837, Fax 323 2260 737.

Red Cross

The oldest of the modern European networks (established 1863), the Red Cross now works throughout the world, helping war wounded and the victims of disasters. National Red Cross societies have expanded Red Cross work to respond to economic and social problems, to help the unemployed, people with learning difficulties and elderly people. In several countries the Red Cross provides homes, hospitals and health centres. The EC Liaison office of the Geneva-headquartered Red Cross represents the 12 national societies of the Red Cross. The Red Cross is a general term applied to a complex organisational structure which comprises the International Committee of the Red Cross (ICRC) and the League of Red Cross and Red Crescent Societies. Between them, the Geneva secretariat has a staff of over 700.

The Red Cross has advisory status with ECOSOC, and it has an annual meeting with the Commission to discuss issues of common concern. The ICRC has a publications catalogue, booklets describing the history and role of the organisation, and an annual report.

■ Liaison office of the Red Cross, rue Stallaert 1, bte 14, B.1060 Brussels, Tel. 322 347 5750.

■ International Committee of the Red Cross, Communications department, ave. de la Paix 19, CH 1202 Geneva, Switzerland, Tel. 42 22 734 6001, Fax 42 22 734 8280/42 22 733 2057.

Salvation Army

The Salvation Army has functioned as an international organisation since 1880. Its headquarters are in London, where the secretary for Europe is also located. The principal services provided throughout Europe are night shelters for the homeless, residential care, and help for prisoners. Although the army has co-ordinated its work and standards at international level, international campaigning has been limited.

■ Salvation Army International Headquarters, 101 Queen Victoria Street, London EC4P 4EP, Tel. 071 236 5222.

Society of St Vincent de Paul

The International Association of Charities of St Vincent de Paul (AIC, for Association Internationale des Charités) goes back to 1617! Societies inspired by St Vincent de Paul provide extensive social services in the southern countries, France and Ireland. It has 200,000 volunteers in 40 national associations world-wide, providing services for the sick, migrants, elderly people, children, the homeless, prisoners, drug addicts and the lonely. The affiliate organisation in the UK is the Ladies of Charity of St Vincent. In some European countries, the society is divided into men's and women's sections.

■ AIC, Place Anneessens 6, B.1000 Brussels, Tel. 322 514 2088, Fax 322 512 3898.

SOCIAL POLICY

Moving on from European networks of organisations providing social services, several networks are concerned with social welfare issues and social welfare policies in general. Some of these are based on professional associations of workers involved in the delivery of social services.

Association Internationale de Techniciens, Experts, et Chercheurs (AITEC)

AITEC is a small French-based international association of researchers with an interest in social policy. In 1989, it joined a number of other networks in making a joint presentation to European housing ministers on the need for shelter and housing for the homeless in Europe. It ran a joint seminar on the relationships between Europe and the third world in the light of the Lomé IV accords, and has a working group on third world debt. It publishes a bimonthly news-sheet with the refreshingly unusual title of *Archimède & Léonard*, which costs 550FFR a year for six issues.

■ AITEC, place de Rungis 14, 75013 Paris, France, Tel. 331 4531 1808, Fax 331 4531 6437.

Basic Income European Network (BIEN)

BIEN is a small network founded in September 1986 to serve as a link between individuals and groups 'committed to or interested in basic income unconditionally granted to all on an individual basis, without means test or work requirement, and to foster informed discussion on this topic throughout Europe'. It has an executive committee of five persons. BIEN publishes a newsletter carrying news and information on the question of a basic minimum income, a theme on which an annual conference is also organised.

■ BIEN, Bosduifstraat 21, B.2018 Antwerp, Belgium, Tel. 323 220 4181.

European Social Action Network (ESAN)

ESAN's purpose is 'to strengthen the voice of the social welfare and social development sector in Europe'. ESAN declares it will 'address the negative effects of European integration on disadvantaged groups and areas regarding their social needs...and will advocate a coherent European social policy as opposed to the more limited workers' charter'. The concept of a European social action network came from the Fondation de France in Paris and the Community Development Foundation in England: the decision to found the network was taken in 1989 with the support of 30 national voluntary organisations, and a director and office were in place early in 1991. Membership costs between 500 and 1500 ECU.

■ ESAN, rue du Trône 98, B.1050 Brussels, Tel. 322 512 7411, Fax 322 512 6673.

International Council on Social Welfare (ICSW)

Established during the early days of modern social work (1928), the ICSW has 10 national committees within the EC countries. It meets twice a year and describes itself as 'a non-governmental agency committed to social development'. ICSW is concerned with all aspects of social welfare and social development issues. It is a bridge between voluntary and governmental sectors from the grass-roots level to the international level, and an agent for their mutual co-operation and co-ordination. It is a forum for the free exchange and articulation of national, regional and international welfare concerns. It has consultative status with the Council of Europe and ECOSOC. It sees its role as defining social needs and finding measures to respond to them, and as promoting the voluntary sector. It organises symposia on broad social themes; the 1991 European conference was on social rights.

■ International Council on Social Welfare, Koestlgergasse 1/29, A.1060 Vienna, Austria, Tel. 431 587 8164, Fax 431 587 9951.

International Federation of Social Workers (IFSW) (European region)

The IFSW dates to 1956 in its present form and is the world-wide federation of 56 national associations of social workers. It is registered in Switzerland, and has consultative status with ECOSOC, the United Nations Children's Fund (UNICEF), and with the Council of Europe. While its primary aim is to promote the social work profession and the standards and quality of social work, the Federation has been prominent in raising social issues of concern to the clients with which its members are working.

In 1978, the Federation established what was termed an EC Liaison Committee, designed to provide a specific, regular point of contact with the European Commission. The Liaison Committee has no legal existence, but takes the form of an annual meeting, dedicated to a specific theme, of European social workers with Commission officials. The Liaison Committee is then charged with preparing a report on the issues arising, for which it is subsequently reimbursed. In the course of the 1984 meeting, for example, the Liaison Committee was invited to identify targets for future EC anti-poverty programmes; at the 1990 meeting, the Liaison Committee discussed the recognition of social worker qualifications across Europe, the position of elderly people, and the need to strengthen the Charter of Fundamental Social Rights. The social workers' Liaison Committee was an early example of a means whereby the European Commission provided a regular interface between organisations working in the social field and its own policy-making machinery.

The UK member of the IFSW is the British Association of Social Workers (BASW).

■ International Federation of Social Workers, rue de l'Athénée 33, CH 1206 Geneva, Switzerland, Tel. 41 22 47 1236, Fax 41 22 46 8657.

A network of occupational social workers called *ENOS* was formed in 1991. It is open to individual members interested in sharing information and improving occupational social work. Existing members come from Germany, Netherlands, Portugal, Sweden, Switzerland and Ireland.

■ European Network of Occupational Social Workers (ENOS), Postbus 131, 4100 AC Culemborg, Netherlands.

CHILD WELFARE

The welfare of children has not hitherto been an area of significant EC interest. The closest involvement of the EC institutions with matters affecting children has been the action plan for women, where attention has been given to child-care arrangements that facilitate women's involvement in the workforce, which is a different issue from the welfare of children with acute social needs.

International Forum for Child Welfare (European Group)

In February 1991, the inaugural meeting of the International Forum for Child Welfare (European Group) was held. This is a British initiative, involving the National Children's Homes, the Children's Society, Barnardo's, Save the Children Fund, the National Children's Bureau and the National Council of Voluntary Childcare Organisations. The European Commission has given a grant to the group to ensure that the needs of children are taken into account by the Parliament and the Commission.

The objectives of the group are 'to improve conditions for and services to children whose rights are violated by individuals or states of the EC, to raise the status of children in general, to provide a means of lobbying the EC on behalf of children, to arrange regular seminars on EC children's issues, and to be a mechanism for the collection and wide dissemination of information relevant to children and NGOs in the EC'. The group has members from Belgium, France, Denmark, Germany, Greece, Ireland, Italy, Luxembourg, Netherlands, Portugal.

■ International Forum for Child Welfare (European Group), Sarah Williams, 8 Wakley Street, London EC1V 7LT, Tel. 071 833 3319, Fax 071 833 8636.

HUMAN RIGHTS

There are several international networks and organisations concerned with the position of prisoners - either prisoners of conscience or political prisoners, remand prisoners or convicted prisoners. Amnesty International is perhaps the best known, but a number of new networks have arisen in recent years. Some have a broad remit in the human rights field.

■ *Grants from Europe*, 68-71.

Amnesty International

Amnesty is one of the best known international human rights organisations in the world. Its Brussels office has been an active contributor to the discussion on human rights, migration, asylum and refugees in Europe.

■ Amnesty International, rue Berkmanns 9, B.1060 Brussels, Tel. 322 537 1302, Fax 322 537 4750.

Conférence Permanente Européenne de la Probation (CEP)

Probation services in Europe are organised in a network called Conférence Permanente Européenne de la Probation (CEP), or Permanent European Conference on Probation. Its purpose is to exchange information, compile documentation, find solutions to common problems and to influence public opinion. It holds an annual seminar, to which probation workers, judges, prosecutors and lawyers are invited, and it has published a book on probation in Europe. CEP has observer status in the Council of Europe. The secretariat of CEP is provided by the Dutch Federation of Probation Institutes. The UK has two affiliate members – the Home Office and Prisoners Abroad.

■ Secretariat, CEP, Zuiderparkweg 280, 5216 HE 's Hertogenbosch, Netherlands, Tel. 31 7312 3221, Fax 31 7389 0990.

Forum for the Re-integration of Ex-offenders

APEX Trust, the national ex-offender employment organisation, is in the process of developing a European network of organisations concerned with the employment of ex-offenders. It is pressing the European institutions for the inclusion of projects for ex-offenders under the European Social Fund and for the improvement of training services for ex-offenders. It hopes to exchange information on 'best practice' work with ex-offenders throughout Europe. In 1991, two MEPs, Steve Hughes and Lode van Outrive (Netherlands) moved a budget line in the European Parliament for such projects.

■ Andrew McCaul, Impact Centre, 12-18 Hoxton Street, London N1 6NG, Tel. 071 729 5979.

Fédération Internationale des Droits de l'Homme (FIDH) (The International Federation of Human Rights)

FIDH (established 1922) brings together human rights leagues from Europe and the rest of the world. Since 1948, its goal has been the implementation of the United Nations Universal Declaration of Human Rights. It works in three ways: the defence of individuals and groups, campaigns to mobilise public opinion and influence governments, and policy proposals on human rights. It sends fact-finding missions to countries to investigate the human rights situations there. It has consultative status with the Council of Europe. The British members are the National Council for Civil Liberties (Liberty) and the Scottish Council for Civil Liberties.

■ FIDH, rue Jean Dolent 27, 75014 Paris, France, Tel. 331 4331 9495, Fax 331 4755 8560.

International Gay and Lesbian Association (ILGA)

ILGA is a world-wide federation of national and local groups dedicated to achieving lesbian and gay rights throughout the world. Founded in 1978, it has more than 200 affiliated organisations from 40 countries. Sixteen British groups have joined. ILGA promotes the right of gay and lesbian people to organise, and for the decriminalisation of homosexuality. ILGA publishes a bimonthly bulletin, and organises a European regional conference. Membership costs between £45 and £80, according to category.

■ ILGA Information Secretariat, rue Marché-au-Charbon 81, B.100 Brussels 1, Tel. & Fax 322 502 2471.

Interrights

Interrights, the International Centre for the Legal Protection of Human Rights, is a UK-based international lawyers' network. It provides free advice on all aspects of international human rights law and assistance and representation in the taking of cases to the European Court of Justice (ECJ) and to the Court of Human Rights under the European Convention of Human Rights. It also makes representations to the Committee of Independent Experts under the

Council of Europe's Social Charter. Specialised advice is also available on European Community law on the free movement of workers. Interrights welcomes enquiries from civil liberties organisations. It has a staff of four and publishes *Bulletin*, which includes international law reports.

■ Interrights, 5-15 Cromer Street, London WC1H 8LS, Tel. 071 278 3230, Fax 071 278 4334.

Penal Reform International (PRI)

PRI describes itself as 'a new world-wide movement to improve prison conditions and promote constructive ways of dealing with offenders'. It was set up in London in 1989, where its head office is located, although it is registered at Groningen in the Netherlands. It was set up to provide an international perspective for individuals and organisations working for penal reform in national states, and to help penal reformers exchange information, knowledge and skills. It promotes non-custodial sanctions, and opposes the death penalty. PRI will not take up individual cases. Membership costs £20 a year.

■ Penal Reform International, 169 Clapham Road, London SW9 0PU, Tel. 071 582 6500, Fax 071 735 4666.

REFUGEES

The attitude of the European Communities in general, and individual member states in particular, towards migrants and refugees has been a source of growing concern in recent years. Fears have been widespread that, as the Communities develop in the 1990s, migrants, refugees, immigrants and ethnic minorities will be treated as second-class citizens of Europe and that they will not have the same rights at law as national citizens. It is estimated that there are now between 8 and 16 million immigrants, migrants and refugees in western Europe. Several networks have emerged in recent years to articulate these concerns and to press for justice and rights for migrants and refugees. Some church-based organisations have taken a lead in this area.

■ See: Migrants' Forum (p.161 below)

European Consultation on Refugees and Exiles (ECRE)

ECRE is a UK-based forum for 55 non-governmental organisations concerned with refugees and the right of asylum. Founded in 1973, its objective is to promote a 'humane and liberal asylum policy in Europe' through analysis, research and information. ECRE participants include national refugee councils in Europe and organisations specialising in human rights issues. ECRE agencies hold half-yearly meetings: the network holds policy and specialised seminars, and has put out a number of publications. Its members are provided with a documentation service.

ECRE has consultative status with the Council of Europe, and has close links with the United Nations High Commissioner for Refugees. It has given expert advice at hearings of the European Parliament. British members include the British section of Amnesty International, the Refugee Council, Refugee Action, the Refugee Studies Programme and the Refugee Unit of the UK Immigrants Advisory Service. Unusually for an EC lobbying network, it is London-based, but Brussels work is contracted to ECAS.

■ ECRE, Bondway House, 3 Bondway, London SW8 1SJ, Tel. 071 582 9928, Fax 071 582 9929.

European Legal Network on Asylum (ELENA)

Within ECRE, there is ELENA, established in 1985 as a forum for legal practitioners and experts promoting human rights standards in the treatment of refugees and asylum seekers through counselling, services, advocacy and legal research. It encourages the exchange of information; lawyers co-operate on emergency cases. ELENA has organised specialist seminars on refugee and asylum law. European refugee case law documentation is being compiled with the Central Refugee Documentation Centre (ZDWF) in Bonn, Germany.

■ ELENA, Bondway House, 3 Bondway, London SW8 1SJ, Tel. 071 820 1156, Fax 071 582 9929.

MIGRANTS AND IMMIGRANTS

Churches' Committee for Migrants in Europe (CCME)

Founded by the World Council of Churches (WCC) in 1964, the CCME 'aims to keep the Churches and public opinion in Europe informed about migration issues and take responsibility in relation to these issues. It encourages churches to take appropriate action to defend the human rights of migrants and their families.' The CCME comprises the protestant and orthodox churches.

The CCME sees itself as a platform where migrants, church representatives and experts meet to exchange information on the present situation in European countries and on developments at international level – in the European Communities and the Council of Europe. In order to do this, CCME has, with Amnesty International, been instrumental in bringing together several European organisations with concerns for migrants, such as Eurocaritas, and the United Nations High Commissioner for Refugees. The CCME runs pilot projects, seminars and consultations, and issues publications. It keeps a close eye on national and international legislation affecting migrants. The CCME has promoted a *Convention of Permanent Residence Right* in the Council of Europe, which is now before its Council of Ministers for approval. This would lay down the concept of a secure residence title for all people now living in the member states.

CCME is one of the publishers of the monthly *Migration News Sheet*, which claims to be the only monthly European digest on policies, practices and law on migration and integration. Subscriptions range from £20 to £43, according to category. Its news-sheet has been opened up to the Commission for Racial Equality (CRE), CRE's equivalent in the Netherlands, the Landelijk Buro Racismebestrijding (LBR), and the Netherlands Centrum Buitenlanders (NCB) (equivalent of the Joint Council for the Welfare of Immigrants). Briefing papers are being circulated. The CCME moved from Geneva to Brussels in 1978. The UK member is the Community and Race Relations Unit of the Council of Churches of Britain and Ireland.

■ Churches Committee for Migrants in Europe, Ecumenical Centre, rue Joseph II 174, B.1040 Brussels, Tel. 322 230 2011/1732, Fax 322 231 1413.

Conseil des Associations d'Immigrés en Europe (CAIE)

Although conferences of European immigrants' organisations had been taking place since 1971, a Council of Associations of Immigrants in Europe was not formed until 1988. It aims to ensure that immigrants play their full part in the economic, social, political and cultural life of the nations where they are resident. To achieve this, it hopes to establish links with the European institutions (EC, UN, and Council of Europe), and ensure that member governments ratify conventions protecting the position of immigrants. CAIE has appointed a permanent representative in Brussels to develop contacts with the European Commission. The Council includes representatives of Moroccans and Kurds in Europe. The British member is the National Ethnic Minority Advisory Council (NEMAC).

■ CAIE, 44 rue de Genève, CH 1004 Lausanne, Switzerland, Tel. 41 21 24 6239.

■ National Ethnic Minority Advisory Council, 2nd and 3rd floors, 13 Macclesfield Street, London W1V 7HL.

International Catholic Migration Commission (ICMC)

ICMC is a small Geneva-based organisation dating to 1951, serving refugees and migrants. More recently, it has concentrated on resettling Vietnamese refugees. Its contact in Britain is the Catholic Women's League, Relief and Refugee Committee. It runs conferences and publishes an annual report, biannual magazine, and quarterly newsletter, *Migration News*.

■ International Catholic Migration Commission, rue de Vermont 39-9, Case Postale 96, CH 1211 Geneva 20 CIC, Switzerland, Tel. 41 22 733 4150, Fax 41 22 734 7929.

Migrants' Forum

On the invitation of the European Commission, a 'migrants' forum' was convened in Brussels in November 1990 in order to found a network where the viewpoints of migrants and their families could be expressed directly to the European Communities. A preparatory committee of 17 persons was elected from the 70 groups present at this constituent assembly to oversee the next stage of its development, such as the adoption of statutes. It may evolve in a manner similar to that of the Youth Forum. The initial work of the forum has been funded by the Commission, and further funding is expected. The Migrants' Forum is important as it provides the first secular Brussels base for those concerned with migration issues. It sees itself both as 'a consultative body and a fighting unit'. The UK delegate was elected as President of the Migrants' Forum at its first meeting. The Forum can be contacted through the European Commission (Tel. 322 235 4893, Fax 322 235 6507).

■ Migrants' Forum, Mr Tara Mukherjee, Confederation of Indian Organisations, 5 Westminster Bridge Road, London SE1 7XW, Tel. 071 928 9889, Fax 0277 200353.

■ *Grants from Europe*, 60-3.

UNEMPLOYED PEOPLE

The level of unemployment in Europe, running at 9.1 per cent in the EC countries in 1991, remains one of its most challenging and intractable social issues. For many years, the European Communities have developed programmes for employment creation and for the promotion of small and medium-sized enterprises (SMEs). Yet only very recently has a network come into existence to represent the interests of the unemployed.

■ *Grants from Europe*, 39-50.

European Network of the Unemployed (ENU)

ENU (in French, Réseau Européenne des Chômeurs) was formed in 1982 and adopted a formal constitution in 1989. ENU has 10 specific aims, which include 'to fight for the elimination of poverty and unemployment; to build up a network for the exchange of information and expertise and to build solidarity' and to 'fight for a policy for, and rights for the unemployed'. ENU currently has eight members in Austria, Portugal, Spain, Ireland, France, Germany, the Netherlands and Britain (NUCC in Liverpool). In 1990, ENU adopted a charter of rights for unemployed people, and is pressing for the Charter of Fundamental Social Rights to be implemented in such a way as to ensure that the needs and rights of the unemployed are taken into account. Its long-term objective is full employment throughout the Communities. ENU membership costs £15. ENU receives funding from the European Commission.

■ European Network for the Unemployed, 48 Fleet Street, Dublin 2, Ireland, Tel. 353 1 6795 316, Fax 353 1 679 2253.

International Network on Unemployment and Social Work (INUSW)

INUSW is a small, Dutch-based network of academics, researchers and activists concerned with unemployment and social work issues. Its members are drawn mainly from the UK, the United States, Canada, the Netherlands, Germany and Sweden. Its English-language newsletter (available for Dfl. 50) reports on publications, research, conferences, movements and organisations, and projects concerned with unemployment.

■ International Network on Unemployment and Social Work (INUSW), c/o NIMAWO, Department of International Relations, Noordeinde 39, 2514 GC The Hague, Netherlands, Tel. 31 70 365 1177, Fax 31 70 356 2825.

POVERTY

A number of European networks are concerned, either directly or indirectly, with various aspects of poverty. Several specialised networks emerged from the Commission's programmes against poverty. In 1989, the Commission decided to sponsor the setting up of a generic anti-poverty network, and brought together about 200 representatives of anti-poverty groups and organisations in Brussels. They in turn elected a working group which, with financial support from the Commission, set about drawing up statutes, aims and objectives, and working methods for a permanent anti-poverty network, now known as the European Anti-Poverty Network (EAPN). Considerable effort was devoted towards ensuring that national delegations to this European network were chosen on as democratic, consultative and representative a base as possible. Draft statutes were presented to a general assembly of these groups in 1990, where an executive committee of 15 persons was elected, including one from each country. Interim funding has since been provided by the European Commission. The UK delegate, Quintin Oliver of the Northern Ireland Council for Voluntary Action, NICVA, was elected as its first president. The UK has eight delegates to the general assembly, divided equally between the four regions of England, Wales, Scotland and Northern Ireland. In December 1990, these four regions agreed a 'concordat' as to how they should co-ordinate their work in the future. A 16-point document was agreed, outlining procedures, values, fields of work, and methods for pursuing financial resources.

■ See: Anti-poverty programmes, chapter 3 of this volume.

■ *Grants from Europe*, 51-5.

The European Anti-Poverty Network (EAPN)

EAPN aims to 'act as a pressure group, promote the analysis of the nature of poverty by research into its causes, promote solidarity, advise on European policies and programmes, promote contacts and exchanges, and analyse and criticise policies which promote social exclusion'. The European Anti-Poverty Network is still at a very early stage. Its present work programme consists of circulating a discussion paper arguing for a greater role for the European Communities in the social field; presenting a policy paper on the meaning of social exclusion and poverty in Europe and the policies which should be adopted to alleviate it; and responding to the European Commission's proposals for a minimum income.

■ European Anti-Poverty Network (EAPN), rue Rempart des Moines 78/4, B.1000 Brussels, Tel. 322 512 1652.

■ *Poverty – a challenge to us all: the foundation of the European anti-poverty network from working group to launch*, Brian Harvey and Judith Kiernan (eds), available from Bronagh Hinds, Northern Ireland Council for Voluntary Action, 127 Ormeau Road, Belfast BT7 1SH, Tel. 0232 321224, Fax 0232 321 204.

ENVIRONMENTAL PROTECTION

The Treaty of Rome did not give the European Communities a specific competence in the environmental field. Despite that, the Communities have undertaken a series of measures in the environmental area, and competence in the environmental area was formally affirmed in the Single European Act, 1987. Networks of organisations concerned with environmental issues are estimated to be some of the most influential in the politics of the European Communities.

■ *Grants from Europe*, 101-10.

Eurogroup for the Conservation of Birds and Habitats (ECBH)

ECBH brings together the main bird protection bodies in the EC. It is viewed as a powerful lobby, concentrating on attempts to control hunting and protect the natural habitats of birds.

■ Eurogroup for the Conservation of Birds and Habitats, c/o The Royal Society for the Protection of Birds, The Lodge, Sandy, Beds. SG19 2DL, Tel. 0767 680551, Fax 0767 692365.

European Environmental Bureau (BEE)

BEE was formed by 25 NGOs in 1974 with EC support. Its present membership has risen to 128. Its objectives are the protection and conservation of the environment, and ensuring that these values are reflected in the policies of the European Communities, especially in agriculture, industry, energy and transport. Its main working relationships are with DG XI (Environment, consumer protection and nuclear safety), which also provides some of its funding. It has developed formal relationships with the Council, and there are meetings between its President and the Executive Committee of the BEE. Once a year the BEE organises a meeting with all the officials of the European institutions with which it has dealings. Every six months the bureau forwards a memorandum to the incoming President of the Council of Ministers. The Green Alliance is one of the UK members. The BEE has a monthly broadsheet newsletter, *Metamorphosis* which provides an up-to-date account on EC environmental developments.

■ European Environmental Bureau (BEE), rue de la Victoire 22-26, B.1060 Brussels.

Friends of the Earth (CEAT)

In 1984, Friends of the Earth established what they term a 'European co-ordination'. It is a regional unit of Friends of the Earth (International) which is located in the Netherlands. Friends of the Earth uses its French-language designation, CEAT (Co-ordination Européenne des Amis de la Terre). CEAT has a membership of 500,000 people in 2,200 local groups in 21 European countries with the goal of promoting the protection of the global environment and the rational use of natural resources. It is developing an information databank, and has in recent years emphasised the provision of scientific information on the environment to the European press and EC institutions. Currently four people work in its Brussels office and two in Bratislava (Czech and Slovak Federal Republic).

Current campaigns (there are many) concern the preservation of the mediterranean environment, water pollution, tropical rain forests, biotechnology, the ozone layer and acid rain. Friends of the Earth International has consultative status with 11 international government agencies, including those of the United Nations. CEAT has recently welcomed new members from Estonia, Latvia and Poland.

■ CEAT, rue blanche 29, B.1050 Brussels, Tel. 322 537 7228, Fax 322 537 5596.

■ Friends of the Earth International, PO Box 19 1991, 100 GD Amsterdam, Netherlands, Tel. 31 20 622, Fax 31 20 627 5287.

Future in Our Hands (FIOH)

FIOH is a small Norwegian-derived organisation concerned with environmental and development issues. There are 13 FIOH branches in Europe and the developing countries.

■ Future in our hands movement, 120 York Road, Swindon, Wilts SN1 2JP. Tel. 0793 532 353.

Greenpeace

Greenpeace International (established 1971) set up what it describes as an EC unit in 1989 with a view to influencing EC policies in environmental matters. It has a staff of nine. Greenpeace International, the parent organisation, has offices in no fewer than 24 countries, including most European countries and Russia – and lists what must be the world's most exotic office address – World Park Base, Antarctica!

Greenpeace is one of the world's premier non-violent direct-action campaigning organisations. It pioneered confrontational, risk-taking, attention-seeking methods with hard-headed political lobbying and research. Some of its many current campaigns include saving the dolphin, protests against toxic waste dumping, the protection of seals and whales, and water quality in the Baltic. Greenpeace made a reputation for itself in its media work, using computer networks to flash news of its activities around the world, and providing the media with its own pictures of its protest actions, getting photos and videos to the newspapers and TV long before officialdom did. It is funded from the subscriptions of its many members and friends. As well as being active in the EC, a significant European focus of Greenpeace has

164

been the Nordic Council. Greenpeace flew a protest balloon over the UN building in Vienna as part of its anti-nuclear campaign.

■ Greenpeace International (EC unit), ave de Tervuren 36, B.1040 Brussels, Tel. 322 736 9927, Fax 322 736 4460.

■ Greenpeace International, Keizersgracht, 1016 DW Amsterdam, Netherlands.

International Conservation Action Network (ICAN)

ICAN is a new international initiative dedicated to the promotion of exchanges of information, expertise, training and personnel between environmental organisations in Europe. Funded by the European Commission, it will initially help European conservation organisations by providing information about working with volunteers, setting up practical projects, working with communities, and advising on habitat management techniques. The British Trust for Conservation Volunteers has been closely involved with ICAN, and already has a partnership with the French conservation action group *Vert Bizness*. ICAN has a newsletter, *Global action*. Working holidays are offered by ICAN: a programme highlight of 1991 was an expedition to save turtles in the Greek islands.

■ The International Conservation Action Network (ICAN), International Development Officer, British Trust for Conservation Volunteers, 36 St Mary's Street, Wallingford, Oxfordshire OX10 0EU, Tel. 0491 39766, Fax 0491 39646.

International Fund for Animal Welfare (IFAW)

IFAW is one of the sharpest lobbying groups in the European Communities. It has concentrated its ample skills on lobbying the European parliament, its first success being a 1983 EC ban on importing products into Europe that were derived from baby seals (whitecoats and black backs). Since 1986, IFAW has employed a Director of Liaison [European Community] to be its roving ambassador within the EC to ensure that legislation, regulations and directives were enacted. IFAW's present priorities are the protection of seals in the North Atlantic and Mediterranean; an end to whaling; banning testing on animals for cosmetic products; captive animals (including zoos and dolphinaria); and the banning of the capture of fur animals in steel jaw leghold traps. IFAW has offices in Brussels, Metz, the Netherlands and Hamburg. It employs a consultant in Italy.

■ International Fund for Animal Welfare, New Road, Crowborough, East Sussex TN6 7QH, Tel. 0892 663374, Fax 0892 665460.

■ International Fund for Animal Welfare (EC office), rue du Taciturne 50, B.1040 Brussels.

International Union for the Conservation of Nature (IUCN)

The World Conservation Union (International Union for the Conservation of Nature - IUCN) is a large, 116-nation conservation alliance, dating from 1948. It initiates and supports conservation projects all over the world, bringing together partners in government and voluntary organisations. Membership costs from $35 to $140,000, according to category. *IUCN Bulletin* is published every three months; in addition, the library has an imposing publications catalogue. Its publications combine a stock of information with news and analysis. Governments and non-governmental organisations are equally welcome as members: 61 states and 121 government agencies are affiliated. Among the most prominent of the 400 NGO members are the World Wide Fund for Nature, the Sierra Club and the Royal Society for the Protection of Birds (RSPB).There are 52 British members.

IUCN activities include information, campaigning, field projects, the promotion of legislation and conventions, policy studies and close co-operation with the environmental work of the United Nations. Some of the hundreds of recent issues tackled by the union include the rainforests, whaling, persistent pesticides, logging, coastal erosion and the preservation of wetlands and plants. A recent initiative was CITES – the Convention on International Trade in Endangered Species.

■ World Conservation Union (International Union for the Conservation of Nature - IUCN), ave du Mont-Blanc, CH 1196 Gland, Switzerland, Tel. 41 22 64 7181, Fax 41 22 642 926.

Ruralité, Environnement, Développement (RED)

RED (established 1980) is a network based in Belgium which spans both environmental matters and rural development. Its programme includes a series of conferences, and transfrontier meetings on environmental issues of common concern. The issues raised by RED include nature parks, river pollution, fauna protection, soil erosion and recycling. Thus far, the work of RED has been concentrated on the common border areas of France, Germany, Belgium and Luxembourg. Since 1990, RED has been working with 12 other

Council of Europe-based international networks to establish a European Centre of Rural Concern. A publications list is available. It has a staff of 4, and 95 affiliated members (3 from Britain); 15 countries are represented. Membership costs 500 BF (individuals), 3000 BF (organisations).

■ RED Association Internationale, rue des Potiers 2, B.6702 Attert, Belgium, Tel. 32 6322 3702, Fax 32 63 21 9870.

TRADE UNIONS AND INDUSTRIAL DEVELOPMENT

Voluntary organisations may wish to consider trade unions as bodies which are worth approaching for their support on economic and social policy issues, all the more so since trade union representatives have a number of important points of influence within the European institutions. For example, their representatives sit on the Economic and Social Committee, the European Foundation for the Improvement of Living and Working Conditions, and they are consulted on many issues by the European institutions. Some trade union-based networks have direct contact with voluntary organisations concerned with community development – such as the committee for workers' co-operatives, the Trade Union Regional Network, and IRENE.

The European Committee of Worker Co-operatives (CECOP)

CECOP (*Comité Européen des Coopératives de Production et de Travail Associé*) is the European Committee of Worker Co-operatives. Founded in 1979, it aims to promote worker co-ops throughout Europe, help its member organisations strengthen and develop, and co-ordinate exchanges. It works to DG XXIII (Social economy), where it advocates the value, importance and role of worker co-operatives. It has two UK members, the Scottish Co-operative Development Committee (Glasgow) and the Industrial Common Ownership Movement (Leeds). Two Czechoslovakian co-operatives have applied for membership.

■ CECOP, ave. de Cortenberg 62, B.1040 Brussels, Tel. 322 736 2030, Fax 322 732 1897.

European Trade Union Conference (ETUC)

European trade unions are organised under the aegis of ETUC, to which 36 national trade union federations are affiliated, representing 44m people. Its purpose is to influence the policies of the European Communities for the benefit of working people. Within the ETUC, trade unions are organised according to 16 sectors (for example, transport, retailing). The ETUC has a number of working groups, which include groups on the status of women, the position of young people and education policy. The research wing of ETUC is ETUI, the European Trade Union Institute, which has over 20 staff. In 1990, the institute's research reports addressed the role of economic and social councils in western Europe, worker representation in the workplace, the future of work, economic reform in central Europe, and EC regional policy. The institute has a documentation centre and publishes a quarterly *Newsletter*.

■ European Trade Union Conference, rue Montagne aux Herbes Potagères 37, B.1000 Brussels, Tel. 322 218 3100, Fax 322 218 3566.

■ European Trade Union Institute, boulevard de l'Impératrice 66, B.1000 Brussels, Tel. 322 512 3070, Fax 322 514 1731.

International Restructuring and Educational Network Europe (IRENE)

The IRENE network on industrial redeployment was set up in 1983, following a survey of non-governmental organisations and trade union bodies engaged in activities in those parts of the EC most affected by industrial change. It examines the effects of international restructuring in industries and services on jobs, the environment, technology, and living conditions.

■ IRENE, Stationstraat 39, 5038 EC Tilburg, Netherlands, Tel. 31 1335 1523, Fax 31 13 350253.

Trade Union Regional Network (TURN)

TURN is a network of self-help regional and local trade union employment initiatives. The initial network included trade unionists from Denmark, Spain, England and Wales, and it is now being expanded to include the other members of the Twelve. Membership of the network is open to trade unions involved in, or about to become involved in employment creation at a regional or local level. It aims to provide access for trade unionists to profiles of existing successful projects, and offer opportunities for bilateral and multilateral projects. Funding for TURN has been made available by two directorates of the Commission – DG V (the section concerned with employment and labour market policy), and DG X (Information). TURN holds an annual workshop which disseminates best practice and good ideas for transnational programmes.

■ Joe Mitchell, TURN Secretariat, 136 Middleton Road, Heywood, Lancashire OL10 2LU, Tel 0706 368691, Fax 0706 626 059.

Other useful contacts include:

■ Association of Co-operative Banks of the EC, rue de la Science 23-5/9, B.1040 Brussels, Tel. 322 230 1124, Fax 322 230 0649.

■ European Club of the Social Economy, rue Haute 28, B.1000 Brussels, Tel. 322 513 2860.

COMMUNITY DEVELOPMENT

Networks of people concerned with community development work in Europe are in their infancy. Community work traditions differ in each country, and many of the new networks are still at the stage of exploring their respective differences.

ATD Quart-Monde

The French title stands for *Aide à Toute Détresse Quart Monde*, or help to those in need in the fourth world. The explanation for this title goes back to 1956 when radical priest Fr Joseph Wresinski set up a solidarity group with poor workers living in the shanty town around Noisy-le-grand outside Paris. He described their conditions as such as to merit the title 'the fourth world', to add to the two developed worlds of the northern hemisphere and the third world. ATD held that about 2 per cent of northern society was excluded from all participation in society and its wealth. Two practical principles are central to ATD community work: volunteers living with the poor and sharing their deprivations, and campaigning for political change. ATD inspired workers, students and young professionals alike to set up similar communities in other European countries during the 1960s and 1970s: there are now national associations in 24 countries, and a Brussels office.

ATD has mobilised an intergroup of 150 MEPs ever since 1979, and contributed to a public hearing on poverty held in the Parliament in 1988. The intergroup meets both during and after parliamentary sessions. ATD has regular consultations with senior officials of the Communities, including, from time to time, the President of the Commission. ATD also holds 'popular universities' in which people living in conditions of poverty share their experiences and present proposals for change: in 1991 ATD held its popular university in conjunction with the EC's Economic and Social Committee. ATD has produced a volume of information, research and analysis of the position affecting the very poor in Europe.

■ ATD Quart-Monde, ave Victor Jacobs 12, B.1040 Brussels, Tel. 322 647 9900, Fax 322 640 7384.

Combined European Bureau for Social Development

Known in abbreviated form as the Combined Bureau, the Combined European Bureau for Social Development brings together community development organisations which include in their activities local action projects, research and training, all geared to the growth and development of local communities. Based in the Netherlands, the Combined Bureau has eleven members drawn from nine European countries. The UK organisation involved is the Community Development Foundation.

The Combined European Bureau hopes to facilitate community development groups looking for partners in other European countries where they could share models of policy and practice; to encourage demonstration projects; and to ensure that the community development approach is given adequate attention and recognition in the development of social policy in Europe. A book is being published which reviews the tradition and inspiration of community development work in Europe.

■ Combined European Bureau for Social Development, PO Box 61677, 2506 AD The Hague, Netherlands, Tel. 31 70 345 4336, Fax 31 70 345 4241.

International Federation of Settlements (IFS) Eurogroup

In Britain in the early part of this century, neighbourhood settlements were a starting-point for the community development tradition: they inspired the community resource centres that flourished from the 1960s onwards. The early work led to an international movement as early as 1926, when IFS was founded. IFS aims to promote social justice and to support the work of its members in communities and neighbourhoods. IFS encourages exchanges of people carrying out community development work and inter-project visits.

The most recent work of IFS has stressed projects that bring together people of different cultures; IFS is also anxious to contribute to the social policy debate on the implications of the completion of the internal market.

The first meeting of the IFS Eurogroup took place in March 1991, with participants from the UK, Netherlands and Denmark. IFS is affiliating to the Council of Europe and is hoping to build links with community development initiatives dealing with unemployment, neighbourhoods and substance abuse in central Europe. Other proposed projects include a database, exchanges, visits and a publication. Individual membership is £15 a year.

■ International Federation of Settlements (Eurogroup), Birmingham Settlement, 318 Summer Lane, Birmingham B19 3LL, Tel. 021 359 3562, Fax 021 359 6357.

HEALTH ISSUES

International organisations and networks concerned with health issues have proliferated. A number were set up in response to the interest shown in health matters by the United Nations through the World Health Organisation (WHO), others through the speedy professionalisation of health services in the years after the war.

■ *Grants from Europe*, 111-15.

Azimut

The Azimut network is a pilot project (1989-) funded by the European Social Fund aimed at job creation for ex-psychiatric patients in small firms and co-operatives. There are participating groups from Greece (the psychiatric hospital in Thessaloniki), Spain (Seville), Germany (Lebenwelten Berlin), Italy, Spain and Ireland.

■ Azimut, NIEP Rome, Via G. Marcova 18-20, 00153 Rome, Italy.

European Association for Special Education (EASE)

EASE (established 1968) has been a forum for contact and co-operation for both professionals and volunteers involved in special educational provision. It has consultative status with the Council of Europe and works with UNESCO, the European Communities and the Nordic Council. Its aims are to improve the education and welfare of disabled people, and to develop an awareness of the educational needs of disabled people in order to promote their social integration. Full membership is open to national associations (it now has 21 such members), and associate membership is open to other organisations, associations or individuals.

EASE arranges conferences and seminars on particular themes concerning special education, produces and disseminates literature, and runs an information service. The 1991 seminar programme, for example, included 12 seminars on such themes as illiteracy, teaching aids, new technologies for disabled people in education, and learning difficulties. The information service costs 80 DKK (Danish kroner), associate membership 275 DKK, and full membership from 550 DKK to 4407 DKK, depending on the size of the national organisation. The UK members are the University of Manchester (associate) and the National Council for Special Education.

■ EASE, Waardsedijk 34, NL-3425 TG Snelrewaard, Netherlands, Tel. 31 3480 17743 and 31 3484 5255.

The European Confederation of European Firms, Employment Initiatives and Co-operatives for People with Psychiatric Disabilities (CEFEC)

CEFEC (established 1987) is registered in Belgium, but its secretariat remains in Berlin. It has 55 members in the EC, Sweden, Japan, the United States, Switzerland and Austria. UK members include the Scottish Association for Mental Health, Rehab Goodwill and the British Institute for Industrial Therapy in Southampton. CEFEC membership costs 70 ECU or £50 for organisations (there is also individual membership for 20 ECU or £15). CEFEC has adopted a charter called 'The right to work for people disabled by mental health problems'. It publishes *CEFEC Newsletter*.

■ CEFEC, Hedemannstraße 14, 1000 Berlin 61, Germany, Tel. 49 30 251 1066.

■ CEFEC UK Alliance, Dr Richard Grove, c/o Richmond Fellowship, 8 Addison Road, London W14 8DL, Tel. 071 603 6373, Fax 071 602 8652.

Health Action International (HAI)

HAI is an informal network of some 100 consumer, health and other interest groups concerned with health and pharmaceutical issues in 60 countries around the world. HAI campaigns for more rational and safer drug use, an improvement in advertising standards, and regulations for the correct production, distribution, marketing and use of drugs. HAI Europe was set up in 1988 to take this campaign to the European political institutions, especially in respect of European drug exports to developing countries. A publications list is available from HAI Europe.

■ Health Action International Europe, J. van Lennepkade 334-T, 1053 NJ Amsterdam, Netherlands, Tel. 31 208 33684, Fax 31 208 55002.

The International Alliance of the Order of St John

The International Alliance of the Order of St John must be the oldest European association in the health area, with a founding date of 1113! Best known in Britain for its ambulance and first aid work, Alliance organisations also provide hospital services, and are active in Germany, the Netherlands and Sweden. It meets annually to exchange information.

■ Order of St John, St John's Gate, Clerkenwell, London EC1M 4DA, Tel. 071 253 6644, Fax 071 490 8835.

International Federation of Anti-Leprosy Federations (ILEP)

ILEP (established 1966) has 22 member associations. The British member is LEPRA. It sees itself as a bridge between the leprosy relief organisations of Europe and other countries in the industrialised world and the 15m sufferers in developing countries. It provides an information service for members servicing 900 projects.

■ International Federation of Leprosy Associations, 234 Blythe Road, London W14 0HJ, Tel. 071 602 6925, Fax 071 371 1621.

International Heart Network (IHN)

IHN is reckoned to be one of the more successful lobbying networks, and is chiefly responsible for EC initiatives against tobacco smoking. Its other objectives are the promotion of a heart-healthy diet, and EC action against cardiovascular disease. Formed in London in 1986, it established a secretariat at the Coronary Prevention Group in London in 1988 before setting up in Brussels in 1990. It has 80 members in 18 countries, and publishes an annual report on its progress. UK members include the British Medical Association, the British Heart Foundation, Action on Smoking and Health UK, the Northern Ireland Chest, Heart and Stroke Association, and the Coronary

Prevention Group. The IHN is funded entirely through membership subscriptions.

- International Heart Network, c/o The Coronary Prevention Group, 60 Great Ormond Street, London WC1N 3HR, Tel. 071 833 3687, Fax 071 487 5692.

- International Heart Network, rue du Trône 98, B.1050 Brussels, Tel. 322 512 9360, Fax 322 512 6673.

International Information Centre on Self-help and Health (IIS)

IIS is a Belgian-based WHO-sponsored network (established 1984) dedicated to co-operation and the exchange of information between health care personnel and community groups. The network includes over 230 self-help groups concerned with health: since 1989, the IIS has devoted its energies to promoting self-help groups of people with AIDS and seropositives. The IIS has an information bank of 6,500 titles of self-help articles, books and publications, of which 250 are devoted to AIDS. It organised an international postgraduate course on self-help groups in Yugoslavia in 1989, and a workshop on the contribution of self-help groups to AIDS-prevention. Its *International Newsletter* goes out to 1800 addresses; it has prepared a directory of self-help groups in Europe. No fewer than 78 British groups participate in the work of the Information Centre, many of them being community councils, self-help centres, mental health projects and women's groups.

- International Information Centre on Self-Help and Health, E Van Evenstraat 2C, B.3000 Leuven, Belgium, Tel. 322 016 283 158.

International League of Societies of Persons with Mental Handicap (ILSMH) – European Association

The ILSMH (established 1960) has 138 societies in 84 countries. It is headquartered in Brussels, but works with the agencies of the United Nations (the Economic and Social Council, the World Health Organisation, UNESCO, ILO) and with the OECD. Its objectives are to work for better services and public attitudes towards persons with mental handicap, to ensure that persons with mental handicap lead lives as close to normal as possible, and to act as an expert pressure group. More recently, the League has made a priority of ensuring that people with mental handicap speak for themselves and take greater responsibility in running the organisation. The ILSMH has a European Association (established 1988) which negotiates with the European Commission. ILSMH has a publications list and an international newsletter. There is provision for three categories of membership – full (for national societies), associate and affiliate. UK members include the Scottish Society for Mental Handicap (SSMH).

■ International League of Societies for Persons with Mental Handicap (ILSMH), ave. Louise 248/17, B.1050 Brussels, Tel. 322 647 6180, Fax 322 647 2969.

World Federation for Mental Health (WFMH)

The WFMH dates to 1948: it was conceived as a consultant to the new agencies of the United Nations, in particular the World Health Organisation. The Federation has expanded: it has 90 member organisations in 39 countries. It describes itself as 'dedicated to advocacy, the transfer of knowledge and consultation aimed at promoting mental health and preventing the disabling consequences of mental illness'. The Federation has promoted the concept of legal rights for mental patients (in 1989, it adopted a *Declaration of Human Rights and Mental Health*) and the setting up of self-help groups. The World Federation encourages individual membership, which costs from $15 upwards.

The WFMH has a European Regional Council (ERC), which includes European countries outside the EC. In the European Communities, the European Regional Council is represented on the Liaison Group of the HELIOS programme. Perhaps its most prominent public campaign in recent years has been to draw public attention to custodial care practices of Greek mental patients in hospitals in Leros and in Daphni. A representative of the ERC has addressed the European Parliament's intergroup on disability. The European Regional Council encourages the formation and development of mental health associations in Europe, works for improvements in mental health care, reports on inhumane treatment or the abuse of psychiatry, and encourages the involvement of the users in the planning and provision of services. UK members include the Scottish Association of Mental Health (SAMH).

■ European Regional Council of the World Federation for Mental Health, Mensana House, 6 Adelaide Street, Dun Laoghaire, co Dublin, Ireland, Tel. 353 1 284 1736, Fax 353 1 284 1736.

DISABILITY

Networks concerned with disabled people have emerged more recently than those concerned with more general health issues, reflecting the growing awareness of the scale of disability in European society, and the need for measures in response.

■ *Grants from Europe*, 64-7.

Action Européenne des Handicapés (AEH) (European Action for Disabled People)

AEH is an EC-based international network (established 1979) dedicated to representing the interests of persons with either a physical, mental or psychological handicap. It does so by putting pressure on the institutions of the European Communities and the Council of Europe for legislation and for the promotion of rehabilitative and preventative measures. Public education about the nature of disability is an important field of work. AEH organises seminars, study visits and regular publications. Countries represented in AEH are Belgium, France, Denmark, Germany, the UK, Greece, Luxembourg and the Netherlands. Nineteen national associations have joined.

■ Action Européenne des Handicapés (AEH), Generalsekretariat, Wurzerstraße 2-4, D 5300 Bonn 2, Germany, Tel. 49 228 820930, Fax 49 228 820 9343.

European Federation for the Employment of the Handicapped (CEEH)

CEEH (established 1990) aims to promote policies and models of good practice in the area of employment for disabled people; to press for the rights of disabled people, and to ensure that the needs of disabled people receive greater attention in legislation, services, training and employment. CEEH has one member in each of the EC states: the British member is RADAR.

■ CEEH, Alpha-Plappeville, rue du Général de Gaulle 18, Plappeville, F.57050 Metz, France, Tel. 33 8732 5285, Fax 33 8732 2898 (M. Bruno Betz, President).

European Association for Creativity for and with Disabled People (EUCREA)

EUCREA was formed in 1987 by representatives of 40 international organisations willing to work in the area of arts and disability. Its board consists of one representative per member state.

EUCREA is directly funded by the European Commission. The objectives of EUCREA are to foster creative activities for people with disabilities, according to guidelines which are agreed with the Commission. It has promoted art displays by people with disabilities, videos, theatre festivals and a database on disability and the arts. Projects must involve at least four member states. Another aspect of EUCREA's work is to promote examples of good practice in the area of arts and disability, and make the public more aware of what is going on in the area. Bursaries will also be available to support the work of artists with disabilities. EUCREA has a brochure of its projects.

■ EUCREA, Sq. Ambiorix 32, B.1040 Brussels, Tel. 322 230 0560, Fax 322 280 6693.

European Blind Union (EBU)

EBU represents the interests and the needs of blind people to the European Communities. Liaison with the EC is currently the responsibility of the Federation of the Blind in Paris.

■ EBU Committee for Liaison with the EC, Fédération des Aveugles, ave Bosquet 58, 75007 Paris, France, Tel. 331 4551 2008.

European Federation of Parents of Hearing Impaired Children (FEPEDA)

FEPEDA is a network of national associations of parents of hearing-impaired children throughout the EC and other countries of northern and central Europe. FEPEDA has a management committee elected from member organisations and holds an annual general assembly and seminar. It has 11 EC countries as full members and four other European countries as associate members.

The primary aim of FEPEDA is to improve the quality of life of hearing-impaired children and young people, to promote the role of parents in their education and development, and to create a forum for international exchange.

■ European Federation of Parents of Hearing Impaired Children, c/o The National Deaf Children's Society, 45 Hereford Road, London W2 5AH, Tel. 071 229 9272, Fax 071 243 0195.

There is already a European Communities Regional Secretariat for the World Federation of the Deaf.

■ European Community Regional Secretariat, 1 Ivor Court, 102 Crouch Hill, London N8 9EB.

Mobility International

This organisation (established 1974) specialises in projects for young people of different nationalities and with different levels of disability. It tries, through its international projects, to give young people (generally aged 18-30) the chance to learn new skills and gain confidence. Mobility International runs projects for experts wishing to explore techniques of working with young people with special needs. Specialised seminars in 1991 included an east-west seminar for voluntary organisations from western and central Europe to share experiences of working in the field of mental handicap; one on techniques of lobbying for access for disabled people; and another on the theme of sexuality and disability. Mobility International offers bursaries for visiting similar institutions in other EC states and for carers attending a disabled person.

Mobility International lobbies the European Commission and the European Parliament to increase the resources of the disability division of the Commission, and for additional money for the European Social Fund. Mobility International *News* is a lively newsletter (subscription, £5 annually) covering international disability issues. Mobility International is currently considering the establishment of a network for the care staff of institutions for the disabled. The organisation is in contact with the new groups of disabled people in Russia.

■ Mobility International, 228 Borough High Street, London SE1 1JX, Tel. 071 403 5688, Fax 071 378 1292.

Rehabilitation International (RI) –European Communities Association

RI (established 1922) is a world-wide federation of 135 national and regional organisations dedicated to preventing disability, for the rehabilitation of disabled people, and for greater equality of opportunity for disabled people in society. It is active in 80 countries, including Russia. It is an advocacy organisation, promoting guidelines for better practice and legislation, and carrying out educational work. It has carried out cross-national studies on social security benefits for disabled people, runs specialised seminars, and has a publications portfolio. Its has links with the International Labour Organisation, UNICEF, and the World Health Organisation.

The European Communities Association of RI has operated informally since the early 1980s and was registered in 1988: it was created within RI to enable closer and more effective co-operation with the Commission. The association has organised seminars on specialised themes of interest to the member states: these have included social security, accessibility, mobility, education, sports and leisure. The association is a member of the HELIOS Liaison Group. There is a national secretary in each country. RADAR is a UK affiliate. RI acts as secretariat of the International Council on Disability, which is grant-aided by UNESCO.

■ Rehabilitation International –European Communities Association, P O Box 30, B.6061 Charleroi (Montingnies), Belgium, Tel. 327 136 1926, Fax 327 147 1934.

HOUSING AND HOMELESSNESS

Housing is not an area of competence listed in the Treaty of Rome, or the Single European Act. Organisations and networks concerned with housing and homelessness have pressed hard for housing to be included within the areas of competence of the European Communities, arguing that to ignore the scale of homelessness and bad housing in Europe would be a fundamental contradiction to a 'social' Europe.

For its part, the Commission accepts that bad housing and homelessness are aspects of poverty which come within the remit of its anti-poverty programmes. In 1990, the Commissioner for Social Affairs took on new responsibilities in the areas of social housing and problems arising from poor housing conditions. There are three main networks operating closely with the Commission in this sector: CECODHAS, EUROPIL and FEANTSA.

In 1989, the European housing ministers met for the first time under the aegis of the French presidency of the European Communities: the ministers agreed to come together yearly thereafter to discuss housing issues of common concern, subsequent meetings being held in December 1990 and September 1991. Both occasions provided opportunities for networks concerned with housing and homelessness to come together to make a united presentation to the housing ministers.

Comité Européen de co-ordination de l'habitat social (CECODHAS)

No fewer than 60m people are housed in social housing schemes in the European Communities in about 20m dwellings. CECODHAS (established 1988) represents 33 national or regional organisations. A French initiative, the formation of CECODHAS was facilitated and encouraged by the European Commission. Asserting that it is the responsibility of society to provide decent secure homes for all citizens, CECODHAS aims to ensure that there is a balanced, pluralistic policy of housing in the European Communities, and that social housing is improved in both quality and availability. Each country is represented on the executive committee, and all national member organisations may send representatives to the general assembly meetings. British members are the National Federation of Housing Associations, the Building and Social Housing Foundation, the National Federation of Housing Co-operatives, the Northern Ireland Federation of Housing Associations, the Scottish Federation of Housing Associations, and the Welsh Federation of Housing Associations.

■ CECODHAS, rue Lord Byron 14, F 75384 Paris, France, Tel. 331 4075 7800, Fax 331 4075 7983.

EUROPIL

Formed in Paris in 1988, EUROPIL's objectives are 'to promote the social re-integration of the poor through housing'. Its title, translated from the French, literally means the European federation for the promotion and resettlement of the underprivileged through housing. It describes its role as to be a focal point for 'observation, exchanges of view, research, training, and support for local initiatives'. It subsequently received financial support from the Commission for the holding of seminars on the theme of housing resettlement. It is a European association registered under French law.

EUROPIL has a general assembly, board of directors, and bureau. Its membership includes 26 organisations from 11 EC countries. Although there were no British groups in the founding membership of Europil, some have joined subsequently, for example the Community Housing Association and the Shettlestown Housing Association, Glasgow. EUROPIL's present projects include the development of a European housing policy and two studies: one on the housing of migrant workers, and the other on the financing of social housing across Europe.

■ EUROPIL, rue de Grenelle 180bis, 75007 Paris, France, Tel. 331 4551 4196/4957, Fax 331 4705 9211.

FEANTSA

FEANTSA (established 1988) is the European Federation of National Organisations Working with the Homeless, but is best known through its French acronym. The origins of FEANTSA go back to 1985 when on the initiative of the National Campaign for the Homeless in Ireland, the European Commission funded the first European seminar on homelessness, held that year in Cork. This seminar recommended that a permanent body be established to monitor homelessness in Europe, and make recommendations to the European institutions for the alleviation and elimination of homelessness. The issue was highlighted when in 1987 the European Parliament adopted a hard-hitting report criticising member governments for their record on homelessness. The Commission decided to allocate financial resources to a European network on homelessness in 1988: FEANTSA was able to open a Brussels office the following year. FEANTSA has 24 members from 11 states (Greece is not yet represented). It provides information, research and policy proposals for the EC institutions, working closely with voluntary organisations, the Commission and Members of the European Parliament.

FEANTSA manages the European observatory on homelessness. Full membership of FEANTSA is, for financial reasons, limited to national organisations, but local projects are welcome to join as associate members. Full UK members are Shelter England, Shelter Scotland and the Council for the Homeless Northern Ireland. Associate members are the Scottish Council for the Homeless, St Mungo's Housing Association and Edinburgh Council for the Homeless.

■ FEANTSA, rue Defacqz 1/17, B.1050 Brussels, Tel. 322 538 6669, Fax 322 539 4174.

Organisation Européenne des Associations pour l'Insertion et Logement des Jeunes Travailleurs (OEIL-JT)

OEIL-JT (established 1990) is linked to the French organisation Union des Foyers des Jeunes Travailleurs, which provides accommodation for young workers throughout France. It has members from six European countries – Denmark, France, Germany, UK, Ireland and the Netherlands. It aims to promote the housing of young people who have left the family home, and to ease the transition to independent life. It campaigns for the modification of national housing policies so that the needs of young people for housing are taken into account. OEIL promotes models of excellence of what it calls integrated service centres which link the housing, training, employment and cultural needs of young people. OEIL has published *Housing for young people – a survey of the situation in selected EC countries*. Shelter is a UK member.

■ Organisation Européenne des Associations pour l'Insertion et Logement des Jeunes Travailleurs (OEIL-JT), avenue du Général de Gaulle 12, 94307 Vincennes Cedex, France, Tel. 331 4374 5356, Fax 331 4374 0429.

Other relevant organisations include:

■ Childhope (World-wide organisation to help street children), 40 Rosebery Avenue, London EC1R 4RN, Tel. 071 833 0868, Fax 071 833 2500.

■ Homeless International (support for community groups providing shelter in developing countries), 5 The Butts, Coventry CV1 3GH, Tel. 0203 632802, Fax 0203 632911.

■ Réseau Européen pour le Respect du Droit au Logement (coalition of tenants' groupings to promote the right to housing), place de Levant 1, 1348 Louvain-la-Neuve, Belgium, Tel. 32 10 47 2314, Fax 32 10 47 4544.

■ Réseau Européen des Chercheurs (network of researchers specialising in housing policy), parc du Saurupt, 54013 Nancy Cedex, France, Tel. 33 8351 4436, Fax 33 8356 6885.

RURAL DEVELOPMENT

The expansion of the European Communities in the 1980s to include Greece, Portugal and Spain led to a sharper appreciation of the problems of poverty, lack of industrial development and rural decline in the European Communities. These problems were by no means confined to the southern countries: people concerned with rural depopulation had long been aware of these issues even in the original Six. Even today, the northern, industrialised image of the EC belies the fact that 50 per cent of the its population lives in rural areas, and the fact that 80 per cent of its land mass is rural.

European Training and Development Centre for Farming and Rural Life (CEPFAR)

CEPFAR is an 80-member strong network of organisations concerned with farming and rural life. Formed in 1972, it covers all the member states of the EC: British members include the National Farmers' Union (England and Wales, Scotland, Ulster); the National Federation of Young Farmers' Clubs, Young Farmers' Clubs of Scotland and Ulster, the Federation of Agricultural Co-operatives, and the National Union of Agricultural and Allied Workers. While reflecting a strong orientation towards the interests of farmers, CEPFAR's brief includes issues of relevance to all those concerned with balanced rural development.

CEPFAR works through information and policy seminars, publications (29 in print), and a newsletter. Its objectives are the development of farming and rural life; and to provide information and training for its members. Activities in 1991 included regional seminars (one in Scotland) on how the structural funds assist the least prosperous regions of the Communities.

■ CEPFAR, rue de la Science 23/5, B.1040 Brussels, Tel. 322 230 3263, Fax 322 231 1845.

The European Council for the Village and Small Town (ECOVAST)

ECOVAST was formed in 1984. 'Rural communities', it declared, were 'undergoing rapid and disruptive social change. Remote areas suffer from economic and social decline. In more central regions, rural communities are disrupted by urban growth.' ECOVAST came together to preserve rural communities, their heritage and environment.

ECOVAST has grown rapidly: it now has 300 members in 25 countries. It is not limited to the EC countries but includes the states of the Council of Europe, with which it has consultative status. Organisations from Poland, the Czech and Slovak Federal Republic, Hungary and Yugoslavia are members. ECOVAST has 24 British members, which include statutory bodies, community councils and development agencies. Membership costs from £10 to £250, according to category. ECOVAST is registered as a non-profit organisation in Alsace (France), although its secretariat is in Namur (Belgium). Despite limited resources, ECOVAST runs a formidable range of activities which include seminars, exchanges and conferences. A journal is published in three languages, accompanied by a news-sheet. ECOVAST has lobbied the European Parliament and other institutions: it was one of the first to draw Europe's attention to the destruction of villages in Rumania by the Ceaucescu dictatorship in the 1980s.

ECOVAST sponsors an innovative educational experiment: the biennial European Rural University. These are mobile study groups which travel by coach touring rural areas and visiting local projects. At the end of the two-week university, a report is compiled for the European Commission, including observations and recommendations arising. The ECOVAST network is funded through membership fees and DG VI of the Commission (Agriculture and Rural Development). One of the UK members is Rural Forum Scotland.

■ ECOVAST, rue de Gembloux 121, B.5002 Namur, Belgium, Tel. 32 81 730 689, Fax 32 81 733 513.

Mouvement International de la Jeunesse Agricole et Rurale Catholique (MIJARC) (International Movement of Agricultural and Rural Youth)

MIJARC is an important rural youth movement with members in 54 countries but not the UK. Founded in 1954, it is committed to the improvement of the rural and village environment. It encourages membership from organisations representing young people, students, workers and the rural unemployed. It is strong in France, and is energetic in international youth organisations.

■ MIJARC, Tiensevest 68, B.3000 Leuven, Belgium, Tel. 32 16 22 8312.

Small Farmers

The small farmers' associations of Britain and Ireland have organised a two-nation network to form a lobbying force to ensure that the needs of small and part-time farmers can be heard, and to ensure that new initiatives or policies will take their needs into account. Members are the Crofters' Union, the Small Farmers' Association of England, the Farmers' Union of Wales, the Northern Ireland Agricultural Producers' Association, and the Irish Creamery and Milk Suppliers' Association.

■ Scottish Crofters' Union (Aonadh Nan Croitearan), Old Mill, Broadford, Isle of Skye, Invernesshire, IV49 9AQ, Tel. 04712 529.

TransEuropean Rural Network (TERN)

The TERN network arose from the second European anti-poverty programme. All of the 13 rural action projects of the programme, anxious to see a continuation of the progress they made and the contacts they had developed, formed the TransEuropean Rural Network in 1990. Its primary aim is to 'actively pursue the evolution of policies which would lead to the redistribution of resources into the marginalised rural areas'. TERN aims to do this by lobbying the EC institutions, through research, by exchanging models of good practice, and by being a channel of information between local projects and the European Commission and vice versa.

TERN is a grass-roots based network, concentrating on active projects rather than national organisations. UK members come from Wales, Stornoway and co Derry. TERN receives funding from DG VI of the Commission (Agriculture and rural development). In 1991, it set up an office within the ECAS secretariat in Brussels. It intends to create a database, develop an information service and establish a political profile.

■ TERN, rue du Trône 98, B.1050 Brussels, Tel. 322 512 9360, Fax 322 512 6673, or

■ TERN, 14A Eustace Street, Dublin 2, Ireland, Tel. 353 1 776421, Fax 353 1 679 6843 (Sr Stanislaus Kennedy).

VIRGILE

VIRGILE is a new (1991) network, comprising ten organisations concerned with agriculture and rural development in eight EC countries. It has two objectives: setting up exchanges, meetings and seminars concerned with training and rural development; and making proposals on rural development to the institutions of the European Communities. VIRGILE will be arguing for balanced rural development which recognises the social, ecological, cultural and political diversity of European's rural communities. The UK member is the Royal Agricultural Society.

■ VIRGILE, c/o CELAVAR, rue des Petites-Ecuries 13015, 75010 Paris, France, Tel. 331 4824 0941, Fax 331 4824 0054.

LOCAL AUTHORITY BASED NETWORKS

Network and lobbying activity in the European Communities in the social arena is by no means confined to voluntary organisations. Statutory bodies outside national governments have found it not only worth their while, but advisable, to organise themselves into networks in order to ensure that their interests in Europe are acknowledged – and they have often pursued issues of interest to the voluntary sector. The two principal ones are described here, though many specialised networks exist or are in the process of formation.

Assembly of European Regions (AER)

AER in its present form dates from 1985. Its aims are to ensure that regional needs are taken into account in the decision-making process in the European Communities. AER's contribution is therefore geared to DG XVI of the Commission (regional policy). Membership of the AER comes from county councils (or their equivalents in other European countries), fees being between 11,000 FFR and 110,000 FFR. Eighteen UK authorities have affiliated: the European total is 160. All the regions in Spain, Portugal and Italy are members.

AER has working groups on regional development, regional culture and the problems of mountain areas. AER organises Eurodysée, a scheme which provides three to six months' training in another country for young people leaving vocational training: about 3,000 young people are now participating in the scheme, whereby the person receives social security and up to 520 ECU a month for training.

■ General Assembly of the Secretariat of European Regions, Immeuble Europe, place des Halles 20, 67000 Strasbourg, France, Tel. 33 8822 0707, Fax 33 8875 6719/33 8822 6482.

■ Eurodysée, sq. Caspan 4, F.25031 Besançon Cedex, France, Tel. 33 8161 6161.

Conference of Peripheral Maritime Regions of the European Communities (CPMR)

CPMR was formed in 1973 in St Malo, Brittany, and now comprises 65 member regions of the EC. The initiative for CPMR came from neglected alpine regions which contended that centralising EC policies were working to the detriment of the regions. The CPMR declared, accordingly, that its objective was to 'redress the balance between the industrialised centre of Europe and the generally undeveloped periphery'; and to protect and add to the values of the maritime and coastal areas. The UK members are Devon, Cornwall, Wales, Dumfries-Galloway, Borders, Fife, Tayside, Grampian, Orkney, Isle of Man, Shetland, the Western Isles of Scotland, Central Scotland and Humberside. It has enjoyed consultative status with the Council of Europe since 1978. CPMR is funded through membership subscriptions and publishes an information bulletin.

The principal achievement of the CPMR to date has been the adoption, by the EC Council of Ministers in 1986 after an eight-year campaign, of the European Coastal Charter. The charter proclaimed objectives that would protect coastal zones, control tourism, and prevent pollution.

■ CPMR, boulevard de la Liberté 35, 3500 Rennes, France, Tel. 33 9931 8181, Fax 33 9978 1221.

Other relevant organisations include:

■ Council of Local Authorities and Regions of Europe, quai d'Orsai 41, 75007 Paris, France.

■ World Federation of Twinned Towns and Cities, 2 rue Logelbach, 75017 Paris, France.

■ International Association of City and Regional Planners, Mauritskade 23, 2514 HD The Hague, Netherlands, Tel. 31 70 346 2654, Fax 31 70 361 7909.

■ European Association for Interregional Cooperation (EUREG), Reinsburgstraße 56, D.7000 Stuttgart 1, Germany, Tel. 49 711 6369 577, Fax 49 711 6369 609.

■ The General Secretary, The International Union of Local Authorities (IULA), PO Box 90646, 2509 LP Den Haag, Netherlands, Tel. 31 32 7032 44032, Fax 31 31 7032 46916; IULA European section, quai d'Orsai 41, 75007 Paris, France.

There is a *European Local Authorities Study and Research Centre* (Centre d'Étude et de Recherche sur les Collectivités Locales Européennes) in Paris for the larger local authorities (defined as towns with a population of more than 200,000 people). Its runs seminars and distributes publications on urban development.

■ Centre d'Étude et de Recherche sur les Collectivités Locales Européennes, rue de la Boétie 59, 75008 Paris, France, Tel. 331 4256 3970, Fax 331 4225 8936.

YOUTH

Youth organisations, institutions and networks are now so well established in Europe that they merit a guide in their own right. This reflects the manner in which 'youth' issues rose to prominence earlier than social issues. European bodies and networks concerned with young people materialised in the period after the explosion of student and youth protest in Europe in 1968. An excellent guide to European youth networks has been published by the King Baudouin Foundation in Belgium. The *Passport for International Youth Relations* (1988) describes the main networks, councils and committees. Price: 500 BF.

■ King Baudouin Foundation, rue Brederode 21, B.1000 Brussels, Tel. 322 511 1840.

The importance of networks of young people for the voluntary sector is two-fold: first, many community organisations, having a membership drawn largely from young people, also see themselves as youth organisations and may wish to consider joining such networks or availing of their services; second, a number of the youth networks have adopted outspoken policy positions on issues of concern to voluntary and community groups: as such, they are possible allies in campaigns for improved social policies in Europe. The youth wings of the main European political parties are active participants in these bodies. The European definition of 'youth' (under 30) is greater than is usually the case in Britain.

The Council of Europe was among the first international bodies to recognise the importance of community and other activities undertaken by youth organisations, and to see the value of youth organisations working on an international basis. The Parliamentary Assembly of the Council of Europe has been discussing youth issues since 1968, and has a subcommittee on youth and sport. The first conference of ministers responsible for youth was held under the aegis of the Council of Europe in 1985. It reached agreement on the importance of promoting the participation of young people in society, and on the need to support the work of non-governmental organisations of young people.

The European Youth Foundation (EYF) was established by the Council of Europe in 1972 to promote and fund international meetings of young people and youth leaders. The EYF endorses the principle of 'co-management': its governing board includes representatives of international non-governmental organisations.

■ European Youth Foundation, Council of Europe, B.P. 431/R6, F 67006 Strasbourg Cedex, France, Tel. 33 8861 4961.

The European Youth Centre, which has also been in operation since 1972, provides a meeting place for international European youth networks and associations in Strasbourg. It is an educational body maintaining conference facilities. The programme of the centre includes study sessions, training and language courses and symposia.

■ European Youth Centre, rue Pierre de Coubertin 30, 67000 Strasbourg Wacken, France, Tel. 338 831 0531.

Council of European National Youth Committees (CENYC)

The national youth committees of Europe set up CENYC in 1963 in order to establish a platform of national youth committees to negotiate with the Council of Europe and the institutions of the European Communities. As well as carrying out a co-ordination role, CENYC organises conferences and seminars on issues of current-day social concern. CENYC issues a free-of-charge quarterly bulletin, *CENYC Contact*. The UK member is the British Youth Council. CENYC is also contact point for the *Framework of All-European Youth and Student Co-operation*, which is a structure for the bringing together of youth organisations of western and central Europe.

■ Council of European National Youth Committee, ave des Courses 8, B.1050 Brussels, Tel. 322 648 9101, Fax 322 648 9640.

ERYICA

The ERYICA network promotes co-operation among youth information and counselling services throughout the Communities and the rest of Europe.

■ ERYICA, quai Branly 101, 75740 Paris Cedex 15, France, Tel. 331 4065 0261.

European Confederation of Youth Club organisations (ECYC)

ECYC (established 1976) is the European network for youth clubs, of which there are estimated to be more than 18,000 with over 3.5m members. As well as promoting exchanges and co-operation (ECYC publishes a *European Youth Clubs Manual*), it acts as a political lobby, and has consultative status with the Council of Europe. It is one of the few Danish-based international networks. The British member is Youth Clubs UK in Leicester.

■ European Confederation of Youth Organisations, Orneej 45, DK-2400 Copenhagen NV, Denmark, Tel. 45 110 8038.

The European Co-ordination Bureau of International Youth Organisations (ECB)

The ECB, launched in 1967 and relaunched in 1977, co-ordinates international non-governmental youth organisations which co-operate with both the European Communities and the Council of Europe. To affiliate, any such INGOs must be active in at least seven European countries. UK-based members are the same as those affiliated to the Youth Forum of the European Communities. It publishes a free-of-charge newsletter, *ECB Info*.

■ European Co-ordination Bureau of International Youth Organisations, rue du Marteau 19, B.1040 Brussels, Tel. 322 217 5632.

The Youth Forum of the European Communities

A desire to involve young people in the construction of the European Communities, and the wish to establish a point of contact between the Commission and Europe's youth organisations, led to the formation of the Youth Forum of the European Communities in 1978. It is designed to act as the political platform of youth organisations, and to facilitate the evolution of policies favouring young people in the European Communities. Accordingly, the forum has established contact with MEPs, the Council of Ministers, the Economic and Social Committee and the Commission; adopted positions on economic and social matters affecting young people in Europe; and run a number of specific campaigns.

Membership consists of international non-governmental organisations (INGOs) and national youth committees from the member states. The national member for the UK is the British Youth Council; British-based INGOs include the European Committee for Young Farmers and 4H Clubs, and the World Association of Girl Guides and Girl Scouts. The forum publishes a lively and attractively-presented magazine *Youth Opinion* (free of charge) which reviews the work of the Forum and the social issues facing young people in Europe.

■ Youth Forum of the European Communities, rue Joseph II 112, B.1040 Brussels, Tel. 322 230 6490, Fax 322 230 2123.

6

The Voluntary Sector in Other European Countries

Writing about the voluntary sector in other European countries presents many problems – of semantics, history and political circumstances. Experts will invariably disagree on how they see the voluntary sector in each country: there will be as many interpretations as there are people. Comparisons between the voluntary sector in one country and another are made difficult because there has been no history of this – either academic or journalistic – although this may now be beginning to change. The level and nature of publications in each country can give us clues as to the nature of the voluntary sector there, but only to a limited extent. In some countries, the voluntary sector is well documented and there is a high output of publications; however, lower levels of publications in other countries do not necessarily mean that the voluntary sector is either inactive or unimportant.

This chapter divides the voluntary sector in Europe into four geographic divisions: the big two of the EC (Germany and France); the other northern countries of the EC; the southern countries of the EC, which share many economic and social characteristics; and other European countries (Scandinavia, the neutral countries, central Europe, and Russia).

It starts by mapping the voluntary sector of the 11 other countries of the European Communities. It examines the main features of the voluntary sector in each country and the social and political climate in which it operates; looks at both traditional and more recent active voluntary and community organisations; and discusses some recent trends. Areas of innovation are discussed, as are those aspects that may be of the greatest curiosity to voluntary organisations in Britain. In the review of the EC countries, prominence is given to the three largest countries: Germany, Italy and France, because of their size and population. Addresses of some of the organisations discussed are given in the Appendix.

The basis on which the voluntary sector is organised differs from country to country. Whereas Britain is used to the idea of a strong, national voluntary sector with firm convictions as to how social policy should evolve, this is not necessarily the case in other countries. In some countries, such as Italy and Spain, the voluntary sector functions on a regional or local basis, and national associations are the exception rather than the norm. In others, voluntary organisations have little experience of presenting social policies to government or media. But first, it is worth looking at the background of the current state of the voluntary sector in Europe.

POLITICAL CHANGE

Two external factors have been important in determining the development of the voluntary sector in European countries in the past 10 years: changes in the priorities of national governments, and decentralisation. The voluntary sector, and its clients, suffered keenly from cutbacks by governments in welfare services in a number of countries with the advent of conservative governments in Denmark (1982), the Netherlands (1980) and Belgium (1980). By contrast, voluntary organisations have expanded their role and services in those countries where governments have expressed a stronger commitment to social development, such as France and Spain.

DECENTRALISATION

Decentralisation is the second important consideration in the development of the voluntary sector in the countries of the European Communities. Several European governments have, in the past 20 years, carried out decentralisation initiatives entailing a tangible shift of power and resources away from the political and administrative centre: for example, Italy (1975), Denmark (1976), Netherlands (1979), Spain (1979) and France (1983). As a result, voluntary organisations have been forced to redefine their role, focus and orientation.

HOW DOES ONE CONTACT
VOLUNTARY ORGANISATIONS IN
OTHER COUNTRIES?

Making contact with, or finding out more about, voluntary organisations in other countries presents a problem in itself. There is no one sure single route, and a combination of methods should be considered by voluntary and community organisations trying to find partners in other European countries. The main possibilities are:

• the national embassies;

• national organisations in contact with other countries (see chapter 3);

• the specialised European programmes (see chapter 3);

• researchers, foundations, institutes and academics (see chapter 3);

• the European networks (see chapter 5); and

• directories and publications (see chapter 7).

National embassies can sometimes be overlooked as a possible point of introduction to voluntary organisations in other countries. Embassies do have a general brief to facilitate enquiries. In some embassies, there may be staff members who have experience of the voluntary sector in their country, or who may have colleagues at home who do - in which case the embassy may be able to name particular organisations to contact. Most embassies will provide the addresses of their department of social affairs, which can also be a useful starting-point. Some of the European specialised programmes will have good links with voluntary organisations - and they will probably be most helpful in getting people in contact with partners. That is, after all, one of the prime reasons why they were set up. The *Poverty 3* programme, to take one example, has direct links into 39 projects, and works with national research and development units which in turn have colleagues and researchers who will be familiar with voluntary organisations concerned with social issues. Some of the large voluntary sector national organisations in the UK will, through networks or otherwise, have contact with the voluntary sector in other countries, and they may well be able to help find partners or contacts.

■ National Council for Voluntary Organisations (NCVO), 26 Bedford Square, London WC1B 3HU, Tel. 071 636 4066, Fax 071 436 3188.

■ Scottish Council for Voluntary Organisations (SCVO), 18-19 Claremount Crescent, Edinburgh EH7 4QD, Tel. 031 556 3882; Fax 031 556 0279.

■ Wales Council for Voluntary Action (*Cyngor Gweithredu Gwirfoddol Cymru*), Llys Ifor, Crescent Road, Caerphilly CF8 1XL, Tel. 0222 869224, Fax 0222 888702, e-mail Geo2:WCVA.

■ Northern Ireland Council for Voluntary Associations (NICVA), 127 Ormeau Road, Belfast BT7 1SH, Tel. 0232 321 224; Fax 0232 438 350.

Contacting voluntary organisations in other countries – whether it be to find partners or simply to ask for information – takes time. The route that finds the appropriate partner may work in one country, but not in others. As is the case in Britain, some voluntary organisations in other European countries are better at responding to information requests than others! Some are information-orientated, respond promptly, and have an informative publications output. Others, by contrast, are less forthcoming. Some voluntary organisations in other countries will have English-speaking members who can reply, particularly in the Netherlands, Germany and Denmark. However, organisations will respond best, and will warmly appreciate, those British organisations that take the trouble of having their request for information or enquiry about partnership translated. Some voluntary organisations may even wish to consider language training courses for their members so as to improve communications with potential European partners.

Voluntary organisations trying to contact small voluntary organisations in other countries may find it convenient to approach large national organisations there first. Small organisations may be affiliated, or be known by them, and they are generally willing to take some trouble to recommend a partner for an organisation in Britain.

There is a limited amount of published English-language information available about the voluntary sector in other countries. A booklet containing an outline of the voluntary sector in the Twelve on a country-by-country basis is available: *The core of the community: volunteers, voluntary organisations and the social state*, by Diana Robbins. It is available from:

■ Department of Social Welfare, Aras Mhic Dhiarmada, Store Street, Dublin 1, Ireland, Tel. 353 1 786444, Fax 353 1 741 909.

In 1991, the National Consumer Council published *Consumer Advice Services in Europe: a directory*. This described and listed voluntary organisations in other EC countries providing not only consumer advice, but legal advice and help to clients in social need (for example, tenants in private rented housing). Many of these bodies listed by the National Consumer

Council may be worth contacting both because they are orientated towards the provision of information and because the remit of consumer advice may cover information in the areas of health, housing, debt, employment and social security.

■ National Consumer Council, 20 Grosvenor Gardens, London SW1W 0DH, Tel. 071 730 3469, Fax 071 730 0191.

Some voluntary organisations and researchers have been known to trawl conference attendance lists with a view to contacting voluntary organisations in other countries. Some people will part with conference attendance lists more readily than others. Trawling conference lists has the advantage of indicating organisations and people in them currently active; but the disadvantage is that such lists and the acronyms found there do not necessarily reveal much about the nature of the bodies concerned. The European Anti-Poverty Network (EAPN)(see chapter 5 in this volume) has a listing of 260 delegates who attended its founding conference, representing a broad cross-section of voluntary and community groups from throughout the EC. Another possibility, which can be productive, is to approach the professional association of social workers in each country: social workers will know the voluntary sector well and will be in a good position to recommend particular organisations.

■ European Anti-poverty Network, rue Rempart des Moines 78/4, B.1000 Brussels, Tel. 322 512 1652.

■ International Federation of Social Workers, rue de l'Athénée 33, CH 1206 Geneva, Switzerland, Tel. 41 22 47 1236, Fax 41 22 46 8657.

THE BIG TWO: FRANCE AND GERMANY

France

France (population: 57m) has a large and flourishing voluntary sector which has provided innovative services and at the same time carved out a robust political role in determining the country's social development.

The election of socialist President François Mitterrand in 1981 inaugurated a challenging period for voluntary organisations in France. The early years of the Mitterrand presidency were marked by the nationalisation of industry and other traditional leftist measures: these were quickly abandoned under the economic difficulties which afflicted all western countries in the mid-1980s. Most of the social measures of the Mitterrand presidency matured in the second half of the decade.

These measures included the decentralisation of administration, the introduction of a minimum income, the passage of a law providing a right to housing, and an urban community development programme that could have a fundamental effect on the way in which urban areas are planned and developed. The decentralisation initiative, called the Defferre law, approved in 1983, made provision for the election of 22 regional councils and gave extra responsibilities (including the planning and delivery of some social services) to the 96 departments of the Republic and the 36,433 local districts (*communes*). Under decentralisation, each department has a social affairs budget: voluntary organisations have been forced both to fight for this budget, and argue with departmental officials as to how it can best be spent, neither of which they were well prepared for.

The introduction of a basic minimum income, the RMI (*Revenue Minimum d'Insertion*) took effect in 1988. Until then, there had been virtually no state provision for people whose social insurance had expired. The RMI provided not only an income floor (set initially at 2,000 francs a month), but schemes of community work and training to help unemployed people back into the workforce (hence the French phrase, insertion, or reinsertion). These schemes were often run by voluntary organisations under contract to the local authorities.

In 1990 a law providing for the right to housing of the homeless, entitled the *Loi Besson*, named after the housing minister, M. Besson, was introduced. This funded local authorities to the tune of 12 billion francs, to draw up plans for the systematic housing of homeless people and those in poor housing. Two further initiatives were launched in 1991: a law to reform the financing of the communes, to ensure that resources were redistributed to the poorer communes; and a town-reform, anti-ghetto law (*orientations pour les villes*). Under this law, towns must ensure housing developments reflect the needs of low-income groups, develop urban rehabilitation programmes, preserve the old quarters of towns, especially those with what are termed 'fragile populations', and carry out rehabilitative and community development programmes. These measures built on the long record of government interest in urban community development. As far back as 1981, the Prime Minister, M. Pierre Mauroy, had set up a National Commission for the Local Development of Neighbourhoods, which pioneered a number of pilot schemes, leading in 1990 to the creation of a government ministerial post for urban development (*Ministre de la Ville*).

These initiatives tested voluntary organisations, which had a key role in overseeing the RMI training and resettlement schemes and *Loi Besson* housing projects. They then found themselves negotiating both with the national government and at local level to improve the manner in which the legislation operated on the ground. The *Loi Besson* was originally thrown out by the national assembly: an angry coalition of housing organisations backed the government, organised nationwide protests, and forced the national assembly to pass the law. Subsequent governmental decrees strengthening the *Loi Besson* reflected the contributions of voluntary organisations in their regular consultations with the housing minister and his officials.

Thus, in the early 1990s, the voluntary sector in France was operating in an environment of government-led social reform, in which it had a relationship of dialogue with that government and the newly-empowered local authorities, and in which it had demonstrated its political effectiveness.

Traditional Organisations
French non-governmental organisations are generally called associations (*associations*). Associations are regulated under a law of 1901: voluntary organisations register with the Minister of the Interior, though ministerial responsibility is actually vested in the Minister for Youth. The term *association* is broad: as few as two persons committed to a common objective (from running a school to a fishing club) can set up an *association*. Many are simply organised community groups concerned with sport, leisure or culture. Private schools also count as 'associations'. There are 3,000 with the status of 'associations of public interest', which means that they can receive property. Many of these are providers of services in the social field. In addition, there are about 500 foundations (*fondations*) in France. When describing the voluntary sector in France, it is important to distinguish linguistically between the world of voluntary organisations (*les associations*) and the ideal of volunteering for unpaid personal social service (*le volontariat*).

There has been a phenomenal growth in associations in recent years: no fewer than 655,521 in the years 1975-91. Over a quarter were in rural areas (many were associations for elderly people). The growth in associations has been strongest in the southern and alpine parts of the country. Over 90,000 associations function in the domain of social action, social services and community development, providing 550,000 places in institutions, employing over 290,000 people, and having an estimated turnover of 465 bn francs. Associations range in size from large national bodies such as the Red Cross, to federations of organisations, and to small, highly localised initiatives. Voluntary organisations play a significant role in the delivery of French social services, providing 86 per cent of places for disabled people, 70 per cent of home care services, 28 per cent of places in old people's homes, and 6 per cent of places in sheltered housing. These services are valued at 30 bn French francs (FFr), of which 80 per cent is state-subsidised.

The long-standing political division between the Catholic and the secular in France is apparent in the voluntary sector. For example, the two main voluntary welfare organisations carry out similar activities - providing low price clothes and food, children's holidays, counselling, training services, initiatives against unemployment - but one is catholic-associated (*Secours Catholique*), the other linked to the political left (*Secours Populaire*). *Secours Populaire* is a large organisation, with over 60,000 volunteers. Even within these divisions of religious and secular, there are political sub-themes: some voluntary organisations proudly trace their origins to the wartime resistance. There is a small but sturdy tradition of Jewish and Protestant social service organisations. The Women's Civic and Social Union (*Union Féminine Civique et Sociale*) (established 1925) is the national women's organisation concerned with consumer protection, social affairs and the environment. An old and well-established (1917) organisation is the federation for the blind (*Fédération des Aveugles de France*); as well as providing services and information for its members, it campaigns for legislation and housing provision for the blind.

Does the voluntary sector come together at national level? It does so in several ways. There are 11 *co-ordinations* (co-ordinations). Environment (which is weak); education (CCOMCEN, which is politically powerful and has over 80,000 member organisations); and *temps libre* (which means leisure, but which includes tenants, squatters and neighbourhood groups) are three co-ordinations. For the outsider, co-ordinations are one of the best routes into the voluntary organisations. Perhaps the most important voluntary organisation in the social affairs area is UNIOPSS (*Union Nationale Interfédérale des Oeuvres et Organismes Privés, Sanitaires et Sociaux*) (Interfederal national union of voluntary social and health bodies). It has 11,000 affiliated members. In addition to providing services for elderly people in hospitals and clinics. UNIOPSS' activities cover the spectrum of social policy in France: elderly people, young children, early school leavers, disabled people and community health. The UNIOPSS activities report covers most issues of interest to the voluntary sector, and records the relationship between the voluntary sector and government. UNIOPSS comments on government social policy and legislation, uniting the voluntary sector around an anti-poverty policy. One of its more successful actions was to convene a national conference on the RMI precisely one hundred days after it came into force. Senior political officials attended and the result of the *100 days on...* deliberation was a sharpening of the RMI legislation so as to make it more effective.

In recent times, the large national organisations have faced criticism on a number of fronts. One is that they have failed to involve clients in their work: few clients can be found on the boards of the large national organisations. A second is that they should be more open about their funding and accountable for how they spend public money - a theme which the media calls 'transparency'.

There are over 500 foundations in France. Perhaps the two most important ones for the voluntary sector are the *Fondation de France* (established 1969) and the *Fondation pour la Vie Associative* (Foundation for the Life of Associations, called the 'Fonda' for short). The Fondation de France is a large grant-making organisation, financing projects in the social field (poverty, handicap, elderly people, illness and family welfare): it promotes the development of voluntary organisations. The Fonda promotes the role of the voluntary sector and provides a forum where the key issues facing the sector can be debated. Its magazine is called *La Tribune*, available for 440 FFr.

In fact, the voluntary sector in France has a prodigious output of publications – it has no fewer than 40,000 titles! Several experts feel the publications process has gone too far, that a newsletter is used more as a validation of an organisation's existence than anything else, and that many newsletters are lifeless in style and content. Many French organisations produce an annual report, called an activities report (*rapport d'activité*), which gives an idea of the issues that each face. Perhaps the best thematic review of social developments and activities is *Union Sociale*. Published monthly by UNIOPSS, it records the texts of all government social decisions in an insert: it is available for 190 FFr. The magazine of the Women's Civic and Social Union (*Union Féminine Civique et Sociale*) *Dialoguer* carries reviews of social developments of interest to the voluntary sector. Many organisations run a standard troika of publications: for example, the large housing resettlement organisation FNARS (*Fédération Nationale des Associations d'Acceuil et de Réadaptation sociale*) (national federation of reception and resettlement centres) is typical, with a monthly gazette, a five-times-a-year magazine called LIR, and a yearbook. The publication which most activists read is *Les actualités socials hébdomodaires*, a weekly leaflet published by the press group *Liaisons*.

CEDIAS (*Centre d'Études, de documentations, d'information et d'action sociales*) (established 1894) is an important documentation centre for social issues in France. It has a library with 80,000 titles, runs conferences and study groups, and issues periodicals (*Vie Sociale*) and directories on different parts of the voluntary sector.

Newer Organisations
The surge of noisy, campaigning grassroots voluntary organisations which broke on most of Europe in the 1960s came early to France. ATD Quart-Monde (*Aide à Toute Détresse Quart Monde*, or help to those in need in the 'fourth world') was perhaps the first of the new wave of voluntary organisations. In 1956, radical priest Fr Joseph Wresinski set up a 'solidarity group' with poor workers: they were joined by volunteers living with the poor and sharing their deprivations. ATD has had close connections with the political system. In 1976, members of the National Assembly from all the political parties agreed to form a consultative group with ATD; a similar group was set up in the Senate (*Sénat*) in 1980. The purpose was to ensure that parliamentarians hear the voices, opinions and frustrations of poor

people who were members of and were represented in ATD. In 1989, ATD organised a meeting in the Senate in Paris, with the strident theme of 'Eliminate extreme poverty in France and Europe before the end of the 1990s!'

Another of the early campaigning voluntary organisations was Emmaus. It too was led by a priest, the Abbé Pierre. Inflamed by the spectacle of poor and homeless people shivering in the streets of Paris during the bleak winter of 1954, he seized a radio station and put out an appeal for the citizens of the capital to bring them food and blankets, which they did. Emmaus grew into a national (and like ATD, an international) movement of solidarity and practical help for the most destitute with food shops, work projects and reception centres. Abbé Pierre is the prophet of radical community action, courted by senior politicians, still throwing himself into campaigning action. A film has even been made of his life, called *Hiver 54* (the winter of '54).

There was a notable expansion of the voluntary sector in France in the 1980s. An example of one of the new and vigorous NGOs was *Médecins du Monde* (Doctors of the world), a humanitarian body set up in 1981 to provide world-wide medical help. In 1986, it set up a Mission France to meet the needs of French people who were not obtaining social assistance or basic community health services. By 1990, it had established 25 medico-socio reception centres with 1,500 volunteers, helping between 500 and 600 people daily. Many of those assisted were either homeless, migrants, refugees or victims of AIDS (SIDA, in French). An original but still small and marginal organisation is a national solidarity group for the unemployed: *Solidarités nouvelles face au chômage* (New solidarity for the unemployed), led by the charismatic Jean Baptiste de Foucauld. By 1990, 24 local branches had been formed.

Another grass-roots organisation was *Restaurants de Coeur*, which were low-price soup, coffee and food shops for the poor and the homeless, set up by France's most famous television clown, Colouche. The work of the organisation was resumed by his widow Véronique after he died in a car crash. Third World solidarity groups are a small and active part of the new French voluntary sector. There is an association in most towns and villages, often linked to doctors, and frequently identified with help to Africa. They are referred to as third-worlders (*tiersmondists*). The two main such organisations are *Médecins du Monde* and *Médecins sans frontières*: they are expert fund-raisers and extremely professional in their campaigning work.

France has numerous immigrant associations, but as a general rule they are shy of taking on an outspoken political role. Many immigrants are anxious to ensure a smooth passage for their children, who automatically become French citizens if born on French soil. Many immigrant associations are involved in cultural work, teaching French, or organising the sending of money home for projects. An exception is *SOS Racisme*, a coalition of immigrants and people concerned about racism and the political growth of the right-wing political party, the National Front (*Front National*). *SOS*

Racisme has been prominent in bringing together the anti-racist forces in France, and functions virtually as a political party. *France Terre d'Asile* is a voluntary organisation helping refugees and carrying out public education work in the area.

Young workers are organised in France through the *Union des Foyers des Jeunes Travailleurs* (UFJT) (established 1955), and they run over 500 reception centres. They have no equivalent in the rest of Europe. UFJT hostels provide accommodation and related services such as counselling and training for young people leaving home in search of work. The UFJT hostels serve 200,000 people, and are managed by 10,000 volunteers and 6,000 paid staff. They are important in the field of community development, for they prepare young people for the transition to independence, and sponsor a network on local employment initiatives (*RILE – Réseau d'Initiatives Locale pour l'Emploi*).

The Commission on Poverty

On the initiative of UNIOPSS, a number of voluntary organisations formed a Commission on Poverty in January 1985 to press for more effective national measures against poverty. It had two general objectives: evaluating government responses to poverty and proposing anti-poverty measures. The members of the Commission on Poverty are an important indicator of those organisations most active on social policy at the national level in France. Its members include Armée de Salut (Salvation Army), Emmaus, Association des Paralysés, ATD Quart-Monde, St Vincent de Paul, Secours Catholique, Entraide Protestant, Fédération Nationale des Centres PACT, Solidarités nouvelles face au chômage, Secours Populaire, Les Petits Frères des Pauvres, Restaurants du Coeur, Croix Rouge, Médecins du Monde, FNARS (Fédération Nationale des Associations d'Acceuil et de Réadaptation Sociale) and UDAADMR (Union Nationale des Associations d'Aide à Domicile en Milieu Rurale). However the Commission's links with anti-poverty research and the academic world remain to be developed.

The Commission on Poverty acts as a liaison point with government, its ministers and officials. It is by no means the only way in which the contribution of the voluntary sector is heard. In addition to the National Assembly and the Senate (together, these comprise the French equivalent of Parliament), France has a broad-based Economic and Social Council, for which there is no direct British equivalent. Its 302 members, a number of whom are drawn from the voluntary sector, must be consulted by the government whenever it proposes social legislation. The Economic and Social Council commissioned a massive report on poverty in France, and appointed as rapporteur Fr Joseph Wresinski, the founder of ATD. Its 1987 findings reflected many of the perspectives of the voluntary sector: comprehensive anti-poverty programmes, investment in social housing and community health, voluntary-statutory partnerships, and new rights for the poor within a legal framework.

In 1983, the government set up a body called the *Conseil National de la Vie Associative* (literally, National Council for the Associative Life), funded through the Prime Minister's office. Its function is to help define the position of the voluntary sector, and to produce an annual report on the state of the voluntary sector in France; it has an elected council. Voluntary organisations regard it with some scepticism, an impression reinforced by the failure of the government to allocate it either staff or a budget.

Despite the shaky evolution of the CNVA, it seems that the French voluntary sector plays an influential, critical, and at times adversarial role with the government – one which the government seems prepared to accept, as witnessed by lively dialogue between it and the voluntary sector. The important function of the voluntary sector in implementing the government's social reforms may also contribute to this relationship.

Germany

The voluntary sector in Germany (population: 80m) is now probably the largest in Europe in its scope, funding and scale. The German voluntary sector, like German society as a whole, is unsettled, as it incorporates the former German Democratic Republic, the GDR, generally referred to as 'East Germany'. The restructuring of East Germany into a market economy has brought serious social consequences in its wake, not least mass unemployment.

Germany has a large immigrant community, estimated to number over four million. About one-quarter come from other EC states, principally Italy and Spain, but no less than 35 per cent are Turks. Immigrants are referred to a guest workers (*gastarbeiter*). Many Turks work in the car factories around Stuttgart and Köln. Yugoslavian immigrants have come to Germany: many have settled near Munich. Immigrants are not politically organised, but they do have cultural associations and can elect representatives to advise the local authorities. The vote in Germany is confined to German nationals: immigrants can apply for citizenship, but the application costs the equivalent of two months' salary, the waiting period is five years, and the home government may, if the application is successful, withdraw citizenship, with consequences for the immigrant's family.

Germany was divided into a federal state in 1945. Whereas income support and guidelines to policies have always been determined nationally, services have been delivered by the 10 different states, called *länder*, to which have been added six regions from the east. The relevant federal government ministry in the social affairs area used to be the Federal Ministry for Youth,

Family, Health and Women, but following the integration of the East, this has now been split into three: Family Policy and Elderly People; Health; and Young People and Women.

The principle of subsidiarity (*subsidiaritätsprinzip*) is enshrined in the German Constitution, termed its 'fundamental law' (*Grundgesetz*). This lays down the concept that the state may intervene to meet a person's needs only after other avenues of help (like the family, or voluntary organisations) have been exhausted. In practice this means that realms of social services, including hospitals, day centres, psychiatric care, rehabilitation establishments, and so on, are provided by voluntary organisations, although generously funded by the state. The fundamental law provides that the state cannot set up a social service if a voluntary one already exists in the area; and it encourages the state (in practice, the *länder*) to invite non-governmental organisations to set up and fund services. This approach to the provision of social and community services was not simply part of the postwar settlement, but dates back to the Weimar Republic of the 1920s and before. A total of 22,120 NGOs were recognised by the state in 1985, including 16,538 self-help groups. The term 'voluntary sector' is not readily recognised in Germany. Germans are more comfortable with the terms 'non-profit sector', 'private sector', 'non-governmental sector', 'non-statutory sector'; the terms 'third sector' and 'intermediary organisations' are also used.

As well as embodying the principle of subsidiarity, the German voluntary sector mirrors the social, religious and political elements of Germany. The voluntary sector reflects the political divisions of Social Democrat and Christian Democrat; the division between religious and secular; the division between large-scale organisation and small-scale initiative; and the division between the religions and the regions (the catholic south and the protestant north).

The voluntary sector in Germany is divided into six main welfare groupings (the 'big six'). English readers may find this structure complicated and the German compound words impenetrable, but it is nevertheless essential in any attempt to come to terms with the voluntary sector in Germany. These are the 'big six':

(i) *Arbeiterwohlfahrt* (Workers' Welfare);
(ii) *Diakonisches Werk der Evangelische Kirche in Deutschland* (affiliated to the Lutheran protestant Church, and referred to as *Diakonie* in shorthand);
(iii) *Deutscher Caritasverband* (Catholic-affiliated, *Caritas* in shorthand);
(iv) *Deutsches Rotes Kreuz* (the Red Cross);
(v) *Zentralwohlfahrtsstelle der Juden in Deutschland* (Central Welfare Office for the Jews)

(the big five welfare organisations); and

(vi)   Paritätischer Wohlfahrtsverband (PWV) (for smaller organisations).

For all of which there is an overall representative body: *Bundesarbeitsgemeinschaft der Freien Wohlfahrtspflege* (BAGFW) (Federal Coalition of Independent Welfare Organisations). In addition, both the private and public social sectors are represented in the *Deutscher Verein für Öffentliche und Private Fürsorge* (in short, the 'Verein').

Voluntary organisations in Germany must belong to the others to be 'recognised' and to obtain public money. This requirement is in article 10 of the Federal Social Assistance Law: the requirement was challenged in the 1960s in the courts, and in the 1980s by the Greens, when they tried to set up a seventh pillar of the German voluntary sector. Both challenges were unsuccessful.

Traditional Organisations

The 'big six' organisations have a long tradition of service which goes back to the eighteenth century. Diakonisches Werk formally began service in 1848, the Red Cross in 1864, Caritas in 1897, the Jewish Welfare Office in 1917, and Arbeiterwohlfahrt, which is associated with the Social Democratic party, in 1919. The Jewish Welfare office operates on a small scale, but is for symbolic reasons treated on a par with the other five; and the others operate on a truly large scale. The church-based organisations are able to draw on the substantial financial resources of their congregations. All citizens (unless they deliberately opt out, which about 10 per cent do) pay church income tax, much of which goes to funding the churches' far-reaching welfare programmes. Church tax raises over five billion marks. Diakonishes Werk, for example, runs 23,000 institutions (hospitals, retirement homes, centres for disabled people, children's centres, and so on) and has 263,000 paid employees. Arbeiterwohlfahrt has 588,000 members. The Red Cross has 4.71m members and 4,795 local groups.

The large organisations provide (1985 figures, West Germany only) 40 per cent of hospital places, 90 per cent of employment for people with learning difficulties, and 60 per cent of places for elderly people. The voluntary sector has 58,086 separate services or institutions, 592,870 permanent employees (2.73 per cent of the total national workforce), 448,838 paid workers, and 1.5m voluntary workers. The worth of the voluntary sector is valued at over nine billion marks. It even has its own bank, the Bank für Sozialwirtschaft!

The large bodies are decentralised and organised at Federal level, *Land* level, city level, district level and local level. Each local group has a substantial degree of autonomy. Although the big six have federal headquarters addresses, much of the real work of their members takes place at local level. Some of the most effective lobbying is done by the local groups at city, rather than federal, level.

The German voluntary sector has a formidable output of publications, the style of which would probably be considered earnest and theoretical by British standards. The main welfare organisations all have journals, such as *Diakonie, Caritaswissenschaft, Nachrichtendienst* and *Theorie und Praxis der sozialen Arbeit*.

The Verein brings together both the public and voluntary sectors in one body. Originally (1880) it was no more than an annual convention of welfare workers and specialists in social policy. Its present importance is generally understated. Verein members are brought on to government advisory bodies, 25 staff produce an interminable stream of publications, and it is consulted by the courts when social welfare claimants bring appeals concerning their entitlements, because the Verein determines an annual calculation on the 'basket of goods' necessary for a minimum standard of living, in effect, a poverty line.

The Reichsbund
There is one influential body outside the big six: the Reichsbund (in full, the *Reichsbund der Kriegsopfer, Behinderten, Sozialrentner und Hinterbliebenen*, or the Imperial association for war victims, people with learning difficulties, tenants and widows). It has hundreds of thousands of members, and is frequently invited to parliamentary hearings concerning social issues. Set up in its present form in 1948, it dates to the strong movement of war victims after the 1918 armistice. Its two political achievements have been the 1923 Social Assistance Act, and the War Victims Protection Law (*Bundesversorgungsbesetz*) of the 1950s. In the 1960s it organised marches on Bonn to demand improvements in pensions; it has a progressive position on social issues and in 1990 launched a new social action programme.

Newer Organisations
A long-standing criticism of the voluntary sector in Germany is that it is dominated by the big six welfare organisations (and within that, the big five), and that they have a lock on debate on social policy and on the allocation of resources. For example, on all committees or advisory bodies or representative institutions concerned with social issues, it is normal to ensure that there is a delicately balanced representation of the big five. Arbeiterwohlfahrt, it is alleged, will not adopt policy positions at odds with the Social Democratic Party, nor will the two religious ones offend the Christian Democrats. The open and vigorous public controversies between the voluntary sector and government that flourish in France are not to be found in Germany. As early as 1924, organisations that did not wish to affiliate to the big five began to organise separately into the Paritätischer Wohlfahrtsverband (PWV), which is now home to over 3,000 small, largely secular organisations. But it too came to be seen as part of the establishment, to the extent that the Paritätischer recently hired Dutch consultants to help it

to redefine its role: it has been modernised and relaunched with a new name (formerly it was the Deutsche...) and new logo.

Several specialised groups represent particular parts of the voluntary sector, in addition to those already within the big six. Two groups working with elderly people are considered influential in determining government policy: the Kuratorium and the Deutsches Zentrum der Altersfragen (DZA) (German Centre for Questions concerning the Elderly). For people interested in the European Social Fund, the Internationaler Bund für Sozialarbeit Jugendsozialwerk (International Association of Social Work) is an important organisation in Germany: it has 260 projects, many of them for the young unemployed. It has 2,500 paid workers. There is a national organisation for single parents in Germany, the Verein der Alleinerziehenden Mütter und Väter (VAMV): poorly funded, its strength varies from city to city. There is no national organisation for immigrants, but there are immigrant bodies located within the big six: Diakonisches Werk (Greeks), Arbeiterwohlfahrt (Turks and Yugoslavs), and Caritas (Spanish, Italians and Portuguese). Each Land now has a person responsible for the position of women within its jurisdiction; there is a large national umbrella body for the welfare of women, the Frauenrat. Deutscher Frauenrat-Lobby der Frauen is a large and influential umbrella and lobbying body for women on social and political questions. Deutscher Frauenrat has an excellent handbook of all the German women's organisations.

Germany was, like France, the home of large-scale community, social and student agitation in the late 1960s. This upheaval generated a proliferation of grass-roots, community, 'base-line initiatives' as they are called in Germany, serving women, families, immigrants, the mentally ill, disabled people and the elderly. Many were, and remain, politically outspoken, and this movement found political expression in the Green party in the 1980s. It is estimated there may now be up to 50,000 self-help groups in Germany, and over 230 networks or federations of self-help groups.

These new groups provided an injection of spontaneity into a voluntary sector that some have seen as leaden, sluggish and procedure-bound. German organisations hold congresses every second year and find it difficult to take policy initiatives or positions in between. Not only are the new voluntary organisations attractive to social activists, but as the result of financial scandals, public confidence in the large welfare organisations has fallen.

Recent Developments

Germany was slow to recognise the persistence of poverty (*armut*, in German): until the 1970s, the word 'poverty' was synonymous only with wartime deprivation and the hardships of the immediate postwar period. Trade unions, government, and even the welfare organisations, found great difficulty with applying the term to contemporary conditions. But poverty is now acknowledged as a social issue, partly due to the work of national organisations which have emerged and which campaign on different aspects of poverty. Although Germany is a federal state, a number of national coalitions (literally, 'federal community work groups') have emerged in recent years to campaign for their sectors and the needs of their constituents:

- Gray Panthers (advocating rights of elderly people);

- *Bundesarbeitsgemeinschaft Wohnungslosenhilfe* (National Coalition for the Homeless);

- *Bundesarbeitsgemeinschaft für Behinderte* (National Coalition for Disabled People);

- *Bundesarbeitsgemeinschaft Soziale Brennpunkte* (National Coalition for Homeless Families);

- *Arbeitsgemeinschaft der Sozialhilfeinitiativen* (National Coalition of Social Action); and

- *Bundesarbeitsgemeinschaft für Schuldnerberatung* (National Coalition against Debt).

The Bundesarbeitsgemeinschaft für Behinderte (National Coalition for Disabled People) is a strong lobbying organisation which was very successful in the 1970s in obtaining resources and allowances for disabled people. Attempts by governments in recent times to reduce these allowances were frustrated by the Behinderten.

Anti-poverty Networks in Germany

There are two important national anti-poverty networks: the informal *Armut und Unterversorgung* (literally, 'poverty and undersupply', or deprivation) and the *Bundesarbeitsgemeinschaft der Sozialhilfempfänge* (National Coalition of Social Service Claimants), one of the most enduring of self-help, client-run, grass-roots organisations. Both are located in Frankfurt am Main. Armut und Unterversorgung arose from an Arbeiterwohlfahrt conference in 1984, and has close relationships with alternative economists who produce an 'Alternative Germany Yearbook' of the social realities of present-day Germany. Armut und Unterversorgung publishes position papers on poverty (*stellungnahmen*), and its documentation and papers are promulgated in the leftist newspaper, *Frankfurter Rundschau*. There is not yet a national coalition for the unemployed, but a network of employment initiatives is in the process of formation (*Netzwerk der Arbeitsloseninitiativen*).

The German universities and polytechnics (*fachhochschule*) have a reputation for the quality of their research into poverty and social issues, and individual researchers will be recommended by the main welfare organisations and the national coalitions, with whom several will have close links. Germany is also well endowed with study groups, institutes, information groups and associations which bring together academics, researchers, local groups and activists. One such group is the *Wohnbund*, which is concerned with housing policy.

The German voluntary sector has devoted much of its attention over the past two years to the question of the east. The old structures, most of them associated with the communist regime, collapsed, and the former voluntary sector there is being integrated into the big six. Voluntary organisations had continued in existence in the East during the period 1945-89, and were active in social services, aftercare help for prisoners being a particular example. These voluntary organisations provided an outlet for citizens anxious to participate in community work, but not in the approved state or party organisations. Over 1989-90 some new groups sprung up, associated with environmental action, the position of women, and care for people with learning difficulties.

Further Information
An English-language booklet published by the *Deutscher Verein für öffentliche und private Fürsorge* outlines the basic principles of welfare provision in Germany, and the role of voluntary organisations (Manfred Wienand, *The social system and social work in the Federal Republic of Germany*: available from the association at Am Stockborn 1-3, D.6000 Frankfurt am Main 50). For a historical and contemporary analysis of the German voluntary sector, see articles by Bauer and Seibel in *Voluntas* vol. 1 no. 1. Basic information and statistics on social affairs in Germany are available in the *Statistisches Taschenbuch* available from the Ministry of Labour and Social Affairs, Press and Information Division, 5300 Bonn 1 (free). The official statistics office is the Statistische Bundesamt. An organisation with a particular interest in social work is the Carl Duisberg company.

THE NORTHERN COUNTRIES OF THE EUROPEAN COMMUNITIES

Belgium

Created only in 1830, Belgium (population: 9m) is divided into three regions – Dutch-speaking Flanders in the north, French-speaking Wallonia in the south, and the bilingual Brussels 'agglomeration' in between. Regional and linguistic divisions were addressed by 'regionalisation' in 1980. Parliament meets nationally, but also divides into a Flemish Council and government and a Walloon Council and government, each with its own departments. Foreign affairs, finance and defence are organised nationally. The political parties likewise operate in three components - in Flanders, Wallonia and the Brussels region. To complicate things still further, parties also divide on a Catholic, socialist and secular basis. These regional and other divisions are important, for they govern the manner in which the voluntary sector is organised and its resulting mosaic of organisations.

Traditional Voluntary Organisations

Churches (Belgium is 90 per cent Catholic) play a prominent role in the non-governmental sector in Belgium, providing services in education, health and social welfare, and hospitals. With the help of government funding, they run old people's homes, welfare centres and psychiatric services. Most of this work comes under the aegis of Caritas (in full, *Katholieke Caritas Confederatie van Instellingen*).

The King Baudouin Foundation is perhaps the most respected foundation in Belgium, and is considered influential in research and the formation of public opinion on social issues. It is deemed to have the finest overall view of social policy and voluntary organisations in the country. Its main fields of action are in the area of poverty, environment, youth, economic policy and social affairs: it has an extensive publications list. The *Vlaams Instituut ter bevordering en Ondersteuning van de Samenlevingsopbouw* (VIBOSO) (Flemish Institute for the promotion and support of constructive social work) is the leading body in Belgium concerned with community development: government-funded, producing research and documentation, it is unchallenged in its field.

Newer Organisations

Many small initiatives by voluntary organisations developed during the 1970s. These included tele-help services (*teleonthaaldiensten*), crisis centres for battered women (*crisisopvang*), low-price food shops (*restaurants du coeur*) and family help services (*familiehulp*). An inventory of anti-poverty groups in Ghent in 1990, for example, listed no fewer than 100 organisations in that city alone. Unemployment in Belgium rocketed in the 1980s: in response, the trade unions set up unemployment advice bureaux. ATD Quart-Monde is one of many organisations which promoted new specialised services, and campaigned for more enlightened policies towards the poor. There are self-help groups of women and migrants. One of the most active third-world charities is the medical help organisation *Médecins sans frontières* which sends young doctors abroad to provide medical help; *Médecins sans frontières* runs a domestic programme for the homeless and the victims of AIDS.

210

Recent Developments
The past 10 years or so have seen the development of voluntary organisation 'platforms' and anti-poverty platforms and forums, where the needs of particular sectors can be articulated. These include, for example, the platform for the voluntary sector (*Platform voor Volontariat* – established 1977), and the Brussels anti-poverty forum, to which 19 anti-poverty groups are affiliated. It publishes a magazine, *L'envers du decor*. There are other, more localised, anti-poverty forums in some of the different counties of Belgium. In Flanders, nearly all the anti-poverty organisations belong to either the independent *Pluralistisch Overleg Welzijnswerk* (POW), or the Catholic, Caritas-associated, umbrella organisation, *Verbond van Instelligen voor Welzijnswerk* (VIW).

Denmark

Denmark (population: 5m) is the image of the model Scandinavian welfare state: cradle-to-grave provision in the areas of health, welfare, housing and social services; high rates of female participation in the workforce (70 per cent); and generous rates of income support which are tempered by very high taxes which command grudging blessing from across the political spectrum. In such a world, could there possibly be any role for non-governmental organisations?

Surprisingly, there is. Comprehensive though welfare services may be, there are many individuals and groups who have been overlooked or for some reason require special attention. Small organisations provide specialised, sometimes innovatory, services for poor people with special needs. There are about 400 national organisations concerned with social welfare, and several thousand local ones. The voluntary sector is small in size compared with statutory provision, but important nonetheless. Advocacy and campaigning organisations in the voluntary sector have a long record in confronting the Danish authorities with the shortcomings of public provision. They exert an influence out of proportion to their size.

In a massive shift of authority and resources, social services were decentralised in Denmark in 1976 to the 14 counties and 275 municipalities. Denmark has had conservative-liberal governments since 1982 which restricted spending on social welfare. Danes have been among the least enthusiastic and most critical members of the EC.

Traditional Organisations
A number of large voluntary organisations were founded in Denmark at the turn of the century, and these continue to play an important role in the provision of services. These are the Church Cross Army (*Kirkens Korshaer* – established 1912), the Salvation Army (*Frelsens Hæer*), the YMCA (*KFUMs Sociale Arbejde*) and, more recently, the YWCA (*KFUKs Sociale Arbejde*). These

211

help the most destitute (for example, there are 13,000 homeless people in Denmark), and they employ both paid staff and volunteers.

Before and during the interwar years (1918-39), a number of predominantly secular voluntary organisations were established to protect the interests of particular client groups, such as disabled people. These organisations were often initiated by relatives or concerned professionals. Until recently, few of them made any attempt to involve the clients in the running or design of these services. They have piloted innovative services and campaigned for improvements in state services. The *Social Security Act, 1933*, gave the public services responsibility for meeting general social needs, but made provision for voluntary organisations to be contracted for the provision of individual services. Many residential homes, kindergartens, detoxification services, and centres for the homeless are delivered by private and voluntary organisations under such paid agreements.

The women's movement has been strong and effective in Denmark, the main organisation being the *Danske Kvinders Nationalråd* (DKN) (National Council of Women in Denmark), founded in 1899, to which 38 organisations are affiliated, with over a million members. DKN has publicised social issues of concern to women, established liaison with MPs and MEPs, promoted women's representation (33 per cent of Danish MPs are now women), played an active international role in the Nordic Forum, the United Nations, the European Women's Lobby, and developed links with sister organisations in central Europe.

Newer Organisations
In the 1960s and 1970s there was an eruption of new, community-based, often politically radical, grass-roots voluntary organisations. Many were concerned with housing, poverty and the position of women. These included such organisations as *Modrehjaelpen af 1983* (to provide social and economic support for children and their families), SIND (to assist the mentally ill), the B-team (to help claimants secure their entitlements), and others helping prostitutes, substance abusers and alcoholics. Several of the new groups have been in the forefront in developing imaginative responses to social need, such as the *Kofoeds Skole*, which has pioneered rehabilitative work for the disabled, and the National Ungbo League, which provides sheltered housing (about 4,000 flats) for youngsters with difficulties. The Danes have also been noted for the quality of residential care and home care for elderly and disabled people. Residents' councils in homes for the elderly were introduced as long ago as 1965.

Recent Developments
There has been a growing level of interest by the government in the development of non-governmental organisations. There has been some suspicion that this is motivated by a desire to see a replacement of state

services by cheaper voluntary provision; however the government has argued that the purpose is to promote innovation and less bureaucratic services.

In 1983, the government set up a 'contact forum' to act as a point of contact between government and non-governmental organisations. The voluntary sector elects seven representatives to the contact forum. The forum has published directories of voluntary organisations in Denmark. Several organisations make active contributions to debate on social issues: the most important are the Danish Institute for Social Research; the Society for the Improvement of the Social Debate (*Selskabet Til Fremme Af Social Debat*) (which publishes *Social Kritik*); the *Social Politisk Forening*; and *SR-Bistand*.

Ireland

Although physically close and presenting fewer problems of language and communication than voluntary organisations in mainland Europe, the voluntary sector in Ireland is not well known in Britain. Church-state relations and the violence in Northern Ireland attract most media attention: social conditions in the Republic (population: 3m) are less well appreciated. The entire island of Ireland is categorised by the European Communities as an 'objective 1 region', and is the poorest of the northern countries in the EC. One-third of the population lives below the poverty line; emigration in 1990 was over 30,000; and the unemployment level at 21 per cent long outstripped its European rivals. Measures of administrative decentralisation which have been popular in the rest of Europe have largely passed Ireland by: critics maintain that Irish social and administrative services are the most centralised west of Poland's river Vistula.

The most important voluntary organisation in Ireland is the Catholic charity, the Society of St Vincent de Paul. It has over 1,000 branches, 10,000 active members, and an annual turnover of IR£20m, which, by Irish standards, is large. It provides help to poor people in almost every parish in the country, from visiting services to cash help and clothes, to the extent that it has been described as a 'shadow state'. Government and local authority funding of voluntary organisations in Ireland may be the lowest in Europe: most voluntary organisations are expected to raise most of their means themselves, largely through traditional fund-raising methods.

In the 1970s a number of new organisations appeared to campaign for single mothers, battered women, the homeless, community law and adult education. The 1980s saw the growth of national federations in order to present a more united viewpoint of the different sectors in the social field. These included the Irish National Organisation of the Unemployed and the National Campaign for the Homeless.

An important body in the social policy field in Ireland is the Combat Poverty Agency, a state organisation established by the *Fine Gael*/Labour party government of 1982-7 and tolerated by subsequent governments. A small, underfinanced statutory agency, it has funded some small projects in the voluntary sector and promoted the general development of voluntary and community organisations. It is a valuable source of information on social policies, local issues and community development. Another statutory body, the National Social Service Board, provides welfare information and advice to voluntary organisations and supports a network of citizens' information centres.

Some voluntary organisations are politically active and with the Combat Poverty Agency, they have made poverty a prominent issue. Some voluntary organisations have developed close links with the political parties and have steered social legislation through the national parliament, the *Oireachtas*.

Luxembourg

Luxembourg (population: 0.38m) is the smallest state in the European Communities. Constitutionally, it is a Grand-Duchy. A number of EC institutions are located there, notably the Statistics Section (EUROSTAT), the Court of Auditors, and the Court of Justice. The languages spoken there are Luxembourgeois, German and French. Two currencies operate in the Grand Duchy: the Belgian franc and the Luxembourg franc, which is fixed at the same rate as the Belgian franc. A basic minimum social security income was introduced in 1986, called the RMG (*Revenu Minimum Garanti*)(Guaranteed Minimum Income).

The principal non-governmental organisations in Luxembourg are Caritas, ATD Quart-Monde (one of the most publicly outspoken), Interactions Faubourgs, ASTI (Association de Soutien aux Travailleurs Immigrés) (Association to help immigrant workers) and Femmes en détresse (Women in Need). State funding for voluntary organisations runs at up to 90 per cent of project costs. The ERGO programme, run under the auspices of CEPS/INSTEAD, has played an important role in bringing together 24 non-governmental organisations concerned with unemployment, community development and social policy issues.

Netherlands

Welfare and social services in the Netherlands (population: 15m) are often contrasted to the Scandinavian countries, where there is comprehensive state provision, and where the voluntary sector is small in size, filling an important niche in other ways. In the Netherlands, by contrast, almost all social services

214

(between 85 and 90 per cent, it is estimated) are delivered by voluntary organisations – but they are funded by the state to do so.

The reasons for this are historical: the voluntary sector reflects the regional, historical and denominational traditions of the Netherlands. The Netherlands has 11 provinces (of which Holland is but one), two main religious traditions (Catholicism in the southwest, and Protestantism in the northeast), and a strong secular and humanist tradition. In the Middle Ages, the trade guilds operated a welfare system for their members, and the voluntary sector today is its linear descendant.

The structure in the Netherlands reflects convenience as much as ideology. When they came to consider the development of social services in the 1920s, Dutch governments avoided setting up state services, preferring instead to channel resources into existing structures. Despite the formal religious divisions of protestant and catholic, less than 50 per cent of Dutch people declare themselves to have a church affiliation.

There are 12 national organisations concerned with poverty and social policy in the Netherlands. Each has local branches. These include the National Organisation for the Disabled (Landelijk WAO berand), the National Organisation for Women on Social Assistance (Landelijk steunpunt komites vrouwen in de bijstand), the National Organisation for the Jobless, and ATD. There are three main church-based societies which provide social services for the poor: the Dutch Council of Churches, the Vincentius Society, and DISK (Church Services in an Industrial Society). DISK is politically active and has close ties with members of parliament.

Traditional Voluntary Organisations

Church-based and secular organisations run hospitals, schools, cultural activities and social services, as well as a large but unknown number of small community-based and self-help groups serving particular interests. By the late 1970s, the voluntary sector in the Netherlands was considered to be the best developed and the most lavishly funded in Europe. There were no fewer than 57 national councils covering the different parts of the voluntary sector, many able to fund consultants and policy development experts.

In addition to government, foundations finance the work of Dutch voluntary organisations. Perhaps the best known is the Queen Juliana Foundation (*Koningin Juliana Fonds*), which has distributed more than 150m guilders to thousands of organisations and groups following its formation in 1948. Funded by lotteries, it grant aids innovative projects and research in social services, community development and mental health. The Queen Juliana Foundation, because of its funding work, has an intimate knowledge of the voluntary sector in the Netherlands. NIMO is the leading body carrying out research into community development.

Newer Voluntary Organisations

Despite having such a strong, established and recognised voluntary sector, the Netherlands by no means escaped the proliferation of small community groups, organisations and projects in the 1970s and 1980s. About 4,000 attracted direct state aid from the national government, which took the view that these projects had a healthy role in providing new services compared to older, possibly stale, traditional organisations.

Their expansion was not to last, for two reasons. Administrative devolution in 1979 meant that funding of these groups was transferred from national to local government, some being more supportive than others. Second, the change of government in 1980 led to substantial cutbacks in welfare spending. Many groups, organisations and agencies succumbed. Of the 57 national sectoral councils and bodies, only a dozen remain – including social work, community development, adult education, housing and health.

Recent Developments

In 1982, a number of women's anti-poverty groups came together to form what is called in shorthand the *Breed Platform*, in full the *Breed Platform vrouwen voor Ekonomische Zelfstandigheid* (Dutch Forum for Women's Economic Independence). A total of 38 organisations are now affiliated, and it has been active in highlighting poverty among women in the Netherlands.

The Netherlands Institute for Care and Welfare (NIZW), was formed in 1989 to promote the improvement of services for young, elderly and disabled people; and for improved home care services and shelter for the homeless. Grant-aided by the Ministry of Welfare, Health and Culture, it has responsibilities in the areas of information, research, and documentation.

Three voluntary organisations in the housing field came together in 1991 to form the Dutch Housing Federation (*Nederlandse Woonbond*). The federation is drawn from LOBH, which is a housing advocacy body with a reputation for innovative community housing projects; LOS (the Urban Renewal Team); and NVH (Dutch Tenants Union).

THE SOUTHERN COUNTRIES

Greece joined the EC in 1981, Portugal and Spain in 1986, and with Italy these four southern countries encompass the poorest regions of the European Communities. The European Commission has been very conscious of the manner in which the allocation of EC resources has been seen as northern European dominated, and for this reason launched a number of what were termed 'mediterranean' initiatives and programmes in the late 1980s. These policies have mainly concerned environmental and regional policy. There is

216

an awareness that the financial levels of social security in the southern countries lag far behind those of the northern countries, and measures to promote convergence between north and south will be a theme of the 1990s.

Italy is included here as a southern country: the southern half of the country is listed as an objective one area, although the northern part of the country has levels of industrialisation and development that would make it more naturally a part of northern Europe.

Greece

Greece (population: 10m) is one of the poorest countries of the EC, with one of the least developed welfare systems. Politically, it suffered from isolation during the period of the rule of the colonels (1967-74); economically it has suffered from depopulation of the rural areas, and dependence on seasonal incomes, not least tourism. The consumer spending power per head in the rural areas is only 40 per cent that of the urban areas. Voluntary organisations are weak, comprising a traditional church-based sector, the Red Cross, and a more recent campaigning segment. During the period 1980-89, when the country was governed by the socialist PASOK party, there was a substantial enlargement of state welfare services, but voluntary organisations were not favoured, promoted or encouraged by the government.

Under Act 57 of 1973, the law states the right of economically weak persons including the poor, the mentally ill, the disabled and the homeless to 'social protection'. Law 1065 of 1980 devolved social and cultural services to the local authorities: however, spending in these areas is limited. Greece does not have comprehensive social security services as they would be understood in the northern countries. Family structure remains more intact than in the north, and there is a sense in which families (and extended families) are expected to look after their own. The level of unemployment payments is low.

Greece is divided into local authorities (*nomoi*, or communes), each with an elected mayor, a chair or secretary. The country is divided French-style into 56 prefectures, each with a prefect appointed by the government: sometimes the local authorities and prefectures overlap geographically, but not always. The church in Greece (95 per cent Orthodox) is divided into 80 bishoprics.

Traditional Organisations: the National Institutes
There is a strong interventionist, statist tradition in Greece, which can be traced to corporatist governments in the 1930s, and to nineteenth-century Napoleonic, centralising administrations. When social problems or groups in especial need are identified in Greece, either in the press or the parliament, the normal course of events is for the government to establish a state body in response: generally this will be termed a national institute or national foundation. Voluntary organisations in Britain wishing to contact bodies

providing similar services in Greece may wish to approach the appropriate national institute, rather than search for what would conventionally be understood as a voluntary organisation.

The institutes, and the small voluntary sector in Greece, are supervised by the state to a greater or lesser degree. They fall under the aegis of one of three government departments: education, religion and cults; economics; and health and welfare, including social services. Legally speaking, there are four types of national institutes: public institutes, public institutes constituted as private companies, private institutes, and co-operatives. Some of these are derived from the former royal institutes from the days of the now abolished monarchy. At local level, services have a pluralistic structure. For example, homes for elderly people, although set up and funded by the state, are governed by a board of trustees consisting of the prefect, the mayor, representatives of the consumers, an appointee of the bishop, and representatives of local government.

There is a national institute for youth, which provides hostels for students and young workers; a National Institute for Nursery Schools; and a National Institute for Social Welfare (PIKPA), which provides social centres, family service units, nursery schools, cash help for the needy, and centres for elderly people. EOP, the National Foundation of Welfare, provides handicraft work, cottage industries, training courses, capital investment loans in rural areas, and cash help to needy families in difficulty. The Mitera (mother) Institute, formerly a royal institute, runs nursery schools, fostering and adoption services, and hostels for single mothers. The Centre for Mental Health, formerly a royal institute, provides day-care centres, educational services, SOS telephone lines, and, with ESF funding, gardening projects, woodwork, and community placements for the moderate mentally ill. Some bodies termed 'unions' and 'national associations' are in practice much the same as national institutes, such as the Union of Deaf People. Help for the unemployed is provided through a state agency, the Organisation for the Employment of the Workforce (OAED). It delivers unemployment assistance, which is available for up to a year, along with training, job-search and counselling.

The national institutes may be the best sources for information on social policy in Greece. Besides PIKPA and EOP, the leading policy institutes are the National Centre of Social Research (EKKE), the Planning and Research Centre (KEPE), and the National Foundation for Youth (EIN). PRAXIS is a new research centre for economic, social and geographical studies, designed to help both the public and the voluntary sector, with an interest in the position of women, training, and poverty.

The tradition of national institutes does not mean that state services in Greece are as comprehensive as they might at first sight appear: it simply means that national institutes are the accepted and standard response to social

218

needs. Greece has attracted criticism for the quality of its institutional care for the mentally ill, for inadequate places for elderly poor people, and for lack of facilities for substance abusers.

Although national institutes are the modern Greek state's conventional response to social issues, there is a long tradition of philanthropic charitable service in Greece: it remains important in the provision of services in specific areas. Service varies from one bishopric to another, and from one parish to another, but most bishoprics and parishes have some kind of philanthropic work and youth work, and run summer camps and Sunday schools. Church-based services are the most important single element in the voluntary sector. One of the activities of bible study circles is collecting clothes for poor children and soldiers. Each parish will have a Friends of the Poor organisation, which will use parish funds to help poor families, single mothers and refugees, through visiting and frequently through cash grants. Normally, Friends of the Poor parish groups are run by women. They can draw on diocesan funds for the more deserving difficult cases. The courts will ask for the views of local Friends of the Poor in juvenile cases. Voluntary and church organisations provide 40 per cent of places for children in institutions and orphanages, 50 per cent of places for people with learning difficulties, 70 per cent of places for the chronically ill, and 96 per cent of places for elderly people.

Recent Developments

The dominance of the national institutes does not mean that national voluntary organisations are absent, though the type of work undertaken by national institutes and national voluntary organisations may not be dissimilar. Some of the larger voluntary organisations are the Christian Fraternity for Young Women, the YWCA (XEN), Caritas, the YMCA, and the Red Cross. The Red Cross is much the most important, being more significant in welfare, medical and nursing circles than any other organisation. It has a substantial and modern welfare branch which is introducing up-to-date ideas and practices. The YWCA (established 1923) has taken on an important social role: it has 25,000 members in 30 centres. It now works with ethnic minorities, migrants and immigrants, single parents, illiterate people, elderly people and drug addicts. The YWCA encourages national policy changes to help women, particularly in the area of family law and job opportunities. The YWCA provides leadership training for women in community work: adult education programmes for women are the main part of its present programme.

Greece has a Union of Large Families (four children or more); and its associate, the Union of Superlarge Families (seven children or more). They dispense cash help for large poor families, and have even provided sewing machines and tractors. They have successfully campaigned for half-price tickets on public transport and for special tax allowances for larger cars for large, and superlarge, families!

Women's organisations are not considered to be strong in Greece. Women's groups are linked to the political parties: the Union of Greek Women is linked to PASOK, and New Democracy has its own group. There are a number of local women's groups, even a philanthropic Union of Athenian Ladies: its very title emphasises the orientation of many voluntary groups to services rather than campaigning.

Most voluntary organisations operate on a localised basis, on a small scale, providing a specific service. There is little tradition of national, sectoral, voluntary organisations campaigning on social issues, although the 1,525-member strong Greek Association of Social Workers has begun to do so. Research into social issues and social problems has been limited, most of what there is having been carried out as part of the second and third anti-poverty programmes. When the Greek section of the European Anti-Poverty Network (EAPN) was being set up, the organisers identified about 50 voluntary organisations concerned with poverty, and of these, 22 subsequently participated in the EAPN. These are compiling a directory of Greek NGOs concerned with poverty.

Communication with Greek organisations is problematic because of the different language and alphabet and distance. Greek translators are scarce, but many Greek organisations will produce at least some documentation in English or French.

Italy

In introducing the voluntary sector in Italy (population: 58m), three features should be noted. These are the decentralised nature of Italian government administration, the ideologically divided nature of Italy's politics and the divisions of wealth between the rich north and the poor south.

Ever since the passing of the decentralisation law in 1976, most social services have been planned, funded and delivered at regional, provincial and communal level rather than at national level. The Minister for Social Affairs is a minister without structures: the minister's duty is to co-ordinate what the regional and local services are doing, and provide information about them. There is no national housing minister at all! The second important element in understanding the voluntary sector in Italy is the ideological nature of Italian politics, which are divided between the PDS (formerly the Communist Party), which is strong in the northern regions and cities, and the Christian Democrats (DC), who have, as a general rule, been strong in the south. As a result, the nature, quality and extent of social services can vary markedly between the richer localities of the north, where the PDS has invested heavily in social and community services, and the southern localities, which are poorer and do not have either the resources for, or political commitment to, social services. The PDS, where it has had political control, has built up state social services, and funded the large-scale development of co-operatives, many with a social orientation. Such development is not as readily evident in Christian Democrat regions, where social services have been left to church-based organisations, generally using unpaid volunteers. There is no national system of unemployment assistance in Italy: some regions provide benefits (*sussido straordinario*), some do not, and rates are set locally.

There is a pronounced gap between the wealth of the industrialised northern regions and the poverty of the south, where farms are marginal, wages low, and where existing wealth is unevenly distributed. Public funding for voluntary organisations in Italy is limited; it is inaccessible without political influence, and in some areas not even worth trying for. There are no substantial national government social programmes with the exception of the funds for the impoverished southern regions (*Il Meridionale*), not yet penetrated by the voluntary sector.

National Organisations
Linguistically, the term 'voluntary sector' is not readily recognised in Italian, and several terms and phrases are used to describe it, such as the third sector (*terzo settore*), the independent sector (*settore indipendente*), and the self-help sector (*self-help* is left untranslated). Italians do make distinctions between voluntarism (*volontariato*) (strictly unpaid, voluntary work), associationism (*associazionismo*) (the world of associations and organised groups) and co-operatives (*cooperativi*) (which imply that they carry out economic activities of a social character). The voluntary sector in Italy spans these three distinctions, and some groups combine co-operative work with unpaid voluntary work within an association. Many personal social services are delivered through co-operatives, and the co-operative form of organisation is often the most attractive one for voluntary organisations. Co-operatives are entitled to charge users, and entitled to apply to the local authorities for subsidies for providing services. They are a useful form of organisation, legally recognised, and it is the form that many voluntary organisations adopt for their work: British community groups interested in contacting 'voluntary' groups in Italy could well find themselves dealing with co-operatives. For example, many of the co-operatives affiliated to the League of Co-operatives (*Lega dei Cooperativi*) provide residential and training services for disabled people and mentally ill people, and health services for women.

Because of the political divisions of the co-operative movement, local funding has tended to favour the co-operative of the local governing party. Some representatives of the voluntary sector have run for election in order to better represent the social needs of their clients, but as independents within the party lists (generally the PDS). Voluntary organisations frequently make their views known not through 'official' channels but through the main political groupings. This is termed clientilism (*clientilismo*). Even the co-operatives in Italy are divided into three federations: the *Lega dei Cooperativi e Mutue* (affiliated to the PDS); the *Confederazione Cooperativa* (affiliated to the DC); and the *Associazione Generale dei Cooperative* (associated with the Republican party). Similarly, many of the voluntary organisations have parallel organisations drawn from their Christian Democrat or Communist or secular counterparts: thus APAS (*Associazione Publiche Assistenze*) is the secular ambulance, first aid, civic defence voluntary organisation; it is paralleled by *Confederazione Nazionale Misericordie d'Italia (Misericordia)*, its direct Catholic equivalent. In some limited cases, the parallel organisations come together to join in common cause: CEIS (*Centro Italiano Solidarietà*) has joined the *Communità di San Patrignano* in the joint struggle against drug abuse through the United Voluntary Movement against Drug Abuse, MUVLAD (*Movimento Unitario Volontari Lotta alla Droga*).

Traditionally, voluntary activity in Italy has been dominated by local, church-based organisations and charities. The largest voluntary organisation in Italy is the church-based Caritas. It provides services for immigrants, gypsies, the homeless, victims of AIDS and mentally ill people. Some of its individual projects are funded by local government. Caritas, organised throughout Italy on a diocesan basis, is a significant provider of services for elderly people – such as residential care, sheltered housing and recreation.

Several attempts have been made to try to measure the size and scope of the voluntary sector in Italy. The most recent (1989) research by the IREF institute and Euresko found that 944,000 people took an active part in the work of associations. In a sample of over 1,000 local voluntary organisations, two Catholic charities comprised almost half the total: Caritas and the charities of St Vincent de Paul (*S. Vincenzo*).

The number of co-operative societies and charities registered in 1985 totalled 146,377. Most are organised at local level. Indeed, perhaps the most striking organisational feature of the voluntary sector in Italy is its fragmented, localised nature. Groups work locally, in villages, towns, cities and regions: they do not have a tradition of national organisation, even though some national organisations are beginning to emerge.

In the past number of years, an attempt has been made to organise people outside these political and ideological structures, and to break away from the system of church and political patronage. Philosophically, the unorganised have been termed 'the sixth estate' (*sesto potere*) (after parliament, judiciary, government, clergy and the press). This attempt to mobilise citizen action has been pioneered by the Democratic Federative Movement (*Movimento Federativo Democratico*). Its history has been depicted by leading Italian social theorist Giancarlo Quaranta, author of *L'uomo negato* ('the denied man'). Its first national convention was in April 1985; in 1991 it adopted a Declaration of Rights for Italian citizens.

222

The Democratic Federative Movement claims its roots in the protest campaigns of the 1960s and its political inspiration from the assassinated Christian Democrat premier Aldo Moro and the late Communist leader Enrico Berlinguer; its motivation is to make Italy a more democratic society of citizen action based on citizens' rights. It has a journal, *Democrazia diretta* ('direct democracy').

Fighting for Patients' Rights
The principal achievement of the Democratic Federative Movement is the Patients' Rights Tribunal (established 1980), an angry coalition of groups formed to fight for better hospital conditions generally and for specific concerns such as privacy, minimum standards of physical comfort, hygiene and food, speedier treatment, the right of hospitalised children to play, and an end to favouritism and under-the counter payments for services, to name just a few. There are now observatories in each region to monitor the situation of patients and progress towards achievement of their rights. There are 350 groups which organise an annual Patients' Charter Day (14 June). Charters of Patients' Rights have now been adopted in 73 cities.

Two early national organisations in the 1950s were the National Association for the Crippled and Civilian Disabled (ANMIC) and the National Association of Invalids and Injured at Work. The Milan-based Federated National League for the Right to Work for People with Learning Difficulties (*La Lega per il Diritto al Lavoro degli Handicapati*) was set up in 1979 and has engaged in aggressive (and successful) national campaigning work, taking authorities to court in order to ensure wheelchair access to buildings and railways. The League has since been active in Disabled Persons International (DPI). In 1990 a national federation for organisations working with the homeless was set up in Brescia, the FIOPSD. The mountainous areas of Italy are represented through UNCEM, the National Union of Communities in Mountainous Areas, which brings together about 300 mountain communities. It is the driving force behind a government body called the 'Advisory committee for the analysis of economic, social and institutional problems in mountainous areas'.

Newer Organisations
The nature of voluntary organisations changed during the decade of the 1970s with an explosion of small, specialised organisations. Figures give an idea of the scale of this expansion: of 15,000 voluntary organisations studied by two researchers (Rossi and Colozzi) in 1985, 40 per cent were founded after 1977. These new community groups and organisations were more democratic in their working methods, user-orientated, and politically outspoken. They used commercial activities to raise income, and they began to make provision for paid work, expenses and salaried workers.

223

These new community groups of the 1970s helped people missed by the traditional charities, such as prisoners, drug addicts, prostitutes and young people at risk. They called themselves groups (*gruppo*, like *Gruppo Abele*, Turin), communities (*communità*, like *Communità de S. Egidio*, Rome or *Communità de Capodarco*) or centres (*centro*, like *Centro Solidarieta*, Genoa), the Italian word often being followed by the place where they were founded or where they operated. The title *Communità* normally denotes a religious, Catholic-based group. The types of services they developed included treatment centres, handicraft shops, day hospitals and agricultural co-operatives. These groups are characterised by their use of a mix of workers – unpaid volunteers, some salaried, and some professional. Many of the volunteers are in their twenties and thirties. While many are secular in their approach, a substantial number are composed of radical Catholic activists, such as Communità de S. Egidio.

Italian refers to what are termed 'marginal people' (*emarginazione*), by which it means homeless people, the victims of unemployment and disabled people who have become isolated from social services: a number of groups are dedicated to helping them, notably MOVI (*Movimento per il Volontariato Italiano*) and CNCA (*Coordinamento Nazionale Communità di Accoglienza*). The number of voluntary organisations caring for immigrants has grown rapidly in recent years. There has been a wave of immigration into Italy from Morocco, Albania, Tunisia, Senegal, Yugoslavia, the Philippines, Peru and Ethiopia; and there are some associations for particular groups of immigrants. The overall body in Italy bringing together groups caring for the welfare of immigrants is FOCSI (*Federazione Organizzazioni Communità Straniere in Italia*). FOPRI is a new organisation helping redundant unemployed people in Italy; at present it runs ESF training activities for 8,000 unemployed people.

There is no national association of unemployed people, but the question of rights of unemployed people is raised actively both by the trade unions and by the influential and well-regarded Young Christian People's Organisation (GOC). Although the feminist movement in Italy may not be strong by international standards, many of the social issues affecting women are raised by the noisy and forceful Italian housewives' association, MOICA (*Movimento Italiano Casalinghe*).

Some attempts have been made very recently to bring together a unifying body for the voluntary sector in Italy. The Convention of Associations (*Convenzione dell' Associazionismo*) has lobbied parliament, unsuccessfully so far, for a better financial deal for voluntary organisations.

Further Information

Research bodies in Italy are generally called foundations (*fondazione*). Several are concerned with social issues. CENSIS, for example, documents voluntary

Table 8 Prominent Italian Voluntary Organisations

Organisation	Specialist Field
Carcere e Communità	Care for prisoners and ex-offenders
Communità di Capodarco	Drug addicts, disabled people, young people at risk, and homeless people
Associazione Nazionale Famiglie Fanciulli e Adulti Subnormale (ANFFAS)	Disabled people
Associazione Ricreativa Culturale Italiana (ARCI)	Large national organisation for young people, consumers and women
Auser	Self-governing services for the elderly
Centro Italiano Solidarietà	Drug addicts
Cooperative di Solidarietà Sociale – Federazione Nazionale	Help for immigrants
Coordinamento Centri Sociali Anziani e orti	Elderly people
Coordinamento Nazionale Communità di Accoglienza (CNCA)	Disabled and 'marginal' people
Comitato Abbattimento Barriere Architettoniche (CABA)	Rights for disabled people; campaigns for disabled access
Gioventu Operaia Cristiana (GOC)	Young workers; projects for unemployed people
Italia Nostra	Environmental action
Lega per l'Ambiente	Environmental action; focus on water quality
Assoc. Nazionale Università della Terza Età (UNITRE)	Elderly people
Movimento Italiano Casalinghe (MOICA)	Italian housewives association

work organisations engaged in social solidarity work. IREF (*Instituto di Ricerche Educative e Formative*) publishes an annual report on voluntary organisations in the social field, listed under different headings (immigration, social assistance, consumers, ecology, and so on) and a directory recording the principal and best known voluntary organisations, detailing their fields of work, date established, size, services and publications. IREF's annual report, *Rapporto sull'associazionismo sociale*, provides an astonishing wealth of detail, including an analysis of recent trends and international comparisons (available from Tecnodid Editrice, Piazza Carlo III, 42, 80137 Napoli for 42,000 lira). Communità de S. Egidio publishes books about immigration in Italy, its two most recent being *Outre il mito – Gli straniere in Italia* (foreigners in Italy) and *Immigrazione, Razzismo e futuro*.

Agenzia Federativa: News Agency for the Voluntary Sector

Voluntary groups in Britain may be particularly interested in two organisations: CERFE and *Agenzia Federativa*. CERFE is the Centre for Research and Documentation (*Centro di Ricerca e Documentazione*). It is in the process of building up a computerised databank on voluntary organisations in Italy and abroad, detailing their activities, policies and publications. Besides this pathfinder project, it reports on the developments in the citizens' movement ('the sixth estate'), and carries out social research and evaluation projects. Agenzia Federativa, which is linked to CERFE, is a news agency devoted to providing news about the voluntary sector to the Italian press, radio and television, and to the voluntary sector itself. Each week it issues snappy, to-the-point news-sheets about developments in the voluntary sector in Italy and abroad (the basic cost is 1m lira per year, about £500).

There is a centre for voluntary work in Lucca. Although its staff numbers are small (about three or four), it is an important clearing-house for information about voluntary organisations, and has published a number of books.

SEI (Società Editrice Internazionale) publishes a series of three guides (editor: Francesco Pionati; available from SEI, Turin) about the voluntary sector in Italy:

- *Volontariato Oggi* (The voluntary sector today) [ISBN 88-05-051-63-2];

- *Dizionario Tematic delle Leggi* (The legal background) [ISBN 88-05-051-64-0]; and

- *Testimonianze* (Interviews) [ISBN 88-05-051-62-4].

Information on the citizens' movement can be found in Giancarlo Quaranta's *Sesto Potere*, available from Liguori Editore, via Mezzocannone 19, 80134 Napoli, ISBN 88-207-1865-0.

Portugal

Portugal (population: 10m) is one of the poorest and least developed EC countries. As in neighbouring Spain, the thrust of providing for the needs of the poor fell on the family and on religious voluntary organisations during the period of dictatorship (1934-74).

There was an eruption of new voluntary and community groups following the April revolution of 1974. Most were small in size and secular in inspiration.

Portugal adopted a new Constitution in 1976: article 63.2 committed the state to organising, supporting, funding and co-ordinating a unified and decentralised social service system. All of Portugal is defined as an objective 1 region. A high percentage of the population lives in the capital, Lisbon, and in the capital of the north, Porto. Rural areas have suffered from the decline of traditional small industry and depopulation.

The activities of non-governmental organisations are regulated under Social Security Law 119/1983 which makes provision for the 'harmonisation of aims and activities of voluntary institutions with those of the social security system'. Some NGOs receive financial assistance from government under what are termed co-operation accords (*acordo de coopertaçao*), the level agreed depending on the service provided and the number of users.

Traditional Organisations

Since the nineteenth century, three main organisations provided social services and assistance throughout Portugal: Caritas, *Santa Casa da Misericórdia* (generally there is one misericordia per commune, or *concelho*), and the Order of Malta (SAOM). Santa Casa da Misericordia, an old charitable order founded in the fifteenth century, concentrates on providing services for elderly people. The Order of Malta provides a chain of services which include hospitals, clothes distribution centres, schools and services for handicapped children, night shelters and workshops for the homeless, and second-chance education for early school-leavers.

Other important providers of services include Casa Pia, Conferências Vicentinas, Cruz Vermelha Portuguesa, Acçao Sócio-Caritativa da Igreja Católica, Exército de Salvaçao and the Comité Português para a UNICEF. Such organisations continue to be important, despite the growth of state welfare provision since 1974, and the arrival of newer voluntary and community organisations. As much as 76 per cent of services for young people, 82 per cent of rehabilitation services, and 79 per cent of services for elderly people are provided by voluntary organisations.

Recent Developments

Non-governmental organisations now operate in five main national federations, of which the main ones are the *Uniao das Instituiçoes Particulares de Solidariedade Social* IPSS (Unions of Social Solidarity), which has 966 services, institutions, groups or branches affiliated; *Mutualités* (388 groups) and *Miséridordias* (121 groups); Caritas (600 groups affiliated); CERCIS (Federation of Co-operatives for Special Education); and UNICOD (Federation for disabled people.). There is a movement for rural solidarity. Thus far, there is little liaison between these bodies to form a united voluntary sector.

Eighteen non-governmental organisations are represented on the Commission for the Status of Women (*Comissao da Condicao Feminina*). The Commission has information not only on women's groups, but on NGOs providing services in Portugal. It co-publishes a national directory of women's voluntary organisations *O Trabalho Voluntário*. There are now some organisations for one-parent families – *Casa de Santo Antonio*, *Lar Luía Canavarro*, and *Casa de Sant'Ana*. The *Cooperativa de Ensino Superior de Serviço Social* is the leading school of social work, carries out a role in local development in northern Portugal, and contributes to the national debate on social policy through its research work.

Spain

Political freedom since the death of General Franco in 1975 has given voluntary organisations in Spain (population: 39m) the scope both to expand their services and role, and to act and speak independently. During the post-Franco period, Spain developed its democratic institutions, adopted a new constitution (one, moreover, which recognised state responsibility for social security and health), and introduced social security provisions (though still far short of what would be expected in Britain). The transformation has been more than administrative. In the long Francoist period, social issues and the care of the poor were seen as the concern of family and church. Since then, Spain has been anxious both to modernise and to define a role for the state in social provision. The voluntary sector is going through a period of growth, with new, specialised campaigning groups coming to the fore.

Spain is a country of contrasts: a rich industrial sector, which makes Spain one of the wealthier countries in the European Communities; one of the highest unemployment rates in the EC (hovering around 15 per cent); a large hidden economy; and depopulating rural areas. Industries protected during the Franco period, such as coal-mining and textiles, have collapsed, and there has been substantial emigration to Germany, France, South America and Britain.

During the period 1980-8, social services in Spain were decentralised to 17 regions or autonomous communities (*autonomías*), following the enactment of the democratic constitution in 1978. Decentralisation reflected not only administrative convenience but recognition of powerful historic and cultural regional traditions. The parliaments of the autonomous regions have the right to pass legislation within their own sphere of competence. Most regions now have their own social security acts which lay down the general principles, organisational framework and details of social services in that region.

Voluntary bodies are, for the most part, organised on a regional and municipal basis: there are few national sectoral organisations. There is cross-party support for the primacy of voluntary organisations in the delivery of social services, the parties believing that such organisations are cheaper, more efficient and carry fewer permanent commitments than statutory services. The work of voluntary organisations and the standards of service provided are monitored and inspected by regional governments.

Although there has been a minimum wage for some time, a basic minimum income (*Renda Mínima Inserció*, RMI) for certain categories of the unemployed was introduced only in the past number of years. The minimum wage, and the RMI, now exist in most, but not all, regions; terms and conditions also vary in each region. To qualify, claimants must be over 25, be a separate family unit, fulfil a residency requirement of up to five years, and must attend courses; even then, it lasts only for two years and is not considered generous.

Voluntary organisations benefit from the 1 per cent of income tax which is earmarked for the Church or for charities (tax-payers can opt for either). Of the allocation for charities, roughly half goes to the Red Cross and Caritas. The funding pattern for voluntary organisations in Spain is as follows. National organisations can receive funding from the Ministry of Social Affairs in Madrid, regional organisations from the regional government, and local organisations from the municipal government. Voluntary organisations are expected to declare themselves as national, regional or local, and are funded accordingly, though some contrive to benefit from at least two of these three tiers of funding.

In practice, the regional governments and local governments are the main funders of social services and voluntary organisations. Regional governments generally fund primary social services, local government helping with specialised services. Lay voluntary organisations derive most of their resources from statutory funding: raising money in the streets or from cake sales is quite unusual. Religious charities take less statutory money, relying more on church resources and funding.

Church-based and National Organisations

There are three national organisations providing services throughout Spain: Caritas, the Red Cross, and ONCE (the national organisation for the blind).

The longest-standing Spanish non-governmental organisation is the church-based Caritas, which provides the bulk of services helping the poor. It has a national structure, although services are actually delivered on a diocesan and parish basis. Caritas has provided documentation on poverty and social policy in Spain for some time, and, because of its church links was in a position to be safely outspoken on these issues as far back as the 1960s. It provides services for elderly people and children, and shelters and work projects for homeless people and is the national organisation which works closest with minorities, gypsies and foreign migrants (mainly from Morocco, South America, the Philippines and the Gambia).

While Caritas is the main campaigning and research organisation in the area of poverty, social services are provided by other religious-based groups, such as the monastic orders, parish, community and lay groups. These groups include the Society of St Vincent de Paul, *Obra Mercedaria*, and *San Juan de Dios*. San Juan de Dios specialises in health services, help for mentally disabled children, and night shelters for the homeless. The Red Cross, while not having the church links of Caritas, is a national provider of social services, home help and aid to refugees.

Savings banks (Caixa de Pensions) are an important element. Facilitated by favourable tax treatment, they run social services, schools for the deaf, day centres for elderly people and disabled people, and provide housing. The *Confederación de Asociaciones de Vecinos de España* is the association of residents' associations. The Committee on Social Welfare is prestigious and meets twice a year in Madrid.

Organising for the Blind
ONCE, the national organisation for the blind, is considered one of the most successful and sophisticated organisations for the blind in Europe, even running its own radio station. It collects money through a national lottery sold in street booths by blind and disabled people, an approach which is criticised as old-fashioned although it is financially lucrative. Services for the blind and teaching for blind children in Spain are considered to be good by international standards.

Newer Organisations
In the past 15 years, new, secular campaigning organisations and providers of services have come into existence, as have a number of protestant charities (*L'Hora de Deu*, for example, and the Salvation Army, which have just begun to provide services). Many of the newer services for disabled people are based on groups of parents. The first of these was ASPANIAS (an acronym for Association of Parents in Spain), which began in Barcelona in the 1960s. Many local and regional groups are based on this model: groups such as ASPANIAS have expanded to employ social workers and start special schools. Self-help associations of elderly people, likewise, have proliferated. Even towns with

a population of only a few hundred people will have associations for elderly people.

Newer campaigning organisations include IRES, Justicia i Pau (*Justice and Peace*) and *SOS Racismo* (modelled on the French anti-racist organisation). IRES is the Instituto de Reinsercion Social (Institute for Social Rehabilitation) and arose in response to the lack of a probation service in Spain. It helps prisoners and young people in difficulty, and pioneered detached youth services in Spain. Despite the progress being made in Spain since democratisation, workers in voluntary organisations are still aware of many areas which require improvement. Areas cited most frequently include community development, care for people involved in substance abuse, services for the deinstitutionalised, probation, and aftercare. Some voluntary organisations have materialised to meet some of these needs. These include APAT, which helps alcoholics and drug addicts; MACI, the Movement for the Care of Children; *Asociacion Proyecto Hombre*, which runs therapeutic communities, and the *Institut Montserrat Montero*, which has pioneered rehabilitative work in Catalonia.

Recent Trends
Several national networking associations are now being established in Spain. These are for the unemployed, gypsies (*gitanos*, to which 34 groups are affiliated), people with learning difficulties, and the victims of AIDS. Three new specialised networks (*red* in Spanish) are in the process of formation, pertaining to substance abuse, human rights and migrants. There is a new group, *Organizaciones no Gubernamentales*, dedicated to the general promotion of the concerns of the voluntary sector, in which Caritas is involved.

Several voluntary organisations, including Caritas, have now become involved in co-operative projects for disabled people and local employment creation. While not as extensive as in Italy, these co-operatives have developed along similar lines, involving agriculture, recycling, painting and repair. These developments include an ex-prisoners' workers' co-operative. Amnesty International has a presence in Spain.

Further Information
Information on voluntary organisations is best sought on a regional level. Some savings banks provide guides to local voluntary services. The regional government in Catalonia provides a detailed guide to voluntary services in its region, called *Guia d'Entitats de Catalunya: associecions, fundacions, cooperatives* (ISBN 84-393-1316-0).

■ Generalitat de Catalunya, Departament de Justicia, Direcció General de Dret i d'Entitats Jurídiques, Barcelona.

ACEBO published in 1989 a description of voluntary organisations in Spain (*Organizaciones voluntarias e intervencion social*), with an analysis of their current state of development (ISBN 84-7103-221).

■ ACEBO, Villafranca del Bierzo 21, Fuenlabrada, Madrid.

The Spanish Committee of Social Welfare has a social affairs publications list. The National Association for Gypsies, PASS is an excellent source of information on social developments in Spain, particularly in the area of immigration and refugees. SIIS operates a large database on social welfare services and mental handicap, adapted to most computer systems now on the market. It has 25,000 references, growing at 7,000 a year. *Gabinet d'Estudis Socials* is a research group specialising in anti-poverty work.

■ SIIS, Reina Regente 5 bajo, 20003 Donostia, San Sebastian, Tel. 34 42 3656, Fax 34 29 3007.

■ Gabinet d'Estudis Socials, Arago 2°2°, Barcelona 08009, Tel. 343 487 3816, Fax 343 215 8815.

AUSTRIA AND SWITZERLAND

Austria

Austria, with a population of 7m people, is a neutral country. It applied to join the European Communities in 1989, though the country remains divided on the issue, fearing increased pressures on its environment and traditional ways of life. It has a developed welfare state and a strong tradition of social and economic planning through joint commissions (called parity commissions) of agriculture, trade unions and industry. The Austrian economy has consistently outperformed its European neighbours, combining rising standards of living with low rates of inflation and unemployment. Social services are delivered at federal, provincial level (there are nine provinces), and commune level. Community development work was a latecomer to Austria, being virtually unknown until the government recognised its importance in a policy document entitled *War on poverty* (1979), published by the Ministry for Social Affairs. As a result, the government introduced a regional and community development programme for the less developed regions of the country.

The Federal Ministry for Employment and Social Affairs publishes a comprehensive 300-page directory of voluntary organisations. Called *Österreich Sozial*, it lists voluntary organisations in each of the nine provinces, and then the national organisations (*zentralstellung*). They are subdivided into categories such as women's groups, elderly people, social justice organisations, disabled people, environment, family services and refugees.

- Bundesministerium für Arbeit und Soziales (Federal Ministry for Employment and Social Affairs), Stubenring 1, A. 1011 Vienna, Tel. 431 222 71100.

- Bundesministerium für Umwelt, Jugend, und Familie (Federal Ministry for the Environment, Youth and Family), Mahlerstraße 6, A. 1015 Vienna, Tel. 432 222 515 070.

Switzerland

Zealously guarding its neutrality, Switzerland (population: 7m) has stayed aloof from the mainstream developments of postwar European politics. Unlike the other European neutrals, it is not contemplating applying for membership of the European Communities. It is a federal state, governed in 22 cantons. The language most commonly used in Switzerland is German, followed by French (western cantons), and Italian (southern cantons). Often advertised as a model of decentralisation, Switzerland has been criticised for being politically backward, women's rights being recognised only belatedly. Switzerland's political isolation has not prevented it from being one of the economic success stories of Europe, with low unemployment, low inflation, and one of the highest standards of living in the world.

Despite that, social problems have persisted. Access to affordable housing is one, principally for immigrants and those on low pay. A number of small housing co-operatives have developed to meet their needs in recent years. In the 1960s and 1970s, what was termed 'the new social movement' (*neue soziale Bewegnung*) emerged, consisting of community action groups, self-help initiatives and environmental protection associations. Many of these were engaged in preserving the old quarters of towns from comprehensive redevelopment. Environmental protection associations concentrated their efforts on trying to clean up the chemical industry, air pollution, and the river Rhine. These groups reflect the political structure of the country, being organised principally on a canton, rather than a national, level. The main organisations which may be of interest to groups in Britain are the *Schweizerischer Verband für Wohnungswesen* (for housing co-operatives), *Pro Infirmis* (for disabled people), *Pro Juventute* (for child welfare), and Caritas. A list of Swiss federal social organisations is available in *Publicus 1990-1 - Annuaire Suisse de la vie publique*:

- Editions Schwabe & Co A.G., Basel.

233

The definitive study of voluntary organisations in Switzerland is *Intermediary Organisations in Switzerland*, by Stefan Rommelfanger. Its full title is *Bewohner beraten, Netze bilden, Organisationen entwickeln...Der Beitrag intermediärer Organisationen zur Entwicklung städtischer Quartiere in der Schweiz*:

■ Dortmunder Vertrieb für Bau- und Plannungsliteratur z.h. Rolf Froessler, Gutenbergstraße 59, 4600 Dortmund 1, Germany.

Up-to-date information on social developments from the perspective of the social work profession is available in the monthly review of the Swiss Association of Social Assistants (in French, the *Association Suisse des Assistants Sociaux Diplômés*, or in German, the *Schweizerischer Berufsverbund dipl. Sozialarbeiterinnen*). The review is called *Travail Sociale* (French version), or *Sozial Arbeit* (German):

■ Association Suisse des Assistants Sociaux Diplômés/Schweizerischer Berufsverbund dipl. Sozialarbeiterinnen, Hopfenweg 21, Postfach, 3000 Bern 14, Tel. 41 31 45 5421, Fax 41 31 45 5466.

FINLAND AND SWEDEN

Finland

There are numerous voluntary organisations in Finland (population: 5m), concentrated on several specific fields of work: child welfare, disability, refugees, and the care of elderly people. Perhaps the most important national umbrella group is the Finnish Federation for Social Security and Social Welfare (*Sosiaaliturvan Keskuslitto* – established 1917). It is a large federation, grouping 209 local authorities, 73 voluntary organisations and 6 trade unions. It is active in policy-making, promoting voluntary-statutory co-operation, information distribution, and the improvement of services. It now has a Euro bureau. Voluntary organisations in Finland are regulated by legislation dating back to 1919, amended in 1989, which lays down procedures for founding an organisation, a model constitution and auditing arrangements.

Voluntary organisations are politically active in Finland: they have good contacts with MPs, some of whom sit on their boards. Voluntary organisations concerned with social issues have formed their own pressure group, the Association of Voluntary Health and Social Welfare Organisations (YTY), which employs a lawyer. It has 98 members, of whom 29 are health organisations, 16 child welfare groups, 26 bodies working with disabled people, 10 caring for elderly people, and 10 engaged in vacation activities.

This breakdown gives an accurate indication on those areas where the Finnish voluntary sector is most active.

The Central Union for the Welfare of the Aged has 220 member organisations throughout the country, providing services and homes for elderly people. It comments on government policy and legislation, and is currently developing new services in the areas of sheltered housing and 24-hour home-help services. The Finnish Association on Mental Retardation (established 1952) has over 60 member organisations: it promotes research and develops housing and rehabilitation services. The Finnish Association of the Deaf (established 1905) is the oldest organisation of people with learning difficulties and has 4,200 members: it campaigns for publicly-funded interpreting and the recognition of the status of sign language, and is exploring the possibilities of the new technologies for the deaf.

The National Association of the Disabled (established 1938) has 140 member organisations, 50,000 members and over 50 centres of activity. It provides information services, vocational training, counselling, rehabilitation, and sporting and holiday programmes. The Council co-operates with the Nordic Council for the Handicapped, Rehabilitation International, and the International Council on Social Welfare. International co-operation of this nature is not unusual. For example, since 1907 the Finnish Association of the Deaf has worked with counterpart organisations in Denmark, Sweden, Iceland, Norway and the Faroe Islands to form the Northern Council for the Deaf. The Red Cross (established 1877), besides its many activities in social services, rescue and disaster relief, works with prisoners and refugees, and is now running pilot projects with AIDS patients.

Gambling with the Social Services

Voluntary organisations in Finland are funded by gambling! A substantial part of their money comes through the Slot Machine Association (RAY) (established 1938), which is owned by 80 non-governmental organisations. RAY has a monopoly on slot machines in the country, and they can be found in restaurants, bars, service stations and supermarkets (RAY is also one of the biggest world suppliers of machines). In 1990, 646 voluntary organisations received 758m Finnish marks from the profits on slot machines.

General information on the work of voluntary organisations in Finland and listings of the principal NGOs are available from the Finnish Federation for Social Security and Social Welfare (*Sosiaaliturvan Keskusliitto*) and from the National Agency for Welfare and Health. The Ministry of Social Affairs and Health has an English language publication about Finland's social services (*Social Security and Health Care in Finland*). Many of the main NGOs also put out first-rate English-language summaries of their work.

Sweden

The modern Swedish state (population: 8m) was largely constructed on nineteenth-century voluntary organisations, called popular movements. These popular movements of the last century – such as the trade unions, the free church movement, adult education societies, sports bodies and the teetotallers movement – are, together with the main political parties, regarded as the elements which built the Swedish nation. Their historical role is still respected today in the manner in which these movements participate in the political process: their views are always solicited when legislation is being prepared and new government policies are being contemplated. Voluntary organisations devote considerable time and energy to this process: the scouting movement, for example, might comment on legislation up to 15 times a year. Voluntary organisations therefore engage actively in the political process, and much of what they say is listened to. Even secondary schools students are organised into an association (with their own 'parliament'); they played an active role in recent educational reforms.

Voluntary organisations in Sweden fill what might be termed a niche role – they carry out specialised tasks in a society considered to have the most comprehensive level of welfare services in the world. Unemployment in Sweden is only 1 per cent. Sweden has the highest rate of female participation in the labour force in the world. There is a high wage – and the span between that wage and the well-paid is quite narrow. Thus the role of voluntary organisations focuses on specific issues and groups: one area where voluntary organisations are especially strong is in the field of disability and handicap, and in campaigning for services dedicated to particular groups in need (cerebral palsy being one example).

Some of the main voluntary organisations in Sweden include:

- Salvation Army (*Frälsingsarmén*), which helps homeless people;

- Save the Children (*Rädda Barnen*);

- Red Cross (*Röda Korset*);

- *Fångarnas Riksförbund*, the trade union for prisoners;

- Consumers movement (*Konsumenternas Riksverbund*);

- *Yrkeskvinnors klub*, for the advancement of women's issues; and

- Swedish Pensioners Association (*Sveriges Pensionäersförbund*).

All this is not to say that Sweden has somehow 'solved' all its social problems – far from it. Rural depopulation remains a serious problem, and rural community development has been neglected. Sweden is considered to

236

have a generous policy for refugees, but a restricted immigration policy. Up to 800,000 Finns work in Sweden, and they are the largest single group of migrant workers; they are followed by the Yugoslavs and the Greeks. Although there is a central immigrants' organisation, each ethnic group also has its own association. The government has now appointed an Ombudsman (the word originated in Sweden) for racial equality. Another group which has generated interest in recent years is the archive worker. Sweden has operated a Freedom of Information Act since 1760, which requires that all government documents are kept and available to citizens. However the monumental filing work that this entails is done by psychiatric patients and people deemed 'unemployable', who are compulsorily employed as archive clerks with little remuneration.

Sweden has applied to join the EC: membership of the Communities was the central theme of the autumn 1991 general election.

CENTRAL EUROPEAN COUNTRIES AND THE CIS

Voluntary Organisations in Central Europe and the CIS

There has been a significant expansion in the voluntary sector in central Europe since the advent of *glasnost* (openness) and *perestroika* (structural transformation) since 1985. The pace of change accelerated rapidly when revolution convulsed all the central European countries in 1989 and the Soviet Union in 1991. Information on voluntary organisations in central Europe is, at this stage, still fragmentary. A clearer, and more comprehensive, picture will undoubtedly emerge over the next few years.

There is a sense in which the voluntary sector never entirely disappeared during the 1945-91 period. Voluntary organisations and societies continued to play a role in the delivery of health and social services; small voluntary associations – many linked to the churches – retained a critical capacity to comment on state services in the health and social field.

The voluntary sector in central Europe is likely to grow in importance over the next number of years. The rapid transition to a market economy is certain to mean that many people, formerly protected by state income support and full employment, will find themselves in acute need for a basic income and for housing. These are expected to be the greatest areas of future social need. Gaps in provision may well be filled by voluntary services which now have full political and economic freedom in which to operate. The growth in non-governmental organisations in the post-1985 period has been uneven. It has been most spectacular in three countries: Hungary, Poland, and the CIS (formerly the USSR), especially its largest republic, Russia.

Many of the new NGOs call themselves 'foundations' or 'social associations'. The term 'voluntary organisation' is not one they would readily recognise. The most prominent sectors of activity for the new central European NGOs are health, environmental action, elderly people and disability.

Barriers that formerly regulated contacts between NGOs in western and central Europe are likely to disappear; indeed some have already done so. Central European NGOs probably need the help of western ones more than the other way round: they will be anxious to learn about how NGOs function, are managed, provide services, and relate to their respective governments. West European NGOs may well see central European NGOs as a source of information on social developments there, not least in the area of migration. Frightening estimates have been given of the numbers of people anxious to migrate westwards in search of work as economic prospects decline and the ready availability of passports make freer movement easier.

The role of voluntary organisations in central Europe and the CIS is now the focus of a spirited public debate. During the pre-*perestroika* period, concepts of charity and voluntary organisations were generally treated with suspicion, either because they did jobs which the state, acting on behalf of all citizens, should now do; or because they were a stalking horse for political dissent. There was a firm political conviction that health care and social services should be national political responsibilities, and people should not be left to the whim and mercy of charity.

The emergence of non-governmental organisations in the CIS after 1985, and in central Europe after the revolutions of 1989, is regarded by many in the field as a mixed blessing. It is regarded positively because of their contribution to political pluralism: views and ideas stifled for many years can now find open organisational expression. Social needs that were denied or ignored for decades can now be addressed by NGOs. On the other hand, there is widespread consternation resulting from the dislocation caused by the move to market economies, and the appearance of mass unemployment, hunger and homelessness, phenomena generally absent from the much criticised postwar communist societies. NGOs know that they can produce only a limited response to these problems.

Obtaining information on voluntary organisations in central Europe and the CIS is inherently more difficult than in the western Europe countries. Exchange schemes with central Europe and the CIS are not yet well developed; their languages are little taught in the schools (Russian has a different alphabet as well); and the voluntary sector there is only now springing into life after many years of suppression. So what are the routes and avenues into central Europe and Russia?

Long before *glasnost*, a variety of western bodies and institutes studied the political, economic and social conditions of central Europe and the CIS. Several sponsored academic journals which may be useful for those anxious to gain a fuller, more up-to-date understanding of developments in Russia and central Europe. CEDUCEE (Centre d'Étude et de Documentation sur l'URSS, la Chine, et l'Europe de l'est, Documentation française) keeps a list of west European research institutes and bodies concerned with central Europe and the CIS, including 10 in the UK.

■ CEDUCEE, quai Voltaire 29, 75340 Paris Cedex 07, France, Tel. 331 4015 7000, Fax 331 4015 7230.

Organisations in Britain Promoting Contact with Central Europe and the CIS, Including Russia

Several organisations in Britain promote contact with central Europe and the CIS:

- the respective embassies;

- the various friendship societies; and

- associations devoted to greater contact between Britain and these countries.

Some British organisations promote contact with the voluntary sector in central Europe and the CIS as part of their general work in furthering the exchange of information, people and ideas.

The Society for Cultural Relations with the USSR (established 1924) offers Russian language courses, library and information services, and contact with organisations in the CIS itself. An educational trust offers small grants for people travelling to the CIS for educational or cultural purposes.

■ Society for Cultural Relations with the USSR, 320 Brixton Road, London SW9 6AB, Tel. 071 274 2282.

The Prince's Trust, London, runs a *Go and see* programme which pays small grants to individuals to make fact-finding or partner-locating visits to European countries (including central Europe).

■ Anne Engel, Prince's Trust, 8 Bedford Row, London WC1R 4BA, Tel. 071 430 0524, Fax 071 831 7280.

A rationalisation has taken place in the manner in which western European organisations are building up contacts with central Europe. There was a danger that the major organisations in each country would independently attempt to set up competing bilateral relationships with central Europe, thus duplicating resources and causing confusion. As a result of this rationalisation, it was agreed that the Charities Aid Foundation, acknowledged experts on contact with central Europe, would deal with the voluntary sector in the Czech and Slovak Federal Republic; the Fondation de France in Poland; and the European Cultural Foundation in Hungary. The Fondation de France office in Warsaw has already opened. In the case of the Czech and Slovak Federal Republic, the Charities Aid Foundation has teamed up with the Charter 77 Foundation, the Civic Forum Foundation, the Committee of Goodwill and the Czechoslovak Council for Humanitarian Co-operation to set up its Prague office.

■ Charities Aid Foundation, 48 Penbury Road, Tonbridge, Kent, Tel. 0732 771 333, Fax 0732 350 570.

■ Charities Aid Foundation, Ul 28 Rijna 5, 110 00 Prague 1, Czech and Slovak Federal Republic, Tel. 422 260 163.

Organisations in the United States Promoting Contact with Central Europe and the CIS

Another route to central Europe goes through the United States, partly because of the large number of emigrés with central European and Russian connections who have settled there in the past 20 years. The Hungarian-born American financier George Soros established foundations in the United States devoted to an improvement in east-west relations. These foundations cover Hungary, Bulgaria, Yugoslavia, Poland (the Stefan Batory Foundation), the Czech and Slovak Federal Republic, Rumania and Russia. Their work is linked to that of the Open Society Foundation in the United States.

■ Open Society Foundation, 888 Seventh Avenue (33rd floor), New York, New York 10106, Tel. 1 212 397 5563, Fax 1 212 974 0367.

The Foundation of Social Innovation (FSI) USA was established in June 1989 to promote contact with Russia in the social field. Its declared aims are 'to foster the development of an independent non-profit sector charitable sector in the USSR, eastern Europe and other countries of the process of profound social restructuring'. FSI (USA) is a partner with FSI (USSR) which was founded in 1986 by Novosibirsk geophysicist Gennadiy Alferenko. FSI(USSR) operates from the newspaper offices of *Komsomolskaya Pravda* where he is special correspondent. Connections between voluntary organisations and the media are by no means unusual, as many voluntary organisations have emerged as a result of the critical social commentaries of newspapers, radio and television. Gennadiy Alferenko organised the first legally established independent youth organisation in Russia in modern times. FSI (USSR) has branch offices in Yakutia and Yerevan in Armenia and plans more in St Petersburg, Kiev (Ukraine), and Magadan (Siberia). A database of Soviet voluntary organisations is now being compiled, with listings of agencies and regions.

Affiliated organisations in the first year of FSI (USSR) included environmental action groups, the association for the struggle against AIDS, and two associations for deaf people.

■ Foundation for Social Innovations (USA), 3220 Sacramento Street, San Francisco, CA 94115, Tel. 1 415 931 2593, Fax 1 415 931 0948.

■ Foundation for Social Innovations (USSR), Yaroslavskaya Street Building, 129243 Moscow.

A United States initiative on central Europe was announced by President Bush in May 1990. This involves the transfer to central Europe of the skills necessary for the building of democratic institutions, the economic infrastructure and entrepreneurial know-how. The encouragement of voluntary organisations is one aspect of this programme. Further information on the development of the initiative, and its newsletter *Focus on central and eastern Europe*, are availble from:

■ Office of Public Communication, Room 6805, Department of State, Washington, DC 20520-6810, Tel. 1 202 647 6316.

Every two years, the Institute for Soviet-American relations publishes a handbook of national non-profit organisations engaged in Soviet-American relations, including a listing of prominent Soviet national organisations. It costs $27.50, from the Institute.

■ Institute of Soviet-American Relations, 1601 Connecticut Avenue NW, (suite 301), Washington, DC 20009, Tel. 1 202 387 3034, Fax 1 202 667 3291.

Environmental groups in the CIS can be contacted through the *Soviet environmental directory*, available for $27.50.

■ Kompass Resources International, 1430 K Street NW (Suite 1200), Washington, DC 20005.

The CIS, Including Russia

The advent of glasnost brought to the surface problems of social deprivation that had been hidden, glossed over, or ignored for the long years of the Brezhnev era (1964-82). These problems were first exposed by the campaigning media, and the work of journalists encouraged voluntary organisations to spring up in response. Newspapers highlighted appalling conditions in children's homes, the sufferings of alcoholics and their families, and the lack of facilities for war veterans disabled in the course of the conflict in Afghanistan.

Social issues, social services and social spending had long been made a low priority in a country geared almost entirely to industrial and agricultural output. Problems such as family break-up, ecological disaster, and the alienation of the young were not even acknowledged, still less written about.

Voluntary organisations did not disappear entirely during the period between the revolution (1917) and perestroika (1985). A limited number of pre-revolutionary associations persisted after 1917, though they were tightly monitored. Three long-standing Soviet NGOs were the Red Cross, the temperance movement, and Timoor (the association of war widows).

Social action was considered important in post-revolutionary society: citizens were expected to work voluntarily on special projects and give up pay for good causes. Once a year, all the workforce would do a day's voluntary work on social projects – these were called *subbotniks* – and young people went on workcamps for longer periods. Enthusiasm for these forms of voluntary action was considered an important test for membership of the Communist Party of the Soviet Union (CPSU) and an integral part of citizenship of the nation. Some critical social discussion survived in the two large Soviet adult education bodies – the *Knowledge Society* and the *People's Universities*. Voluntary organisations were called 'social organisations' in Russia, and their role was referred to positively in the 1977 Constitution. A permit was needed to establish a social organisation on a formal basis.

Social welfare services were always planned and delivered by each of the 15 republics – there was no centralised Soviet department of social services. Personal social services were delivered by district social security departments and by the workplace. Self-help groups were unusual, except for elderly people, where pensioners' councils have existed for some time. Social work was not a recognised profession in the USSR: welfare workers came from backgrounds in law, bookkeeping or economics.

'There are No Disabled People in the USSR'
In the late 1970s, an action group for the defence of the rights of the disabled emerged, but it was harassed: its leaders were exiled. An account of its struggle was subsequently written by founder member Valeri Fefelov with

the illustrative title of *There are no disabled people in the USSR*. Ten million people are now thought to be disabled in the CIS. National groups of disabled people are coming together to campaign for access to buildings and employment opportunities: the two most prominent are the Russian Disabled People's Society and the Moscow Disabled People's Organisation. The Russian Federation of the Deaf is also active. Likewise, confidential phone line services for self-help groups, although first proposed in 1979, encountered many predictable bureaucratic hurdles before they were up and running.

Russian voluntary organisations see information as one of the key elements in the building of the infrastructure of the new voluntary sector. The perversion of information about social conditions by the state has been one of the underlying problems for many years. A new organisation set up to meet this need is Postfactum, a network of independent information agencies in Russia. Another new NGO, linked to Postfactum, is the Volunteer Centre on Prison and Freedom, which does research and practical work to help people in prison and those who have just been released.

Voluntary organisations concerned with the environment were among the first to organise in Russia. Even during the 1960s there were 'conservationist teams': these had a limited political role, but they managed to survive by adopting what they termed a reticular structure (one without identifiable steering bodies or identifiable leaders). New, post-glasnost environmental groups are aggressive: the earliest was a student vigilante group in the Caucasus which first encouraged the idea of a national environmental organisation. This was eventually set up in December 1988 when the Social and Ecological Union was formed, comprising 140 environmental clubs, committees and societies from 89 cities and 11 republics.

Hungary

Voluntary organisations developed quickly after the political thaw in Hungary (population: 10m) in the mid-1980s. There had been a strong organisational life in Hungary prior to 1948 (in fact there were as many as 40,000 associations in the pre-war period), when most of it was forced underground. Some organisations survived thanks to the protection of the churches.

Among the NGOs which rose to prominence in the late 1980s were the greens, who stopped a project to dam the Danube (the Danube circle), and their radical offshoot, who called themselves the 'blues'! Many of the new NGOs were political and emerged from the underground, such as Democratic Forum, but others were concerned with legal rights, such as the Independent service for legal protection, and the Raul Wallenberg Association (for the rights of minorities and gypsies). Another illegal body was the Foundation for Supporting the Poor, *Szeta*, which, dedicated to helping the homeless, the unemployed and gypsies, operated from 1979 as an underground information exchange network (*samizhdat*), but is now a legal foundation.

The government of the Republic of Hungary legalised foundations and associations over the period 1988-9. As a result, several hundred foundations and several thousand associations materialised in the following two years. There is now an association devoted to community development. Homeless people, banned from sleeping in railway stations, have revolted to form a Social Committee for the Homeless. An independent organisation for gypsies has also been formed, and some fledgling women's groups are in the process of getting going. In May 1990, over 80 foundations concerned with social and cultural development came together to form a federation of Hungarian foundations, and there is a Foundation for the Creation of Local Social Networks.

■ Federation of Hungarian Foundations, Budapest, Rottenbiller u.61-22, H.1074 Tel. 361 122 1488.

■ The Women's Information Service of the European Commission has published *Women of Hungary*, by Eva Eberhardt. It is a timely description of the economic and social situation facing women in the country. It is a supplement to the *Women of Europe* series. Commission of the European Communities, Women's Information Section, rue de la loi 200, B.1049 Brussels, Tel. 322 235 9772.

Poland

The population of Poland is 38m. Social problems were not acknowledged in the period before the Solidarity government. Television has, since 1989, played an important role in exposing the whole gamut of social problems concealed by postwar governments. Among the issues revealed were the victims of industrial accidents, the level of AIDS, the lack of school books, overcrowded housing, lack of wheelchairs for disabled people, and the radiation damage inflicted on Poland by the Chernobyl nuclear cloud.

As was the case in the CIS, the first post-glasnost non-governmental associations to set up were environmental. By the time of the election of the Solidarity government in 1989, about 150 non-governmental organisations had come into existence. They ranged from large, national groups with a million members to very small, single-issue local campaigns. Like fellow campaigns in central Europe and Russia, their work was and is hindered by poor telephone services and lack of photocopying and printing equipment. The legacy of the old regime continues to impede the development of NGOs in Poland: Poles are unused to working together in free associations, suspect there may be spies in their midst, prefer to send letters by hand, and distrust the banks with their money.

There are over 70 environmental organisations in Poland, most of them very political in their approach. This should be no surprise, considering the awful levels of industrial contamination in the country. Krakow, its most polluted city, is the base for many. The two principal environmental organisations in Poland are *Wole Bye* and the more radical *Wolnosc i Pokoj*.

Until 1989, the main providers of social services in Poland were the state and the catholic church, the latter running institutions for people with learning difficulties. The church is likely to remain the core of voluntary endeavour in Poland for some time. Caritas existed prior to 1939, survived under the communist regime, and is now in the process of reconstruction. It provides children's homes. The Sue Ryder Foundation has 28 homes in Poland.

The vast majority of new NGOs are city-based, but some are either national or have aspirations to be national. One, called the SOS fund, is rooted in Solidarity and the Citizens' Committees which sustained it during the period of martial law in the early 1980s. SOS has brought together a number of voluntary initiatives, including voluntary services for disabled people, elderly people, haemophiliacs, the deaf and sick children. It provides free meals for the poor. It was set up by a government minister, Jack Kuron, in his spare time, and it is based in the Ministry of Labour and Social Policy. Some of the new organisations include the Foundation for Economic and Social Initiatives, which promotes local employment initiatives; the Brother Albert Aid Society (which helps the homeless and prisoners); Monar (emergency services for the homeless, help for AIDS victims, campaign against drug abuse); the Society for the Protection of Children (equivalent to NSPCC); and the Mother Theresa Missionaries of Charity. Some of the new foundations and social associations raise funds by selling produce; the dividing line between charity and enterprise is not always clear.

Among the foundations established by George Soros is one for Poland – the Stefan Batory Foundation. Its aims include the promotion of social development, research, language training and economic reconstruction. There are now over a thousand foundations in Poland. At a conference sponsored by the Polish Ministry of Labour and Social Affairs in Gdansk in 1990, voluntary organisations present decided to set up an independent council of voluntary organisations. Work was under way on a Polish Foundations Forum during 1991. British voluntary organisations having contact with Poland include:

- VSO, which has sent teachers to Poland;

- Medical Aid for Poland;

- Ockenden Venture;

- PHAB;

- Mobility International; and

- Sue Ryder Foundation.

Some help Poland directly with material aid. Ockenden Venture sends clothing to Poland; Medical Aid for Poland, inspired by doctors, has sent over 270 trucks of medical supplies. Ten British towns or regions are twinned with Polish towns; their local authorities could be a useful point of contact with Poland. These are: Ross and Cromarty (Krosno), Strathclyde (Lodz), Plymouth (Gdynia), Carlisle (Slupsk), Doncaster (Gliwice), Preston (Kalisz), Newark (Mielec), Coventry (Warsaw), and Cleveland (Szczecin).

Rumania, Bulgaria, Czech and Slovak Federal Republic

Little information is available on non-governmental organisations in Rumania. Few survived the Ceaucescu dictatorship which began in the 1960s and fell in the bloody revolution of December 1989.

Similarly, the role of voluntary organisations in Bulgaria was limited, there being only some foundations for disabled people and to help alcoholics. An environmental protest movement came to prominence in the late 1980s, called *Ecoglasnost*. For years, there was one national foundation concerned with social issues, the Lyudmila Zhivkov International Foundation, named after the wife of the Communist ruler.

Voluntary organisations were limited in the Czech and Slovak Federal Republic, although the Red Cross survived the communist governments of 1948-89, albeit under state control and supervision: other voluntary organisations were subsumed into the National Front in 1951. Its monopoly was challenged from the late 1970s onwards by campaigning environmental organisations, such as the Czech Nature Protection Union and the Slovak Nature Protection Union, several of which were, initially at least, illegal. There has been a rapid expansion of Czechoslovakian NGOs since 1989.

7

Information on Europe and How to Get It

There is an abundance of information sources concerning Europe in general, and the European Communities in particular. Even in an information age, it is an information-rich environment. This would suggest that for voluntary organisations, obtaining information about Europe would be a straightforward task. Not so. Of the vast output of information, publications, statistics and data coming out of the European Communities, only a small proportion is likely to be immediately relevant, and finding out where and how to get that information is the all-important task in hand. Not only that, but finding out the most appropriate form in which to get information is also crucial, whether that be through subscription, information office, library, or even electronically.

This chapter describes how the institutions of the European Communities make themselves known in Britain, and introduces their European Documentation Centres (EDCs). It lists some government bodies, and then private and non-governmental organisations providing information about developments in the European Communities. The chapter reviews the types of information sources that are available concerning Europe, such as books and literature, publications and information services of the Communities and their specialised programmes; titles of the other European institutions, like the Council of Europe and the OECD; and publications by voluntary organisations, journals and magazines. Finally, there is a look at the possibilities for voluntary organisations communicating through electronic mail (e-mail).

GRAPPLING WITH THE
INFORMATION ISSUE

People who rush out to collect anything and everything on Europe are likely to find themselves rapidly overloaded. Careful investment in information choices at the early stage of European involvement can prove to be well worthwhile. Some organisations believe that they must travel to Europe to find information, or join a European network in order to receive timely information about developments in the European Communities. Doing these things may give the organisation a better 'feel' for Europe, but this is not strictly necessary purely in order to obtain information. It is possible to be an armchair expert on Europe without going there, but by choosing information sources carefully instead. Having said that, it is certainly true that some representatives of voluntary organisations will make a point of going to conferences to pick up reports, documents and unpublished 'grey' literature. Generally, this is not because such information will never be obtainable, but largely to get hold of it sooner rather than later.

Choosing the right information sources early on requires balancing five different elements: cost, quality, focus, volume and speed. These criteria are worth elaborating. Some information is free, and useful; some free, but not very valuable. Some information is expensive, but available free in other places for nothing; some expensive, not available elsewhere, and worth paying for. Some information is very up-to-date (days old, at most); but invariably some publications will present the same information as red-hot news months later! A voluntary organisation needs to consider its ability to handle information as it comes in – there is no point in obtaining current information if it is not read speedily. Quality is the other issue: although most information is well written and accurate, some betrays the fact that it has been translated from a different, original language.

A voluntary organisation can build up a library from free publications – but it may find that large amounts of the information are repetitive, and not very informative on those issues that it is concerned with the most: allowing price alone to determine what one should receive is probably unwise. The really sharp political operators will spot opportunities for action, or even test cases, in original texts of legislation – opportunities that may escape journalists' summaries. One approach is to combine a mixture of the general material on EC developments, with some sources providing original documents, together with specialised publications covering those matters of greatest concern to the organisation itself. Finally, EC publications will tell you what the EC institutions are thinking and doing: they will not tell you the perspectives of the networks and the voluntary organisations on current European developments.

■ Chapter 5 of this volume, under each network, for listings of publications of the different networks.

Perhaps the most comprehensive analysis of European information from the viewpoint of people interested in social affairs is provided by *Assignation*, the ASLIB Social Sciences Information Group Newsletter (ISSN 0265.2587). Vol. 8 no.4 is devoted entirely to information sources on social issues in Europe.

■ Assignation, National Institute for Social Work, 5 Tavistock Place, London WC1H 9SS, Tel. 071 387 9681.

In order to help the EC-observer come to terms with the specific terminology and the acronyms of the European Communities, Rosters Ltd has published, in association with the Consumers in the European Community Group, an instructive, highly readable paperback, *1992: Eurospeak explained* (price: £5.95, ISBN 1-85631-001-9).

■ Rosters Ltd, 23 Welbeck Street, London W1.

HOW THE EUROPEAN COMMUNITIES MAKE THEMSELVES KNOWN IN BRITAIN

The European Parliament and the European Commission have offices in London, but only the Commission has offices out of London. In London, access to the Commission office is limited, but the Parliament office has a small, well-equipped library and reading room (open 10-1, 2-5). Information material is on display, with brochures, leaflets and videos. Most Commission and Parliament offices have general information and publicity brochures and leaflets available. Enquiries can also be made by phone, and the office will help people try and get in contact with their MEP. It can in any case send out a list of the 81 UK members of the European Parliament, or the 24 members of the Economic and Social Committee.

■ UK information office of the European Parliament, 2 Queen Anne's Gate, London SW1H 9AA, Tel. 071 222 0411, Fax 071 222 2713.

■ Irish office of the European Parliament, Jean Monet Centre, 43 Molesworth Street, Dublin 2, Tel. 353 1 719 100, Fax 353 1 6795 391.

■ Commission of the European Communities, 8 Storey's Gate, London SW1P 3AT, Tel. 071 222 8122, Fax 071 222 0900.

■ 7 Alva Street, Edinburgh EH2 3AT, Tel. 031 225 2058, Fax 031 226 4105.

■ 4 Cathedral Road, Cardiff CF1 9SG, Tel. 0222 371 631, Fax. 0222 395489.

■ Windsor House, 9-15 Bedford Street, Belfast BT2 7EG, Tel. 0232 240 708, Fax 0232 248 241.

■ Jean Monnet Centre, 39 Molesworth Street, Dublin 2, Tel. 353 1 712 244, Fax 353 1 712 657.

The Parliament's office houses the London office of the British Labour Group in the European Parliament (Tel. 071 222 2719) and the Conservative group (Tel. 071 222 1720).

The Commission publishes a concise, to-the-point free-of-charge news-sheet called *The week in Europe* reviewing the main developments in Europe each week (sometimes more frequently). It is a single page, printed on both sides, designed for journalists. Forthcoming EC council meetings and conferences are previewed. It is available, on request, from the Commission office.

The work of the Parliament is reviewed in *EP News* which is a popular, monthly, four-page broadsheet with photographs and diagrams outlining the main parliamentary developments, debates and issues in Strasbourg. The English language edition covers those matters raised by British and Irish MEPs. It is available on request from the London office of the European Parliament.

The European Documentation Centres (EDCs)

The Commission offices are supplied with all the publications of the European Commission. In addition, the EC institutions reach arrangements with a number of universities and polytechnics to stock all their publications. One condition is attached to this arrangement, namely that these publications are available to the public. Places that receive the documentation of the European Communities are termed European Documentation Centres, or EDCs. There are now over 300 EDCs, of which 44 are in the UK.

For voluntary organisations, EDCs offer a number of advantages. EDCs must take *all* documentation coming from the institutions, so (in theory at least) all the publications of the European Communities should be there. This means that voluntary or community organisations can scrutinise such information, and perhaps decide to take up subscriptions after judging the relevance of publications for themselves. Library staff will also be helpful in guiding visitors around the collection. Social affairs information will, of course, be available in EDCs as much as any other category of information.

The principal disadvantage of this walk-in approach to European information is that the quality of EDCs varies. Some EDCs sort and box their material in more attractive ways than others, making it easier or harder to find. Some EDCs can be overwhelmed by the volume of incoming information and as a result are slow to shelve material. This means that although EC publications may arrive on time, there may be delays before they appear on the shelves.

EDCs in Britain include:

■ *Universities* – Aberdeen, Bath, Queen's Belfast, Birmingham, Bradford, Sussex, Brighton, Bristol, Cambridge, Colchester (Essex), Coventry (Warwick), Dundee, Durham, Edinburgh, Exeter, Glasgow, Guildford (Surrey), Hull, Keele, Canterbury (Kent), Coleraine (co. Derry), Lancaster, Leeds, Leicester, QMC London, Loughborough, Manchester, Norwich (East Anglia), Nottingham, Bodleian (Oxford), Reading, Salford, Southampton.

■ *Polytechnics* – Birmingham, Leeds, North London, Newcastle, Sheffield, Wye College (Ashford).

Sign-post Europe Pilot Information Centre

The European Commission, partly to prevent the overloading of its own offices with information enquiries, and partly to make itself more accessible to the regions, encourages people to use the EDCs. It has now established other means of channelling enquiries. A pilot scheme in Newcastle-upon-Tyne is under way to facilitate people in the north, called Sign-post Europe.

■ Sign-post Europe, Princes Building, 11 Akenside Hill, Newcastle-upon-Tyne NE1 3XP, Tel. 091 232 5545.

Euro-Info-Centres and Business and Innovation Centres

For the benefit of small and medium-size enterprises (SMEs), the Commission has set up 21 European Information Centres (Euro-Info-Centres) in Britain, part of 211 Euro-info-centres in the Twelve. A list is available from the European Commission office in London (press release of 17 June 1991). Eight Business and Innovation Centres (BICs) have been located in what the EC terms 'declining industrial areas'; again, specifically to help SMEs. The UK ones are in Barnsley, Calderdale, Cardiff, Cheshire, Derry, Clwyd, Lancashire and Strathclyde. Six hundred SMEs are now being linked together by a Business Co-operation Network, BC-Net, not only in the EC, but in central Europe and the EFTA countries. These networks may be of interest to voluntary organisations engaged in employment creation projects, or as an introduction to other EC programmes and sources of information and advice. Euro-info-centres sometimes hold workshops on general EC matters, and these could be a useful introduction for voluntary organisations anxious to pick up general information about the EC. The Euro-info-centres handled more than 150,000 enquiries in 1990. Helping SMEs is a Commission priority: there are 13m SMEs in the EC, comprising two-thirds of its workforce.

The Department of Trade and Industry

The Department of Trade and Industry issues *Single Market News*.

■ Hotline Tel. 081 200 1992.

It provides publications which will be chiefly of interest to the business community. The Department has available 35 'fact lists' on different aspects of the EC (including one entitled 'The Social Dimension'); and a booklet, regularly updated, on progress toward the completion of the single market (Tel. 071 215 4614). Videos are also obtainable.

The Department of Education and Science

The Department of Education and Science (DES) provides general information and a briefing pack on the EC's education programmes.

■ Department of Education and Science – International Relations Division, Grove House, 2-8 Orange Street, London WC2H 7WE, Tel. 071 321 0433.

The Council of Europe in the UK

■ The Council of Europe has a London Press and Information Office: Tel. 071 720 8781.

ORGANISATIONS PROMOTING INFORMATION ABOUT THE EUROPEAN COMMUNITIES

Europe sans Frontières

Europe sans frontières is the promotional department for Europe of the Confederation of British Industry (CBI). The CBI opened a Brussels office even before Britain joined the European Communities in 1973, and liaises there with the European institutions, the UK Permanent Representation, and the Union of Industrial and Employers' Confederations of Europe (UNICE).

Europe sans frontières is an information service for business, covering European policy issues, and giving early warning of discussions and decisions that may affect business (either positively or adversely). Topics covered include legislation, the social dimension to 1992 and training for industry. The service consists of an information pack, action checklists, and quarterly supplements to bring the information up to date. The annual subscription costs £120 for a non-member.

■ European Affairs Department, Confederation of British Industry, Centre Point, 103 New Oxford Street, London WC1A 1DU, Tel. 071 379 7400, Fax 071 240 1578.

Scottish Community Education Council (SCEC)

SCEC has supported exchange work in Scotland for a number of years, and has promoted training, information and study visits. The Council provides *Eurodesk*, an information service for local authorities, education and training services, and voluntary organisations. It is funded by the Convention of Scottish Local Authorities (COSLA), the Human Resources section of the European Commission, by the Central Bureau for Educational Visits and Exchanges, and privately (through Apple Computers). The service provides information on developments in the European institutions and new programmes, concentrating on education, training and youth. *Eurodesk* includes an alerting service which brings clients up to date with particular developments they have asked to be monitored. About 300 organisations subscribe to *Eurodesk* and its bimonthly magazine *Scan*. Subscription costs between £25 and £100 a year, according to category.

■ Eurodesk, Scottish Community Education Council, West Coates House, 90 Haymarket Terrace, Edinburgh EH12 5LQ, Tel. 031 313 2488, Fax 031 313 2477.

The Local Government International Bureau

The Local Government International Bureau is the European and international affairs unit of five UK local authority associations (Association of County Councils, Association of District Councils, Association of Metropolitan Authorities, Convention of Scottish Local Authorities and the Association of Local Authorities in Northern Ireland). The bureau is directed by a policy board of leading elected members and officers from its parent associations. It acts as the British section of the International Union of Local Authorities (IULA) and its European regional arm, the Council of European Municipalities and Regions (CEMR).

The European Information Service section of the bureau publishes a bulletin entitled *European Information Service* 10 times a year which provides a comprehensive overview of EC legislation and policy likely to affect local authorities. Information sources include official EC documentation, central government memoranda, the press, plus personal contacts in the European institutions and local authorities in the other member states.

The *European Information Service* normally runs to about 60 pages, is A4 size, and is considered to be one of the best information sources of its kind. It reviews EC developments, programmes, and legislation, and provides coverage of seminars and conferences, plus reviews of relevant publications. Available on subscription only, it costs £85 a year for local authorities and registered charities, £170 a year for private organisations. The bureau's 1992 working group has produced occasional papers on 1992.

■ Local Government International Bureau, 35 Great Smith Street, London SW1P 3BJ, Tel. 071 222 1636, Fax 071 233 2179.

■ See also: *Local Europe*, Research library, London Research Centre, Parliament House, Black Prince Road, London SE11, Tel. 071 735 4250.

European Briefing Unit at the University of Bradford

The University of Bradford, which is also a European Documentation Centre, hosts what is called the European Briefing Unit (EBU). It acts as a neutral forum for disseminating knowledge and information about the implications of the single European market, the structural funds, and the implications of

European integration, by providing courses, conferences and workshops for business, commerce, the public sector, voluntary organisations, and educational bodies.

■ The European Briefing Unit, University of Bradford, Bradford, West Yorkshire BD7 1DP, Tel. 0274 733466 ext. 6249.

European Information Association (EIA)

The EIA was formed in 1991, replacing the former Association of EDC (European Documentation Centres) librarians. Membership is open to 'individuals and organisations providing or interested in information services related to the European Communities and related organisations': its membership comes mainly from librarians and information officers. The EIA should be of considerable interest to local authorities and voluntary organisations who have officers or staff responsible for disseminating information about Europe. EIA's objective is to co-ordinate and improve the provision of EC and related information services through fora for the exchange of experience and ideas and by representing the views of providers of services. The EIA will be issuing a newsletter six times a year, as well as publications on EC information sources and databases. Membership costs from £20 to £60, according to category. Training courses have also started.

■ The Administrator, European Information Association, Hilltop, 3 Woolnough Road, Woodbridge, Suffolk IP12 1MJ, Tel./Fax 0394 380 632.

BOOKS AND GUIDES TO EUROPE

Many of the main bookshops now have 'Europe' and '1992' sections. For voluntary organisations anxious to gain knowledge about Europe, these sections present the advantage that they will have books introducing the European institutions and how they function. On the other hand, books dedicated to the social policy aspects of Europe are more difficult to locate. Much of what is commercially available focuses on how industry and commerce are meeting the challenge of the single market. The listing of useful books on Europe here centres on those likely to be of most interest to voluntary and community organisations.

In its efforts to publish a greater volume of information about Europe, a programme was agreed between the National Council for Voluntary Organisations (NCVO) and the Community Development Foundation (CDF) in 1989. There are four books in the series besides this guide:

- *Grants from Europe;*
- *A Citizens' Europe?;*
- *Social Change and Local Action;* and
- *Changing Europe.*

Grants from Europe: how to get money and influence policy was written by Ann Davison and Bill Seary; the sixth edition was published in early 1991. It gives information on key contacts in Brussels and the UK, how to apply for grants, how to assess the chances of success and what problems to expect on the way. The categories of funding covered include women, unemployment, ethnic minorities, poverty, the environment and consumer affairs.

■ Bedford Square Press. Plymbridge Distributors, Estover Road, Plymouth PL6 7PZ. A5, Price: £7.95 by post or from:

■ Directory of Social Change, Radius Works, Back Lane, London NW3 1HL, Tel. 071 435 8171.

A Citizens' Europe – community development in Europe towards 1992 is an anthology of conference papers edited by Charlie McConnell from a variety of British and European contributors discussing the community development field in the new Europe – and asks whether and how community development can play a role in this process.

■ Community Development Foundation, 60 Highbury Grove, London N5 2AG, Tel. 071 226 5375, Fax 071 704 0313. Price £4. ISBN 0-902406-64-7.

Social Change and Local Action – coping with disadvantage in urban areas is by Gabriel Chanan and Koos Vos.

■ Community Development Foundation, 60 Highbury Grove, London N5 2AG, Tel. 071 226 5375, Fax 071 704 0313. Price £5.75, also available from HMSO. An updated version by Gabriel Chanan is forthcoming from the European Foundation for the Improvement of Living and Working Conditions, Loughlinstown House, Shankill, Co Dublin, Tel. 353 1 282 6888, Fax 353 1 282 6456.

Changing Europe – challenges facing the voluntary and community sector in the 1990s by Sean Baine, John Benington and Jill Russell examines the main implications for the voluntary sector of the changes now taking place in Europe. It describes how these changes will particularly affect developments in the fields of poverty and social welfare, the environment, women's rights, health and employment training.

■ NCVO, 26 Bedford Square, London WC1B 3HU. Price £7.95. Tel. 071 636 4066, Fax 071 436 3188.

Funding Opportunities for Voluntary Organisations in Europe

US foundations give about $28m to European charities – about half of which goes to the UK. The Directory of Social Change has published three books on funding the voluntary sector in Europe. These are (add £1.50 P&P):

- *US Foundation Grants in Europe*, by Kerry Robinson (ed.), ISBN 0-907164-52-8, £12.50

- *European Company Giving*, by Brian Dabson (ed.), ISBN 0-907164-74-9, £12.50 and

- *European Tax and Giving*, by Europhil, ISBN 0-907164-79-X, £5.95.

■ Directory of Social Change, Radius Works, Back Lane, London NW3 1HL, Tel. 071 435 8171.

Some Books on Europe

Most of the publications found in general booksellers are supportive of the 1992 programme, and are federalist in approach – favouring the greater integration of Europe. Critical commentaries on the 1992 programme can be difficult to find. A challenging one is *1992 – the struggle for Europe – a critical evaluation of the European Communities*, by T. Cutler, C. Haslam, J. Williams and C. Williams (1989), ISBN 0-85496-596-3.

■ Berg Publishers, 150 Cowley Road, Oxford OX4 1JJ.

The most detailed analysis of the social programme of the EC can be found in C. Brewster and P. Teague, *European Community Social Policy: its impact on the UK* (1989). Price: £30.

■ Institute of Personnel Management, Camp Road, London SW19 4UW.

1991 and All That: civil liberties in the balance, by Michael Spencer (1990), outlines how the single market may affect our civil and political rights. It examines the role of the police in the more integrated European Communities, the dangers awaiting refugees and third country nationals, and the role of the European Charter of Fundamental Social Rights. Price: £3.95.

■ Civil Liberties Trust, 21 Tabard Street, London SE1 4LA, Tel. 071 403 3888.

Presenting your case to Europe by Peter Danton de Rouffignac is an introduction to the lobbying process in Europe and an outline of how the wheels of power turn within the European institutions. Price: £25 + £2 p&p.

■ Mercury Business Books, PO Box 54, Desborough, Northants NN14 2UH.

Some publications on the rights of migrants have come out in the past number of years. These include: Churches Committee for Migrants in Europe (CCME): *On Community Competence in the Field of Migration and Refugees* (1991).

■ CCME, rue Joseph II 174, B.1040 Brussels, Tel. 322 230 2011.

Jan Niessen: *Migrants' Rights in Europe: Residence and work permit arrangements in seventeen European countries* (1990).

■ European Centre for Work and Society. Hoogbrugstraat 436221 CP Maastricht, Netherlands, Tel. 314 321 6724.

Social Work and the European Community (1991) outlines the effect of the European Communities on social work and social policy in the context of the different systems of social work in each member state. Price: £18.95.

■ Jessica Kingsley Publishers, 118 Pentonville Road, London N1 9JN, Tel. 071 833 2307, Fax 071 837 2917.

For those interested in environmental policy in Europe, the most up-to-date and comprehensive account available is *EEC Environmental Policy and Britain*, by Nigel Haigh, Director of the London office of the Institute for European Environmental Policy. Price: £38.50.

■ Longmans, Westgate House, Harlow, Essex CM20 1YQ, Tel. 0279 442601.

The DocTer International Institute for Environmental Studies, Milan, publishes the *European Environmental Yearbook*, a 1,100-page guide with country reports, surveys and details of documentation, legislation and protocols. Price: £63.15.

■ DocTer International UK, Hyde Park House, 5 Manfred Road, London SW15 2RS, Tel. 081 877 1080, Fax 081 874 1845.

The Trades Union Congress has now produced several reports on the 1992 programme, and this is an aspect of work of both the TUC and its members that is likely to grow.

258

■ Trades Union Congress, Congress House, Great Russell Street, London WC1B 3LS. Tel. 071 636 4030, Fax 071 636 0632.

Some Directories and Guides to Europe

Stanley A. Budd and Alun Jones' *The EEC – a guide to the maze* has three editions: not surprisingly, for it is one of the best introductions to the EC, its programme and institutions. It is also attractive for directing the reader to further information sources and for its perspective of the would-be lobbyist of the EC. Price: £10.95 from publishers, Kogan Page.

■ Kogan Page, 120 Pentonville Road, London N1 9JN.

DOD's European companion is a detailed guide to the European Communities. DOD's provides a section-by-section guide to the European institutions: its strength is the provision of 1,400 biographies of the leading civil servants, parliamentarians and politicians of the Communities. At £95 this guide may be too expensive for many voluntary organisations.

■ DOD's Publishing and Research, 60 Chandos Place, London WC2N 4HG, Tel. 071 240 3902, Fax 071 836 8670.

Eurofi has a number of titles of relevance. The two of greatest interest to the voluntary and community sector are likely to be *EEC Contacts* and *Guide to European Economic Community Grants and Loans*.

■ Eurofi PLC, Guildgate House, Pelican Lane, Newbury, Berkshire RG13 1NX, Tel. 0635 31900.

European Directories have published a *1991-2 European Municipal Directory* which they describe as the 'bible' for local government in Europe. In over 1,000 pages it lists the top 10,000 local authorities in 12 European countries, with sections on how to deal with Brussels and briefs written by experts on how local government works in different countries. At £98 it is expensive for voluntary organisations, but should be available in libraries and local authorities, for whom it is specifically designed.

■ European Directories Ltd, Sellarsbrooke Park, Ganarew, Monmouth, Gwent NP5 3SS, Tel. 0600 890 506.

The Landmarks directory of the European institutions, *The European Public Affairs Directory* edited by Alain Fallik, provides a listing of some of the European networks of voluntary organisations. This is a commercial directory, priced at 2470BFr.

■ Landmarks, Chaussée de la Hulpe 185, B.1170 Brussels.

259

HMSO, together with Coventry Polytechnic and the Information Technology Consultancy Unit, has produced one of the outstanding guides to the European Communities. Called *The Europe 1992 Directory* (edited by Antony Inglis and Catherine Hoskyns), it lists the institutions of the EC, useful addresses, databases, pressure groups and organisations, and recent important EC documents. It is A4 in size, and can be recommended for its clarity of presentation. Price: £12.95.

■ HMSO, PO Box 276, London SW8 5DT, Tel. 071 873 8372, Fax 071 873 8463.

One of the most readable guides to the European institutions is the little-known *Churches' Guide to European Institutions* by Jan Niessen (ed.). It describes the Council of Europe, the European Communities, EFTA, the Nordic Council, and the European ecumenical organisations.

■ The Ecumenical Centre, rue Joseph II 174, B.1040 Brussels.

The Times Guide to the European Parliament, edited by A. Wood, is an important source of information on the parliament and the MEPs, listing their addresses and phone numbers (Times Books, 1989, £25).

Vacher's Publications issues a *European Companion and Consultants' Register*, which is A5 and updated quarterly. It costs £9 (single copies) and £25 (annually). It is strongly recommended as a means of keeping up to date with developments in European governments and in the Commission. It provides details of the sections and personnel in the 23 directorates of the Commission, and full information on Members of the European Parliament and the committees and subcommittees which they attend. There is a list of commercial European lobbying consultancies. Finally, there is a national section which provides country-by-country summaries of each nation's government, with lists of government ministers and addresses of government departments. The addresses of the European documentation centres are listed.

■ Vacher's Publications, 113 High Street, Berkhamstead, Herts HP4 2DJ. Tel. 0442 876135.

Forthcoming: a *Directory of EC pressure groups*, to be published by Longmans, edited by Dr Alan Butt Philip. It covers hundreds of EC-based trade, industry and voluntary organisations, giving (in many cases) details of aims, structure, resources and activities, and basic contact information. It includes many more informal networks than the conventional Brussels lobby directories.

■ Longmans, Westgate House, Harlow, Essex CM20 1YQ, Tel. 0279 442601. Price: around £95.

Information about Studying in Europe

UNESCO publishes *Study Abroad*, a comprehensive guide to awards for studying overseas. Price: £12.

■ HMSO, PO Box 276, London SW8 5DT, Tel. 071 873 8372, Fax 071 873 8463.

A Student's Guide to Europe is available from the European Educational Research Trust.

■ The European Educational Research Trust Ltd, 41 The Ridings, East Preston, West Sussex BN16 2TW, Tel. 0903 772494, Fax 0903 787253.

A Student' Guide to Europe has been published by the Conservative group in the European Parliament. Written by Caroline Jackson MEP, it reviews studying opportunities in Europe, the European University Institute in Florence, the College of Europe in Bruges, internships in the European institutions, and student exchanges.

■ The European Democratic Group, 2 Queen Anne's Gate, London SW1H 9AA.

The International Directory of Voluntary Work provides a means whereby people can find out about voluntary work activities in other countries.

■ Vacation Work, 9 Park End Street, Oxford. ISBN 1-85458-000-0.

THE PUBLICATIONS AND INFORMATION SERVICES OF THE EUROPEAN COMMUNITIES AND THEIR SPECIALISED PROGRAMMES

Initial impressions of the EC publications system can be overwhelming, particularly if one is used to dealing with official bodies which are not overgenerous in their information output. However, one can come to terms with the EC system and then select the parts which are relevant and useful. The ground rules are roughly as follows:

• Each of the 23 Directorates of the Commission has its own publications portfolio;

261

- One Directorate (X) is specifically devoted to information services in its own right!

- Each specialised programme run by the Commission has its own information system;

- The Parliament generates its own information;

- So do the Economic and Social Committee and the European Court of Justice;

- So do the independent bodies of the European Communities, like the European Investment Bank or the European Centre for Vocational Training (CEDEFOP); and

- On top of all of this, there is the Office of the Official Publications of the European Communities, and the independent statistical service, EUROSTAT, which have extensive portfolios of publications. Both are based in Luxembourg.

Each of these is discussed in turn, with the exception of the publications of the specialised programmes (see chapter 3 of this volume). Readers wishing to appreciate the nature of EC publications in their entirety should consult: Ian Thomson: *The Documentation of the EC* (Mansell, 1989, £35, ISBN 0-7201-2011-5).

The European Communities do make things easier in a number of respects. There is colour coding. Documents in English are generally published either on purple paper or on paper with a purple side strip; documents in French are blue, and so on. The office for the official publications in the European Communities in Luxembourg also publishes a quarterly catalogue of EC publications.

■ Office for Official Publications of the European Communities, OP 4-4, rue Mercier 2, L-2985 Luxembourg, Tel. 352 499281.

The process for ordering subscriptions from the institutions of the European Communities should be noted. Most are ordered through Her Majesty's Stationery Office (HMSO) rather than directly from Luxembourg or Brussels. Publications are priced in ECU, and HMSO will give customers the current sterling rate. One thing to watch is the calender of subscriptions: generally subscriptions run on a January to December basis. One orders for a calendar year at a time, i.e. all the issues for 1992 or 1993. It is generally not possible to take up a mid-year to mid-year subscription. A second problem is that even if a client orders all the issues of, say, the *Bulletin of the European Communities*, the edition dated January 1991 may not actually appear until May, and December may not appear until some time the following year.

■ HMSO, PO Box 276, London SW8 5DT, Tel. 071 873 8372, Fax 071 873 8463 and personal callers:

■ HMSO Bookshop, 49 High Holborn, London WC1V 6HB.

A European information centre was opened by the Commission in 1991: it's called Info Point Europe, and is designed on an 'all you ever wanted to know about Europe' basis.

■ Info Point Europe, Rond Point Schuman 12, B.1049 Brussels, Tel. 322 236 5555, Fax 322 236 5400.

The Official Journal

Before reviewing the publications and the publication systems of the individual directorates, the official publication system must be noted. The official journal of the Communities records all the decisions and programmes of the European Communities, and in libraries it is entitled OJ-C. Legal texts, and final, agreed legislation are defined as part of the official journal, and they are classified as OJ-L (Official Journal-Legal). A subscription costs 328 ECU. European Documentation Centres receive the journal, and it is probably not worth the while of voluntary organisations to subscribe unless they require it for legislation-based campaigns. A subscription to the OJ includes an *Annual Directory of Community Legislation Now in Force*.

Publication in the journal represents the final stage of the long and often fraught decision-making process, and documents will go through many stages before they reach that far. The most important item to note here is what is called the COM DOC (short for COMmission DOCument). All proposed policies are circulated as COM DOCs, often with informative explanatory memoranda. About 500 COM DOCs are published each year, and they are available in the EDCs.

Extracts from the official journal are available from Her Majesty's Stationery Office through a new system called SCANFAX. Any page of the official journal can be requested by fax, phone or writing and will be faxed back. The charge is 50p per page (minimum charge £4).

■ SCANFAX, HMSO, 51 Nine Elms Lane, London SW8 5DR, Tel. 071 873 8220, Fax 071 873 8416.

Publications by the Commission

The Commission publishes an annual report and a 10-times-a-year *Bulletin*, the latter available for 98.50 ECU. The annual report (more precisely called the

General Report on the Activities of the European Communities) is a hefty 450-page summary of all EC activities under one roof, and whilst it is not exactly light reading, it is a possible starting-point for the really serious EC reader. From time to time the Commission issues a *Directory* listing senior officials. Price: 4 ECU. The directory has come out as often as twice a year, but less frequently of late. Early in the year the Commission publishes its *Annual Programme* (which is sent automatically to bulletin subscribers). The *Bulletin* acts, in effect, as a summary of the official journal, recording the key decisions of the Communities: there are sections on progress towards the completion of the single market, EC foreign policy, the EC budget, actions underway in the Court of Justice and descriptions of 'infringement proceedings' – actions taken against member governments for breaches of the Treaty. The bulletin is useful for people anxious to trace the original texts or sources of decisions.

An appreciation of the complexities of the constitutional, legal and institutional aspects of EC law has been published by the Commission in its *European Perspectives* series. *The Community Legal Order* is by Jean-Victor Louis: it explores the special characteristics of EC law, the sources of EC law, and its relationship to national law. Price: £7.40. HMSO (ISBN 92-826-1665-7).

Individual Directorates' Publications

Each section of the Commission has its own portfolio of publications. The publications of those directorates of greatest interest to voluntary organisations are reviewed here.

Publications by DG V: Social affairs, employment and education
Social Europe is a journal which covers the principal social developments and programmes in the Communities. It includes official texts, statistics and analytical articles. Three issues are published each year, often with supplements and special editions. Issue 2/89, for example, was devoted to poverty in Europe. Issue 1/90 included a series of articles on the Charter of Fundamental Social Rights, with the relevant original texts, and a report on progress towards the development of EC social policy. Supplement 1/91 was devoted to immigration of citizens from third countries into the southern member states of the EC. Available from HMSO, price 87.50 ECU. Each year, DG V issues two reports which may be of interest to voluntary organisations: *Report on social developments* and *Employment in Europe*.

The Task Force on Human Resources, Education, Training and Youth began in its own newsletter in 1991, called simply *Education training*.

Publications by DG XIII –Telecommunications, information industries and innovation
For those interested in the potential of the new information technologies for community development, DG XIII issues a newsletter *Innovation and Technology Transfer*. It is available on diskette.

■ Innovation and technology transfer, Directorate-General XIII/C/3, Office JMO B4/075, L-2920 Luxembourg

Publications of DG XVI – Regional policy
Directorate-General XVI (regional policy) issues periodic bulletins called *Info background*. In 1991 it published *Europe 2000 – outlook for the development of the Communities' Territory*, a handy guide to the regional and demographic issues of the EC.

Publications by DG X – the Information Directorate
Directorate X has the remit of providing information on developments in the Communities. The Women's Information Service was set up within DG X in 1977, in response to an analysis which found that over 20 per cent of all its enquiries concerned women's rights. The section publishes a short, four-page A4 size news-sheet *Women of Europe Newsletter*.

■ *Women of Europe Newsletter*, Commission of the European Communities, Directorate-General X (Information, Communication and Culture), rue de la loi 200, B.1049 Brussels, Tel. 322 235 2860, Fax 322 236 0752.

DG X sponsors the *Symbiosis* programme, designed to advise ordinary citizens on the practical implications for them of the completion of the internal market. Despite some time in preparation, this programme has yet to find its feet in the information arena.

■ Symbiosis, People's Europe Bureau, Directorate-General X (Information, communication and culture), Commission of the European Communities, rue de la loi 200, B.1049 Brussels, Tel. 322 235 0142.

DG X also organises *Eurobarometer*, the series of opinion polls carried out in the EC to test public attitudes on European integration. Two social affairs Eurobarometers were carried out in 1990: one on *The perception of poverty in Europe*; the other entitled *The family and the desire for children*. Some voluntary organisations have quoted Eurobarometer to advantage to show that their proposals enjoy popular support.

Publications Concerning the European Parliament

The Week is published in Brussels by the Central Press Division of the Parliament's Directorate-General for Information and press relations.

not, like Hansard, attempt to record debates verbatim. A4 in size, the average edition is about 40 pages with a monthly index.

■ The editors, *The Week*, Room 367/369, Eastman Building, European Parliament, rue Belliard, B.1047 Brussels, Tel. 322 284 2941.

The Parliament itself publishes reports, working documents and texts adopted. Its documentation is generally not as comprehensive as the Commission, but documentation from the Parliament can be more interesting in highlighting the level of political debate and areas of disagreement. Voluntary organisations following a particular debate may wish to contact the relevant parliamentary committee.

■ The European Parliament, chapter 2 in this volume.

Publications by the Economic and Social Committee

The Economic and Social Committee publishes three principal documents – its *Annual report*, its *Bulletin* 10 times a year (A5), and special reports. The annual report is about 100 pages and outlines the activities of the committee in the previous year, indicating its areas of interest. Price: 12 ECU. The bulletin gives the gist of recent opinions adopted by the committee; its full opinions are, in any case, published in the official journal (OJ-C). Price of the annual report: £3.50. The bulletin is available on subscription: 30 ECU, or £19.80.

Publications by the European Court of Justice (ECJ)

The work of the ECJ is published in *Reports of cases before the court*. These are substantial tomes (the 1989 *Reports* covered almost 4,000 pages in 10 volumes). They include judgments, preliminary rulings, summaries of hearings, and the arguments advanced by both parties. Price: 115 ECU, HMSO. For those requiring more timely information on the work of the Court, the ECJ's information service publishes an A4 *Summary*, which generally runs between 20 and 30 pages. It comes out every two weeks.

■ The European Court of Justice, Palais de la Cour de Justice, L.2929 Luxembourg, Tel. 352 43031, Fax 4303 2600.

Publications by the Independent Bodies of the European Communities

The European Centre for Vocational Training (CEDEFOP) in Berlin has its own publications inventory. CEDEFOP's *Action guidelines* and *Annual report* are free of charge; subscriptions can be arranged for its *Bulletin*.

■ CEDEFOP, Bundesallee, D.1000 Berlin 15, Tel. 49 30 88 4120, Fax 49 30 884 12 222.

The European Centre for the Improvement of Living and Working Conditions has a growing publications list. Its book and reports are presented to a high standard. It has a free-of-charge newsletter, *News from the Foundation*.

■ European Foundation for the Improvement of Living and Working Conditions, Loughlinstown House, Shankill, Co Dublin, Tel. 353 1 282 6888, Fax 353 1 282 6456.

Publications by the Statistical Service of the European Communities (EUROSTAT)

EUROSTAT is located in Luxembourg: it provides the statistical support services for the EC institutions. The strength of the tables published by Eurostat is that they standardise the information of the 12 member states. On the other hand, interpretive commentaries are limited, and layout does not reflect the full potential of current computer graphics packages. To make matters easier for readers, a system of colour-coding is in operation for subject headings: green for agricultural statistics, blue for industrial statistics, red for foreign trade, and yellow for social trends, demography and the labour force. For voluntary organisations interested in less substantial volumes of information, two publications will be of particular interest. First, Eurostat issues a pocket-size handbook called *Basic statistical information about the European Communities*; and second, it puts out what are called *Rapid reports*, which are up-to-date summaries of basic information, including social affairs.

■ Eurostat – the European Commission's Statistical Office, rue Alcide de Gasperi, L.2920 Luxembourg, Tel. 352 43011.

PUBLICATIONS BY THE COUNCIL OF EUROPE AND THE OECD

The volume of information published by the other European institutions (Council of Europe and Organisation of Economic Co-operation and Development - OECD) does not - indeed could not - compare in volume terms to that of the European Communities.

Although OECD publications have an economic focus, they cover social, education and training policy. OECD statistics compare all the developed countries with each other (not just the Twelve). The OECD publishes about 250 new titles a year on economic and related matters. Its periodicals are:

- *OECD Observer* (bimonthly);

- an *Economic Survey* of each member state (annually);

- *OECD in Figures - statistics on the member countries* (each July); and

- *Main Economic Indicators* (monthly).

OECD Observer costs £12 a year. OECD information and statistical tables are attractively presented. The organisation's commentaries are generally considered to be independent and authoritative, and are widely cited in the press and in political circles. Perhaps the greatest advantage of using OECD statistical information is that it provides coverage of countries additional to the 12 of the European Communities.

The Social Affairs, Manpower and Education directorate of the OECD has published social policy studies. Titles include: *Social Expenditure: problems of growth and control, Financing and Delivering Health Care, The Future of Social Protection*, and *Living Conditions in OECD Countries*.

OECD publications are obtained through national sales agents. The UK sales agent is:

■ HMSO, PO Box 276, London SW8 5DT, Tel. 071 873 8372, Fax 071 873 8463 and personal callers:

■ HMSO Bookshop, 49 High Holborn, London WC1V 6HB.

The Council of Europe has a catalogue of its publications:

■ Publications Section, Council of Europe, BP 431/R6, F.67006 Strasbourg Cedex, France.

NEWSPAPERS, JOURNALS AND MAGAZINES

Journals and magazines are sometimes overlooked as sources of information on Europe. Yet many voluntary and community organisations, especially the larger ones, have in-house libraries where material on Europe may already exist in substantial quantities. Alternately, organisations may wish to consider taking up subscriptions to journals which cover European developments.

The European

Daily newspapers vary in the focus of their coverage of European affairs, but the past two years have seen the emergence of a dedicated English-language weekly newspaper. *The European*, available on most news stands, concentrates on political and economic developments in both the EC and the rest of Europe. Its coverage of social affairs has so far been limited.

A Selection of Journals Which Deal with Europe

BIRG Bulletin includes articles on basic income in Europe. Subscriptions cost from £6 to £18, according to category.

■ BIRG, 102 Pepys Road, London SE14 5SG.

The *British Humanities Index* includes a section on the European Communities. Published quarterly, subscriptions cost £174.

■ Library Association Publishing Ltd, 7 Ridgemount Street, London WC1.

Common Market Law Review is published for the British Institute of International and Comparative Law. Quarterly, Fl 420 a year (about £140).

■ Kluwer Academic Publishers, Postbus 17, 3300 AA Dortrecht, Netherlands.

Community Currents is the bimonthly digest of the Community Development Foundation: it notes and summarises new books, articles and grey literature appearing in the field of social policy and community development, including items with a European dimension. Price: £17.

■ Community Development Foundation, 60 Highbury Grove, London N5 2AG, Tel. 071 226 5375, Fax 071 704 0313.

European Social Policy is a new 28-page monthly bulletin published in Brussels, covering legislation, new social policies in the Communities, the social economy, news; it has a monthly interview with an important personality.

■ European Information Services SA, rue de Genève 6-8, B.1140 Brussels, Tel. 322 242 6020.

Birmingham City Council has a monthly four-page, four-colour A4 *Europe briefing*.

■ City Council, Birmingham B3 3 AB, Tel. 021 235 2372.

Euronews (formerly *Euromonitor 92*) is a quarterly four-page newsletter which covers Europe from the perspective of the voluntary sector. It is published with grant-aid from the Charities Aid Foundation, and reaches out to over 8,000 voluntary organisations.

■ Directory of Social Change, Radius Works, Back Lane, London NW3 1HL, Tel. 071 435 8171.

Eurosocial – newsletter and reports has been published by the European Centre for Social Welfare Training and Research since 1974. It is available free of charge.

■ European Centre for Social Welfare Training and Research, Bergasse 17, A 1090 Vienna, Austria, Tel. 431 45050, Fax 431 450519, e-mail: BITNET X θ 261 DAA @ WIUNI11.

Journal of Common Market Studies states that it is 'devoted to the analysis of international integration and the experience of regional groupings throughout the world but its predominant concern is with the European Communities and their relations with the rest of the world'.
The journal is published four times a year. Subscriptions: institutions £58, individuals £31.50.

■ Basil Blackwell, 108 Cowley Road, Oxford OX4 1JF.

Journal of European Social Policy was launched in 1991 to provide independent information and analysis covering the broad range of social policy issues in Europe. Attention will be given to Scandinavia and eastern Europe, as well as the EC. It is aimed at academic social policy analysts and local, national and European policy-makers. Four times yearly, subscriptions cost from £32 (individual) to £64 (institutional).

■ Longman Group UK, Longman House, Burnt Mill, Harlow, Essex CM20 2JE, Tel. 0279 442 601.

New European describes itself as a 'forum for influential people to keep in touch with fundamental thinking about Europe's future'. Leading politicians, academics and statesmen have contributed to *New European*. The periodical encompasses events in central Europe and the Nordic countries. Quarterly, sometimes with special issues. Price: £27 to £60, according to category.

■ MCB University Press Ltd, 62 Toller Lane, Bradford, BD8 9BY, Tel. 0274 499821, Fax 0274 547143.

Welfare Rights Review of the Child Poverty Action Group (CPAG) reviews European Court cases with implications for social security, women and migrant workers.

■ CPAG, 1-5 Bath Street, London EC1V 9PY, Tel. 071 253 3406.

The monthly *Social Services Abstracts* has a European index. Price: £32.

■ HMSO, PO Box 276, London SW8 5DT, Tel. 071 873 8372, Fax 071 873 8463.

The World Today is a monthly journal of international affairs, which includes the member states of the European Communities, published by Oxford University Press.

■ Oxford Journals Subscriptions Department, Walton Street, Oxford OX2 6DP.

Voluntas is a new twice-yearly journal carrying the latest research into the voluntary sector, mainly in Europe and United States. It aims to 'present and discuss current trends and developments and to encourage the exchange of research and ideas at an international level'. Subscriptions: personal £15; institutional £40.

■ Manchester University Press, Oxford Road, Manchester M13 9PL.

ELECTRONIC INFORMATION

Electronic information is beyond the reach of many voluntary organisations. Despite the costs and problems of mastering the technology involved, some organisations, possibly blessed with electronic enthusiasts anxious to develop this aspect of acquiring and disseminating information, have become interested in electronic information. To obtain information electronically is only a step away from word-processing, with which most voluntary organisations are now familiar and comfortable; nor is it far from the world of home computers or prestel systems. France has perhaps reached the highest level of electronic advance in Europe: 1990 figures showed that there were then over five million households with minitel terminals, nine out of ten of all the videotext terminals installed world-wide. Germany comes next – but far, far behind – at 200,000 terminals. Britain has 90,000 prestel users.

The European Communities have moved quickly into the electronic field, and have devoted noteworthy efforts towards making their material available in electronic form. For voluntary organisations, the principal hurdles involved are cost – both of equipment and subscriptions – and unfamiliarity with the technology involved. Electronic processing offers advantages in the volume of information it can handle and in speed. It is an option that may be worth considering.

Electronic Networking by Voluntary Organisations

Before examining the possibilities opened up by voluntary organisations accessing the electronic databases of the European Communities, it is worth asking: what are the possibilities of voluntary organisations using electronic means to share information with each other?

The possibilities for doing so appear to be positive. Several non-governmental organisations already use electronic mail (e-mail for short). The main such users are human rights groups and environmental protection groups such as Friends of the Earth. E-mail not only enables users with the appropriate equipment to connect up with database services, but to transmit messages to an electronic 'mail box', and receive messages left for their 'mail box' in turn. It is a fast, cheap system, but does depend on people having the discipline to check their electronic mail boxes frequently, normally each morning. Some voluntary organisations run what are called 'bulletin boards' with information on forthcoming events, news, as well as 'notes and queries' type items. The best description of how e-mail can work is in *Communications for progress – a guide to international e-mail.*

■ Catholic Institute for International Relations, Unit 3, Canonbury Yard, 190A New North Road, London N1 7BJ.

For voluntary organisations interested in communicating with their counterparts in central Europe, and who find postal or telephone services too much of a struggle, it is best to remember that the telex is perhaps the most appropriate system, even though it is used less and less in western Europe. Britain's non-commercial e-mail system is called Poptel. Poptel believes that its system is 'probably the most important development in written communications since the penny post. Via e-mail, anything that can be written down, of whatever length, can be sent over any distance – from one village to the next, from one end of the Earth to its opposite – and be received almost as soon as sent. Each e-mail user connects his or her computer to an ordinary telephone and transmits text to, or receives text from, a central sorting office computer. Received messages and documents can be printed on paper, or edited on a word-processor and sent on to other e-mail users. E-mail is not only much quicker than the post but usually cheaper, especially for mail-outs, and mail-outs are just as easy to send as individual person-to-person mailings'. The Poptel system is used by peace groups, human rights campaigners, development organisations and trade unions. It has access to the GeoNet system in Europe and the United States.

■ Poptel, 25 Downham Road, London N1 5AA, Tel. 071 249 2948, Fax 071 254 1102.

Electronic Information in the European Communities

The EC now has nearly 40 public databases. These are organised from two centres, which are called 'hosts': Eurobases and ECHO.

■ Eurobases, Commission of the European Communities, rue de la loi 200, B.1049 Brussels, Tel. 322 235 0001, Fax 322 236 0624.

■ ECHO, BP 2373, L-1023 Luxembourg, Tel. 352 48 8041, Fax 352 48 8040.

The ECHO System
ECHO (European Commission Host Organisation) is based in Luxembourg. Responsibility for the service rests with DG XIII, the Directorate-General for Telecommunications, information industries and innovation. ECHO provides an online service 24 hours a day, seven days a week, aided by a customer support team and, during working hours, a help desk. ECHO has now loaded more than 20 databases; those of interest to voluntary organisations include:

• TECNET (vocational training);

• ENREP (environmental research projects);

• JUSLETTER (legislation and court judgments, including human rights, social security, free movement of persons, health, environment and consumer affairs);

• ELISE (local employment initiatives);

- MISEP (employment policies);

- PABLI (development projects)

- ERISTOTE (list of 10,000 studies of European integration); and

- ERGO (initiatives for the long-term unemployed).

The procedure for gaining access to these information systems is as follows. The organisation must first have a microcomputer; a telephone line; and access into the national data network (called PTT contact point). Alternately, one can access ECHO through a minitel or prestel terminal. The organisation then signs a user agreement with ECHO, which in turn provides a password to enter the system, along with a handbook. Using a system that has a printer attached (as most microcomputers will) has the advantage that the user can obtain a print-out of the database in question as a permanent record (this is called downloading information).

■ National PTT contact point, IPSS, National Specialist Sales, Tenter House, 8th floor, 45 Moorfields, London EC2Y 9TH, Tel. 071 250 8719, Fax 071 250 8343.

ECHO publishes a bimonthly free of-charge periodical, *I'M News* (short for Information Market News), providing users and anyone else who might be interested with up-to-date details of developments in electronic information.

European Parliament Databases: CELEX and EPOQUE

The European Parliament has two database systems: CELEX and EPOQUE. EPOQUE stores information on parliamentary debates, resolutions and documents. EPOQUE is designed to help MEPs, their researchers and political groups. Records going back as far as 1979 are now being stored on the system. The procedure is similar to that of ECHO: an application is made for a password.

■ Secretariat of the Division for documentary databases and dataprocessing applications, European Parliament, Bâtiment Schuman 6/38, L-2929 Luxembourg, Tel. 352 43 001.

CELEX is the computerised documentation system for the law of the European Communities. It offers access to the whole body of EC law, data on subsequent amendments, and facilities for determining the state of the law at any given time. It includes the basic treaties, subsequent legal instruments adopted, agreements with third countries, parliamentary questions and the case law of the Court of Justice of the European Communities. Later, it will contain details of national measures taken to implement the provisions of EC law and EC-related decisions of the national courts. The cost of CELEX is 96 ECU an hour when connected.

■ CELEX distribution, Commission of the European Communities, Bâtiment IMCO, rue de la loi 200, B.1049 Brussels, Tel. 322 513 8238.

RAPID (established 1990) is the on-line database accessing the Spokesman's Service in the Commission, and is updated every day at 2pm, normally after the daily press briefing. SCAD is the bibliographic reference database of the EC, referencing not only the activities of the EC but articles published concerning the EC. ECLAS is the database of the Commission's Central Library, covering all EC publications since 1978. All are available on Eurobases.

The Commission office in London now distributes diskettes on a number of themes relating to citizens' rights in the EC. Topics include equality between men and women, social security for migrant workers, free movement and health.

■ Commission of the European Communities, 8 Storey's Gate, London SW1P 3AT, Tel. 071 222 8122.

Databases in Britain

A University of Strathclyde-based company, EPRC, holds three databases with a European dimension: STARS (grants and financial support for UK business), EUROLOC (European financial support schemes), and AIMS (the regulatory environment for business, including European regulations).

■ EPRC, 141 St James Road, Glasgow G4 0LT, Tel. 041 552 4400, Fax 041 552 1757.

SIGLE specialises in 'grey literature' – unpublished material, theses, conference papers and so on. Annual subscription is £59 + VAT; connection charge is £20 + VAT per hour.

■ British Library Automated Information System (BLAISE), 2 Sheraton Street, London W1V 4BH, Tel. 071 323 7078.

EUROLOC is a databank listing sources of finance from the European Communities in the member states, including Britain.

■ EUROLOC, 141 St James Road, Glasgow G4 0LT, Tel. 041 552 4400.

To keep up to date with the rapidly evolving world of EC databases, contact DG X.

275

■ Commission of the European Communities, DG X, rue de la loi 200, B.1049 Brussels, Tel. 322 235 3265, Fax 322 236 0752.

8

Conclusions

Although Britain joined the EC 20 years ago, it has taken the completion of the single market to make ordinary people aware of the consequences of participation in the European Communities. The voluntary sector, apprehensive as to the dislocation which the single market may bring in its wake, is looking for a social dimension to the new Europe. The visionaries of community groups and voluntary organisations fantasise a Europe of full employment, of equality between men and women, where the scourges of poverty, homelessness, racism and social injustice are banished for ever: they are unlikely to settle for the little gestures, the limited expressions of social conscience, that the European Communities have displayed to date.

In one sense, the fact that the social dimension of the EC has been so circumscribed is the fault of the voluntary sector. When the social action programme, the anti-poverty projects and the women's programme were being formulated in the 1970s, the voluntary sector was not there. It was not there to support them, to expand them, to give them a sharp cutting edge, to make them more far-reaching, and to ensure that they led to the level of financial and human investment that would make a real difference.

This time, things are different.

Over a hundred networks of voluntary and community organisations have now formed in Europe. Hard on their heels, several national voluntary organisations have set up shop in Brussels, either on their own or in conjunction with other national voluntary organisations. Many of the networks are rooted in the sobering realities of the European economies: poverty, social misery and passivity in the face of hardship. Despite that, the networks have organised, overcome barriers of language and communication, constructed legal and constitutional structures, and established themselves close to the new centres of power and influence on the continent. They collect information on the hidden Europe of the 3m homeless, the 12m jobless, and the 50m who endure poverty. They now vie for the attention of the highest officials in the European institutions, they importune members of the European Parliament, they knock on the doors of legislators, grant-givers and opinion-makers, and some are even bringing their governments to the European Court. Some of them are staffed by the grisled veterans of the great social campaigns of the 1970s and 1980s: these are people well honed in the skills of coalition-building, appealing to the press and the people over the heads of the politicians, technicians and the experts; they are long experienced in building up a groundswell of support for worthy causes. As the office poster puts it, they have done so much, for so long, with so little, that to do this more holds no terrors for them.

It is not that the lofty idealism of these voluntary and community organisations and networks is always matched by performance. Clearly, it is not. The European networks still have much to learn about communication, about presenting one's case, about combining professionalism with the democratic control of members, and about putting forward concrete political proposals that can make a real difference to people on the ground, the only people who at the end of the day really matter. Some networks are clearer about what they are against, and not so certain how they are going to achieve what they are for. And despite all the causes that they hold in common, the networks still have to learn to talk to each other and learn from each other. Apart from some isolated cases, there is not much evidence that this experience of sharing has yet begun to happen.

The voluntary sector in each country has, under the forces of European integration, begun to change. It is gradually being liberated from the narrow walls of isolation which kept out information about how other countries function, deliver their services, and work with their clients. Rightly, we often bemoan how, within each country, many parts of the voluntary sector still do not converse with each other: but the process whereby the voluntary sector in one country talks to, learns about and discovers the voluntary sector in another has yet to get under way. We are on the threshold of this epoch now, and rich should be the findings as we learn about what other countries do well. We will be inspired by their citizens' rights movements, intrigued with their political practices, roused by their campaigning methods, stimulated by decentralisation, and heartened by what they have been able to achieve. The fact that the voluntary sector has prospered in some countries, and social progress has flourished, is a reminder, where the working environment has been more difficult, that things need not always be so.

By learning from each other, through networks collaborating on projects, social analysis and campaigns, the voluntary sector in Britain and throughout the rest of Europe will be able to make mature, informed choices about the social nature of the Europe that is now at such a critical stage of development. Voluntary organisations will have to decide what social measures can, and should, best be fought for at local, regional, national and European level - and how that should be done. The new European Communities can bring good to the people whose needs, rightly or wrongly, are expressed through the voluntary sector - but it can also bring ill. The revision of the European

278

treaties, the prospect of new members joining the EC, the transformation of society in central Europe and Russia – all these things mean that Europe is in a process of change, flux, uncertainty. It is up to the voluntary sector to forge a fresh destiny for itself in the smithy of the new continent in the making.

APPENDIX

PRINCIPAL EUROPEAN NETWORKS AND LEADING VOLUNTARY ORGANISATIONS IN OTHER EUROPEAN COUNTRIES

Networks concerned with the position of the voluntary sector

Association pour le Volontariat
rue Royale 11
B.1000 Brussels, Belgium
Tel. 322 219 5370.

Comité Européen des Associations
d'intérêt Général (CEDAG)
rue de Varenne 18
F. 75007 Paris, France
Tel. 331 4549 0658, Fax 331 428
40484.

Volonteurope
rue de la Concorde 51
B.1050 Brussels, Belgium

Church-based networks

Commission des Épiscopats de la
Communauté Européenne
(COMECE)
Avenue Père Damien
B.1150 Brussels, Belgium
Tel. 322 771 3678, Fax 322 770 7654.

European Ecumenical Commission
for Church and Society (EECCS)
rue Joseph II 174

B.1040 Brussels, Belgium
Tel. 322 230 1732, Fax 322 231 1413.

European Ecumenical Organisation
for Development (EECOD)
rue Joseph II 174
B.1040 Brussels, Belgium
Tel. 322 230 1732, Fax 322 231 1413.

Catholic European Study and
Information Centre (OCIPE)
rue de la Loi 221
B.1040 Brussels, Belgium
Tel. 322 231 0697, Fax 322 230 0556.

Quaker Council for European
Affairs (QCEA)
square Ambiorix 32
B.1040 Brussels
Tel. 322 230 4935, Fax 322 230 6370,
e-mail greennet qcea

Networks concerned with development issues

European Forum for North-South
Solidarity
rue Jonquy 25
F. 75014 Paris, France
Tel. 331 4539 0862, Fax 322 4539
7164.

Association of Protestant
Development Organisations in
Europe (APRODEV)
rue Joseph II 174
B.1040 Brussels, Belgium
Tel. 322 231 0102, Fax 322 231 1413.

Euro-coopération Internationale
pour le Développement et la
Solidarité (EUROCIDSE)
Avenue des Arts 1-2 bte 6
B.1040 Brussels, Belgium
Tel. 322 219 0080, Fax 322 218 3788.

EUROSTEP
rue Stévin
B.1040 Brussels, Belgium
Tel. 322 231 1709, Fax 322 230 0348.

Handicap International
avenue Clays 111
B.1030 Brussels, Belgium
Tel. 322 735 2008, Fax 322 735 2761.

International Council of Voluntary
Agencies (ICVA)
rue Gautier 13
CH 1201 Geneva, Switzerland
Tel. 41 22 732 6600, Fax 41 22 738
9904.

International Workers
Aid/Entraide Ouvrière
rue Montagnes aux Herbes
Potagerès 37
B.1000 Brussels, Belgium
Tel. 322 219 4882, Fax 322 218 8415.

Médecins sans Frontières
(International office)
boulevard Léopold II 209
B.1080 Brussels, Belgium
Tel. 322 426 5552, Fax 322 426 7536.

Comité de Liaison ONG
avenue de Cortenberg 62
B.1040 Brussels, Belgium
Tel. 322 736 4087, Fax 322 732 1934.

Political groups

European Union of Women
Kärntnerstraße 51
A.1010 Wien, Austria
Tel. 431 515 210, Fax 431 512 2468.

European Young Christian
Democrats (EYCD)
rue de la Victoire 16
B.1060 Brussels, Belgium
Tel. 322 537 4147, Fax 322 537 9348.

Socialist International Women
Maritime House
Old Town
Clapham
London SW4 0JW
Tel. 071 627 4449, Fax 071 720 4448.

**Networks concerned with
women's affairs**

European Network of Women
(ENOW)
rue Blanche 29
B.1050 Brussels, Belgium
Tel. 322 537 7988, Fax 322 537 5596.

European Women's Lobby
Eva Eberhardt
place Quitelet 1a
B.1030 Brussels, Belgium
Tel. 322 217 9020, Fax 322 219 8451.

Associated Countrywomen of the
World (ACWW)
Vincent House
Vincent Square
London SW1P 2NB
Tel. 071 834 8635.

European Forum of Socialist
Feminists
Garden Flat
7 Acol Road
London NW6 3AA
Tel. 071 328 5108.

Women in Development, Europe
(WIDE)
Irish Commission for Justice and
Peace
169 Booterstown Avenue
Blackrock
co Dublin, Ireland
Tel. 353 1 2884853.

World Union of Catholic Women's
Organisations
rue Notre-Dame des Champs 20
F. 75006 Paris, France
Tel. 331 4544 2765, Fax 331 4284
0480.

**Networks concerned with elderly
people**

EURAG, General Secretariat
Schmiedgasse 26 (Amtshaus)
A-8010 Graz, Austria
Tel. 43 316 872 3008, Fax 43 316 872
3019.

Eurolink Age
rue du Trône 98
B.1050 Brussels, Belgium
Tel. 322.512.9360, Fax 322.512.6673.

**Network of older people in
poverty**

Tony Flynn
Beth Johnson Foundation
Parkfield House
64 Princes Road
Hartshill
Stoke-on-Trent ST4 7JL

FIAV (Intl. Fed. Widows and
Widowers)
rue Cambacorès 10
75008 Paris, France
Tel. 331.4007.0432.

Fédération Internationale des
Associations des Personnes Agées
(FIAPA)
rue d'Anjou 24
F. 75413 Paris Cedex 08, France
Tel. 331 4017 7350, Fax 331 4924
9128.

HelpAge International
rue Froissard 123
B.1040 Brussels, Belgium
Tel. 322 230 0872, Fax 322 231 1529.

**Networks concerned with
consumer affairs**

BEUC
lst floor
avenue de Trevuren 36/4
B.1000 Brussels
Tel. 322 735 5110, Fax 322 735 7455.

**Networks concerned with family
issues**

Confederation of Family
Organisations in the European
Community (COFACE)
rue de Londres 17
B.1050 Brussels, Belgium
Tel. 322 511 4179, Fax 322 514 4773.

European Network of One-Parent
Families
325 Bunratty Road
Coolock
Dublin 17, Ireland
Tel. 353 1 481872, Fax 353 1 481116.

Networks concerned with broad social issues

Eurocaritas
rue du Commerce 70-72
B.1040 Brussels
Tel. 322 511 4255, Fax 322 514 4867.

European Association of
Organisations for Home Care and
Help at Home
avenue Lacomblé 69
B.1040 Brussels, Belgium
Tel. 322 739 3511, Fax 322 739 3599.

European Federation of the
Communities of S. Egidio
Vereiniging voor Solidariteit
Lombardenstraat 28
2000 Antwerp, Belgium
Tel. 323 231 4837, Fax 323 226 0737.

Red Cross (EC Liaision office)
rue Stallaert 1/14
B.1060 Brussels
Tel. 322 347 5750, Fax 322 347 4365.

Salvation Army International
Headquarters
101 Queen Victoria Street
London EC4P 4EP
Tel. 071 236 5222.

Association International des
Charités
place Anneessens 6
B.1000 Brussels
Tel. 322 514 2088, Fax 322 512 3898.

Networks concerned with social policy

Association International des
Techniciens, Experts et Chercheurs
(AITEC)
place de Rungis 14
F. 75013 Paris, France
Tel. 331 4531 1808, Fax 331 4531 6432.

Basic Income European Network
(BIEN)
Bosduifstraat 21
B.2018 Antwerp, Belgium
Tel. 323 220 4181.

European Social Action Network
(ESAN)
rue du Trône 98
B.1050 Brussels, Belgium
Tel. 322 512 7411, Fax 322 512 6673.

International Council on Social
Welfare (ICSW)
Koestlergasse 1/29
A.1060 Wien, Austria
Tel. 431 587 8164, Fax 431 587 9951.

International Federation of Social
Workers (IFSW)
rue de l'Athénée 33
CH 1206 Geneva, Switzerland
Tel. 41 22 47 1236, Fax 41 22 46 8657.

Network concerned with child welfare

International Forum for Child
Welfare (European Group)
8 Wakley Street
London EC1V 7LT
Tel. 071 833 3319, Fax 071 833 8636.

Human rights networks

Amnesty International
9 rue Berkmanns
B.1060 Brussels
Tel. 322 537 1302, Fax 322 537 4750.

Conférence Européenne de
Probation (CEP)
Zuiderparkweg 280
5216 HE 's Hertogenbosch
Netherlands
Tel. 31 73 123 221, Fax 31 7389 0990.

Fédération Européenne des Droits
de l'Homme (FIDH)
rue Jean Dolent 27
F. 75014 Paris, France
Tel. 331 43 31 9495, Fax 331 4755
8560.

International Lesbian and Gay
Association
(Information Secretriat)
rue Marché-au-Charbon 81
B.1000 Brussels 1, Belgium
Tel. & Fax 322 502 2471

Interrights
5-15 Cromer Street
London WC1H 8LS
Tel. 071 278 3230, Fax 071 278 4334.

Penal Reform International (PRI)
c/o Secretary General, NACRO
169 Clapham Road
London SW9 0PU
Tel. 071 582 6500, Fax 071 735 4666.

Networks concerning refugees

European Consultation on
Refugees and Exiles (ECRE)
Bondway House
3 Bondway
London SW8 1SJ
Tel. 071 582 9928, Fax 071 582 9929.

European Legal Network on
Asylum (ELENA)
Bondway House
3 Bondway

London SW8 1SJ
Tel. 071 820 1156, Fax 071 582 9929.

**Networks concerned with
migrants and immigrants**

Churches Committee for Migrants
in Europe (CCME)
rue Joseph II 174
B.1040 Brussels, Belgium
Tel. 322 230 1732/2011, Fax 322 231
1413.

Conseil des Associations
d'Immigrés en Europe (CAIE)
rue de Genève 44
CH 1004 Lausanne, Switzerland
Tel. 41 22 2124 6239.

International Catholic Migration
Commission (ICMC)
rue de Vermont 37-9, Case Postale
96
CH 1211 Geneva 20 CIC,
Switzerland
Tel. 41 22 733 4150, Fax 41 22 734
7929.

Migrants' Forum
Mr Tara Mukherjee
Confederation of Indian
Organisations
5 Westminster Bridge Road
London SE1 7XW
Tel. 071 928 9889, Fax 0277 200353.

**Networks concerned with
unemployed people**

European Network of the
Unemployed (ENU)
48 Fleet Street
Dublin 2, Ireland
Tel. 353 1 679 5316, Fax 353 679
2253.

International Network on
Unemployment and Social Welfare
(INUSW)
Department of International
Relations, NIMAWO
Noordeinde 39
2514 GC The Hague, Netherlands
Tel. 31 70 365 1177, Fax 31 70 356
2825.

Networks concerned with poverty

European Anti-Poverty Network
(EAPN)
rue Rempart des Moines 78/4
B.1000 Brussels, Belgium
Tel. 322 512 1652.

**Networks concerned with the
environment**

Eurogroup for the Conservation of
Birds and Habitats
c/o The Royal Society for the
Protection of Birds
The Lodge
Sandy
Beds. SG19 2DL
Tel. 0767 680551, Fax 0767 692 365.

European Environmental Bureau
(BEE)
rue de la Victoire 22-6
B.1060 Brussels, Belgium

Friends of the Earth, European
Coordination (CEAT)
rue Blanche 29
B.1050 Brussels
Tel. 322 537 7228, Fax 322 537 5596.

Future in our hands movement
120 York Road
Swindon
Wilts SN1 2JP.
Tel. 0793 532 353.

Greenpeace (EC Unit)
Avenue de Trevuren 36
B.1040 Brussels, Belgium
Tel. 322 736 9927, Fax 322 736 4460.

International Conservation Action
Network (ICAN)
International Development Officer
British Trust for Conservation
Volunteers
36 St Mary's Street
Wallingford
Oxfordshire OX10 0EU
Tel. 0491 39766, Fax 0491 39646.

International Fund for Animal
Welfare (EC office)
rue du Taciturne 50
B.1040 Brussels, Belgium

International Union for the
Conservation of Nature (IUCN))
Avenue du Mont-Blanc
CH 1196 Gland
Switzerland
Tel. 41 22 647181, Fax 41 22 642926.

RED Association Internationale
rue des Potiers 2
B.6702 Attert, Belgium
Tel. 32 6322 3702, Fax 32 6321 9870.

Trade union based networks

European Committee of Workers
Co-operatives (CECOP)
avenue de Cortenberg 62
B.1040 Brussels, Belgium
Tel. 322 736 2030, Fax 322 732 1897.

European Trade Union Conference
rue Montagne aux Herbes
Potagères 37
Tel. 322 218 3100, Fax 322 218 3566.

European Trade Union Institute
(ETUI)
boulevard de l'Impératrice 6
B.1000 Brussels, Belgium
Tel. 322 512 3070, Fax 322 514 1731.

IRENE
Stationstraat 39
5038 EC Tilburg, Netherlands
Tel. 31 13 35 1523, Fax 31 13 35 0253.

Trade Union Rural Network (TURN)
Joe Mitchell Associates
136 Middleton Road, Heywood
Lancashire OL10 2LU
Tel. 0706 68691, Fax 0706 626 059.

Networks concerned with community development

ATD Quart-Monde
Av Viktor Jacobs 12
B.1040 Brussels, Belgium
Tel. 322 647 9900, Fax 322 640 7384.

Combined European Bureau for
Social Development (CEBSD)
PO Box 61677
2506 AD The Hague, Netherlands
Tel. 3170 345 4336, Fax 31 70 345 4241.

International Federation of
Settlements Eurogroup
Birmingham Settlement
318 Summer Lane
Birmingham B19 3LL
Tel. 021 359 3562, Fax 021 359 6357.

Networks concerned with health issues

Azimuth
NIEP Rome
via G. Marcova 18-20
00153 Rome, Italy

CEFEC
Hedemannstraße 14
1000 Berlin 61
Tel. 49 30 251 1066.

EASE
Waardsedijk 34
NL 3425 TG Snelrewaard
Tel. 03484 5255, 3480 17743.

Health Action International Europe
J. van Lennepkade 334-T
1053 NJ Amsterdam, Netherlands
Tel. 31 20 833 684, Fax 31 208 55002.

Order of St John
St John's Gate
Clerkenwell
London EC1M 4DA
Tel. 071 253 6644, Fax 071 490 8835.

International Federation of
Leprosy Associations
234 Blythe Road
London W14 0HJ
Tel. 071 602 6925, Fax 071 371 1621.

International Heart Network
Rue du Trône 98
B.1040 Brussels, Belgium
Tel. 322 512 9360, Fax 322 512 6673

International Information Centre
on Self-Help and Health
E Van Evenstraat 2C
B.3000 Leuven, Belgium
Tel. 322 016 283 158.

International League of Societies of
Persons with Mental Handicap
(ILSMH)
avenue Louise 248 bte 17
B.1050 Brussels, Belgium
Tel. 322 647 6180, Fax 322 647 2969.

World Federation for Mental
Health (European region)
Mensana House
6 Adelaide Street
Dun Laoghaire
Co Dublin, Ireland
Tel. 353 1 284 1736.

Networks concerned with disabled people

Action Européenne des
Handicapés (AEH)
Generalsekretariat
Wurzerstraße 2-4
D 5300 Bonn 2, Germany
Tel. 49 228 820930, Fax 49 228 820
9343.

CEEH
c/o Alpha Plappeville
rue Général de Gaulle 18
Plappeville
F 57050 Metz, France
Tel. 33 8732 5285, Fax 33 8732 2898.

EBU Commission for Liaison with
the EC
Fédération des Aveugles
avenue Bosquet 58
F. 75007 Paris, France
Tel. 331 4551 2008.

EUCREA
Sq. Ambiorix 32
B.1040 Brussels, Belgium
Tel. 322 230 0560, Fax 322 280 6693.

European Federation of Parents of
Hearing Impaired Children
(FEPEDA)
c/o The National Deaf Children's
Society
45 Hereford Road, London W2 5AH
Tel. 071 229 9272, Fax 071 243 0195.

Mobility International
228 Borough High Street
London SE1 1JX
Tel. 071 403 5688, Fax 071 378 1292.

Rehabilitation International –
European Communities
Association
P O Box 30
B.6061 Charleroi (Montingnies),
Belgium
Tel. 327 136 1926, Fax 327 147 1934.

Networks concerned with housing and homelessness

CECODHAS
rue Lord Byron 14
F 75384 Paris, France
Tel. 331 4075 7800, Fax 331 4075
7983.

EUROPIL
rue de Grenelle 180bis
F. 75007 Paris, France
Tel. 331 4551 4196, Fax 1 4705 9211.

FEANTSA
1 rue Defacqz/17
B.1050 Brussels
Tel. 322 538 6669, Fax 322 539 4174

Organisation Européenne des
Associations pour l'Insertion et
Logement des Jeunes Travailleurs
(OEIL-JT)
avenue du Général de Gaulle 12
F. 94307 Vincennes Cedex, France
Tel. 331 4374 5356, Fax 331 4374
0429.

Networks concerned with rural development

CEPFAR
rue de la Science 23/5
B.1040 Brussels, Belgium
Tel. 322 230 3263, Fax 322 231 1845.

ECOVAST
rue de Gembloux 121
B.5002 Namur, Belgium
Tel. 32 81 730 689, Fax 32 81 733 513.

MIJARC
68 Tiensevest
B.3000 Leuven, Belgium
Tel. 32 16 22 8312.

Small farmers: Aonadh Nan Croitearan (Scottish Crofters Union)
Old Mill
Broadford
Isle of Skye
Invernessshire IV49 9AQ
Tel. 04712 529.

Trans European Rural Network (TERN)
rue du Trône 98
B.1050 Brussels, Belgium
Tel. 322 512 9360, Fax 322 512 6673.

VIRGILE
c/o CELAVAR
rue des Petites-Ecuries 13015
F. 75010 Paris, France
Tel. 331 4824 0941, Fax 331 4824 0054.

Local-authority based networks concerned with rural development and the peripheral regions

Assembly of the European Regions (AER)

Immeuble Europe
place des Halles 20
F. 67000 Strasbourg, France
Tel. 33 8822 0707, Fax 33 8875 6719/33 8822 6482.

Conference on the Peripheral and Maritime Regions (CPMR)
boulevard de la Liberté 35
3500 Rennes, France
Tel. 33 9931 8181, Fax 33 9978 1221.

Networks concerned with young people

Council of European National Youth Committees (CENYC)
avenue des Courses 8
B.1050 Brussels, Belgium
Tel. 322 648 9101, Fax 322 648 9640.

ERYICA
quai Branly 101
F. 75740 Paris Cedex 15, France
Tel. 331 4065 0261.

European Conference of Youth Club Organisations (ECYC)
Orneej 45
DK 2400 Copenhagen NV
Tel. 45 110 8083.

European Co-ordination Bureau of International Youth Organisations (ECB)
rue du Marteau 19
B.1040 Brussels
Tel. 322 217 5632.

Youth Forum of the European Communities
rue Joseph II 112
B.1040 Brussels, Belgium
Tel. 322 230 6490, Fax 322 230 2123.

List of voluntary organisations in other European countries

France

Association Nationale des
Paralysés en France
blvd. Auguste Blanqui 13
F. 75013 Paris

CEDIAS (Centre d'Études, de
documentations, d'information et
d'action sociales)
rue Las Cases 5
F. 75007 Paris
Tel. 331 4551 6610.

Confédération Générale du temps
libre (CGTL)
rue Cadet 9
F. 75009 Paris
Tel. 331 4246 4284.

Comité de coordination des
oeuvres mutualistes et
coopératives de l'Education
nationale (CCOMCEN)
Département associatif
blvd. Garibaldi 63
F. 75015 Paris
Tel. 331 4306 2921.

Comité d'Études et de liaison des
associations à vocation agricole et
rurale (CELAVAR)
rue Paul Escudier 2
F. 75009 Paris
Tel. 331 4874 5288.

Comité national des associations
de jeunesse et d'éducation
populaire (CNAJEP)
rue Martel 15
F. 75010 Paris
Tel. 331 4770 7131.

Conseil National de la Vie
Associative (CNVA)
rue de Varenne 55
F. 75007 Paris
Tel. 331 4548 6400.

Coordination environnement
c/o Maison de Chevreuil
rue Cuvier 57
F. 7531 Paris Cedex 05
Tel. 331 4336 7995.

Emmaus
rue Vaillant Coutourier 183bis
F. 94140 Alfortville
Tel. 33 4893 2950.

Entraide Protestant
rue de Clichy 47
F. 75009 Paris
Tel. 331 4874 5011.

Fédération Nationale des
Associations d'Acceuil et de
Réadaptation Sociale (FNARS)
rue du Faubourg St-Denis 76
F. 75010 Paris
Tel. 331 4523 3909, Fax 331 4770
2702, minitel 3616+fnars.

Fédération des Aveugles de France
avenue Bosquet 58
F. 75007 Paris
Tel. 331 4551 2008.

Fédération Française des Équipes
Saint Vincent
rue des Sèvres 67
F. 75006 Paris
Tel. 331 4544 1756.

Fédération Nationale des Foyers
Ruraux (FNFR) (National
Federation of Villages)
rue Sainte Lucie 1
F. 75015 Paris

Fondation de France
avenue Hoche 40
F. 75008 Paris
Tel. 331 4225 6666, Fax 331 4563
9259.

Fondation pour la vie associative
(FONDA)
rue de Varenne 18
F. 75007 Paris
Tel. 331 4549 0658, Fax 331 4284
0484.

France Terre d'Asile
4-6 Passage Louis Philippe 4-6
F. 75011 Paris.

Intercollectif des ONG de
Développement
rue de la Glacière 49
F. 75013 Paris
Tel. 331 4336 6118.

Médecins du Monde
avenue de la République 67
F. 75011 Paris
Tel. 331 4357 7070, Fax 331 4355
9122, minitel 3615+medmonde.

Médecins sans frontières
rue Saint Savin 8
F. 75011 Paris
Tel. 331 4021 2929, Fax 331 4806
6868, minitel 3615+msf.

Ministry of Health and the Family
avenue de Ségur 8
F. 75700 Paris
Tel. 331 4056 6000, Fax 331 4765
2899.

Mouvement ATD Quart monde
avenue du Général Leclerc 107
F. 95480 Pierrelaye
Tel. 33 3464 6963.

Secours Catholique
rue Bac 106
F. 75341 Paris Cedex 07
Tel. 331 4320 1414.

Secours Populaire
rue Froissart 9-11
F. 75003 Paris
Tel. 331 4278 5048.

Solidarités Nouvelles Face au
Chômage
rue des Couronnes 99
F. 75020 Paris
Tel. 331 4636 5523.

Union des Foyers des Jeunes
Travailleurs & RILE
avenue du Général de Gaulle 12
F. 94307 Vincennes Cedex
Tel. 331 4374 5356, Fax 33 4374 0429.

Union féminine civique et sociale
rue Béranger 6
F. 75003 Paris
Tel. 331 4272 1918, Fax 331 4027
0878.

Union nationale des associations
familiales (UNAF)
place Saint-Georges 28
F. 75009 Paris
Tel. 331 4280 6766.

Union nationale interfédérale des
oeuvres et organismes privés,
sanitaires et sociaux (UNIOPSS)
rue Faubourg Saint Honoré 103
F. 75008 Paris
Tel. 331 4225 1676, Fax 331 4256
4215.

Germany

Arbeiterwohlfahrt
Oppelnerstraße 130
D. 5300 Bonn 1
Tel. 49 228 6685 0.

Arbeitsgemeinschaft der
Sozialhilfeinitiativen
Moselstraße 25
D. 6000 Frankfurt am Main
Tel. 49 69 250038.

Arbeitsgruppe Armut und
Unterversorgung (Working Group
on Poverty and Undersupply)
c/o Institut für Sozialarbeit und
Sozialpädagogik
Am Stockborn 5-7
D. 6000 Frankfurt 50]

Bundesarbeitsgemeinschaft der
Freien Wohlfahrtspflege (BAGFW)
Franz-Lohe-Straße 17
D. 5300 Bonn 1
Tel. 49 228 2261.

Bundesarbeitsgemeinschaft
Wohnungslosenhilfe
Postfach 130 148
D. 4800 Bielefeld
Tel. 49 521 144 3613, Fax 49 521
1442818.

Bundesarbeitsgemeinschaft Hilfe
für Behinderte
Kirchfeldstraße 149
D. 4000 Düsseldorf 1
Tel. 49 211 340 085.

Bundesarbeitsgemeinschaft Soziale
Brennpunkte
Moselstraße 25
D. 6000 Frankfurt am Main

Bundesministerium für Familie &
Senioren (Federal Ministry for
Family policy and elderly people)
Postfach 20022
D. 5300 Bonn 2
Tel. 49 228 308 2300, Fax 49 228 308
2221.

Carl Duisberg Gesellschaft
Postfach
D. 5000 Köln

Deutscher Caristasverband
Karlstraße 40
D. 7800 Freiburg i. Bresgau
Tel. 49 761 200 1.

Deutscher Frauenrat
Simrockstraße 5
D. 5300 Bonn 1
Tel. 49 228 22 3008, Fax 49 228
218819.

Deutscher Verein für Offentliche
und private Fürsorge
Hans Muthesius Hause
Am Stockborn 1-3
D.6000 Frankfurt am Main 50
Tel. 49 69 58013.

Deutsches Zentrum der
Altersfragen (DZA)
Manfred von Richthofenstraße 2
D. 100 Berlin

Deutsches Rote Kreuz
Friedrich-Ebert-Allee 71
D. 5300 Bonn 1
Tel. 49 228 541 1.

Diakonisches Werk
Stafflenbergstraße 76
D. 7000 Stuttgart 1
Tel. 49 711 2159 1.

Internationaler Bund für
Sozialarbeit Jugendsozialwerk
Ludolfusstraße 2-4
D. 6000 Frankfurt am Main 90
Tel. 49 611 770571.

Kuratorium Deutsche
Altershilfe/Whilhelmine
Lübke-Stiftung
An der Pauluskirche 3
D. 5000 Köln 1
Tel. 49 221 313071.

Paritätischer Wohlfahrtsverband
Heinrich Hoffmanstraße 3
D. 6000 Frankfurt am Main 71
Tel. 49 69 6706 0, Fax 49 69 6706 204.

Reichsbund der Kriegsopfer,
Behinderten, Sozialrentner, und
Hinterbliebenen
Beethovenallee 56-58
D. 5300 Bonn 2
Tel. 49 228 3630 7173.

Statistische Bundesamt
Gustav Stresemann Ring 11
6200 Wiesbaden 1

Verband alleinerziehender Mütter
und Väter (VAMV)
Von-Groote-Platz 20
D. 5300 Bonn 2

Wohnbund
Humboldstraße 79
D. 6000 Frankfurt 1.

Zentralwohlfahrtstelle der Juden in
Deutschland
Hebelstraße 6
D. 6000 Frankfurt am Main
Tel. 49 69 4302 6.

Belgium

Bond van Grote en Jonge Gezinnen
(Family League, Flemish section)
Troonstraat
B.1050 Elsene
Tel. 322 507 8811.

Federatie CSW (Federation of
Social Work Centres)
Marnixlaan 19, bus 9B
B. 1050 Brussels
Tel. 322 513 2802.

Fondation Roi Baudouin
rue Brederode 21
B. 1000 Brussels
Tel. 322 511 1840.

Forum Bruxellois de lutte contre la
pauvreté (Brussels Forum Van
Strijd Tegen de Armoede) (Brussels
anti-poverty forum)
av Rogier 45
B. 1030 Brussels
Tel. 322 215 1773.

Ligue des Familles (Family League,
French section)
rue du Trône 127
B.1050 Ixelles
Tel. 322 507 7211, Fax 322 507 7200.

Médecins sans frontières
rue Deschampheleer 24
B. 1080 Brussels
Tel. 322 425 0300, Fax 322 425 3460.

Ministry of Social Affairs
rue de la loi 56
B. 1040 Brussels
Tel. 322 230 1070.

Pluralistisch Overleg Welzijnswerk
(POW)
Diksmuidelaan 50
B. 2600 Berchem-Antwerpen
Tel. 323 366 1380.

Thuislozenzorg
Diksmuidelaan 50
B. 2600 Berchem
Tel. 323 366 0426, Fax 323 366 1158.

Verbond van Instelligen voor
Welzijnswerk (VIW)
Marnixlaan 19
B. 1050 Brussels
Tel. 322 513 2803.

VIBOSO
Handelskaai 18/3
B. 1000 Brussels
Tel. 322 217 5595, Fax 322 218 2810.

World Wide Fund for Nature
Waterloosteenweg 608
B.1060 Brussels
Tel. 322 347 3030, Fax 322 344 0511.

Denmark

Centre for Voluntary Organisations
Contact Committee, Ministry for
Social Affairs (Kontaktudvalget til
det frivilige sociale arbejde,
Socialministeriet)
Slotholmsgade 6
DK. 1216 København K
Tel. 45 3392 3377, Fax 45 3393 2518.

Church Cross Army (Kirkens
Korshær)
Nikolaj Plads 15
DK. 1067 København K
Tel. 45 3312 1600.

Danish Women's Society
Niels Hemmingsensgade 10,3
DK. 1153 København
FAX 45.3817.2720.

Dansk Flygtningehaelp (Danish
Refugee Council)
Borgergade 10, Postbox 53
DK. 1300 København K
Tel. 49 3391 2700, Fax 49 3332 8448.

Kofoeds Skole
Nyrnberggade 1
DK. 2300 København S
Tel. 45 3195 5212.

Landsforeningen Ungbo (National
Ungbo League)
Hejrevej 38
PO Box 909
DK. 1400 København NV
Tel. 45 3834 5600, Fax 45 3833 0061.

National Council of Women in
Denmark (Danske Kvinders
Nationalråd) (DKN)
Niels Hemmingsensgade 10
DK. 1153 København K
Tel. 45 3312 8087, Fax 45 3312 6740.

Social Advice and Aid (Social
Rådgivning og Bistand, SR-Bistand)
Sortedam Dosseringen 3, st.th.
DK. 2200 København N.
Tel. 45 3139 7179.

Society for the Improvement of the
Social Debate (Selskabet Til
Fremme Af Social Debat)
Nansensgade 68
DK. 1366 København K

SOKSOI (Co-ordinating
Organisations for Christian Social
Organisations and Institutes)
Gl. Køge Landevej 137
DK 2500 Valby
Tel. 45 3116 1113.

Ireland

Combat Poverty Agency
8 Charlemont Street
Dublin 2
Tel. 353 1 783355, Fax 353 1 783731.

Department of Social Welfare
Aras Mhic Dhiarmada
Store Street
Dublin 1
Tel. 353 1 786444, Fax 353 1 741709.

Free Legal Advice Centres
49 South William Street
Dublin 2
Tel. 353 1 679 4239, Fax 353 1 6791
554.

Irish Association of Older People
Corrigan House
Fenian Street
Dublin 2
Tel. 353 1 766484.

Irish National Organisation of the
Unemployed
48 Fleet Street
Dublin 2
Tel. 353 1 679 5316, Fax 353 1 679
2253.

National Campaign for the
Homeless
48 Fleet Street
Dublin 2.

National Social Service Board
71 Lower Leeson Street
Dublin 2
Tel. 353 1 616422.

Society of St Vincent de Paul,
National Headquarters
8 New Cabra Road
Dublin 7
Tel. 353 1 384164.

Luxembourg

ATD Quart Monde
blvd Royal 1
L. 2449 Luxembourg
Tel. 352 23 585.

Caritas
rue Michel Welter 29
L. 2730 Luxembourg
Tel. 352 4021 310, Fax 352 4021 3126.

Centre d'Études de Populations, de
Pauvreté et de Politiques
Socio-Économiques (CEPS)
BP 65
L. 7201 Walferdange
Tel. 352 33 3233, Fax 352 33 2705.

Femmes en Détresse
BP 1024
L. 1010 Luxembourg
Tel. 352 44 8181.

Interactions Faubourgs
route de Thionville 9
L. 2611 Luxembourg
Tel. 352 49 2660.

Ministère de la Famille et de
Solidarité (Ministry for the Family
and Solidarity)
avenue de la Gare 14, Luxembourg
Tel. 352 4781/478617, Fax 352
478714.

Netherlands

Anti-poverty working group
(Werkgroep Armoede)
Provinciaal
Samenwerkingsverband
Uitkeringsgerechtigden Limburg
Klinkenberg 22
NL. 6231 BD Rothem-Meersen
Tel. 31 43 643737.

Breed Platform Vrouwen Voor
Ekonomische Zelfstandigheid
Postbus 13174
NL. 3507 Utrecht
Tel. 31 30 340941.

Dienst in de Industriële
Samenleving vanwege de Kerken
(DISK)
Noordermarkt 26
NL. 1015 MZ Amsterdam
Tel. 31 20 228505.

Koningin Juliana Fonds
John F Kennedylaan 101
NL. 3981 Bunnik
Tel. 31 3405 64524.

Landelijke Organisatie
Belangengroepen Huisvesting
(LOBH) (Dutch Organisation for
Special Needs Groups in Housing)
Henri Polaklaan 12b
NL. 1018 CS Amsterdam
Tel. 31 20 223505.

Nederlands Instituut voor de
Maatschappelijke Opbouw (NIMO)
Havensingel 8
NL. 5211 TX 's-Hertogenbosch
Tel. 31 73 137295, Fax 31 73 120650.

Nederlands Instituut voor Zorg en
Welzijn (NIZW) (Dutch Institute
for Care and Welfare)
Postbus 19152
NL. 3501 DD Utrecht
Tel. 31 30 314143.

Nederlandse Woonbund
Nieuwe Achtergracht 17
NL. 1018 XV Amsterdam.
Tel. 31 20 22 3505, Fax 31 20 24 0051.

Ministerie van Welzijn,
Volksgezondheid en Cultuur
(Ministry for Welfare, Health &
Culture)
Postbus 5406
NL. 2280 HK Rijswijk
Tel. 31 70 340 7911.

Greece

Archbishopric of Athens
19 Agias Filotheis Street
GR. Athens
Tel. 301 3231 136.

Centre for Mental Health
58 Notara Street
Exarheia
GR. Athens
Tel. 301 82 10 222.

Centre for Women's Employment
Initiatives
Papafi 113
GR. Thessaloniki 54410
Tel. 3031 917 916.

Confederation of Large Families of
Greece
68 Pireos Street
GR. Athens
Tel. 301 523 5807.

Department of Social Welfare
31 Feidippidou Street
Mitalakopou
GR. Athens
Tel. 301 7710 265.

DIMITRA (Institute of Information,
Training and Development)
Kouma 40
GR. Larissa 421 23
Tel. 3041 287611, Fax 3041 287 521.

DIOTIMA (Women's Research and
Training Centre)
Kekropos 2
GR. Athens 10558
Tel. 301 361 5660.

Foundation of Social Insurance
(IKA)
Division of Social Services
8 Ag. Konstantinou Street
GR. Athens
Tel. 301 52 36061. ext. 51.

Greek Red Cross
1 Lykabitlou Street
GR. Athens
Tel. 301 3613 848.

International Social Service
1 Sofocleous Street
GR. Athens
Tel. 301 3217 758.

National Organisation of Welfare
(EOP)
6 Ipatias Street
GR. Athens 105 56
Tel. 301 322 7060.

National Foundation for the Rehabilitation of the Handicapped (EIAA)
2 Lampsa Street
Athens
Tel. 301 6910 075.

Organisation for the Employment
of the Workforce (OAED)
52 Pireos Street
GR. Athens
Tel. 301 524 2327.

Patriotic Foundation for Social
Welfare (PIKPA)
5 Tsocha Street
Ampelokipi
GR. Athens 115 21
Tel. 301 64 27856.

PRAXIS
12 Matrozou Street
11741 Athens
Tel. 301 923 6710, Fax 301 922 4205.

Re-integration Centre for
Returning Migrants
68 Deinokratous Street
GR. 115 21 Athens
Tel. 301 724 5980, Fax 301 808 3806.

YWCA
11 Amerikis Street
10672 Athens
Tel. 301 362 4292.

Italy

Agenzia Federativa
via F. de Sanctis 15
I. 00195 Roma
Tel. 39 6 372 3240 or 372 3238, Fax
39 6 389969.

Associazione Nazionale Carcere e
Communità
viale di Valle Aurelia 93a
I. 00167 Roma
Tel. 39 6 63 2885 and 638 0327, Fax
39 684 7404.

Associazione Nazionale Famiglie
Fanciullli e Adulti Subnormale
(ANFAS)
via Gianturco 1
I. 00196 Roma
Tel. 39 6 2 946 7131.

Associazione Nazionale Università
della Terza Età
via Principessa Clotilde 97
I. 10100 Torino
Tel. 39 11 768872.

Associazione Ricreativa Culturale
Italiana (ARCI)
via F Carrara 24
I. 00196 Roma
Tel. 39 6 361 0800, Fax 39 6 321 6877.

Caritas Italia
piazza San Calisto 16
I. 00153 Roma

Centro Italiano Solidarietà (CEIS)
via A Ambrosini 129
I. 00142 Roma

Centro Nazionale per il
Volontariato
via A Cataloni 158
I. 55100 Lucca
Tel. 39 583 419 500, Fax 39 583 419
501.

CERFE (Centro di Ricerca e
Documentazione)
via Flaminia 160
I. 00196 Roma
Tel. 39 6 320 0851/2/3, Fax 6 323
0936.

Communità de S.Egidio
Piazza S. Egidio 3a
I. 00153 Roma
Tel. 39 6 58 03548/39 6 589 5945/39
6 580 6883, Fax 39 6 580 0197.

Communità di Capodarco
via Lungro 3
I. 00178 Roma
Tel. 39 6 718 4784 or 718 6733, Fax
39 6 718 7005.

Cooperative di Solidarietà Sociale,
Federazione Nazionale
piazza della Libertà 16
I. 00193 Roma

Coordinamento Centri Sociali
Anziani e Orti
via Becaccino 27
I. 40133 Bologna
Tel. 39 51 63 93080.

Coordinamento Nazionale
Communità di Accoglienza
(CNCA)
via Zumbini 32
I. 20142 Milano

Federazione Organizzazioni
Communità Straniere in Italia
(FOCSI)
via Adua 22
I. 00185 Roma

FIOPSD (National Federation for
the Homeless)
via N. Bixio 10
I.25122 Brescia
Tel. 39 30 46452.

FOPRI (Formazione professionale
reinserimento)
via Vinicio Cortese 147
I-Roma
Tel. 39 6 507 3448 4950.

Fondazione CENSIS (Centro Studi
Investimentiti Sociali)
Piazza di Novolia 2
I. 00199 Roma
Tel. 39 6 826851, Fax 39 6 831 5200.

Gioventu Operaia Cristiana (GOC)
via Vittorio Amedeo II, 16
I. 10100 Torino
Tel. 39 11 515813 or 543156.

IREF (Instituto di Ricerce
Educative e Formative)
via E Bezzi 3
I. Roma
Tel. 39 6 589 7016.

Italia Nostra
via N Porpora 22
I. 00198 Roma

Lega per il diretto al lavoro degli
handicappati
via Morigi 8
I. 20123 Milano

Lega per l'Ambiente
via Salaria 280
I. 00199 Roma
Tel. 39 6 844 2277, Fax 39 6 844 3504.

Ministry of Labour and Social
Security
via Flavia 6
I. Roma

Movimento Federativo
Democratico
via Petro della Valle 1
I. 00198 Roma
Tel. 39 6 689 3535, Fax 39 6 686 1333.

Movimento Italiano Casalinghe
(MOICA)
via B. Castelli 4
I. Brescia
Tel. 39 30 200 3845.

Movimento Volontariato Italiano
(MOVI)
Via Livenza 3
I. 00139 Roma

UMCEM (National Union of
Communities in Mountain Areas)
via Palestro 30
I. 00185 Roma
Tel. 39 6 444 1381.

Portugal

Associaçao dos Professionais de
Serviço Social
Av Casal Ribiero 37-1°
P. 1000 Lisboa
Tel. 351 1 541810.

Associaçao Portuguesa de
Deficientes (APD)
Largo do Rato
P. 1200 Lisboa
Tel. 351 1 689883.

Caritas Nacional
Estrada da Ameixoeira n° 19
P. 1700 Lisboa
Tel. 351 1 759 6046.

Casa de Santo António
Calc. das Necessidades 2-1°
P. 1000 Lisboa

Comissao da Condicao Feminina
Avenue de República, 32-1°
P. 1000 Lisboa
Tel. 351 1 776081.

Comissao Nacional Justiça e Paz
(National Commission for Justice &
Peace)
Avenue Sidónio Pais, 20, 5° Dto
P. 1000 Lisboa
Tel. 351 1 573386.

Cooperativa de Ensino Superior de
Servico Social (ISSS)
Avenue Rodrigues de Freitas 202
P. 4000 Porto
Tel. 351 2 573581, Fax 351 2 563 949.

Cruz Vermelha Portuguesa
(Yellow Cross)
Jardim 9 de abril 1
P. 1200 Lisboa
Tel. 351 1 605490.

Exercito de Salvacao
Rua da Escola do Exercito 11-b
P. 1100 Lisboa
Tel. 351 1 579604.

Instituto de Apoio à Crianca
Avenue de Berna, 56-3°
P. 1000 Lisboa
Tel. 351 1 735875.

Lar Luísa Canavarro
R. de S. Brá 293
P. 4200 Porto

Ministry of Social Affairs
Avenida Joao Crisóstomo 9
P. 1000 Lisboa

Movimento de Solidariedade Rural
(Movement for Rural Solidarity)
Avenue Sidónio Pais, 20-4° dto.
P. 1000 Lisboa
Tel. 351 1 549 752.

Projectos Alternativos de Mulheres
Rua do Cunha 361-2°-Dt°
Paranhos
P. 4200 Porto

Serviço de Assistência Ordem de
Malta (SAOM) (Order of Malta)
Travessa dos Inglesinhos, 46
P. 1200 Lisboa
Tel. 351 2 317595.

Sociedada de s. Vicente de Paulo
Rua Presidente Araújo 6-r/c Esq °
P. 1200 Lisboa
Tel. 351 1 609470.

Uniao das Instituiçoes Particulares
de Solidariedade Social (IPSS)
Rua Amilcar Cabral, Lote 4B -r/c D
P. 1700 Lisboa

Uniao das Misericórdias
Rua Forte de Stª Apolónia lote 4
P.1900 Lisboa

Spain

Asesoria de Programas de
Servicios Sociales, PASS
Valuenzuela, 10
E. 28014 Madrid
Tel. 34 1 532 7478, Fax 34 1 532 2059.

Asociacion de Voluntarios de San
Juan de Dios
Herreros de Tejeda 3
E. 28016 Madrid

Asociacion para la Prevencion del
Alcoholismo y Otras Toxicomanias
Pza Cataluña 9, 4°
E. 08002 Barcelona

Asociacion Proyecto Hombre
Martín de los Heros 68
E. 28008 Madrid

Asociación Secretariado Gitano,
Sede Nacional (Gypsies)
Sagunto 17
Esc. Dcha. 1° Izda
E. 28010 Madrid

Association for Local Economic
Development (ADELA)
C/Fuencarral 138 1° D
E. 28010 Madrid
Tel. 34 1 593 0776, Fax 34 1 593 2388.

Cáritas Española, Sede Nacional
San Bernardo 97
E. 28015 Madrid
Tel. 34 1 445 5300, Fax 34 1 593 4882.

Comité Español para el Bienestar
Social (Commitee for Social Welfare)
Claudio Coello, 35-1°
E. 28001 Madrid

Confederación de Asociaciones de
Vecinos de Espana
San Cosme y San Damian 24-1°
E. 28012 Madrid

Cruz Roja Espanol (Red Cross)
Melchor Fdez. Almagro 216
E. 28029 Madrid

Federacion de Colectivos
Sociosanitarios Prevencion SIDA
(AIDS)
Ardemans 71 D
E. 28028 Madrid

Instituto de Reinserción Social (IRES)
Capellans 2-1°
E. 08002 Barcelona

Institut de Treball Social i Serveis
Socials (INTRESS) (Institute of
Social Work and Social Services)
Placa Catalunya, 9, 4rt
E. 08002 Barcelona
Tel. 34 3 302 6612, Fax 34 3 302 6591.

Ministerio de Asuntos Sociales
(Ministry of Social Affairs)
Dirección Gral. de Acción Social
Infanta Mercedes 94
E. 28003 Madrid
Tel. 34 1 347 7500, Fax 34 1 571 2275.

Austria

Bundesministerium für Arbeit und
Soziales (Federal Ministry for
Employment and Social Affairs)
Stubenring 1
A. 1011 Wien
Tel. 431 1711 00, Fax 431 713 9311.

Bundesministerium für Umwelt,
Jugend, und Familie (Federal
Ministry for the Environment,
Youth and Family)
Radetzkystraße 2
A. 1030 Wien
Tel. 431 1711 58 0, Fax 431 711
584221.

Finland

Centralförbundet för Barnskydd
(Central Union for Child Welfare
in Finland)
Lastensuojelun Keskusliitto r.y.
Armfelintie 1
SF. 00150 Helsinki
Tel. 358 0 625901.

Central Union for the Welfare of
the Aged
Malmin Kauppatie 26
SF. 00700 Helsinki
Tel. 358 0 351 3900.

Finnish Central Federation of the
Visually Handicapped
Mäkelänkatu 50
SF-00510 Finland
Tel. 358 0 396 041, Fax 358 0 396
04200.

Finnish Federation for Social
Security and Social Welfare
(*Sosiaaliturvan Keskuslitto*)
Hämeentie 58-60 A
SF. 00500 Helsinki
Tel. 358 0 735 088, Fax 358 0 738 123.

Finnish Red Cross
Tehtaankatu 1a
PO Box 168
SF. 00140 Helsinki
Tel. 358 0 12931, Fax 358 0 654 149.

Förbundet Utvecklingshämning r.f.
(Finnish Association on Mental
Retardation)
Kehitysvammaliitto r.y.
Viljatie 4 A
SF. 00700 Helsinki
Tel. 358 0 354322, Fax 358 0 353 398.

Invalidförbundet r.f. (National
Association for the Disabled)
Invaliditiito r.y.
Kumpulantie 1 A
SF. 00520 Helsinki
Tel. 358 0 718466, Fax 358 0 739 500.

Kuurojen Liitto (The Finnish
Association of the Deaf)
Ilkantie 4 (PL 57)
SF. 00400 Helsinki
Tel. 358 0 58 031, Fax 358 0 580 3370.

Mannerheim League for Child
Welfare
Toinen Linja 17
SF. 00530 Helsinki
Tel. 358 0 711611.

Ministry for Social Affairs and
Health
Snellmaninkatu 4-6
SF. 00170 Helsinki 17
Fax 358 0 650 442.

National Board for Social Welfare
PO Box 197
SF. 00531 Helsinki

Sweden

Frälsningsarmén (Salvation Army)
Box 5090
S-102 42 Stockholm
Tel. 46 8 663 1700, Fax 46 8 660 9920.

KFUK/KFUMs Riksförbund
(YWCA/YMCA)
Box 2054
S-103 12 Stockholm
Tel. 46 8 145330, Fax 46 8 217522.

Konsumentverket o
Konsumentombudsmannen
(National Board for Consumer
Policies & Ombudsman)
Box 503
S-162 15 Vällingby
Tel. 46 8 759 8300, Fax 46 8 382215.

Rädda Barnen (Save the Children)
Box 27320
S-102 54 Stockholm
Tel. 46 8 665 0100, Fax 46 8 661 5326.

Röda Korset (Red Cross)
Box 27316
S-102 54 Stockholm
Tel. 46 8 665 5600, Fax 46 8 661 2701.

Sveriges Pensionärsförbund
(Pensioners' Association)
Box 26070
S-100 41 Stockholm
Tel. 46 8 679 8850, Fax 46 8 611 5682.

Yrkeskvinnors Riksförbund
(Working Women's Association)
Drottninggatan 59
Stockholm
Tel. 46 8 107415.

Russia

Central Union of Consumer
Societies
B.Cherkassy Per 15/17
Moscow
Tel. 7 095 925 79 80.

Children's Fund
Armyansky Per. 11/2 A
Moscow
Tel. 7 095 242 02 96.

Cultural Foundation of the USSR
121010 Gogolevsky Blvd 6
Moscow
Tel. 7 095 291 26 19.

KMO –Association of Young
Disabled People
7-8 Bogdan Khmelnitsky Street
101846 Moscow

Ministry of Culture of the USSR
Arbat 35
Moscow
Tel. 7 095 241 0709.

Russian Federation of the Deaf
1905 Goda Street 10a
123022 Moscow

Social and Ecological Union
25 Krasnoyarmeeskaya Street, apt
85
125319 Moscow
Tel. 7 095 1516270.

Soviet-American Foundation
13-17 Bolshoi Koslovsky pereulok
Moscow 107078
Tel. 7 095 928 6422, Fax 7 095 288
9512.

Soviet-American Foundation
29 Chaikovsky Street
St Petersburg 191194

Ukraine

Ukranian-American Foundation
Vul Artema 46 Kiev
Ukraine 254053
Tel. 7 044 216 2596, Fax 7 044 216
7629.

Estonia

Open Estonia Foundation
Olevimagi 12
Talinn 200101
Tel. 7 0142 601 980, Fax 7 0142 601
274.

Lithuania

Open Society Fund
Vilnius 22
Vilnius 232600
Tel. 7 122 22 1687, Fax 7 122 22 1419.

Hungary

Association for Community
Development
1011 Budapest
Corvintér 8
Tel. 36 1 35 4300, Fax 36 1 15 3604.

Federation of Hungarian
Foundations
Budapest
Rottenbiller u.61-22
H. 1074 Hungary
Tel. 36 1 122 1488.

Független Cigány Szervexet
(Independent Gypsy Organisation)
Ilka u.30.11.17
H. 1143 Budapest
Tel. 36 1 1 842 917.

Hungarian Association of Social
Workers
Bikszádi u.12/A.1.4.
H.1119 Budapest XI.
Tel. 36 1 1 862 507, Fax 36 1 1 228
853.

Hungarian Women's Alliance
Nepkoztarsasag utja 124
H. 1062 Budapest

LARES Humán Szolgáltató
Szövetkezet (Org. for elderly
people)
V. Tanács krt.2
H. 1051 Budapest
Tel. 36 1 1 176 752.

Org. for handicapped people (c/o)
III. San Marco u.76
H. 1023 Budapest
Tel. 36 1 1 888 951.

Org. for unemployed people
XII. Nagysalló u.13
H. 1124 Budapest
Tel. 36 1 1 860 964.

Soros Foundation
PO Box 34
H. 1525 Budapest
Tel. & Fax 36 1 202. 211.

Poland

Brother Albert Aid Society
Ul. Francuska 47m 36
Warsaw
Tel. 48 22 173185.

Caritas Poland
Ul. Krakowskie Przedmiescie 62
00-322 Warszawa
Tel. 48 2 635 7404.

Missionaries of Charity (Sustry
Misjonarki Milosci)
Ul Grochowska 194
04-135 Warsaw
Tel. 48 2 6100010.

Society for the Protection of
Children
Ul Krakowskie Przmiescie 20/22 m
31
00-325 Warsaw
Tel. 48 22 265907.

Stefan Batory Foundation
ul. Flory 9 IV floor
00-586 Warsaw
Tel. 48 22 499203, Fax 48 22 493561.

Index

voluntary organisations in 293-4
voluntary sector in 211-3
welfare state in 211
women's movement in 212
Department of Education and Science (DES),
	information from 252
Department of Trade and Industry,
	publications of 252
DES *see* Department of Education and Science
d'Estaing, Valery Giscard 17
destitute, aid for in Paris 201
developing countries
	socialist-based network for 135
	support for people of 133-4
development, sustainable 137
development education 133-4
	National Association for 10
development issues
	in Europe, women concerned with 143
	European attitudes to 133
	networks concerned with 280-1
	voluntary organisations concerned with
		135-8
development projects database, PABLI 274
Diakonie 204
Diaz, Antoni 16
Directorate General V: Social affairs,
	employment and education 264
Directorate General X: Information,
	Communication and Culture 265
Directorate General XIII, public database
	system of 273
Directorate General XVI: Regional policy 265
Directorate General XIII:
	Telecommunications, information in
	and innovation 264
Directorates General of European
	Commission, publications by 264-5
directories, of Europe 259-60
Directory of EC pressure groups 260
Directory of Social Change 257
Disability
	International Council on 179
	prevention of 178-9
disability networks 176-9
Disabled Living Foundation, The 72
disabled people
	artistic activities for 177
	in CIS 242-3, 243
	in Denmark 212
	EC legislation for 73
	EC programmes for 71-4
	education for 173, 179
	employment for 176

in Finland 234, 235
in Italy 221, 223
mobility for 179
networks concerned with 287
networks for 177-81
in Poland 245
rehabilitation for 176, 178-9
security benefits for 179
in Spain 230
sports and leisure for 181
transport modifications for 6
young 178
Disabled People International 72
DOD 's European companion 259
drama workshop, international 91
drug addicts, voluntary organisations for in
	Italy 224
drug use, campaign for safer 174
Dutch Federation of Probation Institutes 154

EAA *see* European Environment Agency
e-mail (electronic mail) 272-3
EAPN *see* European Anti-Poverty Network
EASE *see* European Association for Special
	Education
EBRD *see* European Bank for Reconstruction
	and Development
EBU *see* European Blind Union
EC 1992 programme, information about 77-8
EC
	applicants for membership of 8-9
	Basic statistical information about the 267
	budget of 4
	consequences of joining 277-9
	decision-making in 28-9
	electronic databases of 272
	electronic information in 273-4
	formative years of 11
	funding for environmental work by 163, 166
	guide to 260
	history of 2-3
	how to lobby 20-1
	importance of voluntary sector in 277-9
	influencing policy of 113-4
	information services of 261-71
	institutions of 10-1, 30
	international networks affiliated to 118, 119
	introduction to 259
	lobbying of 114
	mediterranean initiatives of 216-7
	organisations promoting information about
		253-5
	prospective new members of 279
	public databases of 273-4

311

publications by independent bodies of 267
redefinition of powers of 29
refugees in 257
relations with central Europe 78-9
relations with the CIS 78-9
role of police in 257
rural development in 182-5
Social Charter of 5
social dimension of 277-9
southern countries of 216-232
special institutions of 23-8
specialised programmes of 46-50
    voluntary organisations attitude to 46-7
treaties of association with 8-9
unemployment in 4
women's influence on policies of 141
EC databases, in Britain 275-6
EC institutions
in Luxembourg 214
EC law 20
advice on 155
computerised documentation system for
    274-5
EC pressure groups, directory of 260
EC Programme for Elderly People 143
EC public databases, gaining access to 274
EC regional policy, report on 168
EC regional programmes, principal 52-3
EC Secretariat for Sports for the Disabled 73
EC specialised programmes
advisory committees for 47-8
of interest to voluntary organisations 48-50
EC statistical service (EUROSTAT),
    publications of 267
EC support programme for women's local
    employment initiatives 64
ECAS *see* European Citizen Action Service
ECB *see* European Co-ordination Bureau of
    International Youth Organisations
ECB Info 190
ECBH *see* Eurogroup for the Conservation of
    Birds and Habitats
ECF *see* European Cultural Foundation
ECHO system 273
ECJ *see* European Court of Justice
ecomonic development, publications on 96
Economic Co-operation and Development *see*
    Organisation for
economic issues, church interest in 131
Economic Policy Research, Centre for,
    publications of 96
economic reform in central Europe, report on
    168
Economic and Social Committee of EC 170

Annual Report of 266
Economic and Social Committee Bulletin 266
Economic and Social Committee of European
    Parliament 18-9, 21
Economic and Social Council, French 202-3
Economic and Social Council *see* United
    Nations Economic and Social Council
economic and social councils in western
    Europe, report on 168
Economic and social situation in the EC, The 19
economic strategies, local 84
Economic Survey, an, of each EC state 268
ECOSOC *see* United Nations Economic and
    Social Council
ECOVAST *see* European Council for the
    Village and Small Town
ECPR News 96
ECPR *see* European Consortium for Political
    Research
ECRE *see* European Consultation on
    Refugees and Exiles
ECU (European Currency Unit) xii
Ecumenical Association for Church and
    Society (EECOD) 131-2
ecumenical international Christian
    associations 130-1
ECYC *see* European Confederation of Youth
    Club Organisations
EDCs *see* European Documentation Centres
Edinburgh Council for the Homeless 181
education
community 54-60
for disabled people 171-2
grants for 98
higher, in Europe 89
multi-cultural 92
new information technoligies in 59
special, provision of 171-2
task force for 14
Education of the children of migrant workers
    programme 55, 59
education information network of EC 60
education policy, trade union research on 168
education policy-makers, programme for 58
Education and Research, Federal Trust for 103
Education and Science, Department of (DES)
    50
information from 252
Education and Social Policy, European
    Institute of 89
Education training 264
educational activities, in Europe 103
educational programmes, of EC 54, 55-6
Educational Research Trust, European 104-5

ERDF *see* European Regional Development
Fund
ERGO, initiatives for the long-term
unemployed database 274
ERGO NEWS 66
ERGO programme of EC 49, 95
in Luxembourg 214
ERGO programme for long-term
unemployed 65-6
ERISTOTE, studies of European integration
database 274
ERYICA network 191
ESAN *see* European Social Action Network
ESF *see* European Social Fund
Estonia, voluntary organisations in 302
ethnic minorities
in Europe 160
fears of 7-8
Ethnic Minority and migrant organisatons -
European directory 108
ETUC *see* European Trade Union Conference
ETUI *see* European Trade Union Institute
EUCREA *see* European Association for
Creativity for and with Disabled
People
European Community Third Action
Programme on Equal Opportunities
for Men and Women 138
EURAG, publications of 144-5
EURATOM *see* European Atomic Energy
Community
Euro Bureau, assistance to Asian residents of
EC countries by 109
Européenne Cooperation Internationale pour
le Développement et la Solidarité
(EUROCIDSE) 135-6
UK members of 133-4
Euro-Info-Centres, in Britain 251
Eurobarometer opinion polls 265
Eurobases 273
Eurocaritas 158
work of 147-8
Eurocities networks 54
Eurocounsel, study of counselling services by
25-6
Eurodesk information service 253-4
Eurodysee training scheme 186
EUROFED *see* European Central Bank
Euroform programme of EC 47
Eurogroup for the Conservation of Birds and
Habitats (ECBH) 163
Eurolink Age 17-8, 72, 144, 145
British members of 143
Brussels office of 120

Bulletin of 143
lobbying by 120-1
parliamentary liason officer of 120
EUROLOC database 275
EURONET 41
Euronews (formerly *Euromonitor* 92) 270
Europaritat 115
Europe 1992 Directory, The 260
Europe 2000 88
Europe 2000 - outlook for the development of the
Communities Territory 265
Europe
applying for grants from 256
books about 255, 257-8
Central *see* Central Europe
change in 1
choosing information sources on 248-9
community development in 256
Council of, Social Charter of 5
Council of *see* Council of Europe
directories of 259-60
guides to 255-7, 259-60
information on 94, 247-76
information on studying in 261
journals dealing with 269-71
lobbying process in 258
NCVO publications on 255-7
women in southern countries of 141
Europe against poverty 76
Europe briefing, of Birmingham City Council
270
Europe Communities Youth Exchange
Bureau 56
Europe sans Frontieres 253
European, The 269
European Act, Single *see* Single European Act
European Action for Disabled People 176
European affairs, in newspapers 269
European Anti-Poverty Network (EAPN) 77,
123, 162, 196
Greek section of 220
objectives of 119
European Association for Creativity for and
with Disabled People (EUCREA) 177
European Association for the Development
of Women's Information & Training
(EUDIFF) 85
European Association for Information on
Local Development 83
European Association of Organisations for
Home Care and Help at Home 147,
148
European Association for Special Education
(EASE) 72, 171-2

European Ecumenical Commission for Church and Society (EECCS) 130-1
European Educational Research Trust, grants from 103
European Environment Agency (EAA) 27-8
European Environmental Bureau (BEE) 163
European Environmental Yearbook 258
European Federation of the Communities of S.Edigio 148-9
European Federation for the Employment of the Handicapped (CEEH) 176
European Federation of Intercultural Learning (EFIL), work of 99
European Federation of National Organisations Working with the Homeless (FEANTSA) 119, 179, 181
European Federation of Parents of Hearing Impaired Children (FEPEDA) 177-8
European Federation for the Welfare of the Elderly *see* EURAG
European Forum for North-South Solidarity 133
European Forum of Socialist Feminists, The 141
European Foundation Centre (EFC) 91-2
European Foundation for the Improvement of Living and Working Conditions 23, 25-6
European Free Trade Area (EFTA) 8, 10
European governments, guide to developments in 260
European Group for Local Employment Initiatives (EGLEI) 65
European Human Rights Foundation, grants made by 97
European ideals, promotion of by voluntary organisations 102
European Information Association (EIA) 255
European Information Exchange Network on Local Development and Local Employment Initiatives (ELISE) 49, 63-4
local employment initiatives database of 273
European Information Service 254
European information weeks 95
European Institute for Social Security 92
European institutions
    guide to 260
    information about 103
European integration, moves towards 9
European Investment Bank (EIB) 23-4
European Journal of Education 89
European Legal Network on Asylum (ELENA) 157

European Local Authorities Study and Research Centre 187-8
European Local Environmental Information Clearing House (ELEICH) 69
European Manifesto of Refugee Forum 110
European Movement, The, aims of 104
1991-2 European Municipal Directory 259
European Network of Occupational Social Workers (ENOS) 152
European Network for One-parent Families 146-7
European Network of Training Schemes for Women 60-1
European Network of Transnational Partnerships (ENTP) 57
European Network of the Unemployed (ENU), work of 160-1
European Network of Women (ENOW) 138, 139
European networks
    origins of 113
    role of 113
    types of 128
    in voluntary sector 128-30
    work of 114-5
European networks of NGOs, history of 117-9
European Nuclear Disarmament 108
European Observatory on Ageing, proposed 83
European Observatory for Cross-border Co-operation 81-2
European Observatory on Employment 82-3
European Observatory on Homelessness 80-1
European Observatory on National Family Policies 80
European Observatory on Social Exclusion 79-80
European Observatory on Social Security 81
European Parliament, The 14-17
    British Labour Group in 250
    Conservative group in 250
    databases of 274-5
    Dublin office of 249
    Economic and Social Committee of 18-9, 21
    guide to 260
    hearing on poverty in 169
    hearings at on refugees 159
    intergroup of the family in 146
    lobbying of by anti-poverty networks 120
    London office of 249-250
    new groups in 15
    new powers for 29
    parliamentary committees of 16-17
    party divisions in 15-16

316

immigration, illegal 7
IMPACT 2 information programme 67
income
  basic minimum 151
  guaranteed minimum, in Luxembourg 214
  minimum 5-6
Independent, The, correspondent of in Brussels 111
Independent Experts, Committee of 34
Industrial Common Ownership Movement 167
industrial decline, EC funds for areas with 22
industrial development 167-9
industrial redeployment 168
Industrial Therapy in Southampton, British Institute for 172
industry, British, representation of in Brussels 111
Info background 265
information agencies, in CIS 243
information programmes of EC 77-8
information sources on Europe, choosing 248-9
information studies, EC funding for 49
InforMISEP 82
INFUSE database 86
initiatives for the long-term unemployed database, ERGO 274
Innovation and Technology Transfer 265
Institute of Family Studies (Wolverhampton Polytechnic) 146
institutes, European 83-93
institutions concerned with Europe, based in Britain 94
Intercultural Education, International Association for 92
Intercultural Educational Programmes (IEP) 99
intercultural learning, European 99
intergroups of MEPS 17-8
  of interest to voluntary organisations 18
internal market, implications of for ordinary citizens 265
International Alliance of the Order of St John 173
International Association for Intercultural Education (IAIE) 92
International Association for Volunteer Effort 130
International Association of Charities of St Vincent de Paul 150
International Association of City and Regional Planners 187

International Association of Crafts and Small and Medium Size Enterprises 37
International Business Club, work of 97
International Catholic Migration Commission (ICMC) 159
International Centre for the Legal Protection of Human Rights *see* Interrights
International Co-operation for Development and Solidarity (CIDSE) 133-4
International Conservation Action Network (ICAN) 165
International convention on the protection of rights of all migrnt etc 42
International Council on Disability 179
International Council on Social Welfare (ICSW) 151-2
International Council of Voluntary Agencies (ICVA) 39, 133, 134-5
International Directory of Voluntary Work, The 261
International Federation of Agricultural Producers 37
International Federation of Anti-Leprosy Federations (ILEP) 173
International Federation of Associations of Elderly Persons 144
International Federation of Human Rights, The *see* FIDH
International Federation of Settlements (IFS) Eurogroup 170-1
International Federation of Social Workers (IFSW) 114, 152, 196
International Federation of Widows and Widowers Organisations (FIAV) 144
International Forum for Child Welfare (European Group) 153
International Fund for Animal Welfare (IFAW) 165-6
International Gay and Lesbian Association (ILGA) 155
International Heart Network (IHN) 173-4
International Information Centre on Self-help and Health (IIS) 174
International Newsletter of 174
International Institute of Humanitarian Law 92-3
International Labour Organisation (ILO) 42-3, 137
  conventions of ratified by UK 41
  Institute for Labour Studies of 42
  work of 94
International Labour Review 42
International League of Societies for Persons with Mental Handicap (ILSMH) 72

work of for persons with mental handicaps 174-5

International Migration 44

International Movement of Agricultural and Rural Youth 184

International Network on Unemployment and Social Work (INUSW) 161

International non-governmental organisations enjoying consultative status with the Council of Europe 116

International Organisation for Migration (IOM) 43-4

International Planned Parenthood Federation 135

International Press Centre in Brussels 111

International Restructuring and Educational Network Europe 168, 169

International Social Development Review 38

International Social Security Association (ISSA) 94

International Social Service (ISS) 93
  work of 94

International Union for the Conservation of Nature (IUNC), work of 166

International Union of Family Organisations (IUFO), UK members of 148

International Union of Local Authorities 187

International Union of Local Authorities (IULA) 39

International Voluntary Service (IVS), workcamps run by 101

International Workers Aid 135

Internationales Arbeiter-Hilfswerk 135

INTERREG programme 52

Interrights 155-6
  Bulletin of 158

INUSW *see* International Network on Unemployment and Social Work

Investment Bank *see* European Investment Bank

IOM *see* International Organisation for Migration

IOM *see* International Organisation for Migration

Ireland
  emigration from 213
  homelessness in 213
  National Campaign for the Homeless in 181
  new voluntary organisations in 213
  poverty of 213, 214
  social policy field in 214
  voluntary organisations in 294
  voluntary sector in 213-4

IRENE *see* International Restructuring and Educational Network Europe

IRIS programme 60-1

Irish Creamery and Milk Suppliers Association 184

Islington Chamber of Commerce 94

ISS *see* International Social Service

ISSA *see* International Social Security Association

Italian citizens, Declaration of Rights for 222

Italian government, decentralised nature of 220

Italian politics, ideological nature of 220-1

Italian social services, regional variations in 220-1

Italian voluntary organisations, important 225

Italian voluntary sector
  national organisations of 221-3
  political nature of 221-2

Italy
  co-operative movement in 221-2
  Democratic Federative Movement in 222-3
  disabled persons in 223
  immigrants in 224
  patients rights in 223
  research bodies in 224, 226
  social research in 224, 226
  unemployed people in 224
  voluntary organisations in 296-8
  voluntary sector in 220-6
  women's issues in 224

IUCN Bulletin 167

IUFO *see* International Union of Family Organisations

IULA *see* International Union of Local Authorities

IUNC *see* International Union for the Conservation of Nature

IVS *see* International Voluntary Service

JEPs *see* Joint European Projects

Jeunesse Européenne Federaliste 105

Jewish social service organisations in France 199

Jews, Central Welfare Office for the, in Germany 204

Joint Council for the Welfare of Immigrants (JCWI) 106, 108

Joint European Projects (JEPs) 56

Journal of Common Market Studies 270

Journal of European Social Policy 270

journals, dealing with Europe 269-71

JUSLETTER, legislation and human rights database 273

Justice
  Committee for the Administration of 106
  see also European Court of

King Baudouin Foundation 91, 188, 210
Komsomolskaya Pravda 240
Kurds in Europe 159

Labour group, British, in European
    Parliament 250
Labour party, in European Parliament 15
Labour Party Women 138
Labour see International Labour Organisation
Labour Studies, ILO Institute for 42
LACE see European Observatory for
    Cross-border Co-operation
Ladies of Charity of St Vincent 150
Landelijk Buro Racismebestrijding 158
language training, for voluntary
    organisations 195
languages
  minority 85-6
  programme for improvement in teaching of
    58
lawyers, working for human rights 155-6
LEADER programme for rural areas 70, 71
League of Nations, The 10
League of Red Cross Societies 39
learning, technologies to facilitate 59
learning difficulties 173
LEDA Magazine 66
LEDA Newsletter 66
LEDA programme of EC 49
LEDA see Local Employment Development
    Action
Left Unity 15
legal rights, in Hungary 243-4
legislation and human rights database,
    JUSLETTER 273
Legislation Monitoring Service for Charities
    109
LEI see European Communities Support
    Programme for Women's etc
LEPRA 173
leprosy relief organisations 173
Les regroupements associatifs en Europe 117
lesbian rights 155
Liason between Actions for the Development
    of the Rural etc (LEADER) 70, 71
liberals, in European Parliament 15
Liberty (formerly National Council for Civil
    Liberties) 106, 108, 155
LIFE, new EC programme for the
    environment 68-9

LINGUA education programme of EC 50
LINGUA programme 54, 55
Lithuania, voluntary organisations in 302
Living and Working Conditions, European
    Centre for the Improvement of 267
Living Conditions, Improvement of see
    European Foundation for
Living Conditions in OECD Countries 268
Living conditions in urban areas 26
LMAs 72
lobbying the EC 20-1
lobbying process, in Europe 258
lobbying through European networks,
    successes of 121
Local authorities and 1992 84
local authorities
  British, represented in Brussels 112
  lobbying by in EC 186-8
  organisations concerned with 187-8
local authority based networks 186-8
local development
  advice on 95, 96
  information on 83
Local Employment Development Action
    (LEDA) 66
local employment initiatives database, ELISE
    273
Local Europe 254
local government, in Europe, guides to 259
Local Government Centre of Warwick
    Business School 77
Local Government International Bureau 53,
    100
  European Information service of 254
local model activities (LMAs) 72
Local and Regional Authorities, Consultative
    Council of with the European
    Communities 53
Local and Regional Authorities in Europe see
    Standing Conference of
Locally-based responses to long-term
    unemployment 26
Loi Besson 197
Lomé IV accords 150
Lothian Foundation, The, work of 104-5
Low Pay Unit 34
Lutheran Protestant Church in Germany,
    welfare work of 204
Luxembourg
  EC institutions in 214
  guaranteed minimum income in 214
  NGOs in 214
  voluntary organisations in 294
  voluntary sector in 214

Luxembourg compromise, the 12

Maastricht Treaty, terms of 29
Main Economic Indicators 268
MANAGAIDS database 86
Manchester, University of 172
MAP-TV programme of EC 78
Marin, Manuel 136
Maritime Regions of the EC, Conference of
  Peripheral 187-8
marriage guidance *see* RELATE
Mauroy, M. Pierre 197
MECU LINGUA programme 58
MECU SPRINT programme 67
MECU xii
Médecins du Monde 201
Médecins sans Frontières 135, 201
  programmes of in Belgium 210
Media, European Institute for the 90
MEDIA programme of EC 78
media programmes of EC 78
Medical Aid for Poland 245
medical help in third world 135
medico-socio reception centres, in France 201
Mediterranean coastline, EC programme for
  68
MEDSPA environmental programme of EC
  68
Mennonites 132
Mental Handicap
  Scottish Society for 175
  work for people with 176
mental health 175
  Greek national institute for 218
mental patients, legal rights for 175
mentally disabled, in Spain 230
mentally handicapped people, in Finland 235
mentally ill people, in Italy 221
MEPs, intergroups of 17-8
Metal Bulletin, correspondent of in Brussels
  111
Metamorphosis, newsletter of European
  Environmental Bureau 163
Midwales, Brussels office of 113
migrant workers
  education of children of 59
  protection for 34
  in Sweden 237
migrants
  in EC 6-8
  rights of 258
migrants in Belgium, self-help groups for 210
migrants in EC 155, 158-60
Migrants Forum of EC 159-60

migrants and immigrants, networks
  concerned with 284
Migrants Rights in Europe: Residence and work
  permit arrangements in seventeen
  European countries 258
migration
  Commission on 94
  information on 84
  into EC 154
  law on 92-3
Migration News Sheet 158
Migration *see* International Organisation for
Millan, Bruce 13
million ECU xii
minimum income
  basic, in France 197
  Commission recommendation on 5-6
minimum wage
  Commission recommendation on 5-6
  in Sweden 236
Ministers of EC, Council of 11-12
MIRIAM programme for rural areas 70
MIRIAM programme on rural development
  49
MISEP 82
  employment policies database 274
MISSOC *see* Mutual Information System on
  Social Protection
Mitterand, President François 196, 197
Mobility International 72, 178
  work in of Poland 246
Moniteur Belge 124
Monnet, Jean 2
Moro, Aldo 223
Moroccans in Europe 159
mountain areas, problems of 187
Mouvement International de la Jeunesse
  Agricole et Rurale Catholique
  (MIJARC) 184
movement, freedom of in single market 3-4
Mutual Information System on Social
  Protection 81, 92

NAC *see* National Advisory Committee
NADEC *see* National Association for
  Development Education
narcotic drugs 7
National Advisory Committee (NAC) 50
National Alliance of Women's Organisations
  139, 140
National Association for Development
  Education (NADEC) 109
National Board of Catholic Women 142

National Campaign for the Homeless in Ireland 181
National Children's Bureau, The 153
National Childrens' Homes 153
National Consumer Council 108, 145, 195-6
directory published by 109
National Council for Civil Liberties *see* Liberty
National Council for Special Education 172
National Council for Voluntary Associations 117
National Council of Voluntary Childcare Organisations 153
National Council for Voluntary Organisations, The (NCVO) 48, 50, 146, 148, 194, 255, 257
National Ethnic Minority Advisory Council (NEMAC) 159
National Farmers' Union 183
National Federation of Housing Associations 180
National Federation of Housing Co-operatives 180
National Federation of Women's Institutes 139, 146
National Federation of Young Farmers' Clubs 183
National Institute for Social Work 249
National Marriage Guidance Council *see* RELATE
National Union of Agricultural and Allied Workers 183
National Women's Network for International Solidarity 109-10, 141
NATO *see* North Atlantic Treaty Organisation
nature conservation programme of EC 68-9
NCVO publications, on Europe 255-7
NCVO *see* National Council for Voluntary Organisations
neighbourhood settlements, in Britain 170
Neighbourhoods, National Commission for the Local Development of, French 197
NEMAC *see* National Ethnic Minority Advisory Council
Netherlands
funding of voluntary sector in 215-6
newer voluntary organisations in 216
recent developments in voluntary sector of 216
traditional voluntary organisations in 215
voluntary organisations in 295
voluntary sector in 214-6
Netherlands Centrum Buitenlanders 158

network, definition of xii
Network on Older People in Poverty, The, publications of 143
networks
concerned with voluntary sector 128-30
directories of 116
for disabled people 176-9
in Europe 277-8
European benefits of joining 126-7
disadvantages of joining 126-7
international, in Europe 117-9
openness of 123
organisational structures of 124-5
reasons for voluntary organisations joining 114-5
with restricted membership 123
New Economics Foundation, The 108
New European 271
New Scientist, correspondent of in Brussels 111
newer organisations of voluntary sector, in Italy 223-4
News from the Foundation 267
newspapers
British, with correspondents in Brussels 111
European affairs in 269
NGO, definition of xii
NGO interest groups, based in Vienna 38
NGO Liason Committee, UK representatives on 136
NGO Liason Committee for voluntary organisations concerned with development issues 136
NGO representatives, accredited at United Nations in Vienna 38
NGOs
advice for 87-8
in Central Europe 238
in CIS 238
consultative status for with Council of Europe 32
contribution of to Council of Europe initiatives 33
in Czechoslovakia 246
in Denmark 212-3
directory of 108
in Hungary 243-4
international
registration of in Belgium 124
registration of in Luxembourg 124
legal status of 33
liason committee of 32-3
in Luxembourg 214
in Poland 244-5

PHARE programme to develop central
European economies 78-9
Pickup Bulletin 59
Pickup Europe programme 59
Pierre, Abbe 201
Pilot Projects to Conserve the Communities
Architectural Heritage 69
Poland
British organisations having contact with
245-6
deaf people in 245
disabled people in 245
elderly people in 245
environmental organisations in 245
funds for 78
homeless in 245
NGOs in 244-5
social problems in 244
voluntary organisations in 303
voluntary sector in 244-6
police, role of in EC 257
POLIS, road traffic information 54
Polish Foundations Forum 245
Polish towns, twinned with British towns 246
political change, effect on voluntary sector
193
political groupings, in European Parliament,
logistic support for 15
political groupings in Europe 136-8
political groups 281
Political Research, European Consortium for,
work of 96-7
political rights, effect of single market on 257
political role of voluntary sector, in France
196
political science, research into 96-7
Political Science in Europe 97
Polytechnic of North London 94
poor
services for 148
in Spain 230
Poptel
non-commercial e-mail system 272-3
use of by voluntary organisations 273
popular universities 170
Portugal
elderly people in 227
NGOs in 228
recent developments in voluntary sector in
228
social services in 227
traditional voluntary organisations in 227
voluntary organisations in 298-9
voluntary sector in 227-8

young people in 227
Poverty 1 and 2 programmes of EC 76
Poverty 3 programme of EC 75-6, 194
poverty
Commission on, French 202-3
in Denmark 212
in EC 161-2
EC programmes to combat 74-7
in Greece 217
hearing on in European Parliament 169
in Ireland 213, 214
networks concerned with 285
perception of in Europe, opinion poll on 265
research into, in Germany 208-9
*Poverty - a challenge to us all: the foundation of
the European anti-poverty network from
working group to launch* 162
poverty in EC 74-5
local projects for 75
poverty in Germany 207-9
poverty in Greece, parish organisation for 219
poverty observatory *see* social exclusion
poverty programmes of EC, research and
development units of 76-7
Power in the European Parliament 108
Presenting your case to Europe 258
pressure groups, in EC, directory of 260
PRI *see* Penal Reform International
Prince's Trust, The 91, 239
grants by 99
PRISMA programme 52
prison conditions 158
prisoners
help for 149
in Spain, help for 231
voluntary organisations for in Italy 224
Prisoners Abroad 154
prisoners of conscience 153
probation services, in Europe 154
problems, common to more than one EC
state, programme for 57
*Proclaiming migrants rights: the new
international convention*, etc 43
prostitutes, voluntary organisations for in
Italy 224
protestant charities, in Spain 230
Protestant churches, representation of in
Brussels 130-1, 132
Protestant development organisations,
Asociation of (APRODEV) 133
Protestant social service organisations in
France 199
psychiatric disabilities, help for with people
with 172

327

psychiatric patients, former, job creation for 172
publishing houses concerned with Europe, based in Britain 95-6

Quaker Council for European Affairs, The (QCEA) 132
Quakers, relationship with NATO 132
Quaranta, Giancarlo 222
Quartiers en crise network 53, 54
Queen Juliana Foundation 91, 215

Racial Equality
Commission for 158
Ombudsman for, in Sweden 237
racial equality in Europe
organisations working for 111
Standing Conference on 110
racism
European Parliament report on 8
in France 201-2
RADAR 176, 179
RAPID, database of Spokesman's service of European Commission 275
Rapid reports published by EUROSTAT 267
RDU see research and development units
RECHAR programme 52
Reconstruction and Development see European Bank for
Red Cross, The 94, 117, 149
in France 198
in Germany 204
in Greece 219
in Spain 229-30
in Sweden 236
Red Cross Societies, League of 39
RED see Ruralité, Environnement, Développement 166-7
reformists, in European Parliament 15
Refugee Action 157
refugee case law documentation 157
Refugee Council, The 39, 106, 157
Refugee Forum 110
refugee law 92
refugee policy 39-40
refugee problems, worldwide 39-40
Refugee Studies Programme, The 157
Refugee Unit of the UK Immigrants Advisory Service 157
Refugees 40
refugees 7
in EC 158-61, 257
in Europe 154
in Finland 234

French voluntary organisation for 202
law on 92-3
networks concerned with 284
organisations working for 110
protection of 135
in Spain 230
in Sweden 237
United Nations High Commissioner for 136
Refugees see United Nations
Refugees Study Programme 135
REGEN programme 52
regional authorities, British, represented in Brussels 112
regional culture 187
regional development 86, 186
advice on 96
Regional Economic Development, Centre for Research in 96
regional funds of EC 112
Regional and Minority Languages, European Charter of 34
regional networks of EC
new 54
funding of 54
specialised 53-4
regions, EC spending on 22
REGIS programme 52
Rehab Goodwill 172
Rehabilitation International 72
Rehabilitation International (R) - European Communities Association 178-9
Reichsbund (Imperial association for war victims) 206
RELATE (formerly National Marriage Guidance Council) 146
Relay Europe 95
Relief and Works Agency of United Nations 39
religious lobby in Brussels, interests of 130-2
religious organisations in Brussels, British members of 133
RENAVAL programme 52
Report on social developments 264
Reports of cases before the court 266
research bodies
European 83-93
in Italy 224, 226
research bodies concerned with Europe, based in Britain 94
research and development units (RDUs), of EC poverty programmes 76-7
Réseau Européen des Chercheurs 182
Réseau Européen pour le Respect du Droit au Logement 182

Security and Co-operation in Europe *see*
   Conference for security policy,
   common 29
seropositives, self-help groups for people
   with 174
Shelter England 181
Shelter Scotland 181
sheltered housing schemes, for elderly 146
Shettlestown Housing Association, Glasgow
   180
shipbuilding areas, EC programme for 52
Sierra Club, the 166
SIGLE database 275
Sign-Post Europe Pilot Information Centre
   251
Single European Act (SEA) 3
   changes resulting from 28-9
   co-operation procedure of 28
   environment in 162
single market, completion of 3-4
single parents in Germany 207
Six, The xiii
Small Farmers' Association of England 184
small and medium enterprises *see* SMEs
SMEs
   creation of 53
   definition of xii
   help for 97
   programmes focusing on 67
   set up by women 62
Social Affairs
   Commissioner for, responsibility of in area
      of housing 179
   European, seminars on 98
   Manpower and Education directorate of
      OECD 268
Social Change, Directory of 257
Social Change and Local Action 256
*Social change and local action - coping with
   disadvantage in urban areas* 26
Social Charter of Council of Europe 5
social deprivation, in CIS 242
Social Development and Humanitarian
   Affairs, Centre for (CSDHA) 38
social dimension, of EC 277-9
Social Economy, European Club of 169
Social Europe 264
social exclusion observatory 79-80
*Social Expenditure: problems of growth and
   control* 268
social field, move for greater EC role in 163-4
Social Fund, European 50-1
social housing, in EC 179-80
social issues

broad, networks concerned with 283
   research into, in Germany 208-9
social issues in France, documentation centre
   for 200
social justice, promotion of 171
social need
   in Central Europe 237-8
   in CIS 237-8
social policy
   French 199
   implications for of Single Market 171
   networks concerned with 283
   researchers interested in 150
social policy in Europe 113
social policy field, in Ireland 214 ·
social problems, in Poland 244
social rehabilitation, in Spain 231
social research, in Italy 224, 226
Social Rights, Charter of Fundamental 5, 8,
   34, 152
   implications of 134
   and women 16
social security
   Commission proposals for improvement in
      6
   European Institute for 92, 93
   International Association of 94
Social Security Association, International
   (ISSA) 93
social security observatory 79, 81
social security programmes of EC 74-7
social security services, in Greece 217
social security systems, improvement of 93
Social Service, International (ISS), work of 93
social service organisations, in EC 147-50
social services, German Ministries for 203-4
Social Services Abstracts 271
social services in Denmark, decentralisation
   of 211
social services in Italy, regional variations in
   220-1
social services in Spain, decentralisation of
   229
social welfare
   grants for 97
   in Greece 218
   International Council on 117
social welfare issues 151
social welfare policy 86-7
   organisations concerned with 150-2
Social Work, National Institute for 249
Social Work and the European Community 258
social workers
   international association of 152

International Federation of 114, 196
    network of 152
social workers Liaison Committee 154
socialist group, in European Parliament 15
Socialist Group in European Parliament,
    objectives of 17
Socialist International 138
Socialist International Women 138
Socialist Society, The 108
Society for Cultural Relations with the USSR
    239
Society of Friends see Quakers
Solidarity, voluntary organisations related to
    245
Soros, George 240
Soviet Union
    social welfare services in 242
    voluntary social work in 242
Soviet Union see also CIS, Russia
soviet-American relations 241
Spaak, Marie 87
Spain
    blind in 230
    changes in since death of Franco 228
    disabled people in 230
    elderly people in 231
    emigration from 228
    homeless in 230
    mentally disabled in 230
    poor in 230
    protestant charities in 230
    refugees in 230
    regional variations in 228
    unemployment in 228
    voluntary organisations in 229, 299-300
    voluntary sector in 228-32
Spanish voluntary organisations
    church-based 229-30
    national 229-30
Spanish voluntary sector
    information on 231-2
    recent trends in 231
SPEC see Support Programme for
    Employment Creation
Special Education, National Council for 174
special institutions, of EC 23-8
Spinelli, Altiero 3
sport for the disabled 73
SPRINT programme of EC 94
St Vincent de Paul, Society of 147
    services provided by 150
Standing Conference of Local and Regional
    Authorities in Europe (CLRAE) 34

Standing Conference on Racial Equality in
    Europe (SCORE) 110
STAR programme 52
STARS database 275
Stauffenberg, Graf Franz von 16
STEP environmental programme of EC 68
Strathclyde Community Business, work by
    for unemployed 51
Strathclyde Regional Council, Brussels office
    of 112
STRIDE programme 52
structural funds
    definition of xii
    of EC, objectives of 22-3, 112
    objective areas of in Britain 23
Student's Guide to Europe, A 261
studies of European integration database,
    ERISTOTE 274
study abroad 100
Study Abroad 261
studying in Europe, information on 261
subsidiarity
    definition of xii-xiii
    principle of, effect on German social
        services 204
Sue Ryder Foundatioin, work of in Poland
    246
Sue Ryder Foundation homes in Poland 245
Summary of cases heard by European Court
    of Justice 266
Sunday Times, The, correspondent of in
    Brussels 111
Support Programme for Employment
    Creation (SPEC) 65
Sweden
    19th-century popular movements in 236
    migrant workers in 237
    minimum wage in 236
    Ombudsman for racial equality in 237
    refugees in 237
    rural depopulation in 236
    unemployment in 236
    voluntary organisations in 301
    voluntary sector in 236-7
    welfare services in 236
Swedish immigration policy 237
Swedish voluntary organisations
    main 236
    part played in political process 236
Switzerland
    environmental protection in 233
    voluntary sector in 233-4
    women's rights in 233
SYMBIOSIS information programme 77-8

size of 205
social divisions of 204
voluntary sector in Greece
National Institutes of 217-9
recent developments in 219-20
state supervision of 218
traditional organisations in 217-9
voluntary sector in Italy
information on 224-6
newer organisations of 223-4
political nature of 221-2
voluntary sector in other countries,
English-language information on 195
voluntary sector in Portugal
recent developments in 228
traditional organisations of 227
voluntary sector in Spain
information on 231-2
newer organisations of 230-1
recent trends in 231
voluntary social and health bodies, French
national union of 199
voluntary work abroad, information on 261
Voluntas 271
Volunteer Centre, The 12, 111, 130
Volunteer Effort, International Association
for 130
volunteering in France (le volontariat) 198
volunteers
charter for 129
role of in social provision in EC 129
Vring, Thomas von der 16
VSO, work of in Poland 245

wage, minimum 5-6
Wales Council for Voluntary Action 195
Wales Women's European Network 140
war, victims of 93-4
war victims, German association for 206
War on Want 135
Week, The 265
Weimar Republic 204
Welfare Organisations, Federal Coalition of
205
welfare provision in Germany, information
on 209
Welfare Rights Bulletin 20
Welfare Rights Review 271
welfare services
cutbacks in made by conservative
governments 193
in Sweden 236
welfare state
in Austria 232

in Denmark 211
Welsh Federation of Housing Associations
180
West European Work and Economy Network
(WEN) 131
Western European Union (WEU) 43
Western Isles, Council of 94
WEU *see* Western European Union
WFMH *see* World Federation for Mental
Health
WHO *see* World Health Organisation
WIDE *see* Women in Development Europe
Widows and Widowers Organisations,
International Federation of 144
wildlife protection 164-6
William Temple Foundation 131
women
black, interests of 141
creation of jobs for 64
EC programmes for 60-3
equal employment opportunities for 84-5
from ethnic minorities, interests of 141
health services for, in Italy 221
long-term unemployed, programme for 61-2
migrant, interests of 141
organisations working for interests of
109-10
participation of in local enterprise projects
64
in public life 137
rights of in Treaty of Rome 138
rural, international organisation for 140-1
in southern countries of Europe 141
status of, trade union research on 168
training for 84-5
Women at Work 42
women in Belgium, self-help groups for 210
Women demand action from the EC 139
Women in Development Europe 109, 141
Women of Europe Award 104
Women of Europe Newsletter 265
women in public life 139
women's affairs, networks concerned with
281-2
women's anti-poverty groups, in
Netherlands 216
women's committee, of European Parliament
62
women's committee of European Parliament,
aims of 16
Women's Forum Scotland 140
women's groups, in Hungary 244
Women's Information Service of European
Commission 139

335

Women's Information and Training,
European Association for the
Development of 85
Women's Institutes, National Federation of
139, 146
women's interests, representation of in EC
141
women's issues, in Italy 224
women's issues in EC 138-42
women's movement, in Denmark 212
Women's National Commission 139
Women's Network for International
Solidarity, National 141
women's networks 138-42
women's organisations
in Germany 207
in Greece 220
national, in France 199
National Alliance of 140
Women's Poverty Tribunal 139
women's rights 20
in Switzerland 233
Work again 65
Work and Society, The European Centre for
(ECWS) 90
workcamps 98
international 101
worker co-ops, in Europe 167
worker representation in the work place,
report on 169
workers, young, accommodation for 181-2
workers in EC, free movement of 156
Working Conditions, Improvement of *see*
European Foundation for
Works Agency for Palestine Refugees 134
World Association of Girl Guides and Girl
Scouts 191
World Bank, The 134
World Council of Churches (WWC) 158
World Federation for Mental Health (WFMH)
campaigns of 177
European Regional Council of 177
World Federation of Twinned Towns and
Cities 187
World Federation of United Cities (FMCU)
100
World Health Organisation (WHO) 37, 40-1,
173, 174
World Ort Union 135
World Park Base, Antarctica 164
World Today, The 271
World Union of Catholic Women's
Organisations 142
World Wide Fund for Nature 166

Wresinski, Fr Joseph 169, 200, 202
WWC *see* World Council of Churches

xenophobia, European Parliament report on 8

YEM *see* Young European Movement
YIPs *see* Youth Initiative Projects
YMCA
in Denmark 211
in Greece 219
young disabled people 180
young employed in Germany, projects for 207
Young European Movement (YEM), aims of
105
Young Farmers' Clubs of Scotland and Ulster
183
young people
at risk, voluntary organisations for in Italy
224
involvement of in EC 192
needs of 182
networks concerned with 288
networks of for voluntary sector 188-91
in Portugal 227
trade union research on 168
vocational training for 56-7
vocational training of, EC funds for 22
Young Women's Christian Association, *see*
YWCA
young workers
accommodation for 181-2
exchange programme for 58
young workers in France, hostels for 202
youth
Greek national institute for 218
task force for 14
youth club organisations 190
Youth Clubs UK 190
Youth for Europe II programme 55, 56
Youth for Europe Programme 102
Youth Exchange Bureau, of EC 56
Youth Exchange Centre, The 102-2
Youth Exchange News 102
youth exchange schemes 98
youth exchanges 102-3
programme for 56
Youth Forum of the European Communities
160, 190-1
youth information services (ERYICA) 189
Youth Initiative Projects (YIPs) 57
youth movement, rural 184
Youth Opinion 191
youth organisations
in CIS 241

Titles on Europe:

Changing Europe: Challenges Facing the Voluntary and Community Sectors in the 1990s
Grants from Europe: How to Get Money and Influence Policy

Other titles in the series:

Artists in Schools: A Handbook for Teachers and Artists
But Is It Legal? Fundraising and the Law
Getting into Print: An Introduction to Publishing
Industrial Tribunals and Appeals: Everything You Need to Know
Opening the Town Hall Door: An Introduction to Local Government, 2nd ed
Organising Your Finances: A Guide to Good Practice
Responding to Child Abuse: Action and Planning for Teachers and Other Professionals
Seeing It Through: How to Be Effective on a Committee
Starting and Running a Voluntary Group
Using the Media, 2nd ed
Who's Having Your Baby?: A Health Rights Handbook for Maternity Care
Working Effectively: A Guide to Evaluation Techniques
You are the Governor: How to be Effective in Your Local School

All books are available through bookshops and can be purchased from NCVO Reception during office hours. To order by post, please contact the NCVO Sales Office for further details.